# SUPERVISING POLICE PERSONNEL

## The Fifteen Responsibilities

*Third Edition*

# SUPERVISING POLICE PERSONNEL

## The Fifteen Responsibilities

*Third Edition*

**Paul M. Whisenand, Ph.D.**
California State University, Long Beach

**George E. Rush, Ph.D.**
California State University, Long Beach

PRENTICE HALL
Upper Saddle River, New Jersey 07458

**Library of Congress Cataloging-in-Publication Data**

Whisenand, Paul M.
    Supervising police personnel: the fifteen responsibilities/Paul
M. Whisenand and George E. Rush.— 3rd ed.
      p.      cm.
    Includes index.
    ISBN 0-13-616673-3 (hardcover)
    1. Police-Supervision of. 2. Police-Supervision of-United
States. I. Rush, George E. (George Eugene), 1932- . II. Title.
HV7936.S8W48 1998
363.2'068'3–dc21                        97-15330
                                                CIP

Production Editor: *Cathy O'Connell*
Acquisitions Editor: *Neil Marquardt*
Managing Editor: *Mary Carnis*
Director of Production and Manufacturing: *Bruce Johnson*
Cover Design: *Marianne Frasco*
Interior Design: *Denise Brown*
Copy Editor: *Nancy Marcello*
Manufacturing Buyer: *Ed O'Dougherty*
Editorial Assistant: *Rosemary Florio*
Formatter/Electronic Art Specialist: *Robin Lucas*
Marketing Manager: *Frank Mortimer, Jr.*

© 1998, 1993, 1988 by Prentice-Hall, Inc.
Simon & Schuster/A Viacom Company
Upper Saddle River, New Jersey 07458

All rights reserved. No part of this book may be
reproduced, in any form or by any means, without
permission in writing from the publisher.

Printed in the United States of America

10  9  8  7  6  5  4  3  2  1

ISBN 0-13-616673-3

Prentice-Hall International (UK) Limited, *London*
Prentice-Hall of Australia Pty. Limited, *Sydney*
Prentice-Hall Canada Inc., *Toronto*
Prentice-Hall Hispanoamericana, S.A., *Mexico*
Prentice-Hall of India Private Limited, *New Delhi*
Prentice-Hall of Japan, Inc., *Tokyo*
Simon & Schuster Asia Pte. Ltd., *Singapore*
Editora Prentice-Hall do Brasil, Ltda., *Rio de Janeiro*

For our Children and their Children.
Love Dad and Granddad
Paul and George

# Contents

—◆—

# Preface

This, our third edition, maintains its original premise—the role of a police supervisor consists of fifteen interlocked responsibilities. Two new responsibilities were added, and two deleted. Some might argue that there are more than fifteen or that some of those that we selected are invalid. We concede to the first part of such an argument while refuting the second part of it. Three convictions undergird our fifteen responsibilities.

First, we are convinced that the initial and most critical step toward being an effective supervisor and leader is accurately knowing your goals, strengths, skills, and abilities. Once this occurs, then you must complete this step by accurately knowing your staff's goals, strengths, skills, and abilities—individually and as a team. Part One provides answers on how to successfully complete this step.

Second, we are convinced that a police–community partnership is impossible to achieve unless the department is similarly structured. A top-down, authoritarian, bureaucratic police agency kills any attempt to link the police to their community. If it isn't happening inside the agency, it certainly won't happen on the outside. We'll justify this assumption in the pages that follow—especially in Part Two. Hence, step two emphasizes the need for developing internal partnerships.

Third, we are convinced that the police must forge an alliance with their community (customers). While overused and misunderstood, we'll refer to this alliance or partnership as community-oriented policing (COP). The third step is the subject of Part Three.

All three steps, all three parts of our book, depend on the implementation of all fifteen responsibilities. The fifteen responsibilities are connected by one common bonding agent—integrity. If you have that, than applying the responsibilities, while not easy, is certainly "do-able."

Our convictions were tested and endorsed by two very supportive reviewers of the third edition. Thank you John J. Sloan III, PH.D. at the University of Alabama and Dana C. DeWitt at Chadron State College.

With the help of the Prentice Hall staff: Cathy O'Connell, Production Editor; Neil Marquardt, Acquisitions Editor; Jean Auman, Editorial Assistant; and Robin Lucas, Formatter/Electronic Art Specialist; and our prized friend and trusted associate, Diane Silleman, we present our book to you.

Paul and George
San Clemente, California

# *The Fifteen Responsibilities*

———◆▶✕◀◆———

> *To be what we are, and to become what we are capable of becoming, is the only end of life.*
>
> —Robert Louis Stevenson

You're a supervisor! In fact, you've probably been one for twenty or more years. Let us explain our reasoning for such an assertion. Since you were two to three years of age, you have been responsible, more or less, for supervising at least one person—yourself. (In your opinion, how have you done so far?) *The effective supervision of people starts with effective self-supervision.* What follows has a twofold application. If read and practiced, you will become more successful in supervising yourself daily and supervising other people in an organizational context.

First and foremost, successful supervisors (police sergeants, civilian supervisors, and the like) have demonstrated an ongoing capability for holding themselves accountable for the pursuit and completion of specific tasks and goals. Those who have failed in meeting this requirement, and are supervising others, are substandard in the performance of their job.

OK—to sum up our thinking about supervision. First, we're all responsible for supervising ourselves and sometimes other people. Second, if we do a good job on the self, we'll probably do a good job with others. Third, the reverse is also true. Finally, our role as a police supervisor consists of achieving certain key responsibilities—in this case, fifteen of them.

## THE "R" WORD

We see a disturbing and growing trend in our nation, and in other countries too, of people ducking responsibility while telling everyone else what to do. Obviously, the two of us are not a part of this malformation. It's all of those other folks who fail to stand and be accountable while simultaneously casting guilt on others

Several years ago, a pilot for Japan Air Lines landed a Boeing 747 at the San Francisco International Airport and proceeded to run the aircraft off of the tarmac and into the bay. Fortunately, no one was injured, but the plane suffered considerable damage. Naturally, this was a lawyer's dream accident. On the first day in Superior Court, Captain Asoh was summoned to the witness stand. The lead attorney for the plaintiffs stared at him and coldly inquired, "Captain Asoh, why did your airplane end up in the San Francisco Bay?" Without hesitation and looking directly at the lawyer, he replied in accented English, "I screwed up!" No blaming other flight crew, air traffic controllers, the aircraft manufacturers, a dysfunctional youth, racial prejudice, whatever. Now that's responsibility!

Have you noticed that those who shirk their responsibilities refuse to be held accountable, and frequently attempt to slide the blame for irresponsibility on to someone or something else? It is sucking us into behavioral and political absurdities and discontents. This phenomenon can be observed in both private and government organizations. We see it happening in some police agencies.

Our nation's legal language on rights is highly developed, but the language of responsibility is meager. This situation has hamstrung self-reliance, inner autonomy, and risk taking. A society, an organization, a police agency, can't operate if everyone has rights and no one has responsibilities.

<hr>

> A society, an organization, a police agency, can't operate if everyone has rights and no one has responsibilities.

<hr>

The blame game is perpetuated by a low intolerance for mistakes. This is especially prevalent in police work. Many police managers are quick to profess, "In our agency, we want our employees to take risks!" After a while, some believe that taking a calculated risk for all the right reasons will be supported. Then someone takes a risk and fails, and all hell breaks loose. Ridicule, sanctions, tainted career, and more come down on the risk taker. Is it of any surprise that many police organizations have a culture of risk avoidance: "Risk taking— that's not my responsibility. Let some other fool try it."

> Police supervision is a job that holds one responsible for helping others in the achievement of value-added public services. We see this job as being comprised of fifteen responsibilities. Assuming the fifteen responsibilities is the crux of our message.

*Additionally, the underlying hope is about deepening our responsibility to delivering quality police service.* We have the language of service. We serve our country; we call ourselves a service economy; we choose the police service as a profession; we have committed to serve customers. What is missing is the experience of service. Our experience is sometimes to find ourselves surrounded by self-interest, even inside our police departments. The ways we govern, supervise, and lead can be a testimony to self-interest and non-responsibility.

## OPTIMISM

With what we've painted thus far, you may have inferred that our vision is one of despair and gloom. Not so. *We are indelible optimists about police supervision and police work.* Daily, we see and hear about more and more police supervisors willing to chance it on being held accountable.

One example of accountability we have learned about involved a police sergeant who decided to deploy his crew in such a fashion that residential burglaries would be reduced in one portion of his assigned patrol area. For five days, his patrol officers targeted a specific area. His exposure paid off but, unfortunately, to the burglar. A single burglar stole over $15,000 in household goods during this time. The chief asked to see the sergeant and admonished him on an overconcentration of patrol resources. He then said, "That's all." The sergeant exclaimed, "That's all? I thought I would get a written reprimand or days off without pay." The chief smiled and said, "Days off! We've just spent $15,000 in educating you."

There are literally scores of responsibilities encased in the role and job of a police supervisor. We believe the fifteen that we'll cover in the pages that await you are the most central and important in getting the results that your agency and its customers want—top-drawer police services.

Thus far, we have sought to establish what is needed in police supervision (responsible supervisors) and why (to provide quality services). In between the two is a key linkage—*partnership*.

Keep in mind that using a partnership to galvanize responsibility with results is one of many linkages or procedures. Another type is telling (raw authority) others what must be done and when. Yet another is selling (the power of persuasion) others on their job performance. Coaching (showing) others is one more approach. We are convinced that developing a partnership is the most effective method for *bonding a supervisor's responsibilities with the results his or her officers produce, and the results his or her customers receive.*

## A PARTNERSHIP

There is a desire in each of us to commit to things that matter, and to have the police organization in which we work be successful. Our task is to insure that when we step aside, our job, or at least our organization, will still exist for the next generation (no easy task in this environment). What follows is also about living out democratic values, using the workplace as the focal point. One of its goals is to quicken our efforts to improve our police organizations in order to guarantee service to the community in the broadest sense.

We have struggled with the use of the terms "customer" and "community." Our rationale finally favored "customer" over "community." Granted, *community-oriented policing (COP)* appears to be more than another short-lived fad. Nevertheless, when COP is implemented, dissected, and evaluated, it translates into *customers served*. Some of the customers are criminals, but most often not. Typically, they are customers looking to their government, their police, for help and advice. Most importantly:

Community-oriented policing is impossible until an agency decides to partnership internally (department-employee) and externally (employee-community).

## Partnership: Customer Service

*Partnership* is the set of principles and practices which have the potential to make dramatic changes in our police system. It is concerned with creating a way of policing ourselves that produces a strong sense of ownership and responsibility for outcomes at the bottom of the police organization. It means empowering line personnel and giving more influence to customers. Partnership creates self-reliance on the part of all who are touched by the institution. The answer to police problems is not more money; it is to focus on quality, service, and participation first. This is what will put us closer to our community. It is the connection with our customers that is the answer to our concerns about police services.

———•◦••◦•———

It means empowering line personnel and giving more influence to customers.

———•◦••◦•———

A partnership begins with the willingness to be responsible for some larger body than ourselves—an organization, a community. Partnering springs from a set of beliefs about reforming organizations that affirms our choice for service over the pursuit of self-interest. When we choose service over self-interest, we confirm that we are totally accountable without choosing to control the world around us. It requires a level of trust that we are not used to accepting.

In its commitment to service, a partnership forces us to yield our desire to use good overseeing as a basic form of supervision. We already know how to be good supervisors at work. The alternative—partnership—is something we are just learning about. Our difficulty with creating partnerships is that supervising—and its stronger ally, control—is so deeply ingrained in our muscle, memory, and practice that we are unaware that we are doing it.

Besides engendering partnership, genuine police service requires us to act on our own account. We cannot be stewards of an institution and blame someone else for its mistakes. Stewardship is the choice for service. We serve best through partnership, rather than a hierarchy of authority. Dependency is the opposite of partnership and thus *empowerment* is involved.

———•◦••◦•———

Besides engendering partnership, genuine police service requires us to act on our own account.

———•◦••◦•———

A partnership is more profound than simply asking who is at the top of our police organization or what supervisory style enjoys popular support at the moment.

## Three Questions

What we have just covered is clearly a different approach to supervising others. On closer examination, one can detect that deciding whether to use a partnership approach or not raises three questions for a supervisor and a police department to answer. If the leadership of the agency considers the questions that follow, and answers all in the affirmative, then it is highly probable that the partnership approach will occur.

Implementing a partnership is possible, but not easy. It challenges the old organizational styles and working relationships and thus will meet with resistance that can vary from moderate to uncompromising. If the police supervisor opts in favor of partnering and the department does not, with a lot of individual effort and personal risk, the supervisor can cause it to happen. Obviously it is highly preferable that both entities choose to operate in a partnership fashion. This type of partnership deals with internal decision making and will be covered in many of the fifteen responsibilities (especially the one on teamwork).

There is a second partnership that must be evaluated. This one focuses on the degree of mutual influence or interdependency sought by the department with its community. A decision to partnership produces the foundation for COP. (Note that COP is one of the fifteen responsibilities.) A decision not to partnership precludes a COP program. Unfortunately, some police agencies loudly profess a COP functioning philosophy but, in reality, operate within the traditional walls of a rigid and closed hierarchy. Now the three questions.

---

A decision to partnership produces the foundation for COP.

---

**WHO CONTROLS?** In deciding how to supervise, one critical choice is between autocracy and partnership. An autocracy expresses the belief that it is those at the top (e.g., police chief/sheriff) who are totally responsible for the success of the agency and the job satisfaction of its members. These people manage and supervise our police agencies by consistency, control, and predictability.

A top-down unilateral authority breeds dependency, low commitment, groupthink, and poor quality of services. Partnership carries the intention to balance power between ourselves and those around us. It brings into question the utility of maintaining consistency and control as cornerstones of police supervision. It comes from the choice to place control close to where the work is done and not hold it as the prerogative of the middle and upper managers. Partnership also flows from the choice to yield on rigid consistency in how we supervise and thus to support line units in creating policies and practices that fit local police conditions.

> Hierarchies push decisions to the top of an organization. Partnerships push decisions to the bottom of an organization.

**DEPENDENCY OR EMPOWERMENT?** Another choice is between dependency and empowerment. Dependency rests on the belief that there are people in power who know what is best for others, including ourselves. We think the task of these leaders is to create an environment where we can live a life of safety and predictability. Dependency also holds those above personally responsible for how we feel about ourselves and for how much freedom we have. We will never forget hearing a police officer say to his sergeant, "I want my freedom, if it is OK with you."

Empowerment embodies the belief that the answer to the latest crisis lies within each of us and therefore we all saddle up for adventure. Empowerment bets that police employees at our own level or below will know best how to organize to prevent crime, serve a customer, and get it right the first time. We know that a democracy is a political system designed not for efficiency, but for participation and effectiveness. Empowerment is our willingness to bring this value into the workplace: to claim our accountability and commit ourselves to making the police organization work well, with or without the assistance to those above us. This requires a belief that my safety and my freedom are in my own hands. This is no easy task, but well worth the endeavor.

> Authority is bottom up! It is you who temporarily grants it to an organization. You have the freedom to take it back!

**SERVICE OR SELF-INTEREST?** A pivotal choice one must make in a police career is between service and self-interest: theoretically an easy one; in reality an exceedingly tough decision. Self-interest, me-first, you owe it to me, has a compelling attraction. We live in an era of self-interest.

Nevertheless, there are some people—some police supervisors—who commit to a higher purpose. They shun the "what's in it for me?" and search for a purpose. They're ready to sacrifice, risk, and actually enjoy the adventure of producing a worthwhile work product. This is the deeper meaning of customer service and therefore COP.

The fundamental goal of police leadership and supervision is to create organizations that line personnel can believe in, in order to make police work a dedication rather than a demand.

---

A choice for service and community becomes the only practical answer to our underlying temptation about self-interest.

---

The fifteen responsibilities are divided into three areas of concentration. To begin with, a police supervisor must know the job or role. Basically, the focus is on the character and abilities of the incumbent supervisor. Next, we shift our sights to building partnerships within the department. Much of the learning acquired in the first area is also needed and applied here. However, this group of responsibilities are designed to prepare line personnel to perform their work. Finally, all of the foregoing responsibilities are used in conjunction with the last set to effectively produce value-added police services by forming partnerships with the community.

## CHANGE

A partnership for accomplishing fifteen responsibilities is the umbrella idea of this book for achieving basic change in the way we lead and supervise our police organizations. As such, it emphasizes responsibility rather than control. I am not implying the role of supervisor should not include the control of others. On the contrary, making certain that the line personnel perform their assigned duties in the right way is essential. There is a shift in emphasis, however. This shift is making certain that everyone shares in the responsibility for doing a high-quality job. This shift is not a minor one. In fact, it challenges the traditional "one best way" or "we've always done it this way" of supervisory thinking and practices.

Since this book will present opportunities and problems associated with change, it is best that we talk about it.

---

If you can't talk about it, you can't fix it.

---

### Managing Change

There has been considerable discourse and literature on the topic of managing change. In reality, *there is very little that we can do to manage change.* Change happens! "The answer is, the answer changes." However, what we can do is manage (supervise) our response to change. It is critical that a police supervisor adapt to change, and while this is not easy, it can be accomplished.

Keep in mind that organizational change is not temporary or unusual: Change is constant and inevitable. An old adage states that "There are two things in life that you can depend on—death and taxation." That epigram should be expanded to include "change."

> You can't control change, but you can control yourself.

## Accepting Uncertainty

In accepting change as a natural and normal part of our lives, we must also accept ambiguity and uncertainty. Pinning down your job as a police sergeant or civilian supervisor today is like trying to nail Jello-O to the wall. Most of us seek structure and certainty, while what we get is ambiguity and uncertainty. A rapidly changing world (it always has been, only the velocity is steadily increasing) deals ruthlessly with police organizations and police supervisors who refuse to change. If you attempt to ignore incoming demands for change (e.g., COP), then you're setting yourself and your department up for failure.

As a supervisor, you should develop a capacity for creating role clarity for yourself. Chase down the information you need. Show initiative in getting your bearings, and in aligning your efforts with the agency's larger strategy. Guesswork will become a critical skill. Improvising will become an artform.

> How many people take their cue from you? What kind of influence do you carry? When change hits, remember to move yourself first, so you don't get in the way of others.

## Expect Resistance

Resistance is the most common human response to change. If you don't encounter it, you should wonder if you've really changed things much. Change triggers the organization's immune system. Like antibodies, we automatically attack the incoming change as if it were a virus.

Some 20 percent of the people are "change-friendly." They're clear advocates who willingly embrace the change. You can depend on them to help drive the program. Another 50 percent of the folks sit on the fence. They assume a so-called neutral position, trying to figure out which way to lean. They're not necessarily hostile to change, but they're not helping either. The remaining 30 percent are the resisters. They're antagonistic toward change and often deliberately try to make it fail.

Guess which group makes the most noise? And who do you think soaks up the most supervisory time and energy? The resisters, of course. This is the group that gives you the least return on the efforts you invest. And giving resisters your attention often just *reinforces* their problem behavior.

It makes more sense to spend your time trying to convince the fence-sitters. You have far better odds of winning them over. You also should devote generous attention to the 20 percent who are driving the change. They deserve it the most, but ordinarily they're taken for granted.

What you are really after are *hard results*, rather than getting employees to feel happy about what's going on. Never presume that you must have buy in from everyone before you move forward. For a good percentage of people, buy in will only come later—if at all—*after* the results are in which prove that the change was both appropriate and successful.

Resistance cuts two ways. As a protective shield, it may fend off a bad idea. Or it may block a much-needed idea. The degree of resistance has nothing to do with the merit of an idea. The resistance barometer measures the magnitude of the new idea.

> Any organizational change generates human resistance. It is up to you to decide if it is worth championing or opposing.

### Flexible and Fast

Under turbulent and uncertain times, it is vital that a police supervisor be adaptable and quick. Your organization will keep reshaping itself, shifting and flexing to fit a rapidly changing world. Look for it to restructure, outsource, downsize, subcontract, and form new alliances.

You also can expect flexible ways of working. Duties will be constantly realigned. Short-lived assignments will be common. Maybe you'll work on a contract basis or spend time on several project teams. You might even end up working for more than one department at a time. You'll probably have a constantly new set of co-workers and more new bosses.

You're not going to like some of this. Chances are, nobody will like it *all*, even those who push it at the top. But the question is, will you get with the program anyhow? And, if so, how fast can you align yourself with the new program *and* make it work. A considerable portion of your work performance will be measured on your flexibility and speed during change.

> Hold yourself professionally responsible for quickly adapting to change.

## QUALITY

The first edition of this book was subtitled, *Back to the Basics*. We meant by this a return to greater effectiveness. And, naturally, effectiveness included "quality." Wrong!

The icon kicker, Tom Peters, has bluntly stated, "Quality and flexibility through skilled labor have never been an American custom." He acknowledges that we are great at mass-producing goods and services. Regretfully, quality hasn't been a prominent part of our national game plan. The private sector is joining in the quality movement and so is government. And *our police are getting started.*

We see many passing facts in police work. Producing quality services—in this case police services—is not one of them. Making certain that the consumer gets quality police services represents the most profound, comprehensive alteration in supervisory theory and practice for this decade and the next. Until a few years ago, police executives focused on the cosmetics of quality, bottom-line statistics, while ignoring the foundations, *leadership and people.*

## Quality: Who Decides?

W. Edwards Deming taught the Japanese what quality was all about in the late 1950s and 1960s. As a result, we witness the success of such Japanese corporate giants as Sony, Toyota, Canon, and many more. Deming rejected the notion that programs or hardware such as the following spelled out quality: hard work, management by objectives (MBO), management information systems (MIS), computer hardware, pay for performance, officers with college degrees, and so forth. These elements may contribute to good police services, but they by no means assure it.

Deming realized that quality resides effectively in the eye of the beholder— it is what you and I believe it to be. Thus, for the police officer, quality may be pride or workmanship; for the chief, decreasing crime; and for the citizen, reasonably priced police services that protect and help him or her.

Ultimately, then, the test of quality is what the citizen judges it to be. No other stakeholder of a police agency—city council, police chief, officers, neighborhood watches—can long survive while ignoring the demands of the judge of quality, the citizen. Thus, all quality initiatives must be customer focused.

But how do we achieve quality in the judgment of consumers? Dr. Deming contends that quality, the *result*, is a function of quality, the *process*. The fifteen responsibilities follow the principles and application tools necessary to activate the two ingredients most essential to this *quality process: partnerships within the agency and partnerships between it and its community.* If you wonder how quality should look, merely ask the people you serve!

---

If you think the customer is unimportant, then think again.

---

## WHAT FOLLOWS

Thus far, we have sought to convince you that:

- All of us are supervisors in one or more ways.
- The ultimate goal of a police supervisor is to deliver quality services.

- The primary judge of what is or is not quality is the user—the customer.
- The goal of quality services is best achieved through a leadership style that evolves into a partnership.
- Various degrees of change, along with resistance to it, are natural and to be expected.
- A police agency that functions via a series of *internal working partnerships* and *external working partnerships* is most likely to succeed in implementing and sustaining community-oriented policing (COP).

## About the Fifteen Responsibilities

The fifteen responsibilities that follow reflect timeless, basic principles of effective human interaction. They are not easy, quick-fix solutions to personal and interpersonal decisions. Rather, they are foundational principles that, when applied consistently in countless specific practices, become behaviors enabling the transformation of individuals, work units, and organizations into a series of partnerships for producing quality police services. Police supervisors are becoming more tuned into the reality that employees are actually capable and want to do good work. Further, they want to reach their full potential. To encourage police supervisors who lead their employees into a full partnership for getting quality results is the hope and substance of this book.

The fifteen responsibilities are divided into three functional groups:

- Know your job
- Internal partnerships
- External partnerships

**KNOW YOUR JOB.** It may seem like a paradox that *to know your job you must first know yourself*. This means you must understand yourself—your values, interests, and drives. Once you are aware of what makes you tick, you're in a position to comprehend the workings and people that compromise your job purview. Responsibility One is devoted to *values*.

The next step involves ethics and professional standards—the do's and don'ts in your organization and in your profession. Where are the integrity lines drawn? Can you fully recognize absolutes and courageously condemn the bad and champion the good? Responsibility Two focuses on *ethics*.

We're now able to take values and ethics and blend them into a vision. The vision sets us up to be a potential leader. "I can see where we ought to be going, let me show you how it looks, follow me. I'll empower you." With a vision comes Responsibility Three—*leadership*.

To share a vision you must communicate it to others. Leaders know and fulfill Responsibility Four—*communications*.

All of the preceding requires time, not just mere time but top-priority time. And we all know that time is tough to come by or control. "Oh, if I only had more time" is a common complaint. Either we manage it or it manages us. Thus, Responsibility Five is *time management*.

**INTERNAL PARTNERSHIPS.**    The first five responsibilities have set the stage for you as a supervisor to forge internal partnerships. Remember, they're the people who will, or won't, get quality results for you and your police agency. This section will show you how to make the efforts of a few people into what appears to be the efforts of many. This is referred to as "synergy." Basically, synergy is adding one plus one and coming up with six, sixty, six hundred.

Why build partnerships? You wouldn't be able to unleash their motives if you didn't. Motivation and inspiration are interrelated. The prefix "in" means inside or within. Inspiration then translates into helping someone letting what's within, without, and then guiding it. Simply put, Responsibility Six is *motivation*.

If you haven't a distinction in mind, any route will get you to where you're going. We need to know where and why we're moving in a particular direction. We need goals! In the late 1950s, Peter Drucker conceptualized the process of MBO. We've modified it here for our purposes and refer to it as supervision by objectives (SBO). A goal is a desired end, a hoped for result. SBO supplies that plus some means for getting there. Hence, Responsibility Seven is *goals*.

The next characteristic focuses on making everyone feel and behave as though they're 100 percent responsible for their work output. Two methods are available for building individual accountability. First, empower people to do their work. Second, ensure that they participate in decisions that affect them. Empowerment is the guts of an internal partnership. Responsibility Eight is employee-oriented supervision, or *empowerment*.

After goals are set in place, measuring their attainment becomes critical. Goals are most often achieved by brainpower and physical energy. In measuring goal fulfillment, we're actually evaluating the individual and group efforts of police officers, cadets, civilian dispatchers, corrections officers, and more. Thus, Responsibility Nine is *performance*.

Each of us enters into jobs, relationships, and situations with certain unspoken expectations. And one of the major causes of "people problems" in police organizations is unclear, confusing, or unfulfilled expectations. Conflicting expectations regarding rules, roles, and goals cause most of us pain and problems, adding stress to working relationships. Responsibility Ten is likewise employee oriented—*conflict*.

Despite all the "wellness" literature to the contrary, there is no easy way of coping with stress. Stress is change: stress or change is natural and inevitable. How we handle it is up to us. We can choose our response to any circumstance or condition. When stress impacts us, we can choose to unleash within ourselves a winning or whining response, a growth or grinding experience, a healthy or harmful reaction. Responsibility Eleven is *stress*.

**EXTERNAL PARTNERSHIPS.**    External partnerships have two dimensions: *quality* and *commitment*. Quality comes from the heart, commitment from involvement. Commitment and quality produce results—total quality results.

By this point in the book, you'll know how to know your job; you'll know how to construct a partnership with your staff; and, thus, it's time to go to work. Basically, you'll be applying all of the previous eleven responsibilities in developing a partnership with your customers. *This partnership is customer driven, quality conscious, results-oriented—we know it as community-oriented policing.*

*Organizing* is Responsibility Twelve. You now know what you and your crew are capable of doing and what and why to do it. Your challenge here is to create a work unit that is quick to respond to change while not abandoning the underlying values and goals of the department. Essentially, the supervisor must balance values with velocity, constancy with change, and efficiency with effectiveness.

One might view organizing as a needed structure or skeleton for arranging things or people. Teamwork adds the movement or muscle for action. A team works together almost daily. It is constantly aware of its own performance, and it must be in tune with its own values. Responsibility Thirteen, *teamwork*, serves as the linkage between internal partnerships (supervisor–officers) and external partnerships (supervisor/officers–community).

For decades our police managers have hammered on their staffs to be more efficient (doing things right, bottom-line statistics). The supervisors reacted by demanding more and more quantity of services from the line officers. "Lower the crime rate; move, move, move; faster, faster." The late 1960s saw a repudiation of such policies and practices; this was labeled "police community relations." Later other titles were applied such as "team policing" and "neighborhood policing." With only slightly differing approaches, these programs sought to link the police to their community better. Underlying all of these programs was a nearly unrecognized hope to produce better and better services via *community-oriented policing (COP)*. Related to COP is *problem-oriented policing (POP)*. Some police agencies are attempting to be "problem driven" as compared to just driven. They're seeking to pinpoint the root of a police problem, and not some evasive and random set of occurrences. Responsibility Fourteen is therefore *COP + POP*.

The supervisors should be on constant alert for incoming changes. Anticipating change is as important, if not more so, as coping with it. In fact, the more skilled one is in spotting change, the better one is in dealing with it. I am not implying that police supervisors struggle to be futurists. However, I am holding them responsible in Responsibility Fifteen for *anticipation*.

Soon you'll be studying and, we hope, practicing the fifteen responsibilities.

- Acting on a few of the responsibilities and ignoring the others won't work.
- Doing the fifteen responsibilities is not easy—but, after all, if supervising were easy, everyone would be doing it.
- COP and POP hinge on a police supervisor performing all fifteen responsibilities.

# PART ONE

# *Know Your Job*

## RESPONSIBILITIES

- One—Values

- Two—Ethics

- Three—Leadership

- Four—Communications

- Five—Time Management

# RESPONSIBILITY ONE

———◆◆◆———

# *Values*

| | |
|---|---|
| *The police supervisor is responsible for developing consensus within the work group on its values and then insuring that it behaves accordingly.* | *What lies behind us and what lies before us are tiny matters compared to what lies within us.* |
| | —Oliver Wendell Holmes |

**Values provide the character, courage, and consciousness for determining where the work unit is going and how it is going to get there.**

Find a quiet place to read and think about the next few paragraphs. Make a conscious effort to project yourself into the following situation.

Picture yourself driving to a retirement dinner for a co-worker who is also a close friend. You park your car and walk inside the restaurant. You locate the assigned ballroom and enter. As you wander in, you notice the banners and flags. You spot the smiling faces of your co-workers and their spouses. You sense gaiety and happiness in the room.

As you approach them, you look up at the head table and see your name card on it. You also see the name cards of your spouse and three children. Overhead on a banner is printed in large letters your name and, "Congratulations for Twenty-Five Years of Service." Below that banner is another that reads, "A Happy Retirement to You." This is your retirement! And all of these people have come to honor you, to express feelings of appreciation for your work.

You're escorted to the head table where your spouse and children join you. You're handed a program. There are five speakers. The first is your spouse. The second is one of your children. The third speaker is your closest friend. The fourth speaker is an employee who is currently working for you. The final speaker is your boss. All of these people know you very well but in differing ways.

Now, think carefully. What would you expect each of these speakers to say about you and your life? What kind of spouse, parent, and friend would you like their words to reflect? What kind of supervisor? What kind of subordinate?

What values would you like them to have seen in you? What contributions, what achievements would you want them to remember? Look carefully at the people who have gathered to wish you well. What difference would you like to have made in their lives?

Take a few moments and write down key values that you think they would attribute to you.

## VALUES: AN OVERVIEW

Our values play a crucial role in our professional and personal lives. Basically, a *value* is something for which we have an enduring preference. As a police supervisor, one could be expected to value supervising and police work. Although associated with other concepts, such as needs and attitudes, values differ from them and are much more fundamental.

Values serve a variety of purposes, including acting as filters, generation builders, individual distinctions, standards of behavior, conflict resolvers, signs of emotional states, stimuli for thinking, and forces that cause one to behave. Our values are primarily derived from the early, formative years. Values change over time, and we have a choice as to what we will value and its priority in our value system.

We are what we value, and thus will supervise ourselves and others accordingly. *Moreover, values become the beliefs that guide a police organization* and the behavior of its employees. Responsibility One focuses on individual value systems. Later in Responsibility Thirteen we'll look at organizational values, or teamwork.

## VALUES: UNDERSTANDING AND RESPECT

The ability of the police supervisor to perform his or her role successfully is directly linked to an understanding and respect for the values and attitudes of assigned personnel. With this understanding and respect, the supervisor is fortified to influence and lead others in the accomplishment of their assigned duties. The focus must be twofold, however. The supervisor must first comprehend his or her values and attitudes. Once accomplished, the supervisor is in a better position to accurately understand those values possessed by other employees.

### We Are What We Value

Human values are important to us, because they *are* us. Simply stated, our past values have determined who we are and what we are pursuing in life; our present values are likewise shaping our life today, and our futures will be primarily shaped according to the values that we possess at each coming point in time.

It is vital for the police supervisor to know and appreciate human values because they serve as a destiny (an end or a goal) and as a path (a means or guide) toward reaching that destiny. In summary, then, each of us should know his or her own values because they underpin one's character, personality, and supervisory style and performance. This chapter assists you in clarifying your own value system so that you can eventually apply it in a way that will support, rather than detract from, your responsibility for being an effective police supervisor.

———◆•◆••◆—————

All that we value becomes a part of us. And thus, we are what we value and…we supervise ourself and others according to our value system!

———◆•◆••◆—————

### Worker Attitudes

Our human values, in conjunction with the organizational setting and our personal lives, shape for each of us work-related attitudes. We would underscore the "personal side" because what we feel and think about our job is very much influenced by personal or private events, and vice versa. Even if we do not want this connection or spillover from one arena to another, it happens. This is simply a manifest reflection of our holistic nature. An understanding of attitudes, attitude formation, and attitude change is important for several reasons.

1. Attitudes can be found in every aspect of police work. We have attitudes about most things that happen to us, as well as about most people we meet. In view of this universal characteristic of attitudes, an understanding of their nature is essential for supervisors.
2. Attitudes influence behavior. Much of how we behave at work is governed by how we feel about things. Therefore, an awareness of attitudes can assist supervisors in understanding human behavior at work. Changes in police employee behavior can be expected to the extent that supervisors can change or control employee attitudes.
3. Bad attitudes on the job cause problems. Poor job attitudes can be reflected in subsequent poor performance, citizen's complaints, equipment abuse, turnover, and absenteeism, all of which result in direct costs to the police agency.

## DEFINITION, SOURCES, AND CHANGING OF HUMAN VALUES

*The modern individual is assailed from every angle by divergent and contradictory value claims. It is no longer possible, as it was in the not too distant historical past, to settle comfortably into the value system of one's forebears or one's community and live out one's life without ever examining the nature and the assumptions of that system.*

—Carl R. Rogers

The term "value" has a variety of uses. For example, one may value one's family, value one's leisure time, value one's reputation, value one's position as a police manager, or value jogging. Each of these five values is different in several respects. One is a goal-oriented value: one's reputation. Another value, jogging, is a means to another desired state: one's physical and mental health. Yet another value, one's position as a police supervisor, is temporal; that is, it is a temporary position. We have a tendency to forget that what some persons may value highly, others may not. (For example, you may place a high value on the promise of a promotion, while someone else, satisfied with his or her present job, may not.) In fact, people are alike or are different due to the commonality or the incongruence of their professional, personal, and societal values.

## Values Defined

A *value* is an enduring belief that a specific mode of conduct or end state of existence is personally or socially preferable to an opposite or inverse mode of conduct or end-state existence.[1] Because each of us possesses more than a single value, it is essential that we think in terms of a *value system*, which is an enduring organization of beliefs concerning preferable modes of conduct or end states of existence in a hierarchical ranking of relative importance.[2] Hence, a value is an enduring but changeable belief that a particular means to a particular goal is to be preferred over another option. However, one should not be deluded into thinking that there is always a one-to-one connection between a means and a goal. One usually has approximately eighteen end-state values (goals) and sixty to seventy modes of conduct values (means).[3]

---

A value is both a *goal* and a *means* toward accomplishing the goal.

---

## Sources of Our Values

The process of value creation may actually begin long before birth, as argued by many sociobiologists and popular authors such as Carl Sagan in *The Dragons of Eden* and Desmond Morris in *The Naked Ape*. Many experts suggest that *some* behavior patterns in our primitive ancestors might have been encoded in the DNA, which in turn now guides *our* behavior patterns. Whatever the degree of genetic input, for our purposes it is enough to assume that genetics shape broad patterns of human behavior. Our concern is with behavior patterns that are learned from the moment of birth forward.

Our value-programming periods can be divided into three periods: imprinting, modeling, and socialization.[4]

**IMPRINTING.**  During the first six to seven years of age, in addition to *physical* behavior development, a tremendous amount of *mental* development takes place. The popular analogy, "As the twig is bent, so the tree shall grow," is perhaps so

[1]For more on values see Milton Rokeach, *The Nature of Human Values* (New York: Macmillan, 1973), pp. 33–65.

[2]Rokeach, *The Nature of Human Values*, pp. 33–65.

[3]Rokeach, *The Nature of Human Values*, pp. 33–65.

[4]This typology is based on Morris Massey, *The People Puzzle: Understanding Yourself and Others* (Reston, Va.: Reston Publishing Company, 1979).

obviously simple that we frequently fail to apply it to children. The early years of childhood may be compared to the foundation and frame of a building. The foundation determines the quality and strength of the structure that goes on top. The completed structure depends on its base, even if additions are built. The foundation of a person is the child as formed in his or her early years. The key figures here are Mom and Dad and a few others. Even though real "formal" learning does not start in the preschool period, there are many important stages that determine how, how much, how well, and what the child will learn as she or he develops. The question that we must answer and comprehend is "By *whom*, and *how* were we (or they) imprinted in our formative years?"

**MODELING.** From seven or eight to thirteen or fourteen years of age, the process of identification—initially with the mother, then the father and important "others" around the child—expands. The child shifts into intense *modeling*, relating to family, friends, and external "heroes" in the surrounding world. People the child would "like to be like" are carefully observed. As a result, our initial close models give way to more expanded contacts. Soon, group membership begins to exert its influence. We identify not only with play groups or gangs as a whole but also with certain "important" individuals within them. New values and behavior patterns are combined with the ones we absorbed from our family. Once in school, the process of identifying extends to the heroes of history and fictional stories. Furthermore, our increasing involvement with media during this period will bring in characters from movies and television as additional heroes. We use these models to construct our internal ego ideal, the person we would like to become. We are not a complex composite of absorbed inputs. The programming accelerates.

The hero models in our lives are very critical people. They are the people we try to behave like, the people that we want to be like when we become adults. The modeling period is a critical period during which we absorb values from a diverse selection of models. Do you remember your own modeling activities? When you were ten years old, whom did you want to grow up to be like? Whom did you secretly look up to, try to imitate in the way you talked, the way you walked, the way you dressed, the way you wanted to be? What about your co-workers? Who were their potential role models at the age of ten or eleven?

**SOCIALIZATION.** From thirteen or fourteen to around twenty years of age, our social life becomes structured primarily in terms of our friends. This intense *socialization* with one's peers results in people of common interests (values) grouping together for reinforcement. During the period of adolescence, we are in the process of defining and integrating values, beliefs, and standards of our particular culture into our own personalities. It is during this period that we achieve full physical maturity and a dominant value system. This system determines our basic personality. During this period of socialization, we engage in experimentation, verification, and validation of our basic life plan. From about age twenty on, our value system programmed during childhood and adolescence locks in, and we then repeatedly "test" it against the reality of the world.

People of like interests, behavior, and developing value systems associate intensely with one another and reinforce each other in their development. Who were your friends? What was your "best friend" like? What did you talk about? What about sex? Were you a leader or follower, a joiner or loner? Did your friends have a nickname for you? What did you do together? How long have your friendships lasted? These same questions should be addressed about your co-workers.

## Changing Our Values

Our values, while enduring, can be changed. This transition can occur in one of two ways. The first is a traumatic or significant emotional event (SEE). The second revolves around major dissatisfaction. Let us look at each condition more closely.

SIGNIFICANT EMOTIONAL EVENTS. The common denominator of SEEs is a challenge and disruption to our present behavior patterns and values. In job situations or family relationships, such challenges might be artificially created (e.g., being fired or promoted), but, more likely, SEEs occur in an unplanned, undirected manner (e.g., being seriously injured, or winning an athletic contest). We must be careful to distinguish between SEEs, which actually change our gut-level value system, and external events, which simply modify our behavior. For example, a departmental order imposed on us may demand that we pay attention to the needs of the employees. Our behavior may change accordingly, but our values remain the same. The closer such events occur to our early programming periods, the more likely significant change will occur. The less dramatic the event, the longer we hold our programmed values, and any change in values will occur more slowly, if at all. It is possible to "teach an old dog new tricks," but the learning is much more difficult than for the younger animal. SEEs are neither good nor bad. Their frequency, type, and how we cope with them determine if they are positive or negative for us.

PROFOUND DISSATISFACTION. To be successful in this most difficult of transitions—psychological growth—requires a special combination of inner and, to a degree, outer circumstances. These are set forth with splendid simplicity by psychologist Clare Graves.[5]

Graves says that a person must possess three attributes if he or she is to make a substantial psychological step forward:

**1.** The individual must be deeply dissatisfied. Otherwise, why change?
**2.** The individual must possess much psychological and physical energy. Few things are harder to break than old bonds, old views, old prejudices, old convictions, old loves.

---

[5]Adapted from Clare W. Graves, *On the Theory of Value*, mimeographed paper, 1967.

**3.** The individual must have or acquire the psychological insight to know what will slake the driving dissatisfaction. Without this, the effort to change will be directionless, ceaseless, and pointless.

Only when all three of these factors are present simultaneously will a person have the motivation to change, the drive to act on the motivation, and the foresight to know where to go and when he or she has arrived. See Figure 1-1, which graphically describes this section.

## VALUES: WHAT DO THEY DO FOR US?

In a general sense, values tell us much about who we are, as individuals, as citizens, as consumers, as a nation, and as a police supervisor.[6] As you examine the remainder of this section, keep in mind the following:

- The total number of values that each person possesses is relatively small (thirty to sixty is a flexible range).
- Everyone everywhere has the same values, to different degrees.
- Values are organized into value systems.
- The origin of human values can be traced to one's formative years, culture, institutions, society, and—to some limited extent, perhaps—one's unique genetic makeup.
- The consequences of one's values will be manifested in virtually all that one feels, thinks, and does.

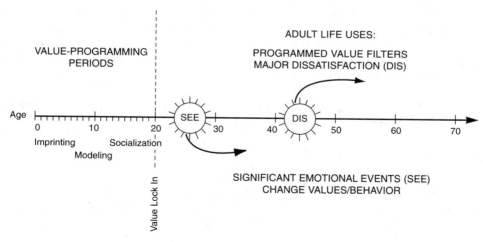

**Figure 1-1**   Value-Programming Periods and Change

[6]A well-documented scientific study of our current and emerging value systems can be found in Arnold Mitchell, *The Nine American Lifestyles* (New York: Macmillan, 1983).

- A large part of a police supervisor's effectiveness, or lack of it, is dependent on his or her value system.
- Enhanced or continued effectiveness is directly linked to a police supervisor's awareness of his or her values *and* the values of co-workers.

---

The effectiveness of a police supervisor is directly linked to an awareness of values—his own and others.

---

## Filters

Literally everything is sifted through the fundamental value systems operating in each of us. Values are our subjective reactions to the world around us. Although some items are purely functional and can be viewed rationally and objectively (chalkboards, picture books, light bulbs, rulers, etc.), most items involve the subjective reaction, especially when our feelings come into play. Gut-level value systems automatically *filter* the way we view most of the things around us. Your filters operate in degrees and shades of good/bad, right/wrong, normal/not normal, or acceptance/rejection.

## Generation Gaps

In recent decades, the acceleration in the rate of change of technology, legal dimensions, social behavior, education, and economic systems has created vastly diverse programming experiences between generations. The differences in these experiences have created a spectrum of widely varying value systems within our society. Recently a popular label was "the generation gap"—but it is much more. In volumes of material, people have attempted to reconcile differences between generations that, in reality, are irreconcilable—perhaps *understandable*, but *nonnegotiable*. The fundamental value systems are, in fact, dramatically different between the generations that presently exist simultaneously in our society. Police organizations can reflect as many as four or more generations within their employees. Obviously this can, and usually does, present a problem for the supervisor.

## Individual Differences

Value programming is not simply a process of indoctrination. Nor is the behavior of people the result of a series of processes that simply overlay a particular culture on the biological core of individuals. Rather, society shapes a person's inherited temperament, but it does not transform that person into a complete opposite of his or her own basic nature. We each emerge with somewhat distinctive ways of behaving, despite the influences in our generation's programming. Our basic physical and mental abilities are influenced by a wide range of inputs. In broad categories, the major sources of programming experiences for all of us were (1) family, (2) educational experiences of a formal nature, (3) religious inputs, (4) the media, (5) our friends, (6) where we grew up geographically, and (7) the amount of money that provided a base for these other factors.

## Standards

A value system acts as a set of standards and thus guides our conduct. It causes us to take a position or to abandon one previously adopted, predisposes us to accept or reject certain ideas or activities, gives us a sense of being right or wrong, aids us in making comparisons, acts as a basis from which we attempt to influence others, and affords us an opportunity to justify or rationalize our actions. Thus, our value system is, in effect, our individual "code of conduct."

## Conflict Resolvers

We frequently find ourselves in conflict with another person because of individual value system disparities. In an intrapersonal way, however, value systems more often than not support us in making choices. "I prefer blue over brown" or "I choose to allocate my police personnel in a crime-prevention program over a crime-specific program" are illustrations of this. Briefly, one's value system assists in making decisions. Nonetheless, when individuals possess different values, they are apt to conflict with one another.

## Emotional Indicators

Most people give the value of "fairness" a high rank. As a consequence, when seeing or experiencing wrongful personnel practices, one's emotional threshold is normally breached and one becomes angry, depressed, or threatened, or a combination of all three. If one has been the perpetrator of the unjust act, then the emotion of guilt is probably triggered within oneself. The police supervisor who disciplines an errant employee with reasonable cause may feel some sadness because of his or her value for the family unit, feeling that the employee well deserved being disciplined, but also feeling sorry for the employee's spouse and children.

## Thought Provokers

If we value being an effective police supervisor, does it not make sense that this value should provoke us into thinking about what means (e.g., enhancing one's job knowledge) would best achieve the desired outcome (success)? Fortunately, there are techniques for the recording and exploration of one's thoughts in a meaningful way so that we can put these thoughts to use. The techniques range from keeping a diary to following planned exercises. We will cover a number of such techniques later; in the meantime, remember that values generate thoughts as well as guide them.

## Motivators

The terms "motivation" and "motive" denote desire or actual movement toward an identified end. A person's value system motivates him or her to choose one path (means) as compared to any others. Thus, one can feel or see one's motivations by inspection of or introspection on one's behavior. What moves a person to act, or to want to act, in a particular manner stems from his or her own value system. In essence, one's values underpin and generate one's motives. As a result, if you value supervision, it is reasonable for you to be motivated to become a police supervisor. This sense of being motivated further serves as a motivation for acquiring the skills, knowledge, and abilities necessary for supervising a group of police officers.

Your value system determines how you relate to your family, what products you buy, and how you vote. It dictates your leisure-time activities, what information you absorb, and your religious convictions. Of relevance here is that your values decide how well you perform your job as a supervisor. Figure 1-2 summarizes this section.

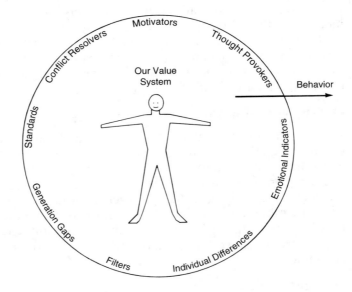

**Figure 1-2**   How Our Values Affect Our Behavior

## VALUE CLARIFICATION

*What you are [value] speaks so loudly I cannot hear what you say.*

—Ralph Waldo Emerson

Select any one of your values (e.g., your job), and if you can answer each of the following questions with a "yes," you have identified and confirmed one of your values.[7]

---

[7]Adapted from L.E. Rath, M. Harmon, and S. Simon, *Values and Teaching* (Columbus, Ohio: Charles E. Merrill Publishing Co., 1966), p. 30.

In terms of a particular value, are you

**1.** Choosing freely?
**2.** Choosing from options?
**3.** Choosing after thoughtful consideration of the consequences of each option?
**4.** Prizing being happy with the choice?
**5.** Willing to make a public affirmation of the choice?
**6.** Doing something with the choice: performance?
**7.** Using the choice in a pattern of life?

## Choosing Freely

The values that are chosen freely are those that one will internalize, cherish, and allow to guide one's life. Society or one's physical environment may impose a value, but it does not necessarily become one's own.

## Choosing from Options

It follows that, if there are no options, then there is not a freedom of choice. One would be hard-pressed to convince someone that he or she valued employment with a specific police department when in fact it was the only one that would hire him or her.

## Choosing after Thoughtful Consideration

A value must be *freely* chosen after a careful review of the consequences of each option. In other words, the consequences must be known to whatever extent possible. After all, if we do not realize the consequences of a particular alternative, we do not know what is likely to occur and therefore cannot have freely chosen that alternative.

## Prizing

Briefly, a value is something that we cherish, respect, and show pride in.

## Public Affirmation

If one values a person, an object, or a concept, it seems only reasonable that one would profess it openly. Are you pleased and proud to tell others that you are a police supervisor or not?

## Performance

What one does reflects one's values. The importance of a particular value (such as acquiring a college education) can be assessed in line with how much time is spent on it (such as taking three units a semester rather than nine). There is an obvious difference between thinking about a value and acting on it. Thinking about a value (such as losing ten pounds) may be an early indication that one is forming a specific value, but it is in performing the value (an actual loss of weight) that one can attest to its being a full value.

**Pattern of Life**

Values, because one acts on them, become a dominating influence in one's life. They establish patterns in thought and deed. Consequently, they motivate us to attend church or not, to get married or not, to have children or not, and to *supervise effectively* or not. It is interesting that we frequently think that we possess a value that, in reality, we no longer hold. We assume that because we once held a particular value that we continue to hold it, and we may be shocked to find that it is no longer a value, or at least no longer an important one. There are two value-clarification exercises in this chapter to assist you in analyzing your value system.

### *Structured Exercise 1-1*

Let us take the next few minutes and explore some of your individually held values. The following two exercises can be accomplished either alone or in a group setting.

To begin with, complete the Value Indicator List by quickly writing down the ten things that you enjoy (value) doing in your professional, social, or personal life. In other words, of all the things you do in your life, list the ten that you enjoy the most. (They range from the tangible [e.g., money, car, family] to the intangible (e.g., love, respect, freedom). We are value driven, and consequently it is critical for us to know what values reside in our value system.

**Value Indicator List**

| Rank | Value | Symbol |
|------|-------|--------|
| _____ | 1. _____ | _____ |
| _____ | 2. _____ | _____ |
| _____ | 3. _____ | _____ |
| _____ | 4. _____ | _____ |
| _____ | 5. _____ | _____ |
| _____ | 6. _____ | _____ |
| _____ | 7. _____ | _____ |
| _____ | 8. _____ | _____ |
| _____ | 9. _____ | _____ |
| _____ | 10. _____ | _____ |

Now study your list and rank your values on the left side of the list in order of priority. The number 1 indicates the most valued, 2 the next most valued, and so on. Next, where they apply, place the following symbols on the right side of the list.

**1.** Put a "$" by any item that costs forty dollars or more each time you perform it. (Be certain to look for hidden costs.)

**2.** Put a "10" by any item that you would not have done ten years ago.

**3.** Put an "X" by any item that you would like to let others know you do.

**4.** Put a "T" by any item that you spend at least four hours a week doing.

**5.** Put an "M" by any item that you have actually done in the last month.

**6.** Put an "E" by any item that you spend time reading about, thinking about, worrying about, or planning for.

**7.** Put a "C" by any item that you consciously choose over other possible activities.

**8.** Put a "G" by any item that you think helps you to grow as a police supervisor.

**9.** Put an "R" by any item that involves some risk. (The risk may be physical, intellectual, or emotional.)

In looking at your list, the more markings you have put next to an item, the more likely it is that the activity is a value for you. This list is not necessarily a compilation of your values; rather, it may be an indication of where your values lie. Count the number of marks next to each item—the activity with the most marks being first, and so on. Now compare your first ranking (left side) with your second ranking (right side) and note the following:

**1.** Do your rankings match?

**2.** Is your highest value in the first ranking the one that has the most marks next to it?

**3.** Can you see any patterns in your list?

**4.** Have you discovered anything new about yourself as a result of this activity?

**5.** Is there anything you would like to change about your preferences as a result of this exercise?

If you are studying as a group, you may want to divide into subgroups of four or five members each and share what you have learned about your values. This was an *awareness exercise* and *not* a test. Hence, its accuracy is measured by *your* judgment and not some outside criteria. Basically, if there are more symbols next to the values that you ranked the highest, then you've achieved "confirmation." Conversely, if the highest ranked values have few symbols, then you're looking at "discovery." Finally, if the pattern is erratic, you're probably seeing both some confirmation and some discovery.

The main thing is—you have identified ten core values.

### Failing to Act On Our Values

We fail to act on our values when we . . .

**1.** Concentrate on short-term objectives which do not relate to our long-term goals.
**2.** Relive past failures.
**3.** Succumb to the "we can't change" syndrome.
**4.** Substitute egocentrism for altruism.
**5.** Allow conformity to overpower courage.
**6.** Ignore our purpose in life and, in so doing, place the ladder of success against the wrong wall.

## POLICE SUPERVISOR AS VALUE DRIVEN

Figure 1-3 shows the supervisor's job environment as being a highly normative (value-laden) process. Following is an explanation of each of the boxes.

### Position and Person

The position of the police supervisor serves best as a starting point. This component is value free. The position of police supervisor alone does not contain

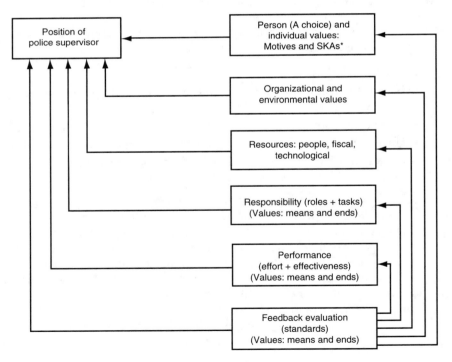

*SKAs - skills, knowledge, and abilities

**Figure 1-3**   The Police Supervisor: Value Driven

values. Obviously, it may be valued by someone. Once a person is inserted into a position, it takes on values. Once staffed, it will reflect not only the individual supervisor's preferences but also those of the agency and the community (organizational and environmental preferences). Hence, we find a human being who chose to be a supervisor and possesses a unique value system inserted into the position, and his or her value system is supported or challenged by incoming external values to varying degrees.

---

> The position of a police supervisor does not contain values. . . Once a person is inserted into the position, it takes on values.

---

## Organizational-Environmental and Resources

Next, the organizational and environmental values component acts on the police supervisor and determines, to a large extent, the amount and types of resources the supervisor will have to administer. Certainly, the input resources will significantly constrain or promote her or his ability to perform effectively and achieve results. The type and amount of resources are evidence of an agency's values.

## Responsibility

Figure 1-3 identifies responsibility as a key supervisory value. The responsibility component subsumes the role concept (job behavior) and various tasks (such as planning, communicating, morale, control, etc.). Here is where values can operate in a dual sense. To illustrate, the value of assuming responsibility for effectively supervising a police unit has a futuristic connotation or *end state*. Simultaneously, acting responsible is a daily phenomenon and thus is more of a *means* toward a given purpose.

## Performance

In being and acting responsibly, the police supervisor expends effort to perform effectively. Again, many value considerations crop up in the performance component; for example, the questions of how much effort should be given to the job of supervising compared with being a spouse and parent, or how much emphasis should be placed on organizational output compared with individual officer job satisfaction.

## Feedback

Finally, we arrive at feedback. To be valid and reliable, feedback must be related to standards of performance and to methods for program and individual evaluation.

What one decides to measure is largely determined by what one values. The setting of standards is similarly linked to the police supervisor's individual (internal) value system as modified by the agency's and the community's (the organizational and environmental) respective set of values.

### *Structured Exercise 1-2*

Let us take another approach that is more supervisor-oriented. Complete the Supervisor Value Priority Rankings statements by assigning 1 to the highest priority, and then in descending rank order, 2, 3, and 4.

As with the first exercise, if possible, form groups of four to five members each for the purpose of discussing individual rankings. The groups can create a single group response by consensus. Look for commonalities, trends and surprises.

**1.** I think that the best police supervisor is one who:

_____ tells you what should be done.

_____ consults with you on important issues.

_____ persuades you to live up to your ideals.

_____ facilitates a consensus on important issues.

_____ other: _____

**2.** For recreation, I prefer:

_____ conversation in a small group.

_____ doing something together in a group.

_____ watching TV.

_____ reading the newspaper.

_____ other: _____

**3.** In my role as a police supervisor, I like to:

_____ work by myself.

_____ work with others.

_____ delegate responsibility to others.

_____ other: _____

**4.** I like to use my free time to:

_____ be by myself.

_____ visit my friends.

_____ catch up on work.

_____ other: _____

**5.** In my retirement, I would want to:

_____ work on my hobbies.

_____ travel.

_____ take a part-time job.

_____ other: _____

**6.** For my professional future, I should:

_____ stay just as I am.

_____ take on new interests.

_____ renew present interests.

_____ drop some of my present interests.

_____ other: _____

**7.** With police supervisor colleagues, it is best to:

_____ keep quiet about yourself and your work.

_____ ask for help, advice, or consultation when you need it.

_____ be friendly, but not talk about personal or important business matters.

_____ tell them about yourself and your work.

_____ other: _____

**8.** Does this list leave out any important areas? If so, add other areas, including possible approaches to that area, and then rank them as above.

---

## A VALUES STATEMENT

Several police departments have "mission statements." Fewer have values statements and very few have ethics statements.

No police agency is a single-minded entity . . . they're all run by an "internal values committee" to include power, ambition, envy, caring, trust, humor, loyalty, creativity, dependency, freedom, and many more. As a "member of the committee," you have to get in touch with all members of the values committee to make sure that they are compatible and not confrontational. Hence, the goals and the means to their attainment are in harmony.

Remember, *When our values collide, we divide.*
And, *If you can't talk about it, you can't fix it.*

---

If you can't talk about it, you can't fix it.

---

Figure 1-4 displays a values statement. This statement did not pop out overnight. It was the culmination of hundreds of hours of work by many people.

### *Structured Exercise 1-3*

Search for the values in the values statement (Figure 1-4). How many can you identify? Once identified, attempt to rank order them in order of importance. If asked by a line employee for a definition of each one, what would you say?

## FROM VALUES TO ETHICS

*The capacity to care is the thing which gives life its deepest significance.*

—Pablo Casals
Spanish cellist, composer, conductor

Let us transcend from a caring about values to a more profound caring about ethics. In review:

- A value is something for which we have an *enduring preference.*
- An *enduring preference* means that a value is both a *goal* and a *means* for its pursuit.
- We supervise ourselves and others according to our value system.

   As a preview to Responsibility Two:

- *Our values serve as the birthplace of our ethics.*
- Some values are ethical in quality. Hence, all ethics are values.
- *Our ethics become a part of us.*
- *We supervise ourselves and we supervise others according to our ethics.*

## KEY POINTS

- We supervise ourselves and others according to our value system.
- A value is a means or a goal, or both.
- Our values stem from three periods in our life: imprinting, modeling, and socialization.
- Although enduring, our values can be modified.
- Our values play eight significant functions in our personal and professional lives.
- Our values can be clarified, and it is important that we do so.

# VALUE STATEMENT

We, the members of the Riverside County Sheriff's Department, fill a variety of difficult and demanding roles as we provide law enforcement and related services to our communities. We recognize that trust and support are not automatically granted but must be earned.

To achieve and maintain superior service we proudly commit ourselves to exercise and display the following values:

**I.** *__INTEGRITY__*

We are dedicated to honesty and integrity in all our actions and will uphold our ethical beliefs regardless of the consequences. Our actions must be above reproach. We will:
- Promote and recognize ethical behavior and actions.
- Demand honesty over loyalty.
- Prevent abuse of the law and violation of civil rights.
- Report and confront employees who violate laws and the basic values of the organization.

**II.** *__LOYALTY__*

We are dedicated and loyal to the citizens of our communities, our Department, and our co-workers. Above all, we will be loyal to the Law Enforcement Code of Ethics. We will:
- Reward and recognize those who contribute to the development of more effective ways of providing the policing service.
- Take all reasonable steps and precautions to protect both the employees' and the Department's interest in incidents that present either danger or civil exposure.

**III.** *__PROFESSIONALISM__*

We will serve with honor and vitality. Our professionalism dictates critical self-appraisal and objective analysis, with a commitment to community betterment. We will maintain the position of honor entrusted to us by those we serve. We will:
- Openly discuss both ethical and operational issues.
- Promote an atmosphere that encourages reasonable risk-taking and recognizes that growth and learning may be spawned by honest mistakes.
- Recognize that it is our duty to prevent, report, and investigate crimes; pursue, apprehend, and prosecute lawbreakers.
- Require professional performance for all members of the Department.

**IV.** *__LEADERSHIP__*

We are mandated by law and public expectation to be leaders. We will lead by example and by adherence to our professional ethics and values. We will:
- Listen to and promote suggestions emanating from all levels of the Department.
- Review and react to individual performance based upon the totality of the circumstances surrounding a decision or action.
- Publicly acknowledge and praise employees who excel at their jobs.

**Figure 1-4**    (Courtesy of Riverside County Sheriff's Department)

- The police supervisor is value laden.
- Certain values are ethical in quality.

## DISCUSSION

**1.** How does the phrase "we are what we value" pertain to the police supervisor?

**2.** Indicate what was the most significant input to your value system during each of the three value-programming periods.

**3.** Has anyone had a SEE lately? What did it do to your value system?

**4.** Identify a value—any value (e.g., "personal safety"). Discuss how this value acts as a filter, reflects generation gaps, produces individual differences, creates standards, resolves conflicts, triggers emotions, provokes thoughts, and motivates us.

**5.** What values are of an ethical nature (e.g., trust)?

# RESPONSIBILITY TWO

———◆▸✦◂◆———

# *Ethics*

The responsibility of a police supervisor is to insure that the employees understand and adhere to a professional code of ethics.

*It is the eternal struggle between these two principles—the right and wrong—throughout the world. They are the two principles that have stood face to face from the beginning of time; and will ever continue to struggle.*

—Abraham Lincoln

Earlier you were informed that we supervise ourself and others according to our value system (R-1). Likewise, we also supervise ourself and others according to our ethical standards (R-2). In the next chapter, we will see (R-3) how important it is for the supervisor to constantly communicate and consistently reinforce both.

———

Certain types of values are *ethical values*. Values and ethical values are a branch of philosophy. Ethics is concerned with *moral duties* and how we *should* behave regarding both ends and means. Police work is an intrinsically practical service enterprise that judges its employees and acts only in terms of the effective use of power and the achievement of results.

Ethos is the distinguishing character, moral nature, or *guiding beliefs* of a person, group, or institution. What are your guiding beliefs, those of your work group, those of your department? Does the ethos support or conflict with the ethics? For example, the following are ethical values:

- Honesty
- Fairness
- Trustworthiness
- Integrity

- Respect for others
- Thoughtfulness
- Compassion
- Honor

- Law abidingness
- Loyalty
- Accountability

Let us assume that you possess the preceding values. Now, do your ethos or guiding beliefs agree? Further, do your acts reflect them? There are three vital steps to ethics:

**1.** Knowing what is right.

**2.** Being totally committed to it.

**3.** Doing it.

Here are some useful definitions that will assist us as we progress with this responsibility:

- Ethics   = Body of moral principles or values
- Moral   = Right conduct
- Honesty = *Intending* to act morally and thus subscribing to ethical principles
- Integrity = *Behaving* in a moral way and thus manifesting ethical principles

      Integral = wholeness

### *Structured Exercise 2-1*

Imagine that you are a police officer and you're at roll call training. Your newly assigned sergeant starts the training by introducing himself and then adds, "If you have any doubts about how I want you to treat our citizens, treat them *exactly* the way I treat you!"

Now imagine that you're a police sergeant and you've just introduced yourself to your newly assigned shift officers. One officer raises her hand and asks, "How do you expect us to treat the citizens?" What is your reply? On a sheet of paper or in the margin of this page write down your response. Share this information with others in your group.

## COURAGEOUS CHOICES

*The leader's integrity is not idealistic. It rests on a pragmatic knowledge of how things work.*
—Tao Ti Ching (500 B.C.)

Courage is what gives ethics vibrancy. So many people espouse ethics about integrity, trust, loyalty, and the like until the dilemma is theirs. Then, because of their particular circumstances, selfish needs, and uncomfortable feelings, the ethics become negotiable. Clearly, to resist the inner drive toward self-indulgence over character, requires an ethical code that judges some behaviors as better than others—along with a specialty known as *courage*.

Over the years we have seen and read about officers, supervisors, and managers wrestling with some "hard choices" and some not-so-hard choices. It is important to recognize that there is a constant conflict between the practical realities of politics, personal ambition, and the democratic ideal of selfless public service. Ethics and the "real world" place very different demands on us that are not easily reconcilable. Are we in an ethics vacuum in this nation? Do you perceive a "sleaze factor" in our society? Is there a materialistic excess that has spawned a "me era"?

———◆◆◆◆◆———

Being a police supervisor is a public trust.

———◆◆◆◆◆———

*Public office (e.g., police sergeant) is a public trust.* This axiom, supported by the related idea that participatory democracy requires public confidence in the integrity of government, lays the very foundations for the ethical demands placed on police personnel and the laws establishing baseline standards of behavior. Laws and rules are especially useful concerning choices on brutality, stealing, perjury, and bribe taking. Although the choice here is not always easy, it's clear and straightforward. Laws are needed to define *minimum* standards of conduct.

Referring to such laws and rules as "ethical laws" or "ethical standards" is misleading and actually counterproductive. It is misleading because the laws deal only with a narrow spectrum of ethical decisions facing police employees. It is counterproductive because it encourages us to accept only existing laws as ethics. We accept narrow technical rules as the *only* moral criteria of conduct. Hence, if it's legal, it's ethical. It would be like using the penal code as a substitute for the Bible, Talmud, or Koran.

One reason ethics is much easier said than done is that the legal kind of unethical behavior has become so very ordinary, as we can see from these generic examples.

- Embellishing claims
- Scapegoating personal failures
- Shirking distasteful responsibilities
- Knowingly making unreasonable demands
- Stonewalling questions
- Acting insincerely
- Reneging on promises
- Covering up
- Making consequential decisions unilaterally
- Loafing and loitering

None of these behaviors is scandalous. But each, nonetheless, violates a sense of what is the morally correct behavior (e.g., the behaviors of personal responsibility, honesty, fairness, etc.), increases cynicism and distrust, undermines integrity, and can be a stepping-stone to wrongful behavior.

Though laws can secure compliance within limited margins, they are far too narrow or minimum to act as a substitute for ethics. We expect too much from laws and demand too little from people.

---

Though laws can secure compliance within limited margins, they are far too narrow or minimum to act as a substitute for ethics.

---

The easy choices typically involve clear-cut laws and rules. You take a bribe, the choice may result in the obvious—you're fired and go to jail. The hard choices deal with moral issues and ethical considerations such as a discretion, rule infractions (e.g., sleeping on duty), deception in police investigations, the use of deadly force, the use of physical force, off-duty behavior that may or may not be job related, and so on.

Ethical decisions—courageous choices—are much more difficult than we would like to think. It is not simply a matter of character or upbringing. Ethical decision making requires an alert and informed conscience. It requires the ability to resist self-deception and rationalization. It requires courage and persistence to risk disapproval of others and the loss of power and prestige. Finally, it requires the capacity to evaluate incomplete or confusing facts and anticipate likely consequences under all kinds of pressure.

*Some of us overestimate the costs of being ethical and underestimate the costs of compromise.*

—Michael Josephson

### Structured Exercise 2-2

---

What ethics are reflected in the short story that follows?

> *One of two brothers fighting in the same company in France fell by a German bullet. The one who escaped asked permission of his officer to go and bring his brother in.*
>
> *"He is probably dead," said the officer, "and there is no use in your risking your life to bring in his body."*
>
> *But after further pleading the officer consented. Just as the soldier reached the lines with his brother on his shoulders, the wounded man died.*
>
> *"There, you see," said the officer, "you risked your life for nothing."*
>
> *"No," replied Tom. "I did what he expected of me, and I have my reward. When I crept up to him and took him in my arms, he said, 'Tom, I knew you would come—I just felt you would come.'"*

*There you have the gist of it all; somebody expects something fine and noble and unselfish of us; someone expects us to be faithful.*

———◆·▪◆·◆———

## ETHICAL DECISION MAKING

Ethical decision making is a skill that can be learned. The first step is to know what the ethics are. Figure 2-1 presents an ethical code—if you're a law-enforcement officer (public and private), you should know it. Take a few minutes to read it now; you'll find it loaded with ethical values that are much broader than a set of criminal laws.

### *Structured Exercise 2-3*

———◆·▪◆·◆———

When faced with a decision that involves ethics, ask the following questions of yourself or your work unit.

1. Will the decision I make violate the rights or goodwill of others?
2. What is my personal motive and spirit behind my actions?
3. Will it add to or detract from my reputation?
4. If I were asked to explain my decision in public, would I do so with pride or shame?
5. Even if what I do is not illegal, is it done at someone else's personal expense?
6. Does what I do violate another's reputation?
7. If it were done to me, would I approve or would I take offense and react in pain?
8. What are the basic principles which govern my actions and decisions?
9. When I am in doubt, to whom can and will I go to check my decisions?
10. Will my decision give other people any reason to distrust me?
11. Will my decision build the credibility of my work or profession?

———◆·▪◆·◆———

Ethics in the workplace cannot be left solely to each officer's conscience for two obvious reasons. First, temptations and pressures in the workplace may overcome conscience. Second, a person's unethical behavior invariably affects other officers, Ethics, therefore, must be a departmental as well as an individual responsibility.

Most police personnel want to do the right thing. In fact, this desire is so compelling that some will unintentionally engage in rationalizations to justify ethically doubtful behavior. Building on this tendency, it is possible to increase the likelihood that police employees will act more ethically more often if they're taught how to do it.

We know a police manager who taught himself ethical decision making. When asked how he did it, he replied, "Simple. Every time I have a hard choice to

# Police Code of Conduct

All law enforcement officers must be fully aware of the ethical responsibilities of their position and must strive constantly to live up to the highest possible standards of professional policing.

The International Association of Chiefs of Police believes it important that police officers have clear advice and counsel available to assist them in performing their duties consistent with these standards, and has adopted the following ethical mandates as guidelines to meet these ends.

## Primary Responsibilities of a Police Officer

A police officer acts as an official representative of government who is required and trusted to work within the law. The officer's powers and duties are conferred by statute. The fundamental duties of a police officer include serving the community, safeguarding lives and property, protecting the innocent, keeping the peace and ensuring the rights of all to liberty, equality and justice.

## Performance of the Duties of a Police Officer

A police officer shall perform all duties impartially, without favor or affection or ill will and without regard to status, sex, race, religion, political belief or aspiration. All citizens will be treated equally with courtesy, consideration and dignity.

Officers will never allow personal feelings, animosities or friendships to influence official conduct. Laws will be enforced appropriately and courteously and, in carrying out their responsibilities, officers will strive to obtain maximum cooperation from the public. They will conduct themselves in appearance and deportment in such a manner as to inspire confidence and respect for the position of public trust they hold.

## Discretion

A police officer will use responsibly the discretion vested in his position and exercise it within the law. The principle of reasonableness will guide the officer's determinations, and the officer will consider all surrounding circumstances in determining whether any legal action shall be taken.

Consistent and wise use of discretion, based on professional policing competence, will do much to preserve good relationships and retain the confidence of the public. There can be difficulty in choosing between conflicting courses of action. It is important to remember that a timely word of advice rather than arrest—which may be correct in appropriate circumstances—can be a more effective means of achieving a desired end.

## Use of Force

A police officer will never employ unnecessary force or violence and will use only such force in the discharge of duty as is reasonable in all circumstances.

The use of force should be used only with the greatest restraint and only after discussion, negotiation and persuasion have been found to be inappropriate or ineffective. While the use of force is occasionally unavoidable, every police officer will refrain from unnecessary infliction of pain or suffering and will never engage in cruel, degrading or inhuman treatment of any person.

## Confidentiality

Whatever a police officer sees, hears or learns of that is of a confidential nature will be kept secret unless the performance of duty or legal provision requires otherwise.

Members of the public have a right to security and privacy, and information obtained about them must not be improperly divulged.

## Integrity

A police officer will not engage in acts of corruption or bribery, nor will an officer condone such acts by other police officers.

The public demands that the integrity of police officers be above reproach. Police officers must, therefore, avoid any conduct that might compromise integrity and thus undercut the public confidence in a law enforcement agency. Officers will refuse to accept any gifts, presents, subscriptions, favors, gratuities or promises that could be interpreted as seeking to cause the officer to refrain from performing official responsibilities honestly and within the law. Police officers must not receive private or special advantage from their official status. Respect from the public cannot be bought; it can only be earned and cultivated.

## Cooperation with Other Police Officers and Agencies

Police officers will cooperate with all legally authorized agencies and their representatives in the pursuit of justice.

An officer or agency may be one among many organizations that may provide law enforcement services to a jurisdiction. It is imperative that a police officer assist colleagues fully and completely with respect and consideration at all times.

## Personal-Professional Capabilities

Police officers will be responsible for their own standard of professional performance and will take every reasonable opportunity to enhance and improve their level of knowledge and competence.

Through study and experience, a police officer can acquire the high level of knowledge and competence that is essential for the efficient and effective performance of duty. The acquisition of knowledge is a never-ending process of personal and professional development that should be pursued constantly.

## Private Life

Police officers will behave in a manner that does not bring discredit to their agencies or themselves.

A police officer's character and conduct while off duty must always be exemplary, thus maintaining a position of respect in the community in which he or she lives and serves. The officer's personal behavior must be beyond reproach.

THE INTERNATIONAL ASSOCIATION OF CHIEFS OF POLICE

**Figure 2-1** Police Code of Conduct (Reprinted with permission of the International Association of Chiefs of Police.)

make, I imagine my Dad standing in front of me and looking into my eyes. At the same moment, I imagine my ten-year-old daughter looking over my shoulder. With this picture in my mind, a hard choice converts into an easy one for me."

## STRATEGY FOR FOSTERING INTEGRITY

A police employee can be dishonest, break commitments, and be unfair and unaccountable (e.g., the abuse of sick leave) without breaking the law.

Whey the concern for building a strategy to combat unlawful or unethical conduct? First, wrongful conduct reduces public confidence in the police and thus inhibits citizens from cooperating in crime prevention and control. Second, it enhances criminal activity. After all, if the police are corrupt, others may decide to follow their example. Third, it destroys effective police management and supervision. Finally, departmental morale goes down the drain.

We propose a five-point strategy for fostering integrity as follows:

1. *Live it.* The chief, command staff, and supervisors must, minute by minute, speak with integrity and act with integrity. Line personnel do pay careful attention to what their bosses think and do!
2. *Accountability.* Poorly managed and supervised departments are breeding grounds for slimy behavior. Every police manager and supervisor must be, first of all, answerable for his or her conduct as well as the conduct of the staff.
3. *Moralistic discretion.* The decisions by the police must be compatible with the overarching values of society and especially their community. All police activity should be subjected to the light of truth—this light is a combination of legal constraints and ethical propositions.
4. *Outside help.* Gaining the backing of the city manager, city council, and board of supervisors is of help. Much of their support would manifest itself in them speaking about and acting with integrity. Other criminal justice agencies (the prosecuting attorney and criminal courts) are also important in pushing integrity.
5. *Ethics learning.* Values can be learned, leadership can be learned, public speaking can be learned, and so on. Most crucial, ethics can be learned. A police department program that does nothing more than keep behavior legal, while no small accomplishment, would not be a bona fide ethics program. It would be more of a "law-enforcement" program. Laws and regulations are not the answer to keeping behavior above the bottom line of ethics. Training is.

## ETHICS TRAINING

All of us have been trained to read, write, and calculate numbers. We've been trained to operate a computer, a fax machine, an automobile. We've learned how to protect ourselves from being victimized. We learned many, many more things. How many of us, have you, taken a course on ethical conduct? Ethics training for police employees has been nonexistent or superficial. This is changing. There is, fortunately, an accelerating trend to train ethics.

It is possible for police agencies to create a positive ethical culture that nurtures and rewards moral behavior and discourages bad conduct.

It is possible for police agencies to create a positive ethical culture that nurtures and rewards moral behavior and discourages bad conduct. There are four ways to enhance ethics.

1. Inspiration
2. Collaboration
3. Education and training
4. Integration

### Inspiration

Inspiration is fostered by the following:

**LEADERSHIP BY EXAMPLE.** *We preach a better sermon with our life than with our lips.* We've heard sergeants comment with detectable frustration, "The officers don't pay attention to me." Nonsense. They do pay *careful* attention to their supervisors and managers. For most officers, leadership either occurs or not based on their relationship to their sergeant and, to a lesser extent, the middle manager. They rarely have direct contact with the administrators. Essentially, they see them on occasion and basically know them secondhand through what the sergeant may have to say about them. We're aware of some supervisors who imply that "management is the enemy." Little do they realize that the officer is likely to take such a warning one step further—"If they're my enemy, you're best not trusted either." Remember, *your staff does pay careful consideration to what you say and what you do!*

**VALUE ORIENTATION.** *Assure that everyone, especially newcomers, knows and understands the laws, rules, and values that should guide their hearts and behavior.* This establishes a culture of ethics. If your agency has a mission statement, a code of ethics, or a set of goals, periodically review it with your staff. Reinforce it with the decisions you make—live it minute by minute.

With all cultures there are countercultures. Some countercultures may be good (e.g., a group of officers who refuse to accept bribes when others do so). Alternatively, we may see an agency striving very hard to provide high-quality services, whereas a counterculture of officers is advocating that the public (or most of it) is the enemy.

Culture building is not a one-shot endeavor. It takes time and a lot of reinforcement. People want to know the rules, the laws, the goals, and the values that guide and measure their activity. Far too often we've been told by officers (sometimes by sergeants and higher-command personnel), "I do not know what our mission is here. I do not know if we have a set of goals. I really have a sense of aimlessness." The answer, if there isn't a mission statement or set of values or goals, is—create them for your staff. Use the International Association of Chiefs of Police or the National Sheriffs Code of Ethics as a start. Remember, one of your responsibilities is to build a culture that is value laden—especially with ethical values.

**LIMITATIONS OF LAWS AND RULES.** *The technical compliance with laws is necessary but not always enough!* A person can be dishonest, break commitments, be unfair and unaccountable without breaking the law. Laws cannot replace the need for a sensitive conscience or free one of the moral duty to adhere to traditional *ethical principles.* To encourage good faith acceptance of the moral obligation to abide by both the letter and spirit of the law, every opportunity must be used to (1) clarify the reasons for the rules; and (2) emphasize the importance of the "appearance of wrongdoing" test.

Good ethics are expected and appreciated by supervisors. The line personnel are no different—good ethics are expected and appreciated by them, of their supervisors. Those supervisors who use the legal do's and don'ts, who impose the "should" and "should not" of rules are missing their main power source—ethical values.

## Collaboration

Collaboration can be achieved by the following:

**UNIFYING THE GROUP.** *Unify individuals behind the traditional ethical values.* One way is to appeal to the common interest all personnel have in ethical behavior of every individual. All should be informed that it is to everyone's advantage that police personnel (sworn and civilian) be, and be perceived to be, ethical. the goal here is shared esteem for duty and honor, and where it is obviously unacceptable for any member to place self-interest (e.g., taking extra rewards such as free meals) above the public trust.

We've listened to a sheriff admonish his staff about not accepting gratuities. "Not one dime, not one cup of coffee," he asserted. Later, he signed a permit to "carry a concealed weapon" for one of his key campaign donors. Something doesn't jibe here. A colleague of ours had the courage to tell a story on himself. He sermonized a group of newly appointed sheriff's sergeants on the virtues of honesty. For thirty minutes he extolled them on morality. He then proceeded to play a pirated VCR tape. Naturally, the duplicated tape was politely called to his attention by members of the group. He was embarrassed, he blushed, he was speechless. He learned a lesson, however. If you're going to preach something, you'd darn well better be practicing it.

**SPECIFYING GUIDELINES.** *Specify guidelines and approaches for deciding on hard choices.* This task involves the development and pronouncement of minimum standards of behavior for various situations. It also involves guidelines for coping with the totally unanticipated circumstances.

We recall a police sergeant that reprimanded one of his officers for poor performance with, "Maynard, you've only given the minimum here since I've been your supervisor!" Maynard snapped back, "Sergeant, if the minimum wasn't acceptable, it wouldn't be the minimum!" Either the "minimum" had not been conveyed, or it should be elevated. Hard choices require known guidelines.

### Education and Training

Ongoing educational programs focusing on *issue spotting*, reasoning, and other decision-making skills are vital ingredients of an ethics program. We believe the following should be included in the program.

• **No sermonizing.** *Moralizing about ethics is not very effective in sustaining or changing attitudes and behavior.* Traditional lectures on ethics should be scrapped and replaced with group discussions. We're confident that if police personnel were asked in the early 1980s, "Where might our major vulnerability for corruption be?" the answer would have been, in most cases, "Drug money and drug usage." The officers knew this but, regretfully, few administrators asked them.

No one likes to be "should upon." We've attempted to avoid doing that here. If we fell prey to sermonizing, we apologize.

Our intent here is to emphasize:

- Ethics as a subset of values
- What ethics are all about
- Ethical standards at times makes for hard and courageous choices
- Ethics can be trained
- Supervisors often make decisions involving ethical matters
- Individual acts of moral courage are never wasted—each instance of ethical fortitude provides a lasting example that teaches and inspires.

• **Practical problem solving.** *"Seeing ethics" is easier than "doing ethics."* The first involves *consciousness* and the second emphasizes *commitment*. We must learn how to better evaluate facts and make reasoned decisions on ethical conduct. There are some people who overestimate the costs of being ethical and underestimate the "costs of" compromising ethical values. Decisions that include deceit or coercion often cause secondary risks that are not seen or properly evaluated. If you wonder what we mean by this last statement, merely scan the front page or business section of a daily newspaper.

An ethics course should attempt to build competency in creative, practical problem solving. This can be accomplished by helping others to identify optional approaches for staying on the "high road" and avoiding the lower one.

---

"Seeing ethics" is easier than "doing ethics."

---

• **Recognizing ethical issues.** *People should be educated and trained in early detection of ethical issues.* They should be sensitized to the eight factors that tend to defeat ethical instincts.

- Self-interest
- Self-protection
- Self-deception
- Self-righteousness

- Rationalization
- Groupthink
- Greed
- Envy

Self-interest tends to impede one's ethical awareness. When our personal interests subordinate our professional code of conduct, objectivity is next to impossible. In such cases, there is a tendency to push the importance for the questionable conduct.

An example of this occurred when a bright and respected police chief we know submitted an application for a nationally recognized award for his department—not himself. The award involved no monetary gain for anyone. Someone disclosed that the department had not met the requirements for the award, and the chief knew it. He resigned. He apologized and emphasized that his action was not for his "self-interest." He deceived himself and lost his job as a consequence. If he'd only spoken to a few, trusted associates, they would have likely caused a "reality checkpoint" for him. He might have heard, "Don't do it! You're deceiving yourself."

One means for determining if you're becoming a victim to the preceding eight factors is asking yourself or your work unit to review the following:

- "Ethics is not performance."
- "Ethics is behavior, and behavior and results are the two parts of performance."
- "Ethics is too subjective to be measured."
- "Ethical behaviors can be appraised."
- "It's an overseeing big brother."
- "Not if done right, like self-appraisal with exceptions."
- "It makes ethics confrontational."
- "Unethical behavior needs to be confronted."
- "We hold people accountable in other ways."
- "What ways and how well?"
- "It's implicitly understood."
- "Ethics and its communication are too important to be left to mind reading."

### *Structured Exercise 2-4*

Some of the following comments are signposts of ethical wrongdoing. Have you heard, or are you now hearing, them in your organization? Discuss this exercise as a group.

### Denying or trivializing its significance

- "Show me a victim."
- "It's not illegal."

- "You can't legislate morality."
- "It's just a technicality."

## Invoking the double standard
- "Morality is a personal matter."
- "I don't mix business with my personal feelings."

## Arguing necessity
- "It's cutthroat out there."
- "If I don't do it, someone else will."
- "It's my job."
- "It will save some jobs."

## Arguing relativity
- "It's not illegal elsewhere."
- "In the United States, ideals are turned into laws."
- "No act is inherently illegal."
- "We are no worse or better than society at large."

## Professing ignorance
- "I wasn't told."
- "Ethics is a gray area."
- "The rules are inscrutable."

---

- **Anticipating ethical problems**. Typically, those in the best position to anticipate ethical challenges are supervisors. After all, they've recently experienced identical or similar hard choices. Any ethics program must be custom built by and for a particular agency. What may be an ethics problem for one agency may not be for anther.

Members of an agency should be surveyed to discover ethical problems and issues. Once the critical concerns have been spotted, then training scenarios and simulations can be constructed. Similar to a finely tuned and expertly trained athlete, all of us can be conditioned to make, when necessary, the right choices, which frequently are the courageous choices.

- **Own reward**. An ethics course should acknowledge that integrity, trust, and honor may not give immediate rewards or gratification, and they can be career-threatening (e.g., informing the chief that a lieutenant is stealing). The absence of integrity, trust, and honor may go undetected and unpunished. In fact, great wealth and power may be gained. Therefore, being ethical must be its own reward.

- **Temptations.** Being ethical does not mean we're temptation free. There are going to be exciting temptations toward which we will feel drawn. It is at that moment we have the opportunity to make a choice for time-honored rules of conduct, including everything from etiquette to morality, to get us through the situation without acquiescing to it, because we know that, ultimately, it is likely not to be in our best interest to succumb.

---

*Assessing motives is usually pointless and often harmful.*

---

- **Motives.** Assessing motives is usually pointless and often harmful. It is pointless because motives are almost impossible to determine. We often don't know our own let alone those of others. It is harmful because we almost always exaggerate the purity of our own motives and assign evil motives to those of others.

The solution to this problem is: We should judge *actions*—our own and those of others—not motives. An ethics course should emphasize that it is what we *do*, not what we *intend*, that counts!

---

*A police department can survive a serious crime condition but not its officers' lack of ethical conduct.*

---

- **Basically good.** The belief that employees are inherently good is one of the most widely held beliefs in society. Yet is is both untrue and destructive. As far as our proposition about "inherently good," look around and you'll detect numerous infractions of rules and policies. The destructiveness occurs when people concentrate on the external forces (e.g., "My mom forgot to cut the crust off my sandwiches") rather than the human will. Those who believe in innate human goodness view the battle for a better world as primarily a conflict between the individual and society. We think that, especially in a free society, the battle is between the individual and his or her character. A police department can survive a serious crime condition but not its officers' lack of ethical conduct.

## Integration

Basically, this step involves combining *inspiration, collaboration, education,* and *training* into a comprehensive package that daily becomes a viable influence within our lives and our organizations. Unfortunately, exercising moral restraint does not ensure that others will do likewise. On occasion it places the ethical person at a disadvantage in competing with persons who are constrained by ethical principles.

Do you agree, or not, that it is better to lose than to sacrifice integrity? One person quipped, "The trouble with the rat race is that even if you win, you're still a rat." We cannot turn moral commitment on and off as it suits us or the situation. An ethically based person cannot win by being dishonest, disloyal, or unfair any more than one can truly win a tennis match by cheating.

*The most important human endeavor is the striving for morality in our actions. Our inner balance, and even our very existence, depends on it. Only morality in our actions can give beauty and dignity to our lives.*

—Albert Einstein

## PARADIGMS

You are quite literally unable to to perceive data right before your very eyes. Stop for a moment and reread the preceding sentence. Anything unusual about it? Look again. Read it slowly. Did you catch the second "to"? If not, you've experienced the paradigm affect. And it is capable of either helping or hindering you in making choices about your decisions. You'll see how later. First, let us define and describe it so that you'll appreciate its enormous strength.

---

A paradigm is a set of rules and regulations (written or unwritten) that does two things: (1) It essentially establishes or defines boundaries; and (2) it tells you how to behave inside the boundaries in order to be successful.

---

**DEFINITION AND DESCRIPTION.** A paradigm is a set of rules and regulations (written or unwritten) that does two things: (1) It establishes or defines boundaries; and (2) it tells you how to behave inside the boundaries in order to be successful. If we equate being successful with being ethical, ethical behavior can be measured by the choices you make when solving problems—problems from trivial issues to matters of honor.

A police organization is a forest of paradigms. There are management paradigms, promotion paradigms, deployment paradigms, loyalty paradigms, and so on. In our personal life, there are even more paradigms—how we raise our children; the foods we eat; the friends we keep; the music we listen to; our political choices; our choice of marriage partners, and so forth.

A paradigm tells you how to play the game of life according to the rules. However, the rules are subject to change. Watch for people messing with the rules, because that is the earliest sign of significant change.

### *Structured Exercise 2-5*

---

Very quickly add up the following numbers and record your addition. This completes the exercise.

                1000

                 40

                1000

                 30

                1000

                 20

                1000

                 10

———————◆━►◆◄━◆———————

Incidentally, what was your bottom-line number—5,000? You just applied your addition paradigm. By the way, the correct number is 4,100.

What is your paradigm of "work ethic"? Are you alone in subscribing to it, or is it pervasive in your department? Remember, you see your world through your paradigms. As a consequence, they significantly influence what you think is right or wrong. For example, your work ethic may be one that rules out accepting anything that is normally paid for as free (e.g., food). Someone else, perhaps a co-worker, has a work ethic paradigm that rules in free meals.

Another case in point could be "honesty." What do you say when someone asks you "How do I look?" and the individual appears to be seriously ill. Do you respond, "Very sick" or "Just fine"? Which one is dishonest? Or could it be that, according to one's paradigm, they're both honest?

- *"The phonograph…is not of any commercial value."* Thomas Edison, remarking on his own invention to his assistant Sam Insull, 1880.
- *"I hereby request that the U.S. Patent Office be closed because everything that can be invented has been invented!"* U.S. Patent Office Commissioner, 1889.
- *"Sensible and responsible women do not want to vote."* Grover Cleveland, 1905.
- *"There is no likelihood man can ever tap the power of the atom."* Robert Millikan, Nobel Prize winner in physics, 1920.
- *"[Babe] Ruth made a big mistake when he gave up pitching."* Tris Speaker, 1921.
- *"Who the hell wants to hear actors talk?"* Harry Warner, Warner Brothers Pictures, 1927.
- *"I think there is a world market for about five computers."* Thomas J. Watson, chairman of IBM, 1943.
- *"Americans are destined to have nuclear power that is too cheap to meter."* Popular Science, 1965.
- *"The computer will create the paperless society."* Some misguided moron, circa 1970.

- *"There is no reason for any individual to have a computer in their home."* Ken Olsen, president of Digital Equipment Corporation, 1977. (In 1960, Olsen created the minicomputer. DEC grew in eight years to a $6.7 billion company. Olsen could not see or react to the "personal computer" and was forced to resign.)

### *Structured Exercise 2-6*

Individually, or better as a group, generate two lists of paradigms that pertain to police organizations. One list should be "old and disproved" (e.g., women can't function as police officers) and the other "currently held" (e.g., empowerment leads to better decisions).

**PARADIGMS ARE COMMON.**   Paradigms abound in our lives. Many are non-consequential. Some pack major impacts (e.g., an ethical decision involving one's loyalty). But all paradigms—major and minor—have the same effect of giving a person special vision, understanding, and problem-solving methods.

**PARADIGMS ARE FUNCTIONAL.**   We need paradigms. We need rules and boundaries to help us live and work in this turbulent society. They are functional because they help us distinguish data that is important from that which is not. The rules tell us how to look at the data and then how to deal with it. With my paradigms, I can solve certain classes of problems. With your paradigms, you can solve another class of problems. It is our *diversity* as a group that lets us deal with the complexity of the world through their application.

**PARADIGMS REVERSE SEEING AND BELIEVING.**   In some cases, we have to know the rules or principles to see a concept. In other words, you have to believe it before you're in a position to see it. Whether music, a painting, or a new program (community-oriented policing), you typically must believe in the rules (principles) before you can fully grasp the contents of what lies before you.

I'll see it when I believe it.

This explains why some new police employees have a difficult time of adjustment. What they are really doing is adjusting to the paradigms of the department, and until they know those rules, they will literally be unable to see things that are obvious to people who have been there for a while. The temptation is to think that these people are not intelligent enough to handle the job. The fact is, they may have more than enough intelligence; they simply lack the understanding of the particular paradigm.

**PARADIGMS ALMOST ALWAYS PROVIDE MORE THAN ONE RIGHT ANSWER.**  By changing my paradigm, I change my perception of the world. That does not have to mean I must have contradictory perceptions; rather that I am seeing another part of the world that is just as real as the part that I saw with the other rules. But because one paradigm gives me one set of information and another paradigm gives me another set, I can achieve two different, yet equally accurate explanations of what is happening in the world.

---

Even with ethics there may be more than one choice.

---

Anyone who assumes there is only one right answer is missing the point of paradigms. Even with ethics, there may be more than one right choice. After all, there are usually several wrong choices attached to an ethical decision.

**PARADIGM PARALYSIS.**  Paradigm paralysis is, unfortunately, an easy illness to get and is often fatal. It grows from a situation of power. We all have our paradigms, but, when one is successful and in power, there is a temptation to take our paradigm and convert it *into the* paradigm. After all, isn't it what made us successful? Once we have the paradigm in place, then any suggested alternative has to be wrong. "That's not the way we do things around here." This problem can occur at all levels, in all police organizations and in the long run will discourage new ideas.

**PARADIGM PLIANCY.**  Paradigm pliancy is intentionally seeking out new ways of doing things. It stimulates innovations and creative problem solving. Here are three questions that trigger imagination. Once asked, be quiet and listen. You'll be surprised at how many good ideas you will hear.

1. "What do I believe is impossible to do in my field but, if it could be done, would fundamentally change my work?"
2. "I never thought about it that way before. Can you tell me more?"
3. "Who, outside my field, might be interested in my unsolved problems?"

To ignore the power of paradigms to influence your judgment is to put yourself at significant risk as a police supervisor. To be successful, you have to be ready and able to change your paradigms.

**PARADIGMS CAN BE CHANGED BY HUMAN CHOICE.**  Human beings are not genetically programmed with only one way of looking at the world. In fact, our freedom of choice gives us the capability to look at the world in a wide variety of ways. We may not be able to change our paradigm or those of another, but we always retain the choice of how we react to them. As a human being, it is one of our rights.

The paradigms that you hold about ethics are of your choice. And you can either agree or disagree with those held by others.

> You will be what you will be
> But failure finds its false content
> In that poor word environment
> But spirit scorns it and is free.

## KEY POINTS

- Ethics focuses on moral duties and how we should behave.
- Ethos is the distinguishing quality, moral nature, or guiding beliefs we hold.
- Certain values serve as ethical values.
- Obeying the law is an easy choice as compared with an ethical decision that can be a hard choice.
- Self-deception and rationalization will cause us difficulty with hard choices.
- Ethics training involves inspiration, collaboration, education, and integration.
- Education and training in ethics best:
  - avoid sermonizing,
  - promote practical problem solving;
  - help in recognizing ethical issues;
  - show how to anticipate problems;
  - emphasize that ethics is its own reward;
  - identify temptations;
  - concentrate on actions, not motives; and
  - accept the fact humankind is not basically good.
  - Paradigms determine what we can easily understand, and what is difficult for us to comprehend.
  - Typically, there is more than one correct answer to being honorable.

## DISCUSSION

1. Develop a group setting. Identify and rank order what you as a group believe to be the seven most important ethical values that a police supervisor should hold. Next, rate yourself against each value with a number of one (low) to seven (high). Discuss your highest and lowest ratings with your associates.
2. What does *ethos* mean to you? Cite a guiding belief that *you* believe represents your police agency.

**3.** Relatively, obeying the law is an easy choice. Making ethical decisions is a hard choice. Why? Do you have examples?

**4.** Identify a recent motion picture that portrays "moral courage." Describe an act or activity. Why did you select it? What does it tell us?

**5.** What has this responsibility not covered? Where did it push or sermonize? Where did it seem uncertain or lacking?

**6.** How do paradigms influence our ethical decision making?

# RESPONSIBILITY THREE

---

# *Leadership*

The *police supervisor* is responsible for cultivating the characteristics of a leader and then applying them in a productive, positive, and caring manner.

*I would sooner fail than not be among the greatest.*

—John Keats

With your values (R-1) and ethics (R-2) in mind, you have established both a basis and a framework for exercising leadership (R-3), which depends on your ability to communicate (R-4) it.

---

There is a big difference between supervision and leadership. Leaders and supervisors differ in orientation, mission, assumptions, behavior, organizational environments, and ultimately results.

Leadership is the process of moving police personnel in some direction, mostly through their willingness to go. Supervisors are more short term, control-oriented, and report focused. Leaders think longer term, comprehend the relationship of larger realities, think in terms of renewal, have social perception, cause change, emphasize values, and achieve unity.

There is nothing wrong with being a supervisor. Clearly, we've needed them in the past and will do so in the future. Our hope here is for *the police supervisor to also take on the mantle of a leader.*

---

There is a big difference between supervision and leadership.

---

We've looked at numerous definitions of leadership and have a few of our own. We believe Warren Bennis exposes it when he writes that the leader is the person *who knows what he or she wants, communicates it to others, positions himself or herself correctly, and then empowers others to perform their duties successfully.* If this definition is too long for you, then we'd merely say that *leadership is self-expression.*

## AUTHORITY AND POWER

Leadership can and ought to be a logical addition of a paramount strength to the position of police supervisor. As you have perhaps seen or surmised, not all supervisors are leaders. Alternatively, not all leaders are supervisors. Supervision and leadership can occur together, which is highly preferable, or they can operate separate from one another. The single linking pin between the two functions is *influence.*

### Authority

Once, in a police agency, we noticed that the police chief "managed" and that his assistant chief managed and "led." Briefly, the chief used the *authority* of his office to gain compliance and provide direction for *achieving results.* Authority is the "right" to command. The assistant chief had the same right and executed it at times. However, he most often relied on his leadership, or his individual capacity for managing. Although both were successful managers, the assistant chief demonstrated more *effectiveness* in achieving results than did the chief.

Authority is the *right* to command. All police supervisors have it. As a police supervisor, your authority originates in your *position.* Your position grants you the right to reward and sanction the behavior of those who work for you. In other words, all three—position + rewards + sanctions—provide you with authority. And, when you exercise your authority, you are attempting to influence the attitudes and behavior of others. If they comply, then your authority is working well.

**POSITION.** By its very definition, your position is to command or influence the acts of others. The statement of your duties, your stripes, your salary, your training, and so on, attest to the responsibilities of the job.

**REWARDS.** Your authority to reward is based on the right to control and administer rewards to others (such as money, promotions, or praise) for compliance with the agency's requests or directives.

**SANCTIONS.** Your authority to sanction is based on the right to control and administer punishments to others (such as reprimand or termination) for noncompliance with the agency's requests or directives.

### Power

Supervisors, because of the responsibilities of their position, acquire the right or the authority to command. With this right or authority goes influence. Hence, police supervisors are strategically located for moving an agency toward goal attainment. It is the effective supervisor who develops his or her talent for leading others, and consequently possesses a significantly enhanced influence (authority + power) for achieving results—for *achieving results effectively.*

---

Authority is the right to command. Power comes from expertise and example.

---

Fundamentally, your power is person based as compared with position based. Your power to lead others is derived from your *expertise* and *example.* Both combine to attract others to follow you.

**EXPERTISE.**     Expert power is based on a special ability, skill, expertise, or knowledge exhibited by an individual. For example, a new police sergeant may have some questions regarding the functioning of a piece of equipment. Rather than ask the lieutenant, the supervisor contacts the individual who previously held the sergeant's position for assistance because of his or her previous knowledge or expertise with the equipment.

**EXAMPLE OR REFERENT.**     Referent power is based on the attractiveness or the appeal of one person to another. A leader may be admired because of certain characteristics or traits that inspire or attract followers (charisma is an example). Referent power may also be based on a person's connection with another powerful individual. For example, the title of "assistant" has been given to people who work closely with others with titles such as sheriff or police chief. Although the title of assistant to the sheriff may not have reward or coercive (or legitimate) power, other individuals may perceive that this person is acting with the consent of the boss, resulting in his or her power to influence. The sheriff's assistant is perceived as the sheriff's alter ego. Many will wonder if the assistant is acting for the sheriff or on his or her own. Rather than take a chance, one typically opts in favor of the former possibility.

Keep in mind that *power is the capacity to command.* All police supervisors have it. Not all police supervisors use it. Hence, only some police supervisors are leaders.

## FORMAL AND INFORMAL LEADERS

Not all police leaders have sergeant's stripes or lieutenant's or captain's bars. For a number of reasons, there are informal leaders. These people surface in all organizations to fill a one-time or ongoing need. For example, if a particular expertise is required, then the person who possesses it will provide leadership. This could occur if the victim of a crime can communicate only in Spanish. A Spanish-speaking officer thus may temporarily lead in an investigation. Another occurs when the supervisor fails to establish followership because of either inadequate expertise or a poor example. The work group will commonly fill this void by creating an informal leader.

The reasons for an informal leader emerging determine if it is helpful or harmful to the work group. Informal leaders are a normal phenomenon in an

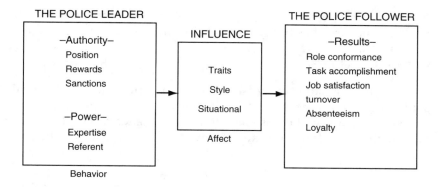

THE POLICE LEADER

−Authority−
Position
Rewards
Sanctions

−Power−
Expertise
Referent

Behavior

INFLUENCE

Traits

Style

Situational

Affect

THE POLICE FOLLOWER

−Results−
Role conformance
Task accomplishment
Job satisfaction
turnover
Absenteeism
Loyalty

**Figure 3-1**

organization. They can be extremely useful to a supervisor if they act in concert with and support of the group's goals.

*Leadership* is a relationship between two or more people, in which one attempts to influence the other(s) toward the attainment of a goal or goals. Figure 3-1 summarizes the relationship between power, influence, and leadership.

The key to the concept of leadership is to look at it as an influence process. It is a process that includes the elements of the *power base* of the leader and of the degree of acceptance with the characteristics, needs, and decision role of the subordinate(s).

## LEADERSHIP AND SUPERVISION

*The dominant principle of organization has shifted, from supervision and management in order to control an enterprise, to leadership in order to bring out the best in people and to respond quickly to change.*

—John Naisbett and Patricia Aberdene

Please reread the above quotation. Think about it for a few moments. This is not the "police leadership" officers so often call for when they really want a father figure to take care of all their problems. It is a participative yet demanding leadership that respects people and encourages self-management, autonomous teams, and problem-oriented policing.

While we differentiate leadership from supervision, we are not knocking people who supervise only. However, we need to recognize that someone can be a successful supervisor and a lousy leader. The reverse is equally true—someone can be a lousy supervisor and a competent leader. We would all like that wonderful balance of leader-supervisor, but one role usually dominates the other. Basically, a supervisor relies on *organizational authority* to get the job done, while a leader uses *personal power*.

- The supervisor administers; the leader innovates.
- The supervisor has a short-range view; the leader has a long-range perspective.

- The supervisor asks how and when; the leader asks what and why.
- The supervisor has his eye on the bottom line; the leader has his eye on the horizon.
- The supervisor accepts the status quo; the leader challenges it.

Leadership skills are possessed by a majority but used by a minority. It's something that can be learned by anyone, taught to everyone, denied to no one. Nonetheless, Warren Bennis has asserted that leadership is like the Abominable Snowman whose footprints are everywhere but is nowhere to be seen.

————◆◆◆◆◆————

Many police departments have overmanaged and underled.

————◆◆◆◆◆————

*The problem with many police organizations, and especially the ones that are deficient, is that they tend to be overmanaged and underled.* Supervision and leadership are equally important. Supervisors do things right, and leaders do the right thing. The first concentrates on efficiency, and the second requires effectiveness. (Please reread this paragraph—it's fundamental to everything that follows.)

We are convinced that leadership is *the* pivotal force causing ordinary organizations to be successful organizations.

## THREE THEORIES OF LEADERSHIP

Three major theories of leadership will be examined: the *trait theory*, the *behavioral theory*, and the *situational theory*. The basic foundation of each approach is summarized in Table 3-1.

**Table 3-1**   Major Theories of Leadership

| Theory | Emphasis |
|---|---|
| Trait (1940s–1950s) | There exists a finite set of individualized *traits* or characteristics that can be used to distinguish successful leaders from unsuccessful leaders. |
| Behavioral (1950s–1960s) | The most important aspect of leadership is not the traits of the leader, but what the leader does in various situations. Successful leaders are distinguished from unsuccessful leaders by their particular *style* of leadership. |
| Situational (1970s) | The effectiveness of the leader is determined not only by his or her style of behavior but also by the *situation* surrounding the leadership environment. Situational factors include the characteristics of the leader and the subordinate(s), the nature of the task, and the structure of the group. |

## Trait

During my basic (preentry) police training, platoon leaders were selected by the cadre. Each was one of the tallest members of our sixty-six-person academy class. Being only average in height, I was excluded from consideration. Apparently, leaders are tall (Alexander the Great, Napoleon, and Hyman Rickover) or psychologically powerful (Franklin D. Roosevelt, Helen Keller, Mohandas K. Gandhi). Although the results of these trait considerations appear to be helpful in identifying certain salient characteristics of leaders, little has been provided for understanding or predicting leadership effectiveness. The list of important leadership traits is endless and grows with each passing year. It has not yet been shown that a finite set of traits can distinguish successful from unsuccessful leaders. Although such aspects as personality do appear to be significant factors, they are only a few of the many factors that can contribute to leadership effectiveness.

Also, focusing on individual traits does not show what a police manager actually does in a leadership situation. Traits can identify who the police leader is, but not the behavioral patterns he or she will exhibit in attempting to influence subordinate actions. The trait theory has ignored the police subordinates and their effect on leadership. The effectiveness of leadership depends to a large extent on the situation within the environment of the leadership or influence process: A particular leadership pattern may be effective for a group of uniformed police officers, but may be totally ineffective for a group of detectives. Interactions among the many factors of the situation must be examined before any predictions about leadership effectiveness can be made.

## Behavioral

During the 1950s the dissatisfaction with the trait theory of leadership led behavioral scientists to focus their attention on the actual behavior of a leader—what leaders do and how they do it. The foundation for the style-of-leadership approach was the belief that effective leaders applied a particular style to leading individuals and groups to the achievement of certain goals, resulting in high productivity and morale. Unlike the trait theory, the behavioral theory focused on *leader effectiveness*, not on the emergence of an individual as a leader.

A number of definitions of leadership style were developed. Although many terms were assigned to the different leadership styles, two factors were emphasized in each approach: task orientation and employee orientation. *Task orientation* is the emphasis that a leader places on getting a job done by such actions as assigning and organizing the work, making decisions, and evaluating performance. *Employee orientation* is the openness and friendliness exhibited by a leader and the leader's concern for the needs of his or her personnel.

In their search for the most effective leadership style, the researchers' findings suggested that a universally accepted "best" style was inappropriate for the complexities of modern organizations. For a supervisor's leadership style to be effective, other situational factors must be considered.

## Situational

During the late 1960s, researchers recognized the limitations of the behavioral theory and began to develop a new theory of leadership, focusing on the more complex situational factors. The work of the trait and the behavioral style theorists provided a significant foundation for the study of leadership within organizations, because the results of these researchers strongly suggested that the most effective way to lead is a dynamic and flexible process that adapts to particular situations.

---

*One of the most important functions of a supervisor's role is to diagnose and evaluate the many factors that may have an impact on leadership effectiveness.*

---

One of the most important functions of a supervisor's role is to diagnose and evaluate the many factors that may have an impact on the effectiveness of his or her leadership. Diagnosis involves the identification and understanding of the influence of factors such as individual differences, group structure, and agency policies and practices. A careful study of each situation is a crucial process for leaders contemplating the application of a particular style. For example, a group of uniformed police officers working under conditions of extreme stress to control a riot will require a different type of leadership style than would a group of detectives who routinely investigate the properties of a criminal event. The accurate diagnosis of a situation requires an examination by a supervisor of four important areas: (1) supervisory characteristics, (2) subordinate characteristics, (3) group structure and the nature of the task, and (4) organizational factors.

1. *Supervisory characteristics.* The leader's behavior in any given environment is dependent on the forces or characteristics of the individual. The important factors include
   a. Personality characteristics
   b. Needs and motives
   c. Past experience and reinforcement

2. *Subordinate characteristics.* Before a police leader decides on a particular leadership style, he or she should assess the individual characteristics and behavioral patterns of the staff. The staff members, like the police supervisor, have internal factors that may affect their behavior. Some of these factors include
   a. Personality characteristics
   b. Needs and motives
   c. Past experience and reinforcement

3. *Group structure.* Groups are a prominent feature in society and organizations. The particular characteristics of the group usually have a significant impact on a police supervisor's ability to lead his or her personnel. Some of the important group factors include

   **a.** Group development stage (Where the group is in its development can influence the effectiveness of a particular leadership style. The supervisor's behavior during the orientation stage may not be appropriate during the internal problem-solving stage, in which conflict resolution is a frequent occurrence.)

   **b.** Group structure

   **c.** Group task (The nature of the task has an important impact on the success of any leader's influence activities. For example, groups working on ambiguous tasks may require a completely different type of leadership than groups involved with routine tasks.)

4. *Organizational factors.* Among the most crucial yet least understood factors in the leadership situation is the type of organization. Some of the most important considerations are

   **a.** Influence base (What is the foundation of a police leader's influence base? Does it consist of authority, reward, coercion, expertise, and referent power, or some subset?)

   **b.** Rules and procedures (Agencies vary in the manner in which rules, policies, standards, and procedures are used to guide the work of police employees. Many police departments have developed extensive policy systems, such as manuals and standard operating procedures, that may dictate the type of police-leader behavior required.)

   **c.** Professionalism (Highly trained police professionals, such as criminal investigators, may depend more on their educational backgrounds or experiences than on the police leader to guide their work, which may limit the ability of the leader to influence them.)

   **d.** Time (If an immediate decision must be made, or if there is a high level of tension and stress, the involvement of personnel may be difficult, if not impossible. However, there is usually ample time to elicit the opinion of those who will be affected by the pending decision.)

## Old and New Situations

Table 3-2 presents a listing of old and new situations. The situational leader is expected to modify or move his or her work unit/organization from the old to the new. For instance, at one time it was thought that a large organization was better at solving problems. Presently, many police agencies and private businesses are reconfiguring their resources into smaller interdependent units for purposes of greater efficiency and effectiveness.

**Table 3-2**  OLD VERSUS NEW LEADERSHIP SITUATIONS

| Old Situations | New Situations |
| --- | --- |
| Bigness | Smallness |
| Closed | Open |
| Some change | Chaotic change |
| Predictability | Uncertainty |
| Continuity | Flexibility |
| Hierarchy | Empowerment |
| Process centered | Problem centered |
| Hiring | Outsourcing, overtime, contracting |
| Product orientation | Customer orientation |
| Unionization | Independent contracting |
| Management | Leadership |
| Human labor | Automation |
| Middle managers | Computers |
| 8 to 5 work schedules | Telecommuting, modified workweeks |
| Local hiring | Nationwide competition for labor |
| Rank as power | Information as power |

## *Structured Exercise 3-1*

As situational leader is by definition a highly adaptive person, open to change, and free from conditioned responses. If you want to see whether you have learned the skills that make someone adaptable (e.g., a situational leader), answer the following questions as they apply to you, assigning the following points:

| | |
| --- | --- |
| Almost never applies | 0 points |
| Sometimes applies | 1 point |
| Usually applies | 2 points |
| Almost always applies | 3 points |

1. When I am first confronted with a problem and have no idea how it can be solved, I take the attitude that the right answer will emerge.

2. Events in my life happen with their own right timing.

3. I feel optimistic about my future.

4. When someone rejects me, I feel hurt, but I accept that the decision was theirs to make.

5. I feel the loss of family and friends who have died, but the grief resolves itself and I move on—I don't try to bring back what cannot be brought back.

6. I feel committed to ideals larger than myself.

7. When I'm arguing with someone, I defend my position, but I also find it easy to acknowledge the rightness in the other side.

8. I vote the person, not the party.

9. I donate time to worthwhile causes, even if they are unpopular.

10. I am considered a good listener. I don't interrupt others when they talk.

11. If someone has a lot of emotion at stake in something, I will hear them out without expressing my views.

12. Given a choice between a high-salaried job that is fairly boring and a job I like doing at half the pay, I'll take the job I love to do.

13. My style of supervising other people is to allow them to do what they want rather than try to control them. I interfere as little as possible.

14. I find it easy to trust others.

15. I am not prone to worry; the ups and downs of difficult situations affect me less than most other people.

16. In a competitive situation, I am a good loser—I will say, "Good game," not, "I wasn't at my best."

17. Being right in every situation isn't all that important to me.

18. I feel comfortable playing games and laughing.

19. I don't think about my moods very much.

20. I can easily feel what someone else is feeling.

21. Quiet people make me feel comfortable. Nervous people don't make me nervous.

Total score: _____

*Evaluating your score:*

50 points or over:

You are an exceptionally adaptable person. Others seek you for guidance. You place a high priority on your ability to remain comfortable under pressure. You pride yourself on being able to resolve conflicts well.

30–40 points:

You are reasonably adaptable to everyday challenges. You are the kind of person whom others consider easygoing, but you are likely to have more worries and regrets. Conflicts upset you, and you tend to fall under the influence of people with stronger emotions than yours.

20–30 points:

You have definite ideas of right and wrong behavior and put a high priority on defending your point of view. You are likely to be well organized and decidedly goal-oriented. If you find yourself in a situation of conflict or competition, you really want to be on the winning side.

Under 20 points:

Your sense of "self" needs considerable work. You fear rejection and become upset or critical when others disagree with you. You have your way of doing things and do not like surprises. You are likely to be obsessively orderly, with lots of hidden worry, or else very disorganized, reacting strongly to one external event after another.

The purpose of the findings is not to make anyone feel superior or inferior, but to spur conscious growth. The common denominator of all situational leaders is that they actually work, on a daily basis, at keeping their awareness open.

———◆◆◆◆◆———

## POLICE DEPARTMENT: VOLUNTARY ORGANIZATION

Authority is bottom up! If you really do not want to work for an organization anymore, you can quit. You have that freedom of choice. (There are a few select organizations, such as prisons, where quitting is not an option.)

When you commence working as a police officer, you temporarily loan the department over you. If they abuse it or foul up in some way, you can merely take it back. As Johnny Paycheck sings, "You can take this job and shove it. I'm not working here anymore." Granted, finding another job may be difficult. The fact remains you do have a choice.

———◆◆◆◆◆———

Authority is bottom up.

———◆◆◆◆◆———

Paradoxically, employees who are free to leave, who are independent thinkers, who question established approaches are a leader's best source of accurate information and the key hope for providing top-drawer police services.

## MISSION: DEPARTMENTAL AND PERSONAL

Earlier, we discussed ladders, or vision. To be of use, the vision and its mission must be communicated (Responsibility Four) to others. If they do not comprehend the big picture, they're unable to do their fair share of painting it.

We're surprised when a police manager or supervisor criticizes a line employee (in some cases one another) for "not seeing the big picture." Our first reaction is—were they ever informed? Second, is the leader daily reinforcing the vision by what he or she thinks and does?

*The police work force will assist the organization to achieve its mission if it can achieve its own personal goals as well.* This is a plus for both parties—if the personal goals include achievement, security, creativity, and rewards. Obviously, there are personal goals that should be rejected such as self-aggrandizement, doing as little as possible, and advancement at all costs.

The overarching vision must encapsulate both organizational and personal goals. By doing so, the leader is in a much better position to sell it to others. And, it is the "others" who get the job done.

———◆◆◆◆———

Visionaries are not necessarily leaders.

———◆◆◆◆———

One final note: Visionaries are not necessarily leaders. How can you tell the difference? Visionaries have great ideas about the future. But when they look behind them, no one else is following. Leaders always have people behind them.

### Front-Line Bias

Loyalty, commitment, respect, and trust of the front-line officer is gained by the supervisor.

- Emphasizing their welfare
- Giving them top priority in everything
- Rewarding staff personnel on how well they support the line people

Review your actions at the end of each work shift. Have you made your bias for the front line—and those on staff who vigorously support them—convincingly clear? A few police managers and supervisors look on and treat front-line employees as necessary cogs in a wheel. When this occurs, front-line police work suffers from a distinct lack of care and nurturing. This malady must be cured, and the police leader is responsible for seeing to it.

## MISSION STATEMENTS

**MISSION AND VISION STATEMENTS ARTICULATE THE PURPOSE OF AN ORGANIZATION.** In Responsibility One, we examined values and value statements. At this point, we will focus on mission statements. In Responsibility Seven, we will shift our analysis to individual goals and roles.

Mission and vision statements articulate the purpose of an organization. In a leadership-oriented department, it is incumbent upon management and supervision to develop these statements as strategies for providing a uniform basis for thinking and working in the agency. Creating a mission and values statement that is both convincing and operable isn't easy. There are three organizational hurdles: (1) lack of ownership, (2) lack of consensus, and (3) lack of teamwork.

***Mission statements can and should be a major component of a performance rating system (see Responsibility Nine).*** The sheriff of the Los Angeles County Sheriff's Department created a task force to design a new mission statement. After several months of arduous thinking and interaction with all units of the department, the following mission statement (Figure 3-2) was mailed to every employee in the department with a cover letter from the sheriff. (Incidentally, it took a while because there are more than 10,000 employees.) As you peruse the statement, take your high-lighter or writing instrument and point out the values that are included. Essentially, when you see members of a department doing what is stated in its mission statement, they're conforming and should be commended. Conversely, if you see personnel doing the opposite then they should be corrected. While everyone may not be in conformance, they all know what is expected of them and what they stand for. And thus the stage is set for pursuing organizational excellence!

### *Structured Exercise 3-2*

There are several excellent motion pictures that portray leadership characteristics and strategies. The movie *Mr. Holland's Opus* is one example. Identify a movie that you can borrow or rent. (Be certain the movie depicts an actual leader.) View the movie and analyze it for leadership characteristics. Look for the successes and mistakes that he or she experienced. Record what you see. When the movie is finished, discuss with one another what you saw in the leader's behavior (values, vision, positive self-regard, integrity, etc.).

## LEADERSHIP PARADIGM

A few years ago Warren Bennis committed two years of his professional life to investigate leadership. He conducted ninety interviews, sixty with acknowledged successful business chief executives (CEOs) and thirty others. From corporate boardrooms to sport coaches to public officials, he ardently inquired of these people: "How did you become a leader?" His research led to their *four strategies for leadership*, which follow:

**1.** Riveting one's attention via vision

**2.** Creating meaning via communication

**3.** Building trust via positioning

**4.** Deploying yourself via positive self-regard and trying[1]

[1]This section is adapted and modified from the work: *On Becoming a Leader*; in conjunction with Burt Nanus, *Leaders: The Strategies for Taking Charge* (New York: Harper and Row, 1985).

# OUR MISSION

**T**he quality of neighborhood life, its safety and welfare comes from the commitment of each of its citizens. The **Los Angeles County Sheriff's Department** takes pride in its role as a citizen of the community; partners with its members in the delivery of quality law enforcement services. We dedicate our full-time efforts to the duties incumbent upon every community member. As we act, we are universal citizens deriving our authority from those we serve. We accept our law enforcement mission to serve our communities with the enduring belief that in so doing, we serve ourselves. As professionals, we view our responsibilities as a covenant of public trust, ever mindful that we must keep our promises. As we succeed, our effectiveness will be measured by the absence of crime and fear in our neighborhoods and by the level of community respect for our efforts. In accomplishing this all important mission, we are guided by the following principles:

To recognize that the primary purpose of our organization is not only the skillful **enforcement** of the law, but the delivery of **humanitarian services** which promote community peace.

To understand that we must maintain a level of professional **competence** that ensures our safety and that of the public without compromising the constitutional guarantees of any person.

To base our decisions and actions on **ethical** as well as practical perspectives and to accept **responsibility** for the consequences.

To foster a collaborative relationship with the public in determining the best course in achieving **community order**.

To strive for **innovation**, yet remain **prudent** in sustaining our fiscal health through wise use of resources.

To never tire of our **duty**, never shrink from the difficult tasks and never lose sight of our own humanity.

**Figure 3-2** Mission Statement (Reprinted with permission of the Los Angeles County Sheriff's Department.)

The preceding strategies form a cause-effect equation. If I create a vision, the effect will be your attention. If I convey communications, the effect will be meaning. If I position myself (knowing who I am), the effect will be trust. And, if I manifest high regard for myself plus (to the best of my ability) do my job, the effect will be experiencing me as a dedicated police supervisor.

### Attention through Vision

Vision *grabs*. At first it grabs the leader and, if effectively projected, it convinces others to get on board. The leader's vision is intended to be magnetic. Winning coaches transmit an unbridled clarity about what they want from their players. If coaches can do it, so can police supervisors—if they want to.

The first thing you do with your vision is to *convey* it to others. Your staff has to know what you see. Second, they must *understand* it. The understanding may be vague or incomplete, but they have at least a fundamental concept of what you're proposing. Third, the people must be convinced that the vision is of *paramount importance*, even if it initially appears impossible. It excites people and drives them. Fourth, the leader pays close *attention* to the vision and uses it as transaction between himself and his followers. It becomes a subtle link that forges the leader and follower as one. Coach and team. Sergeant and officers.

Vision grabs.

Once the preceding steps have been taken, the leader must

- Closely live the enabling vision
- Use it to prioritize (quality first, quantity second, etc.)
- Adapt to vision of changing needs and new opportunities

If you understand your values, the values of your department, and the values of your profession, then visioning is possible for you. You merely allow your *imagination* and *conscience* to take charge. Through imagination, you can visualize the uncharted wealth of potential that lies within *yourself* and *others*. Through conscience, you can compare your ideas with universal laws or principles as well as your personal standards.

We'll take a few moments here to illustrate the preceding process. Captain Jim Nunn, his department, and his profession hold "quality" as a cornerstone value. He is currently in command of one of his sheriff department's nine patrol stations. The area served will soon incorporate as a city. The city will either form its own police agency or contract for police services with the sheriff. His imagination causes him to envision the newly elected city council opting to contract for sheriff coverage. His vision also included an approach to furthering this goal—provide top-quality police services. Nothing less than the very best! He conceived a rather risky motto, "Treat those that you serve exactly the way I treat you." Finally, he foresaw a comprehensive training program that would ignite the interest, and secure the follow-through, of his entire staff.

You're Sergeant Ortega and you learn of his vision, see its importance, and make a commitment to its implementation. You present the vision to your line employees with enthusiasm and total endorsement. You likewise adopt the captain's motto. However, you add an energizing concept of your own, "We're 100 percent responsible for everything that *we* do." Your imagination has locked on to *teamwork*. Consequently, you start training, praising, rewarding, and reprimanding team, not individual, efforts.

Your conscience informs you that *fair play* is a critical principle while introducing a new program. It also tells you that you'll be the example, and you'll set the standards. As you pay close attention to your staff, they'll be paying equal (if not more) attention to what you are doing regarding quality police services. Finally, your inner voice says that every act, no matter how small, counts.

In conceiving our vision, many of us discover nonproductive thoughts, inconsistent guidelines, and unworthy habits. We don't have to live with them. We are "response-able" to apply our imagination and creativity to go beyond our present horizon in search of new opportunities for organizational and personal excellence. *Supervisors realize that they have choices; leaders act on them.*

## Meaning through Communication

Responsibility Four provides an expansive coverage of this strategy. We underscore it here because Bennis's research demonstrated that all of the leaders he studied mastered communications. It was inseparable from effective leadership. It isn't just information or facts—it's the *context* of presentation, the overall meaning.

*All* police organizations depend on the existence of shared meanings and interpretations of reality, which facilitate coordinated efforts. "Meaning" surpasses what is typically meant by "communications." Meaning has little to do with facts or even knowing. Facts and knowing pertain to technique, tactics, with "knowing how to do things." That is useful and often necessary. But thinking is much closer to what we mean by "meaning" than knowing. This is not a subtle difference. Thinking prepares one for what *ought* to be done.

---

To depend on facts, without thinking, may seem all right, but in the long run, it is dangerous because it lacks direction.

---

To depend on facts, without thinking, may seem all right, but in the long run, it is dangerous because it lacks *direction*. The distinctive role of leadership (especially in a volatile police environment) is that the "know-why" occurs before the "know-how." This logic shows, once more, one of the basic differences between leaders and supervisors.

Police supervisors primarily engage in a mental process known as problem solving. Problem solving includes a problem, a method, and a solution based on the former two factors. A creative mental process outcrops when neither the problem nor the method, let alone the solution, exists. There's no rule, manual or guru, to turn to. Hence, it's up to the supervisor to discover the *real* problem. Creativity uncovers a "hidden problem"—one that requires attention from the start to the finish. *The highest type of discovery always centers on problem finding!*

Why do people align behind one solution, direction, or vision, and not another? We believe that endorsement of a vision—or any new idea or change—requires that the employees be interested in paying attention to the hoped-for destination.

Let us forewarn you—new ideas of visions are never judged solely by their inherent quality or goodness. (Adolph Hitler had a lot of visions, all of which proved to be disastrous.) Even the prudent ideas are only as good as their capacity to attract attention. Police organizations are by nature unpredictable; they can reject a good vision just as easily as a bad one.

Leadership, by communicating meaning, generates a confederation of learning, and this is what successful police agencies proudly possess. *Lack of clarity makes police organizations little more than simple devices for the avoidance of responsibility.*

We've conducted more than 2,000 team-building workshops for police and sheriff's departments. (We've also conducted similar workshops for fire departments, city councils, and a variety of business firms.) With rare exception, the number one issue in the workshop is the failure to communicate with one another. Far too often the participants state with detectable anger, "I never got the word." "Everything moves, but there's no feedback." "I've expressed my ideas before, but they could care less." And the worst one is, "I don't know our priorities, let alone our goals."

If our body's arterial system does not touch base with our cells, they'll eventually die. *Similarly, if our police organizations' communication system does not contact, with meaning, its human resources—the staff may not be dead, but they might as well be.*

## Trust through Positioning

Trust encompasses accountability, predictability, reliability, and faith. Technically, it is a noun. But to achieve it, there must be a mental or physical act. Something must happen for me to trust you or vice versa. You tell me that you'll be at work on time, and you are—I start the "trust process."

Trusting involves a trust bank account (TBA). You consistently arrive at work on time, and your TBA prospers. You make many daily TBA deposits in a variety of ways. You open new TBAs with people that you meet. Depending on your working relationships, family members, and friends, you may have hundreds of TBAs in existence. You could be *trust rich*. Conversely, you could be *trust poor*.

It takes a lot of deposits to build a strong TBA with another person. Making a mistake, for example, lying to another person, can wipe out your TBA. It could send you into indefinite, maybe permanent, bankruptcy with the other party. It could also destroy a working relationship, a marriage, a friendship. TBAs take considerable time to build and only one second—in some cases, one word—to dissolve.

Kids have a remarkable memory. A few years ago, one of your authors told his wife that he'd *never* made a promise to their four-year-old grandson that was not fulfilled. As most good spouses will do, she said, "Let's see what his opinion is." I asked, "Derek, Grandpa has always done what he said he would do—right?" The split-second retort was, "No. You said you'd take me fishing. You didn't do it." I do not recall making such a promise. To this day, I'm certain that he was correct. (To the best of my knowledge, I've not made any other withdrawals from my Derek TBA.)

We cannot imagine a police organization that does not have some level of trust among the working personnel. It may be very little, but still it's there. The lower the trust, the weaker the leadership.

Although TBAs are very fragile, they are very resilient at the same time. If we have a healthy TBA, let us assume a trust bank (TB) of 200,000 with others, we can make small withdrawals of TB 5,000 from time to time. Those concerned will understand and tolerate it. For instance, we may need to make a very unpopular unilateral decision, because of time pressures, without involving others or even explaining it to them. In doing so, we make a TB 5,000 withdrawal, leaving TB 190,000 on deposit. Perhaps the next day, we can explain what we did and why we did it, thus redepositing the TB 5,000. Obviously, outright lying and so on to a co-worker can result in a "closed account."

---

Leaders who are trusted make themselves known and make their positions known.

---

Leaders who are trusted make themselves known and make their positions (e.g., values, principles, vision) known. Followers do not stay with shiny ideals and cute words. *Only relentless dedication to a position on the part of a police leader will engage trust.*

Positioning is a set of actions necessary to implement the vision of a leader. Through establishing the position (by action), the followers are given the chance to *trust—trust in the leader and trust in the position; they're synonymous.*

*For a police organization to foster trust, it first must present a sense of who it is and what it is to do—in other words, a position.* The police leader is responsible for seeing to it that the position of the department is known to employee and community members alike. This is not easy because people form different perceptions. The police leader may see the position of the department as *X*, the employees as *Y*, and the citizens as *Z*. If the three positions are contradictory, then trust is hard to achieve.

The greater the agreement on what the position of the department is, the more one is able to trust it. If I know what you stand for, and believe in it, I'll trust your leadership.

*Second, positioning needs courageous patience.* The leader has to stay with it. With time, he starts managing trust. Change may occur, and innovations may be needed; thus the position must be carefully shifted and then maintained.

We know of a large-scale local law-enforcement agency that took the position of full stress during basic academy training. This position was trusted and, hence, vigorously endorsed by the leaders. One innovative employee questioned the position of full stress—he didn't trust its results. The results of his research caused a shift in basic training from full stress to modified stress. A new position was identified, and it caused enhanced trust in the training program.

Positions must adjust, as appropriate, to maintain trust. The police leader must recognize when to maintain the steady course or change direction. *Trust in the leader's ability to lead depends on his or her decision to retain or shift a position.*

## Deployment of Self through Positive Self-Regard

The higher you advance in a police organization, the more interpersonal and relational the working environment. This deployment of self makes leading a profoundly personal activity. Such a deployment depends on one's positive self-regard. *Positive self-regard* is a three-sided triangle consisting of (1) competency, (2) positive other-regard, and (3) the Wallenda factor.

---

The deployment of self makes leading a profoundly personal activity.

---

**COMPETENCY.** Positive self-regard is not self-aggrandizement, conceitfulness, or ego mania. Essentially, it is confidence in who you are and what you are capable of doing. It is prudent self-esteem and self-respect.

The first step in building positive self-regard is *recognizing your strengths and compensating for your weaknesses*. The next step involves the constant *nurturing of skills*. The final step is astuteness in *evaluating the fit between your perceived skills and what the job requires*. Being good at your job and knowing why sums up one side of positive self-regard. We label this "competency."

**OTHER-REGARD.** Those that have high regard for themselves typically have the same for others. Having positive self-regard is contagious. Potentially everyone can catch it. *Positive self-regard creates it in others*. It seems to exert its force by generating in others a sense of confidence and high expectations.

Positive self- and other-regard encourages the development of five key people skills.

1. The ability to accept individuals as they are, not as you would like them to be. This ability is fundamental to leading a culturally diverse work force.
2. The capacity to approach people and problems in relation to the present rather than the past.
3. The ability to deal with those that are close to you with the same active listening ear and courtesy that you give to citizens and casual acquaintances.
4. The ability to trust in another person's dedication and capabilities.
5. The ability to function without constant approval or even support from others.

**WALLENDA FACTOR.** In his research, Bennis found that the leaders he studied simply didn't think about failure. In fact, they didn't use the term. The closest they would identify with it were through words such as "mistake," "setback," or "error."

Failure to them was like learning to ski. At first you're destined to fall; with persistence and perspiration you'll eventually master the art of skiing. It's the same with leadership. *They used their mistakes as a lesson on what not to do as well as what to do next.*

Failure and mistakes can open you up to self- or other-criticism. It can erode both positive self- and other-regard. The more valid it is, the more bothersome it is to us. The successful leader accepts it, but then twists it into a useful message. Remember, *feedback is the breakfast of champions.*

Karl Wallenda was one of the premier high-wire aerialists. He fell to his death in 1978 while walking a seventy-five-foot-high tightrope. After his fall, Mrs. Wallenda commented that for three straight months before the accident all he thought about was not falling. He substituted his past successful thinking about walking the tightrope with falling.

Karl Wallenda would likely tell the police supervisor, pour your energies into success (walking the tightrope) and not failing (or not falling). To worry places barriers in the path of clear thinking. An absence of clear thinking can cause *mistakes* for those who possess positive self-regard. An absence of clear thinking can cause *failures* for those that do not have it.

**THREE SIDES OF POSITIVE SELF-REGARD.** The three sides combined look like the following diagram:

**Figure 3-3**

Your positive self-regard is a direct derivative of

- Your competency—you have what it takes and you know it.
- Your capacity for instilling it in others by having high other-regard for them.
- Your conviction of an outcome—the expectation of success.

For effective leadership to occur, there has to be a fusion of competency, capacity, and conviction. It is similar to the archer who builds his prowess to the point where the zeal to hit the center of the target is obliterated, and man, bow, arrow, and target become one, united. Positive self-regard magnetically attracts and gradually empowers people to join the police supervisor, the police leader, in a quest for quality services that are good for police departments and for society.

## *Structured Exercise 3-3*

Warren Bennis discovered four critical characteristics or strategies that proven leaders had. What four would you add to his list? First of all create your own list; then along with your colleagues, get consensus on a joint list of four strategies.

## THE TWO BIGGEST MISTAKES A LEADER CAN MAKE

The worst mistake a leader or supervisor can make is ducking accountability. If others see the leader attempting to slide away from a bad situation, worse yet, try to blame others for it, the TBA is zero. Leadership is down the tubes and is extremely difficult to restore.

A good leader rarely takes credit.

A second common trap for even those leaders practicing the four tenets discovered by Bennis is—taking too much credit. In fact, a good leader rarely takes credit. We've found that the people who most quickly gain trust, loyalty, excitement, and energy in an organization are those who pass on the credit to the people who have really done the work. If you're the top supervisor, you may be getting more credit than you deserve.

Most good leaders have strong character and positive self-regard, but they shouldn't let their egos get too big. Their egos need to be strong enough to handle the kind of anger or abuse they will sometimes incur and to appreciate contrary feedback. But an ego should not be so big that you lose your associates' respect.

## BEYOND LEADERSHIP

All organizations want to demonstrate progressive forms of change. We know there is a need for progress; we are less clear about how to achieve it. Most of our theories about making change are clustered around a belief in leadership. We think that leadership, in this case police leadership, is the key to fitting agencies to their communities and fitting people to their agencies. If the agency fails, it is the leader's head we want. It is this pervasive belief in leaders that slows genuine progress and success. A few are beginning to see stewardship as the answer to this problem.

## Stewardship

Stewardship is the willingness to be accountable for the well-being of the larger organization by operating in service, rather than in control, of those around us. Stated simply, it is accountability without control or compliance. And, the underlying value is—deepening our commitment to *service*. Hence, stewardship requires that we reject self-interest and rely on mutual trust.

---

> Stewardship is the willingness to be accountable for the well-being of the larger organization by operating in service.

---

**PARTNERSHIP.** In its commitment to service, stewardship forces us then to yield on our desire to use good parenting as a basic form of leadership. The alternative, partnership, is something we are just learning about. Our difficulty with creating partnerships is that parenting is so deeply ingrained in our spinal cord and armature that we don't even realize we are doing it.

When we decide to resist efforts to treat others like children (which feeds our need for dependency), we can then serve the department best by creating a place of our own choosing. The well-worn term for this is "empowerment."

**SIGHTINGS.** Stewardship cannot at this point be identified as a clear-cut trend. However, there are more frequent sightings of it: when you see a department make a full commitment to service; when you see this commitment as a partnership; when you see people rebelling against dependency. You'll be looking at a work group, a police department, that practices empowerment through stewardship.

## KEY POINTS

- Authority is the right to supervise, and power is one's capacity to do so.
- Both authority and power seek to influence the behavior of others.
- There are two types of authority: sanctions and rewards. Also, there are three types of power: position, expertise, and example.
- Informal leadership is a natural phenomenon in an organization.
- There are three schools of thought about how leaders emerge: trait, behavioral, and situational.

- There is no one best way to become a leader—but there are ways.
- The police work force is changing by being educated; supplanting loyalty with professional growth; becoming more diverse in composition; having a greater percentage of civilian employees; being more difficult to recruit and hire; and having a greater need than ever before for leadership.
  - The police organization is a voluntary organization, and its goals should complement those of its work force.
  - Many police organizations are overmanaged and underled.
  - Successful leaders demonstrate four common patterns of behavior. They consistently (1) get your attention through a vision they have; (2) create meaning through communication; (3) build trust via positioning; and (4) project positive self-regard.
  - Leadership can be learned.
  - All of us, therefore, are capable of becoming a leader.
- The greatest mistakes a leader can make are ducking accountability and assuming too much credit for good work.
- There is a movement to supplant leadership with stewardship.

## DISCUSSION

1. Discuss authority and power. How do they differ? What is their common bond? If you could only have one, which would you choose?
2. Realizing that you, the police supervisor, are a formal leader, how do you explain the likelihood that there are informal leaders in or around your assigned work unit?
3. Give a specific illustration of each theory (trait, behavioral, and situational) of leadership. Try to use an example from your own department.
4. What other changes can be seen in the police work force today? What changes may be anticipated within the next five years?
5. What is meant by positive self-regard? How does one acquire it? Who do you know that has this characteristic?
6. Have you witnessed leaders either avoiding accountability or frequently taking credit? If so, discuss what you saw and what occurred as a result of it.
7. Have you had any "sightings" of stewardship? If so, discuss what you saw.

# RESPONSIBILITY FOUR

# *Communications*

The police supervisor is responsible for communication with others in such a manner that employee understanding, trust and mutual support are engendered.

*cy-ber-net-ics*
*The theoretical study of control processed in biological, mechanical and electronic systems.*

—From Greek
Kubernêtês, governor

At this point, your values (R-1) and ethics (R-2) have been explored for the purpose of developing your capacity to function as a leader (R-3). The next step is to convey it (R-4), and that takes time (R-5).

Communication is our most important human skill. Everything that we've done, are doing, and wish to do revolves around it. It's, therefore, axiomatic that everything a police supervisor does involves communicating. Not a few things, but everything! You can't make a correct decision without information. That information has to be communicated. Once a decision is made, again communication must take place. Otherwise, no one will know a decision has been made. The most creative suggestion or the finest plan cannot take form without communication. Supervisors, therefore, need effective communication skills. We are not saying that solid communication skills alone make a successful police supervisor. We can say, with confidence, that ineffective communication skills can lead to a continuous stream of problems for the supervisor.

## Structured Exercise 4-1

**Instructions**. Each participant is to take a piece of posterboard and one or more felt-tip pens. Divide the posterboard into eight areas. Use symbols, pictures, or words to depict each area as follows:

Area 1. My immediate major job challenge is…

Area 2. Professionally, I am looking forward to…

Area 3. In the past six months I have assisted another department/team member by…

Area 4. In the past six months I have received assistance from another department/team member in the way of…

Area 5. In the past twelve months my major accomplishment was…

Area 6. In the past twelve months my major failure was…

Area 7. Presently, or soon, I will need team support in…

Area 8. I wish to thank (*team member*) for

You have twenty minutes to complete your chart. Then each person will stand and make a three-minute presentation explaining each area.

## COMMUNICATIONS: LEADERSHIP, DECISION MAKING, AND TRUST

We began Responsibility Four by asserting that "communication is our most important skill." Not one of many, but *the* most important skill. Our ability to communicate effectively and directly determines our success on becoming a *leader*, our success in making accurate *decisions*, and our success in being *trusted*. Let's explore these three dimensions in more detail.

### Leadership

Communication is the vehicle for supervisory leadership. In other words, the police supervisor is a key person in building and maintaining effective organizational communications as he or she interacts with subordinates, peers, superiors, and the citizenry.

A communication, or in terms of an organizational setting, a communication system, provides the means by which information, statements, views, and instructions are transmitted through a department. Although one often speaks of the "flow" of communications, this flow actually consists of a series of discrete messages of different length, form, and content. These messages are transmitted through certain channels (or lines of communications), which make up the communication system or network. Each message is sent by a transmitter (an individual, a group, a division, a computer) to a receiver or several receivers. Significantly, the supervisory role and function are filled with a heavy volume of transmissions and receptions.

### Decision Making

A police supervisor decides issues based on information received in conjunction with previously developed strategies, procedures, or rules. Consequently, the communication process is necessary because the flow of proper information to the decision points throughout the organization is such a vital requirement for task accomplishment. In fact, if supervision were thought of primarily as decision making and if the decision process were considered essentially a communication process including a network of communication systems, then supervision could be viewed as a communication process. The closer we look at leadership and decision making, the more we become aware of the significance of information exchange.

### Trust

Later on we'll cover the concept of a trust bank account (TBA). The most important ingredient we put into any relationship is not what we say or what we do, but what we are. We do this by communicating. How do you react to the person who does not share with you his ideas, values, hopes, and ethical standards? Do you grow to trust him? Probably not. He either refuses or is incapable of making deposits into your TBA. In fact, if this individual persists in being closed, he'll likely make withdrawals from your TBA. *Trust and communications are linked.* For one to be high, the other must be high. You lower one (reduced communication), and you'll lower the other (reduced trust).

---

Communications and trust are linked.

---

## WHAT IS COMMUNICATION?

Communication is the transfer of meaning. If no information or ideas have been conveyed, communication has not taken place. The supervisor who is not heard or the writer who is not read does not communicate. For communication to be successful, the meaning must be not only sent but also comprehended. Therefore, communication is the movement and understanding of meaning. Perfect communication, if such a thing were possible, would exist when a transmitted thought is perceived by the receiver exactly the same as envisioned by the sender.

---

Communications is the movement and understanding of meaning.

---

Good communication is often erroneously defined by the communicator as agreement rather than clarity of understanding. If someone disagrees with us, it's not unusual to assume the person just didn't fully understand our position. What happens is that many of us define good communication as having someone accept our views. But a supervisor can very clearly understand what you mean and not agree with what you say. In fact, often when observers conclude that a lack of communication must exist because a conflict has continued for a prolonged time, a close examination reveals that there is plenty of effective communication going on. Each fully understands the other's position. The problem is one of equating effective communication with differences in values, responsibilities, and roles.

## WHAT WE KNOW ABOUT COMMUNICATIONS

What knowledge exists about communications is scattered over numerous disciplines and fields and is often contradictory. In many ways, what we know about communications has been derived from our failures rather than our successes. Thus it is in the residues of our discovered imperfections that we are better able to predict what might work. Sufficient evidence is now before us to conclude that communications: (1) is perception; (2) is expected; (3) makes demands; (4) is related to but different from information; (5) and is marginal when one-way. These five premises are explained next.

**1.** *Perception.* Paradoxically, it is the recipient who communicates rather than the person who emits the message. (Therefore, the truism—a leader cannot lead until he or she has a follower.) While the communicator speaks, writes, or gesticulates a message, communication does not occur until the receiver(s) perceives it. Keep in mind that perception is a total experience as opposed to logic. And receivers vary in their sensory and mental capacities to perceive data inputs. Hence the first question that the communicator must ask prior to the sending of a message is, "Can the receiver perceive it?" That is, are the receivers sensorially and cognitively capable of ingesting and conceptualizing the message? The second question concerns the values, attitudes, and emotions of the recipient. Thus the query, "What is the receiver's particular mental set at this time?" The communicator is therefore dealing with psycho-physiological tolerances and conditioning factors that determine *if* the message is received and *how* it is interpreted.

**2.** *Expectations.* In most instances we perceive what we expect to find in the message. The unexpected or unwanted data are frequently ignored or filtered in line with our expectations. Basically, our human mind seeks to fit incoming data into a preestablished pattern of expectations. Consequently, before we attempt to communicate, we must predict what the recipient expects to hear or see. And we should keep in mind that minor discongruities will probably be rejected or distorted to fit the pattern. Thus, if the data are important, the communicator may find it necessary to apply sufficient "shock" or drive to the message so that it disturbs the pattern and alerts the recipient that the unexpected is occurring.

**3.** *Demands.* The prime usage of communications is to influence or control. Therefore, it is always making demands on us to change or continue to do what we are doing, believe or not believe, and act or not act. Usually such demands are gradual or subliminal in that major demands are frequently resisted because they do not comply with the existing pattern of expectations.

**4.** *Related to information.* Information and communications, although different, are nevertheless interdependent. Information is formal and logical. Conversely, communication is personal and psychological. Indeed, communications can occur without information. As an example, we can share in an experience while not receiving the logic of information. Also of interest is the difference between effective information and effective communication. The former is specific, terse, and structured; the latter is subjected to varying perceptions, expectations, and demands. It is debatable whether information once freed from these three conditions becomes more informative or whether, on the contrary, it tends to lose its meaning. Am I communicating this thought to you? What is your *perception*?

**5.** *Two-way is best.* One-way communication typically fails. It is ineffective for the obvious reason that we do not know if or how the recipient has perceived the message. Listening is important, but not sufficient to ensure that one has communicated. Moreover, the answer to better communications is clearly *not* more information. Usually more information tends to widen the communications gap between the sender and the receiver (information overload). Are not most of us today in need of more communications and less information?

**A SOLUTION.** The solution is threefold: (1) develop an understanding of the perceptions and expectations of the recipient, (2) assess the demands made in your message, and (3) seek feedback regarding the perception and reaction to your message. *Communications is best a two-way process.*

Communications is best a two-way process.

## TYPES OF COMMUNICATION CHANNELS

Various channels of communication are available to the police supervisor for exchanging information. Commonly, a communications system is divided into formal and informal channels. The informal communication channels have three subclasses: subformal, personal task directed, and personal nontask directed.

### Formal Communication Channels

All organizations develop formal communication channels as a response to large size and the limited information-handling capability of each individual. The formal channels adhere to the recognized official structure of the organization. Accordingly, the formal communication channels transmit messages expressive of the legitimate structure of authority. Hence, one usually sees formal orders and directives, reports, official correspondence, standard operating procedures, and so on. Those persons who emphasize going through channels are doing so in deference to the unit of command principle within the formal hierarchy.

Strict compliance with formal channels can be disruptive.

Strict compliance with formal channels can be disruptive. These disruptions are primarily in terms of time, creativity, and experience. To explain, first, it takes a long time for a formal message from a supervisor in one division to pass to another supervisor in another division. Second, formal messages are on the record and thus restrict the free flow of ideas. As an example, police officers may not want to expose their ideas to their supervisors for the time being, even in rough form; yet any formal communication is immediately routed through the originator's supervisor. Third, in practice a formal communication system cannot cover all informational needs. Informational needs change quite rapidly, while the formal channels change only with considerable time and effort. Therefore, the most urgent need for informal communication channels is to plug the gaps in the formal channels.

## Informal Communication Channels

Regretfully, there are some who consider formal communication channels as the only way to transmit information so necessary to the functioning of the organization. However, this precept is no longer as sacred as it once was. Not only are we witnessing an interest in acquiring a better understanding of the informal organization, but along with it has come an awareness of its potential use. This interest and awareness quite naturally leads to a different perspective on the structuring of communication flow. In essence, this perspective does not confine organizationally useful communication to purely formal channels. It includes all the social processes of the broadest relevance in the functioning of any group or organization. Consequently, we now treat informal and personal communications as a supportive and frequently necessary process for effective functioning.

The prevalence of informal channels means that formal channels do not fully meet the important communications needs in a police department. Therefore, it is futile for police administrators to establish formal channels and assume that those channels will carry most of the messages. Ironically, the more restricted the formal channels, the greater is the growth of informal ones.

We next proceed to an analysis of three kinds of informal communication channels. The first two are task, or goal, oriented, while the third is oriented toward the individual.

**SUBFORMAL.** Subformal channels carry those messages arising from the informal power structure existing in every police organization. Every member of the department must know and observe informal rules and procedures about what to communicate and to whom. Such rules are rarely written down and must be learned by experience and example, a necessity that causes difficulties for newcomers.

There are two types of subformal communications: those that flow along formal channels, but not as formal communications, and those that flow along purely informal channels. Both types have the distinct advantage of not being official; therefore, they can be withdrawn or changed without any official record being made. As a result, almost all new ideas are first proposed and tested as subformal communications. Significantly, the vast majority of communications in police organizations are subformal.

While in general it has been indicated that subformal channels meet the communication requirements not met by formal channels, they become all the more necessary under certain conditions. First, the greater the degree of interdependence among activities within the department, the greater is the number and use of subformal channels. Second, the more uncertainty about the objectives of the department, the greater is the number and use of subformal channels. When the environment is relatively unpredictable, people cannot easily determine what they should be doing simply by referring to that environment. Consequently, they tend to talk to each other more to gain an improved understanding of their situation. Third, when a police organization is operating under the pressure of time, it tends to use subformal channels extensively, because there is often no time to use the formal channels. Thus, police administrators reach out for information whenever they can get it from whatever channel is necessary. Fourth, if the divisions of a police organization are in strong competition, they tend to avoid subformal channels and communicate only formally. Conversely, closely cooperating sections rely primarily upon subformal communications. Hence, strong rivalry has significant communications drawbacks. Fifth, subformal communications channels are used more frequently if departmental members have stable, rather than constantly changing, relationships with each other.

**PERSONAL TASK DIRECTED.** A personal task-directed communication is one in which an organization member deliberately reveals something of his own attitude toward the activities of his own organization. While personal, this communication is also in terms of the goals or activities of the organization. Thus we can refer to it as task directed. It possesses the following characteristics: First, task-directed personal channels are nearly always used for informing rather than for directing. Second, before a person acts on the basis of information received through personal channels, he or she usually verifies that information through either subformal or formal channels. Third, this channel transmits information with considerable speed because there are no formal mechanisms to impede its flow. Fourth, because task-directed personal messages are transmitted by personnel acting as individuals, they do not bear the weight of the position emitting them. To this extent, they differ from subformal messages, which are transmitted by individuals acting in their official capacity—but not for the record.

**PERSONAL NONTASK DIRECTED.** As suggested by its title, this form of communication apparently does not contain information related to the task of the organization. Note the word "apparently." Paradoxically, this channel may handle information on occasion far more valuable to the achievement of organizational goals than any other channel, including the formal ones. An example of this channel is the supervisor learning through a friendly subordinate of the reasons for growing job dissatisfaction. A discussion of its characteristics should provide an explanation of its utility. First, nontask-directed channels furnish a vehicle for an individual to satisfy his or her social needs. In doing so, a person experiences a certain degree of need fulfillment that carries over into the job, and, as described in earlier chapters, a person is more likely to remain with an organization if satisfied. Second, this channel provides a way for an individual to blow off steam over things that are disturbing. This pressure-release valve often reduces a person's level of tension to a point where she or he does not engage in acts injurious to the functioning of the organization. Third, nontask-directed channels frequently supply useful feedback information to the management and supervisory levels. This feedback is normally comprised of unexpected information not obtainable in any other way. Fourth, personal channels offer the best medium for a person to become socialized in the organizational setting. Unwritten standards, group values, and "the way we do things here" are conveniently expressed through nontask-directed channels.

## METHODS OF COMMUNICATING

Let's review the various methods that we can use to convey information and assess their strengths and weaknesses.

### Oral

The method most used by people to communicate with one another is oral. Popular forms of oral communication include speeches, formal one-on-one and group discussions, and the informal rumor mill or grapevine.

The advantages of oral communications are speed and feedback. A verbal message can be conveyed and a response received in a minimal amount of time. If the receiver is unsure of the message, rapid feedback allows for early detection by the sender and for correction.

The major disadvantage of oral communication surfaces whenever the message has to be passed through a number of people. The more people a message must pass through, the greater the potential for distortion. In a police agency where decisions and other information are verbally passed up and down the authority hierarchy, considerable opportunity exists for messages to become distorted.

### Written

Written communications include memos, letters, organizational periodicals, bulletin boards, or any other device that transmits via written words or symbols.

Written messages have advantages because of the fact that they are permanent, tangible, and verifiable. Typically, both the sender and receiver have a record of the communication. The message can be stored. If there are questions concerning the content of the message, it is physically available for later reference. This is particularly important for complex or lengthy communications. A final benefit of written communications comes from the process itself. More care is taken with the written word than with the oral word.

Written communications are more likely to be well thought out, logical, and clear. After all, they appear as departmental orders and regulations.

Of course, written messages have their drawbacks. They're time-consuming. You could probably say the same thing in ten to fifteen minutes that it takes you an hour to write. Thus, while writing may be more precise, it also consumes a great deal more time. The other major disadvantage is feedback, or lack of it. Oral communications allow the receivers to rapidly respond to what they think they hear. However, written communications do not have a built-in feedback mechanism.

## Nonverbal

Some of the most meaningful communications are transmitted neither verbally nor in writing. These are nonverbal communications. A loud siren at an intersection tells you something without words. A supervisor teaching a group of officers doesn't need words to tell when the trainees are bored. The size of a person's office and desk or the clothes people wear also send messages to others. However, the most well-known areas of nonverbal communication are verbal intonations and body language.

- Verbal intonations refer to the emphasis someone gives to words or phrases. A pleasant, smooth tone creates a different meaning than an intonation that is abrasive with strong emphasis placed on the last word.
- Body language includes everything from facial expressions to our sitting or standing posture.

**UNDERSTAND FIRST—EMPATHIC LISTENING.** *The key to influencing another person is to first gain an understanding of that person.* As a supervisor, you must know your staff to influence them. Most of us are prone to want the other person to open his or her mind to our message. Wanting to understand the other person requires that *we open our mind to him or her*.

---

The key to influencing another person is to first gain an understanding of that person.

---

Consider this scenario. Sergeant Ker is speaking to Sergeant Paulson, "I can't understand Officer Hooper. He just won't listen to me." Sergeant Paulson replies, "You don't understand Hooper because *he* won't listen to *you?*" Ker answers, "That's what I said." Paulson remarks, "I thought that to understand another person, *you* need to listen to *him!*" Ker realized that he didn't communicate with Hooper because he didn't understand him.

When we seek to understand, we are applying the principle of "empathy." *Empathy* is a Greek word. The "em-" part of *empathy* means "in." The "-pathy" part comes from *pathos*, which means "feeling" or "suffering." Empathy is not sympathy. Sympathy is a form of agreement, a form of judgment. We have empathy, then, when we place ourselves within the other person, so to speak, to experience his feelings as he experiences them. *This does not mean that we agree, simply that we understand the other viewpoint.*

Once we understand, we can proceed with the second step of the interaction: seeking to be understood. But now it is much more likely that we will actually be understood, because the other person's drive to be understood has been satisfied.

- To understand another person, we must be willing to be open to that person's thoughts.
- When we are open, we give people room to release their fixed positions and consider alternatives.
- Seeking first to understand lets us act from a position of knowledge.
- By seeking to understand, we gain influence in the relationship.
- Seeking first to understand leads people to discover other options.

When we seek to understand, people become less defensive about their position. They become more open to the question, "How can we *both* get what we want?" As they get their position out of the way, they begin to see their values more clearly so that they can use them as guidelines for creating and evaluating other options.

Empathic listening is particularly important under three conditions.

- When the interaction has a strong emotional component
- When we are not sure that we understand
- When we are not sure the other person feels confident that we understand

The following three steps, if practiced, will measurably assist you in listening with an empathetic ear.

***Listening with the eyes.*** *To truly understand, we must listen to more than words.* Words are weak compared with the richness and complexity of the ideas that we need to express. They are particularly poor at expressing feelings, for example, and yet feelings are often the thing that people most want us to understand. So when we seek to understand, we must look beyond the surface issues that the words describe, to consider how people feel.

***Win-win.*** The most vital part of empathic listening is developing a win-win attitude. *Win-win requires a nexus of courage and consideration.* It will give us success even when we are not adept at the skill. As we learn the skill, we will be that much better.

Empathic responses will destroy understanding if the attitude behind them is wrong. The danger of empathic listening is that we may use it because we believe that it "works." We may see it as a tool for getting what we want, or for manipulating people. If we use it with wrong intentions, we corrupt the skill. Empathic listening creates positive results only when we accept it as a useful principle and use it solely with the intent to understand.

***Now to be understood.*** Once we understand, we can then proceed to be understood. This is related to the earlier comment that win-win is a balance between courage and consideration. Understanding the other person shows consideration. Being understood takes courage. Both are necessary conditions for win-win agreements.

If, in the course of being understood, we sense resistance, we have another opportunity to choose again either to be defensive, or to seek to understand. So we may find ourselves moving back and forth between seeking to understand and seeking to be understood. The process is complete when both parties feel understood, and when their interaction has given them a foundation for discovering other options. *This is what empowerment is all about* (see Responsibility Eight).

### Structured Exercise 4-2

Complete this exercise by yourself. Then, if others are available, brainstorm the possible answers as a group.

**1.** Identify a situation in which you should use the skill and attitude of empathy.

_____

_____

_____

**2.** What benefit might occur from your use of empathy in this situation?

_____

_____

_____

**3.** What may happen if you don't use empathy?

_____

_____

_____

**4.** Would it be helpful to inform the other person of your intention to try to be a better listener and to ask for his or her support as you try out this approach? Why or why not?

_____

_____

_____

_____

## COMMUNICATIONS: DOWN, UP, AND LATERAL

Earlier we saw that communications flow in more than a single direction. Traditionally, communication flow was envisioned as being exclusively downward and synonymous with the pattern of authority. The pattern of authority provides, of course, the structure of an organization, but almost invariably it is found to represent an idealized concept of what the organization is like. The formal and informal channels indicate the three directions of communications in an organization. Furthermore, the content of the message varies with the direction of flow. The three directions possible for a message to flow are downward, upward, and laterally (horizontally). We begin our discussion by a look at the downward flow of messages.

### Downward

Communications from supervisor to staff are of primarily five types.

**1.** Specific task directives: *job instructions.*
**2.** Information to produce the understanding of the task and its relation to other organizational tasks: *job rationale*
**3.** Information concerning organizational *procedures and practices*
**4.** *Feedback* to the subordinate officer about his performance
**5.** Information to instill a sense of mission: *indoctrination of goals*

   **1.** *Job instructions.* The first type of message is most often given priority in police organizations. Instructions about the position of police officer are communicated to the person through direct orders from the supervisor, training sessions, training manuals, and written directives. The objective is to ensure the reliable performance of every police officer in the organization.

   **2.** *Job rationale.* Less attention is given to the second type, which is designed to provide the police officer with a full understanding of his or her position and its relation to related positions in the same organization. Many police officers know what they are to do but not why. Withholding information on the rationale of the job not only reduces the loyalty of the member to the organization but also means that the organization must rely heavily on the first type of information, detailed instructions about the job. If a person does not understand why he or she should do something or how his or her job relates to other jobs performed by co-workers, then there must be sufficient repetition in the task instructions so that the individual behaves automatically. This problem is dramatically illustrated in the conflict about the information to be given to police officers about their functions. Some city and police administrators are in favor of reducing the police officer's behavior to that of a robot; others want to use the officer's intelligence by having him or her act on an understanding of the total situation. It can be seen, therefore, that the advantages of giving fuller information on job understanding are twofold: If an officer knows the reasons for an assignment, he or she will often carry out the job more effectively; and if the officer has an understanding of what the job is about in relation to the overall mission of the department, he or she is more likely to identify with its goals.

**3.** *Procedures and practices.* Information about organizational procedures supplies a prescription of the role requirements of the organizational member. In addition to instructions about the job, the police officer is also informed about other duties and privileges as a member of the police organization.

**4.** *Feedback.* Feedback is necessary to ensure that the organization is operating properly. It is also a means for motivating the individual performer. However, feedback to the individual about how well he or she is doing in the job is often neglected or poorly handled, even in police organizations in which the managerial philosophy calls for such evaluation. Where emphasis is placed on compliance to specific task directives, it is natural to expect that such compliance will be recognized and deviation penalized.

**5.** *Organizational goals.* The final type of downward-directed information has as its purpose to implant organizational goals, either for the total organization or a major unit of it. Consequently, an important function of a police supervisor is to describe the mission of the police department in an attractive and novel form.

SIZE OF THE LOOP.    The size of the loop in downward communications affects organizational morale and effectiveness. In terms of morale, communications about the goals of the police organization cover in theory a loop as large as the organization itself. In practice, however, the rank-and-file officers are touched only minimally by this loop. Their degree of inclusion within the loop depends mainly upon how they are tied into the police organization. If they are tied in on the basis of being rewarded for a routine performance, information about the goals and policies of the overall structure will be of no interest to them. Therefore, the police supervisor should make every effort to see that the employees are involved members of the organization.

Next, the size of the loop affects the degree of understanding contained in a communication. Messages from top management addressed to all organizational personnel are often too general in nature and too far removed from the daily experiences of the line police officer to convey their intended meaning. To be effective, messages about departmental policy need to be translated at critical levels as they move down in the organization.

Hence, the police supervisor is required to translate a received message into specific meanings for subordinates. This does not necessarily mean that a police officer should get all his or her job directives from a single supervisor, but it does mean that additional supervisors should be used only if they are experts on a specialized function. To illustrate, the patrol officer, in addition to complying with the orders of an immediate supervisor, on occasion can also find relevant direction from a superior of a traffic, vice, or juvenile unit.

## Upward

Communications from subordinate to supervisor are also of chiefly five types.

**1.** Information about his or her *performance* and *grievances*
**2.** Information about the *performance* and *grievances* of others
**3.** Feedback regarding organizational *practices* and *policies*
**4.** Feedback concerning what needs to be *done* and the *means* for doing it
**5.** Requests for *clarification* about goals and the mission

**1.** *Performance and grievances—me.* By our very nature, we want to know "Why?" This is especially so when it comes to performance evaluations. Good, bad, or standard, we want to know the reasons for such judgments about our work. We want examples, the facts about our rating. To get this information, we have to communicate upward. Similarly, when it comes to feeling unfairly treated, we seek an upward appeal—a second opinion—about what befell us.

**2.** *Performance and grievances—others.* We likewise want to ask similar questions about our co-workers. This is a touchy one, because in some cases, it may not be any of our business. However, if we're reprimanded for a mistake, and someone else commits the same one and is not—we'll want to know why.

**3.** *Feedback on policies and practices.* Feedback is one form of two-way communications. Indeed, it may be *the* most important. "Do I understand this policy/practice correctly?" is a critical inquiry deserving the singular attention of the person being asked.

**4.** *Feedback on objectives and methods.* Later on, we'll be covering managing by objectives (MBO) and how it motivates people into action. You'll find that without feedback, it crashes. The supervisor should be in a position to clarify, explain, and justify the objectives of the work unit and how the employees ought to proceed in their accomplishment.

**5.** *Goal clarification.* Similar to the above, the police supervisor should be able to clarify, explain, and justify the overall goals and mission of the department.

**UPWARD IS TOUGH.** There are enormous constraints on free upward communication for a variety of reasons. Most prominent is the structure itself. Simply stated, bureaucracies or highly formalized organizations tend to inhibit upward informal communications. In doing so, a tremendous amount of important information never reaches the upper-level decision centers.

Other factors adversely affecting the upward flow of messages are as follows. Superiors are less in the habit of listening to their subordinates than in talking to them. Furthermore, information fed up the line is often used for control purposes. Hence the superior is not likely to be given information by subordinates that would lead to decisions affecting them adversely. They tell the superior not only what he or she wants to hear but also what they want the supervisor to know. Employees do want to get certain information up the line, but generally they are afraid of presenting it in the most objective form. Full and objective reporting about one's own performance and problems is difficult.

For all these reasons the upward flow of communication in police organizations is not noted for spontaneous and objective expression, despite attempts to formalize the process of feedback up the line. Importantly, it is not a problem of changing the communication habits of individuals, but of changing the organizational conditions responsible for these habits.

## Horizontal

Communications between people at the same hierarchical level are basically of four types.

**1.** Information necessary to provide task *coordination*

**2.** Information for identifying and defining *common problems* to be solved through cooperation

**3.** Feedback from co-workers that fulfills *individual* needs

**4.** Information needed to provide *professional* (not organizational) *guidance* for a group so that it can maintain the members' compliance with its standards and values

**1.** *Coordination.* Confusion, conflict, and frustration emanate from a lack of coordination between work units. If not emphasized, detectives and narcotics could be investigating the same crime; one patrol unit could be messing up the operations of another; and so on.

**2.** *Common problems.* Weak horizontal communications nearly guarantee that the root causes of a police problem will go undetected. When we discuss problem-oriented policing in a subsequent chapter, you'll gain an appreciation for a comprehensive (versus narrow) view of a police problem.

**3.** *Feedback on individual needs.* Most of us want to know what others think about our efforts. "Am I doing a good job?" "Am I trusted?" are of concern to us. Some of this feedback occurs within the work unit. Clearly, it is also valued from co-workers in other work units.

**4.** *Professional guidance.* The sharing of information among work units increases the probability that the various groups are acting in concert with approved service values and quality standards.

A BALANCE. Organizations face one of their most difficult problems in procedures and practices concerned with lateral communication. In essence, a working balance must be found between unrestricted and overrestricted communications among peers in an organization. To explain, unrestricted communications of a horizontal character can detract from maximum efficiency because too much nonrelevant information may be transmitted. At the opposite extreme, efficiency suffers if an employee receives all his or her instructions from the person above, thus reducing task coordination.

Communicating across boundaries is usually overrestricted. If we had to choose between too much or too little, we would opt for the former. Teamwork depends on the speed and ease of movement of information from one departmental sector to another.

The type and amount of information that should be circulated on a horizontal basis is best determined by answering the question, "Who needs to know and why?" To put it another way, the information transmitted should be related to the objectives of the various units in the police organization, with primary focus on their major task. An interesting hang-up in horizontal communications occurs when people overvalue peer communication to the neglect of those below and above them. Sergeants talk only to sergeants, and lieutenants only to lieutenants. However, in many instances the really critical information is at levels below or above them.

---

Communications across boundaries, or laterally, is by far the toughest to achieve.

---

Moving information from one decision center to another is not easy. Of the three directions, clearly communicating across boundaries, or laterally, is by far the toughest to achieve.

### *Structured Exercise 4-3*

David Packard is one of the founders of Hewlett-Packard. He has lectured and written about the "HP Way" of managing. One of its management practices is "managing by wandering around" (MBWA). It guarantees face-to-face, two-way communications. It is based on the following set of assumptions:

- Quality requires minute attention to every detail.
- Everyone in an organization wants to do a good job.
- Written instructions are seldom adequate.
- Personal involvement is essential.

Straightforward as it sounds, there are some subtleties and requirements that go with MBWA. For one thing, Mr. Packard recognized that not every manager finds it easy and natural to do. And if it's done reluctantly or infrequently, it just won't work. It needs to be frequent, friendly, unfocused, and unscheduled—but far from pointless. And since its principal aim is to seek out people's thoughts and opinions, it requires good *listening*.

Linked with MBWA is another important management practice at Hewlett-Packard, and a basic tenet of the HP Way. It's called the "open door policy." Like MBWA, this policy is aimed at building mutual trust and understanding, and creating an environment in which people feel free to express their ideas, opinions, problems, and concerns.

The open door encourages employees, should they have problems of either a personal or job-related nature, to discuss these with an appropriate manager. In the vast majority of cases, this will be the employee's immediate supervisor. But, should the employee be uncomfortable talking with the supervisor, he or she can go up the line to discuss misunderstandings or any other problems with a higher-level manager. HP has found that people do not seem to be particularly averse to bringing up any problems or concerns they may have, and managers usually are able to find satisfactory solutions fairly quickly.

It must be clearly understood by supervisors and managers that people using the open door are not to be subjected to reprisals or to any other adverse consequences.

The open door policy is very important at HP because it characterizes the management style to which it is dedicated. It means managers are available, open, and receptive. Everyone at HP, including the CEO, works in open-plan, doorless offices. This ready availability has its drawbacks in that interruptions are always possible. But at HP, managers have found that the benefits of accessibility far outweigh the disadvantages. The open door policy is an integral part of the management-by-objective philosophy. Also, it is a procedure that encourages and, in fact, ensures that the communication flow will be upward and horizontal as well as downward.

HP believes that it can operate more effectively and comfortably in a truly informal and first-name atmosphere. In no way do charts dictate the channels of communication used by HP people. Managers want their people to communicate with one another in a simple and direct way, guided by common sense rather than by lines and boxes on a chart. To get the job done, an individual is expected to seek information from the most likely source.

HP is convinced that employee publications, e-mail, and fax are useful communications media, but nothing beats personal, two-way communication for fostering cooperation and teamwork and for building an attitude of trust and understanding among employees—this is the HP Way.

Have you seen the HP Way practiced—all or in part—in a police agency? If so, describe what you saw. Is MBWA of benefit to a police agency? What might fit and what might be rejected? Why? Why not?

———⬥✕⬥———

## COMMUNICATION NETWORKS

The vertical and horizontal dimensions in departmental communications can be combined into a variety of patterns or into what is referred to as communication networks.

### Five Networks

Five common networks are shown in Figure 4-1; these are the chain, Y, wheel, circle, and all-channel. In Figure 4-1, the chain network represents a five-level vertical hierarchy where communications can move only upward or downward. In a police department, this type of network could be found in direct-line authority relations with no deviations. For example, the officer reports to the sergeant, who in turn answers to the lieutenant, who reports to the captain, who is responsible to the chief of police.

If we turn the Y network upside down, we can see two subordinates reporting to a supervisor, with two levels of hierarchy still above the supervisor. This is, in effect, a four-level hierarchy.

If we look at the wheel diagram in Figure 4-1 as if we were standing above the network, it becomes obvious that the wheel represents a police supervisor with four officers. However, there is no interaction between the subordinates. All communications are channeled through the supervisor.

The circle network allows members to interact with adjoining members, but no further. It represents a three-level hierarchy in which there is vertical communication between superiors and subordinates and lateral communication only at the lowest level.

Finally, the all-channel network allows each subject to communicate freely with the other four. It is the least structured. While it is like the circle in some respects, the all-channel network has no central position. However, there are no restrictions; all members are equal. This network is best illustrated by a task force, where no one member either formally or informally assumes a dominant or take-charge position.

### Which Is Most Effective?

Which network is most effective totally depends on your purpose. No single network will be best for all situations. If speed is critical, the wheel and all-channel networks are preferred. The chain, Y, and wheel score high on accuracy. The structure of the wheel facilitates the emergence of a leader. The circle and all-

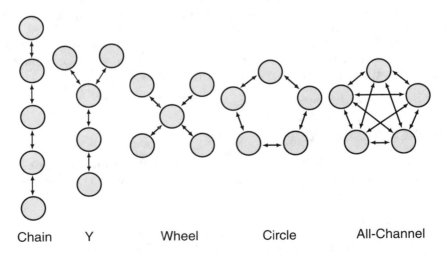

| Chain | Y | Wheel | Circle | All-Channel |

**Figure 4-1**   Common Communication Networks

channel networks are best if the goal is to have high employee satisfaction. Again, what are your intentions as a police supervisor in transmitting a particular message? This determines which network you should employ.

## MESSAGES: VOLUME AND TYPES

Communication is costly. Every message involves the expenditure of time to decide what to send, time for composing, the cost of transmitting the message (which may consist of time or money, or both), and time spent in receiving the message. Consequently, the volume of messages in an organization is of real concern to everyone. *The more communication there is, the more difficult it is for communication to succeed.*

Every individual has a saturation point regarding the amount of information that can be usefully handled in a given time period. In this case, both the volume and the length of the message can overload an individual beyond the saturation point. When overloaded, a person will be unable effectively either to comprehend the information provided or to use it. All of this means that the particular methods used by a police organization to collect, select, and transmit information are critically important determinants of its success. First, we take a closer look at the volume of messages; second, at the types of messages.

### Volume

The volume of messages in a police organization is determined by six basic factors.

- The total number of members in the organization
- The nature of its communications networks (downward, upward, or horizontal)
- The transmission regulations controlling when and to whom messages are sent
- The degree of interdependence among the organization's various activities
- The speed with which relevant changes occur in its external environment
- The search mechanisms and procedures used by the organization to investigate its environment

High message volume usually results in overloading. Attempts are automatically made to reduce any overloading. Police supervisors can react to this situation in one or more of the following ways. First, they can slow down their handling of messages without changing the organization's network structure or transmission rules. This action will cause the police department to reduce its speed of reaction to events, and thereby lessen its output. Second, they can change the transmission rules so that their subordinates screen out more information before sending messages. This reaction also reduces the quantity of the department's output. Third, they can add more channels to the existing network to accommodate the same quantity of messages in the same time period. This reaction provides more opportunities for message distortion and is more expensive. Fourth, they can relate tasks within the organization so that those units with the highest message traffic are grouped together within the overall communications system. This action reduces the volume of messages sent through higher levels in the network and facilitates the coordination of effort. Fifth, they can improve the quality of the messages in order to reduce the time needed for receiving, composing, and transmitting them. Furthermore, besides bettering the content and format of the message, the supervisor can decide on more advantageous methods for handling them. In conclusion, a police organization compelled by its functions to maintain a high volume of messages must inevitably suffer certain disadvantages over a department functioning with a low message volume.

## Types

Messages vary in content and form. There are reports, statements, inquiries, questions, accounts, comments, notes, records, recommendations, rejoinders, instructions, and so on. Messages can be transmitted one of four ways:

- Written reports
- Face-to-face communications
- Telephone conversations
- Electronically/digitally

**WRITTEN REPORTS.** There are six basic characteristics to a well-written report. Each of these is equally important to the completion of a well-written report.

1. *Accurate*. Accurate means in exact conformity to fact.
2. *Clear*. Clear means the report is plain or evident to the reader; the meaning is unmistakable.
3. *Complete*. Reports must have all the necessary parts and include the who, what, when, where, why, and how. Crime reports must include the elements of the crime.
4. *Concise*. Concise means to express all the necessary information in as few words as possible. It does not imply leaving out part of the facts in the interest of brevity.
5. *Factual*. A fact is something real and presented objectively. Facts are things the officer can prove or disprove. Inference and unsubstantiated opinion are not facts and must not be written in police reports. Unsubstantiated opinions are usually based on premises; however, sometimes they are based on prejudice and bias.
6. *Objective*. Objective police reports are not influenced by emotion, personal prejudice, or personal opinion. Officers should record all the facts, remembering there is more than one side to each story.

There are six types of written reports as follows:

- *Routine report*. A routine report is a message that supplies information as part of a standard operation. There are two ways in which a report can be created: (1) time triggered: a report called for at set time intervals (e.g., a police supervisor is required to send weekly reports on the activities of subordinates); and (2) event triggered: a report called for when certain tasks are completed (e.g., a report is to be sent when a case is finished or when certain training has been provided to subordinates).

In each of these examples, the initiative to make a report does not lie with the supervisor; the circumstances under which a report is issued are clearly specified by organizational procedures. The supervisor is required only to determine that the circumstances conform to the specifications. Frequently, the contents of the report are prescribed, either in the format the report is to take (as in the case of a predesigned form) or in the information it is expected to furnish, although the supervisor can exercise limited initiative as to the content and coverage.

- *Memorandum.* A memorandum also supplies information, but not as a part of a routine procedure. A memorandum can be (1) *a statement of fact*, submitted in response to an inquiry, to aid in evaluating a problem or to prepare proposals for action; (2) *a statement that is event triggered*, released when circumstances have changed in an unprescribed manner, calling for some initiative by the transmitter in drawing attention of others to the change so that a plan of action can be formulated; or (3) *a comment*, made in response to some other statement to add information or to give a different interpretation of data.

There is a distinction between a prescribed event, which triggers a report, and an event that generates a memorandum: The first is described by "*When* event such and such occurs, then …," the second, by "*If* the following event occurs, then …," The first describes an event that is expected to occur; the second, an event that may occur. This is the basic difference between the circumstances that lead to reports and those that lead to memoranda.

- *Inquiry.* An inquiry is a message requesting information to assist in evaluating a given problem, usually before making recommendations for action. The response to such a request would be a memorandum, which would include a statement with the necessary information and an analysis of the data. An inquiry usually involves information not included in reports, unless the reports are time triggered and the information is required before the next report is due. Relatedly, an inquiry may meet with a comment, which asks for clarification or points out the difficulties in providing certain information in the time specified. Such a comment is usually generated when the inquiry is ambiguous.

- *Query.* A query is a message defining the characteristics of a problem and asking for instructions or proposals about courses of resolution. A query is often made by a subordinate concerning problems not fully covered by standing regulations, either because of the novelty of the situation or because of ambiguities or inconsistencies in procedures. Furthermore, a query may also be generated by a supervisor seeking advice and direction from peers or subordinates.

- *Proposal.* A proposal describes a course of action the writer feels should be taken. It can be the result of several exchanges of queries, inquiries, reports, and memoranda. It may be generated by a subordinate, on her or his own initiative, or at the instigation of a supervisor; or it may be created by a supervisor wishing to test the reactions of peers or subordinates. A response to a proposal may take the form of a comment or a counterproposal. The absence of a reaction to a proposal is usually viewed as tacit approval.

- *Decision.* A decision states the action to be taken. This message may be of two kinds: (1) a decision that affects recurrent events, which provides direction, not only on how to handle the particular event that caused the discussion prior to the decision, but also similar events in the future (such a decision is made to avoid handling similar problems on an ad hoc basis in the future and to delegate the action for such problems to a lower level in the organization); and (2) a decision on an ad hoc problem, which does not formally affect future procedures.

A decision can take a number of forms. It may begin with a request to review the causes that necessitate making a decision to resolve certain problems; it may continue by outlining alternative courses of action and explaining the reasons for the rejection of some; it may then specify what has been decided and how the decision is to be implemented; next it may indicate what feedback is expected to keep the decision maker informed of progress in implementation.

**ORAL MESSAGES.** Oral messages are of two varieties: meetings (face to face) and telephone conversations (ear to ear).

- *Meetings.* A meeting involves a discussion among two or more people. Meetings have four purposes: (1) to provide a means for exchanges to take place quickly, (2) to provide a job environment in which members are stimulated to new ideas by the rapid exchange of views between individuals, (3) to reduce the amount of semantic difficulties through face-to-face interaction, and (4) to get the members attending the meeting committed more strongly to given proposals or procedures than they would be otherwise.

There are two types of meetings: routine meetings, such as those of permanent committees, and ad hoc meetings, called to discuss particular issues. The difference between a routine meeting and an ad hoc meeting is similar to that between a routine report and a memorandum. Like a routine report, a routine meeting can be either time or event triggered, whereas an ad hoc meeting may either be called in regard to a request to consider a particular problem or be event triggered. Furthermore, a meeting can result in the issuance of any one or several of the messages, listed earlier: a report, a memorandum, an inquiry for further information, a request for instructions, a proposal, or a decision. Significantly, a meeting can also fizzle out and end inconclusively.

- *Telephone conversations.* Many of the comments made on meetings are pertinent to telephone communications. The distinction made earlier between routine and ad hoc communications may be useful here. There are, however, some noteworthy differences between the two media: (1) A telephone conversation is generally confined to two participants, and (2) it lacks certain unique characteristics of interaction that take place in a face-to-face exchange. The preceding two differences are being rapidly erased by technology that supports teleconferencing and its electronic partners—telecommuting and cellular telephones.

**TECHNOLOGICAL COMMUNICATIONS.** The phrase "information age" has come to denote the explosion in information technology and its impact upon society. The industrial age manufactured things, whereas the information age is intended to provide knowledge. The computer, and especially the personal computer (PC), is presently the driving force of our information age or revolution. The PC has given us new applications, online systems, Internet connections, electronic mail, multimedia titles, and a host of games.

Technological advancements are racing toward us all, creating a world in which information is both advantage and freedom. This is a world where time and space are shortened; where computers operate faster, taking up a fraction of the space, and communicating across networks without borders. We hear it every day: "cyberspace," "wired," "on demand," "seamless access," "virtual reality," and "fun." But what does it all really mean to you? Does it make your job easier? Does it make your life better? We are becoming a society that is in touch, but...not touched!

———◆◆◆◆◆———

> The current information revolution, with all of its unresolved confusion and challenges, is but a porous foundation for the incoming second revolution in communications.

———◆◆◆◆◆———

Microsoft's Bill Gates asserts that the current information revolution, with all of its unresolved confusion and challenges, is but a porous foundation for the incoming second revolution in communications. (In fact, he refers to the present global information highway as more like a lot of country lanes.) The dimensions of the second revolution are still vague but likely to involve increasing speeds, inexpensive communications, global interconnections, and customer-driven applications. The most fundamental difference we'll see in future information is that almost all of it will be digital. The latter point means that the cyber-executives will ask us what we want, and then they'll build it for us. Bill Gates sees technology as responsible for providing us with more flexibility and efficiency.

Forward-looking police supervisors will have numerous opportunities to perform better in the years ahead if they are able to strike a balance between "high-tech" and "high-touch." An overconcentration on the high-tech will cost them leadership. An overemphasis on high-touch will cause them obsolescence. Earlier we wrote about Hewlett-Packard, a high-tech company that has a strong belief and trust in people. And, MBWA was used—not computers or e-mail or teleconferencing—to nurture dignity and creativity in the workplace. While the Internet, e-mail, and fax machines have enhanced the movement of information, they in turn are impeding interpersonal communication. There is no substitute for face-to-face communications. We see "fax potatoes" emerging. They'll fax or e-mail you a message rather than walk a few feet to communicate with you in person. We're getting tons of information with only a few pounds of knowledge. Technology is frequently sold as the panacea of all work-related problems. It is alluring and habit forming to the detriment of much needed person-to-person contacts. We would urge that all computers be programmed to periodically shut down, thus ensuring the supervisor MBWA time.

## BARRIERS TO EFFECTIVE COMMUNICATION

*Today, communication itself is the problem. We have become the world's first overcommunicated society.*

—Al Ries and Jack Trout

Unfortunately, positioned in between you, the sender, and the receiver are a number of barriers or distorters that create confusing or misinterpreted messages. The more salient are:

- *Filtering.* This involves either the sender or receiver intentionally manipulating information.
- *Selective perception.* The receiver, in the communication process, selectively sees and hears based on his or her needs, motivations, experience, background, and other personal characteristics. The receiver also projects his or her interests and expectations into communications in decoding them.
- *Emotions.* How the receiver feels at the time of receipt of a communication message influences how he or she interprets it.
- *Words.* Words mean different things to different people. Age, education, and cultural background are three of the more obvious variables that influence the language people use and the definitions they give to words. Senders tend to assume that the words and terms they use mean the same to the receiver as they do to them. This, of course, is often incorrect and thus creates communication difficulties.
- *Information overload.* Technology makes it possible for police supervisors to have, at their fingertips, a wealth of up-to-date information on those activities for which they are responsible or that they need to know about. Supervisors are forced to ignore or give only a cursory review of many messages. The result is that some messages are overlooked or misinterpreted.
- *Nonverbal signs.* When nonverbal cues are inconsistent with the oral message, the receiver becomes confused and the clarity of the message suffers. The lieutenant who tells you that he sincerely wants to hear about your problem and then proceeds to read his mail while you talk is sending conflicting signals.
- *Time pressures.* Supervisors frequently function under time pressures. These pressures can create communication problems when, to expedite matters, formal channels are short-circuited, leaving some people in the dark, and when messages that are transmitted are incomplete or ambiguous to the receiver.

## REMOVING THE BARRIERS

Human beings have been communicating with each other by gestures and signs since the origin of the species, by spoken words for perhaps half a million years, and by some form of writing for more than four thousand years. We should be experts at it by now! The major problem today is not that we are not experts at communication, but that the demands now being placed on human communication threaten to exceed its capacity. Since communications is a human activity, even though machines may be used to assist people in interacting, we emphasize a fundamental principle: The effectiveness of communication tends to be directly proportional to the degree to which both the sender and the receiver regard and treat each other as "human" in the sociocultural context of the event. The following techniques or basics for effective communication should be evaluated and implemented with this principle in mind.

A tremendous number of techniques have been developed whereby supervisors may remove or bypass the blockage at each point in the communication process. The major techniques may be broadly classified in terms of the blockage they remedy. There are five areas where blockage might occur in a communication system: (1) senders, those who initiate a message; (2) message, the vehicle for transmitting information; (3) symbol, the content and format of the information; (4) channel, the means for interchanging messages; and (5) receivers, those who receive a message. The major techniques for overcoming the blockages follow.

**Overcoming Sender Blockage**

The sender of a message should:

- Create special positions or units whose function is to disseminate information inside or outside the organizations.
- Use formal and informal reporting systems.
- Use the grapevine.
- Solicit feedback.
- Simplify language.
- Use appropriate nonverbal cues.

**Reducing Message Blockage**

The content of a message can be clarified by:

- Using more than one medium (e.g., written and verbal).
- Regulating the timing to avoid periods of information overloads.
- Repeating the message at a certain time interval.
- Developing format standards for the reports.
- Summarizing long or complex messages.

**Decreasing Symbol Blockage**

The symbols we transmit, or words, are more apt to accurately depart the sender and access the receiver if:

- All are trained in the use of special terms and acronyms (DOA, FTO, 211, TA, etc.).
- Visual aids, graphs, charts, and so on are used.
- One is alert for emotionally charged symbols and nonverbal cues.

## Coping with Channel Blockage

Communications channels can be cleared by the following practices:

- Carefully routing messages into the most proper channel (e.g., face-to-face conversation).
- Developing openness and human trust.
- Using more than one channel.
- Being concise.
- If the channel you use bypasses someone who should be informed, making certain that she or he is made aware of that particular message. No surprises!

## Combating Receiver Blockage

The receiver should endeavor to:

- Opt for more than a single message.
- Ask for definition of all symbols that are ambiguous or are subject to more than a single translation.
- Know thyself. What are your predilections and biases?
- Seek the advice of others when interpreting the contents of a message.
- Listen actively.
- Watch for nonverbal cues.

## Point

The use of such techniques is, by itself, no guarantee of better communication. Any one of them, in helping to cope with one source of blockage, may create still another kind. If many of them together resulted in much more communication, the result could be a serious increase in the information overload. The appropriate use of well-known techniques and the invention of new ones are rooted in the broader reasoning of police supervisors who have acquired an interest in the communication process and the ability to communicate. The supervisor with an interest in communication is one who, instead of taking communication for granted, is always aware of the possibility of blockage at any point.

## Counterpoint

Given our knowledge that information can be a significant source of power in a police department, it should not come as a surprise to find that supervisors do not always seek to achieve maximum clarity in their communication. There are very few police supervisors who will publicly come out against better communication; however, a few resist initiatives to improve communications because it works against their personal interests and those of their unit. Keeping communications fuzzy cuts down on questions, permits faster decision making, minimizes objections, reduces opposition, makes it easier to deny one's earlier statements, preserves freedom to change one's mind, helps to preserve mystique and hide insecurities, allows one to say several things at the same time, permits one to say "no" diplomatically, helps to avoid confrontation and anxiety, and provides other similar benefits that work to the advantage of the supervisor.

## CONCLUSION: A CHALLENGE

As a supervisor, you are a gatekeeper. It is through you that information is channeled to the top of the department. Too often the greatest mistake made by supervisors is thinking that information is independent of the manner in which it is communicated. It is not, nor should it be. The voluminous report may speak well of effort but speak not at all of insight, implication, or value added. The summary page may be cleverly composed but may lose all the richness and depth of understanding embodied in preliminary material.

Review the nature of the information that leaves your desk by deed, voice, or written word. Is it just information? Or are you genuinely and personally excited by the intriguing nature of what is contained in your document or presentation? Have you truly considered your audience and what would motivate it to act on your information? Is there enough in what you have to say that is new? Have you made pronouncements of change in a threatening manner, or have you skillfully assured the recipient that opportunity is to be had from seemingly threatening new circumstances? Have you thought through the internal political consequences of the information you are transmitting, even to the extent of having done some preliminary work in building a broad-based constituency in support of your information or suggested actions? And, most important, do you undermine yourself by appearing to believe that you are smarter than those to whom you are delivering the information and therefore oversimplify or excessively repeat the contents of your presentation? Finally, have you taken advantage of opportunities made available to you to bring others along in the acquisition and acceptance of information about change?

With values and ethics in mind, and an enhanced awareness of why and how to convey them, we are positioned to assume the responsibility for leading others.

*The management of meaning, mastery of communication, is inseparable from effective leadership.*
—Warren Bennis and Bart Nanus

## KEY POINTS

- Supervising is basically a communication process.
- Communications is the sending and understanding of a message.
- Communications is influenced by our perceptions and expectations, makes demands on us, is related to but different than information, and is best when not "one-way."
- Communication channels are of two types: formal and informal.
- We transmit messages three ways: orally, in writing, and via nonverbal cues.

- Empathic listening is based on first understanding another person and then making one's self understood.
- In an organization, messages can travel downward, upward, and laterally.
- Managing by wandering around (MBWA) has proven to be a valuable communications tool.
- There are five communications networks. Each has its own unique purpose and limitations.
- Information can be transmitted in writing, in person, by telephone, and by electronic technology.
- The personal computer is setting the stage for a second revolution in communications.
- There is too much information and not enough knowledge.
- There are seven barriers to effective communications, ranging from filtering to time pressures.
- Steps can be taken to reduce the adverse influence of each barrier.
- Your effectiveness as a supervisor and communicator is directly tied to your motivations to be effective.

## DISCUSSION

1. What is the key link between the supervisor serving as a leader and acting as a decision maker?
2. What information do we usually find moving in a formal channel as compared to the informal channels?
3. Of the three main methods for communicating, which is best?
4. In which direction is it most difficult (up, down, horizontally) for a supervisor to communicate? Why?
5. Of the five communications networks, which is best? Why?
6. What have you or your organization done to improve the human communication process?
7. When have you either performed or observed empathic listening? What did the listener actually do?
8. How has communications technology helped you in your job? How has it caused you problems?

# RESPONSIBILITY FIVE

---

# Time Management

The police supervisor is responsible for self-management which assures precious freedom for making prudent decisions on job-related matters.

*Success generally depends on knowing how long it takes to succeed.*

—Montesquieu

Now that you have acquired a greater understanding and appreciation of your values (R-1) and ethics (R-2), and how to communicate (R-4) as a leader (R-3), you are prepared to manage yourself, and in turn your time (R-5), in their application.

---

Have you ever heard or used the expression, "I'll save some time by taking this approach?" Or, "I really lost a lot of time by doing it that way?" Time is not ours to bank or spend. It is a precisionally measured period of seconds, minutes, and hours that eventually become a day and, with a great deal of time, we arrive at a millennium (e.g., the year 2000).

> On May 6, 1954, Roger Bannister achieved a major breakthrough in time—he ran a 3:59:6 mile. Now, many track athletes have run a sub–four-minute mile. Will the years 2000 see a sub–three-and-a-half-minute mile, or a sub–two-minute-mile marathon? The athletes that eventually will succeed in doing so will not be managing time, they'll be managing themselves.

Once you've finished this chapter, you'll be managing your time by better managing yourself. This responsibility will, if you truly intend to manage your time, require much more thought and effort than the mere number of pages would suggest. If done properly, this responsibility will require twice the investment of time as compared with the other fourteen responsibilities. You'll discover that much of what you will do depends on the accomplishment of the four prior responsibilities. If you have those well in mind, you'll find the necessary steps for fulfilling Responsibility Five to be richly rewarding and even fun. Moreover, you'll be incrementally closer to what we earlier assumed you sought to become—an effective police supervisor.

## A Couple Of Questions For You

On a sheet of paper write down a short answer to the following questions. (Later on you'll find that your responses are important—be certain to write your answers.)

First, what one thing could you do consistently (i.e., you're not doing it now) that would make a significant change in your personal life?

Second, what one thing in your career life would cause similar results?

## Our Mission

*We gain control of time and events by understanding how they relate to our mission.* Responsibility Five is the exercise of our independent will for becoming a more effective supervisor, which automatically means a more effective person. We do not lead a compartmentalized life. The various roles that we play out in life definitely overlap and influence one another. If you spot a wise time manager at work, you'll probably discover that this individual also prudently manages time as a father or mother, family member, sports participant, hobby enthusiast, and so on. Conversely, the worker who is managed by time, misses deadline dates, is late for work, or is unprepared to do the tasks, is probably the same way in attempting to fulfill other life roles.

---

Our approach to time management *must* involve the total you.

---

Hence, our approach to time management *must* involve the total you. Dealing with your role of supervisor exclusively would be meaningless, or at best a long list of "to-do's," many of which would never get done. Obviously we'll concentrate on making your time at work more productive. At the same time, remember when we use the term "mission" we mean your comprehensive mission in life—the total you.

## People, People, People

A nationally recognized business leader wrote, "My firm basically is comprised of manufacturing, service and people. In order of importance they are: people, people, people."

Ken Blanchard had produced a business around the concept of a "one-minute manager." His logo is a one-minute readout from the face of a modern digital watch. The log is intended to remind us to take a minute out of each day to look into the faces of the people we supervise and to realize that *they* are our most important asset. Our proposition is that clearly much more than one minute should be devoted to this interaction.

If you accept the preceding premise that people are a police agency's greatest asset, then supervisors must understand how to bind them together in a culture wherein they feel truly motivated to achieve high goals. Face-to-face communication, ongoing training and development, creative incentive programs, and job security all display the sort of sensitivity that nurtures strong departmental cultures. Every strong culture derives from management's sensitivity. Without it police employees feel unmotivated, underused, and even exploited. Building the kind of work culture and work team you want obviously takes time. Quality time. Priority time. In the next few pages we'll show you how to do it.

## TIME DIMENSION

> Time\tim\n[Me,fr]: the measured or measurable period during which an action, process, or condition exists or continues.

One complexity is ever present in every supervisory job: Every decision, every action demands due consideration of the time dimension. Supervisors have to assess both today and tomorrow—the present and the future. Little Orphan Annie sang in the musical of the 1980s, "Tomorrow, tomorrow, tomorrow is only a day away." The astute supervisor understands and reacts to the tacit message conveyed in this lyric.

The challenge of harmonizing today and tomorrow exists in all areas and especially with people. The time dimension is inherent in supervision because supervision is concerned with decisions for *action*. The time dimension influences decisions for *progress* (e.g., crime reduction, crime prevention). Finally, the supervisor's time dimension entails the *future*. One international airline's motto is "Being prepared in everything." The successful police supervisor is in constant preparation for the incoming future—the next event, the next decision, the next risk, all the while knowing that they'll be different. Again, time for action, time for progress, and a time for tomorrow—you've got to get a grip on this threefold time dimension.

## SELF-MASTERY OF TIME

One of Albert Einstein's brilliant contributions to modern physics was his intuition that linear time, along with everything happening in it, is superficial. Time seems to flow and move; clocks tick off their seconds, minutes, and hours; eons of history unfold and disappear. But ultimately, Einstein held, this vast activity is all relative, meaning that it has no absolute value.

Einstein displaced linear time with something much more fluid—time that can contract and expand, slow down or speed up. He often compared this to subjective time, for he noted that spending a minute sitting on a hot stove seems like an hour, while a man spending an hour with a beautiful girl seems like a minute. What he meant by this is that time depends on the situation of the observer.

---

Whenever you take an attitude toward time, you are really saying something about yourself.

---

We all have a sense that time expands and contracts, seeming to drag one moment and race the next, but what is our constant, our absolute? It is "me," our core sense of self. The clock doesn't lie about how much linear time has elapsed "out there." But subjective time, the kind that exists only "in here," is a different matter. If you're bored, time hangs heavy; if you're desperate, time's running out; if you're exhilarated, time flies; when you're in love, time stands still. In other words, whenever you take an attitude toward time, you are really saying something about yourself. Time, in the subjective sense, is a mirror.

## Time Pressure

Time pressure causes stress hormones to be released into the body, which in turn elevates heartbeat. If the person struggles against this reaction, his situation only gets worse. Now his heart has to put up with time pressure and frustration. When heart patients are given demanding tasks under a deadline, a significant number grow so agitated that their heart muscles actually suffer "silent" heart attacks ("silent" meaning that damage is occurring but without any sensation of pain).

The element of time pressure also alters behavior, attitudes, and physiological responses. So subjective time can be an incredibly powerful force. It's no accident that the word "deadline" contains the word "dead."

Some people are much more sensitive to time pressure than others. One feels time pressure as a threat, the other as a challenge. One feels thrown out of control; the other feels impelled to test his sense of control and improve upon it.

## Boundaryless Time

---

Being able to identify with a reality that is not bounded by time is extremely important; otherwise, there is no escape from the tyranny that time inevitably brings.

---

We are the only creatures on earth who can change our biology by what we think and feel. Being able to identify with a reality that is not bounded by time is extremely important; otherwise, there is no escape from the tyranny that time inevitably brings. Linear time (the clock) fools us into thinking that one minute follows another with equal spacing, but change your reference for a moment to *subjective time*: Two seconds sitting on a hot stove are much farther apart than two seconds with a loved one. You can catch a glimpse of timelessness with a simple mind-body exercise.

### *Structured Exercise 5-1*

Choose a time of day when you feel relaxed and unpressured. Sit quietly in a comfortable chair and take off your watch, placing it nearby so that you can easily refer to it without having to lift or move your head very much. Now close your eyes and be aware of your breathing. Let your attention easily follow the stream of breath going in and out of your body. Imagine your whole body rising and falling with the flow of each breath. After a minute or two, you will be aware of warmth and relaxation pervading your muscles.

When you feel very settled and quiet inside, slowly open your eyes and peek at the second hand of your watch. What's it doing? Depending on how relaxed you are, the second hand will behave in different ways. For some people, it will have stopped entirely, and this effect will last anywhere from one to perhaps three seconds. For other people, the second hand will hesitate for half a second, then jump into its normal ticking. Still other people will perceive the second hand moving, but at a slower pace than usual. Unless you have tried this little experiment, it seems very unlikely, but once you have had the experience of seeing a watch stop, you will never again doubt that time is a product of perception. The only time there is, is the one you are aware of.

Eastern philosophy and Western science together informs us that:

- While perception appears to be automatic, it is in fact a learned phenomenon. The world you live in, including the experience of your body, is completely dictated by how you learned to perceive it. If you change your perception paradigm, you change the experience of your body and your world.
- Time does not exist as an absolute, but only eternity. Time is quantified eternity, timelessness chopped up into bits and pieces (seconds, hours, days, years) by us. What we call linear time is a reflection of how we perceive change.

## TIME AND PRODUCTIVITY

Most of us want to feel productive. Those who do, do not want to waste their time. After all, time is our most perishable resource. There is nothing less productive than idle time of capital equipment (patrol cars) or wasted time of highly paid and able police employees. Equally unproductive—even counterproductive—may be jamming more work effort into time than it will comfortably hold; for instance, the attempt to provide full patrol coverage by repeatedly paying overtime to officers that are daily becoming more fatigued and less quality conscious. The most productive—or least productive—time is that of the supervisor him or herself. Yet it is usually the least known, least analyzed, and least managed factor of delivering police services.

Time and productivity are causally linked. You have to pay attention to both factors. However, *solid time management is the forerunner of highly productive supervisors.*

## OVERLOADS

Many years ago you would hear police supervisors complain, "I don't get enough information to do my job." The 1950s started to flip such statements to where today we hear, "Good grief, there's just too much information. I don't have the *time* to process it!"

There has never been more media—new television networks and channels, video and film, record numbers of new magazines, newsletters, journals, and newspapers—dedicated to delivering you the changing news of the day. Compounding this is the computer—desktop, laptop, in-car terminals, and even wrist-top. You don't have to look for a telephone today—they're in airplanes, trains, automobiles and frequently seen on a person's hip. We have e-mail and voice mail. Then there is the omnipresent fax. Finally, we have the advanced photocopying machines—"Let's make a copy for everybody!"

What are you absorbing? Do you have the time to process the multitude of incoming messages, much less add yours to the information glut? Incidentally, have you noticed that the so-called paperless society actually has more paper than before? And, while you're receiving and sending more information much faster, much of it doesn't make sense, or you haven't the time to make sense out of it.

> *Without a structure, a frame of reference, the vast amount of data that comes your way each day will probably whiz right by you.*

Probably in reaction to the overloads of this day, Lao Tzu wrote nearly 4,000 years ago to the leaders of China:

> *Endless drama in a group clouds consciousness. Too much noise overloads the senses. Continual input obscures genuine insight. Do not substitute sensationalism for learning.*
>
> *Allow regular time for silent reflection. Turn inward and digest what has happened. Let the senses rest and grow still.*
>
> *Teach people to let go of their superficial mental chatter and obsessions. Teach people to pay attention to the whole body's reaction to a situation.*
>
> *When group members have time to reflect, they can see more clearly what is essential in themselves and others.*

It takes time for reflection. Overloads attempt to block such time allocation. The supervisor must assign it a high priority. If not, any endeavor to manage one's time is doomed to fail. Mark McCormack (sports consultant) puts it this way—"You must take some time to take control of your time."

## Structured Exercise 5-2

### Questionnaire: How Do You Experience Time?

Read the following sentences and check off each one that applies to you fairly often or that you generally agree with. Some of the statements in Part I may seem to contradict others in Part II, but that doesn't matter. Even if you have seemingly opposed traits and opinions, answer each statement on its own.

**Part I**

_____ **1.** There's barely enough time in the day to do all the things I have to do.

_____ **2.** I'm sometimes too exhausted at night to get to sleep.

_____ **3.** I've had to abandon several important goals I set for myself when I was younger.

_____ **4.** I'm less idealistic than I used to be.

_____ **5.** It bothers me to let unpaid bills sit around.

_____ **6.** I'm more cautious now about making new friends and entering serious relationships.

_____ **7.** I've learned a lot from the school of hard knocks.

_____ **8.** I spend more time and attention on my career than on my friends and family.

_____ **9.** I could be a lot wiser about how I spend my money.

_____ **10.** Life is a balance of losses and gains; I just try to have more gains than losses.

_____ **11.** In a loving relationship, the other person should be counted on to meet my needs.

_____ **12.** It sometimes hurts to remember the people I have let down.

_____ **13.** Being loved is one of the most important things I can think of.

_____ **14.** I don't like authority figures.

_____ **15.** For me, one of the most frightening prospects about old age is loneliness.

**Part I score** _____

**Part II**

_____  **1.** I do what I love. I love what I do.

_____  **2.** It's important to have a greater purpose in life than just family and career.

_____  **3.** I feel unique.

_____  **4.** Near-death experiences are very real.

_____  **5.** I often forget what day it is.

_____  **6.** I would describe myself as a carefree person.

_____  **7.** It's a good thing to bring sexual issues out in the open, even when they are disturbing.

_____  **8.** I work for myself.

_____  **9.** It doesn't bother me to miss reading the newspaper or watching the evening news.

_____  **10.** I love myself.

_____  **11.** I've spent time in therapy and/or other self-development practices.

_____  **12.** I don't buy into everything about the New Age, but it intrigues me.

_____  **13.** I believe it is possible to know God.

_____  **14.** I am more leisurely about things than most people.

_____  **15.** I consider myself a spiritual person: This is an area of my life I work on.

**Part II score**  _____

### EVALUATING YOUR SCORE

Although everyone usually checks at least a few answers in both sections, you will probably find that you scored higher in one section than the other.

_If you scored higher on Part I,_ you tend to be time-bound. For you, time is linear; it often runs short and will eventually run out. Relying on outside approval, motivation, and love, you have not grappled with your inner world as much as with the external one. You are likely to value excitement and positive emotions more highly than inner peace and nonattachment. You may cherish being loved by others too much and lose the opportunity to find self-acceptance.

_If you scored higher on Part II,_ you tend to be timeless in your awareness. Your sense of loving and being loved is based on a secure relationship with yourself. You value detachment over possessiveness; your motivations tend to be internal rather than external. At some time in your life, you have a sense of being larger than your limited physical self; your life may have been shaped by decisive experiences of a spiritual nature or your higher self. Where others fear loneliness, you are grateful for your aloneness—solitude has developed your ability to know who you are.

————◆◆◆◆◆————

## If It's Worth Doing, It's Worth Doing Poorly

Take a moment and reread the title of this section. This comment was made by a very successful person. Think about it. Before reading further attempt to develop some type of a rationale for refuting or confirming, "If it's worth doing, it's worth doing poorly."

Let us now add—*to make the best use of your time, you have to make a habit of using it flat out.* Conversely, do you not agree with the proposition that working hard is not necessarily the same as working smart? One more thought—are working hard and working fast synonymous?

Many of us prefer fast decisions to slowness and wrong ones to none at all. Throughout his writings Tom Peters challenges us to "move, move, move." The preceding heading essentially means that if something is vitally important, make a decision quickly. It may cause less than perfect results (even poor results), but the fact remains someone is taking on the problem. It's the quick and timely response, with the underlying knowledge that you're doing the best you can. Now the big *but—slow decisions are usually better than fast ones.* It has been demonstrated again and again that shared or participative decision making produces significantly better results. Further, shared decision making typically builds in a commitment on the part of those involved to implement it.

Fast or slow—which should it be? No doubt both approaches impact on your truly irreplaceable commodity—time. We believe the answer to this puzzle is both—sometimes a fast, sometimes a slow application of time. Both have their place in police organizations. An emergency situation (e.g., robbery in progress) obviously requires fast decisions, a fast time frame. Many supervisors fall prey to all decisions being made fast, when in most cases there is ample time to involve those in the decisions that are going to affect them. Getting one or two really good ideas normally requires getting a lot of ideas at first. Later we'll consider "empowerment." Fast decisions impede empowerment.

We're not against fast decisions. At times they're needed. What we are arguing for is flexibility. Sometimes fast, sometimes slow—it all depends on the situation.

## Four Generations of Time Management

According to Steve Covey (management consultant), there are four generations of time management. Each one builds on the other. The first three conform to the axiom: *Organize and execute around priorities.* The first generation is characterized by notes and checklists. It essentially recognizes the varying demands made on our time. The second generation is epitomized by calendars and appointment books. Here we see an endeavor to schedule ahead. The third generation portrays the more prevalent form of time management. It takes the above two and adds the dimension of prioritization. It focuses on values toward which time and energy are allocated. (The higher the priority of a value—the more time spent.) It is planning with a purpose. The emerging fourth generation recognizes that "time management" is misconstrued! The challenge is not to manage time; after all, time by its very nature manages itself. Rather than concentrating on *activities* and *time*, the fourth generation emphasizes preserving and enhancing *relationships* and on getting results through *teamwork*.

———◆▸◀◆———

The challenge is not to manage time; after all, time by its very nature manages itself.

———◆▸◀◆———

### Time Management Matrix

The matrix that follows categorizes activities or things as fast or slow, and critical or noncritical. Fast activities press us to respond now. Critical matters have to do with results, the fulfillment of our job duties. Let's examine Table 5-1.

Category I is both fast and critical. All of us operate on occasion in this area. Regretfully, some become habitual crises persons. Push, push, faster, faster. These people are frequently experienced as task driven and aggressive. Unfortunately, they beat themselves up while tackling the crises (e.g., stress, burnout, overloads, always putting out fires). When exhausted they often retreat to Category IV, with little attention paid to Category II. There are others who expend a lot of time in Category III, believing that they're in Category I. They are confronting crises all right, only the issues are relatively unimportant in

**Table 5-1**   TIME MANAGEMENT MATRIX

| Fast | Slow |
|---|---|
| I | II |
| Activities | Activities |
|    Crises (shots fired) |    Prevention of conflicts |
|    Pressing problems (computers down) |    Relationship building |
|    Deadline-driven projects (staff reports) |    Recognition of new opportunities |
| |    Planning, recreation |
| |    Team building |
| III | IV |
| Activities | Activities |
|    Interruptions, some calls (open door) |    Trivia, busy work |
|    Some mail, some reports (in-basket) |    Some mail |
|    Some meetings (roll call) |    Some phone calls |
|    Proximate, pressing matters (evaluation) |    Time wasters |
|    Popular activities (code 7) |    Pleasant activities |

terms of their mission. In fact, they are likely responding to the values and expectations of others. *Those of us who spend most of our time in Categories III and IV basically lead irresponsible lives.* Effective supervisors stay out of Categories III and IV because, urgent or not, they aren't critical.

Category II is the crux of managing ourselves. It deals with things that do not require a fast response but are critical, such as building trust, enhancing candid communications, long-range planning, physical exercise, preparation, and renewal. These are high-leverage, capacity-expansion activities.

Stop—now take a look at the two answers you wrote down earlier. What category do they fit in? They probably relate to Category II. But because they do not require a ready-aim-fire response, we neglect them. Your effectiveness will measurably grow if you focus on them. They will make a tremendous, positive difference in your professional and personal lives.

Tom Peters describes a Category II activity that he discovered at Hewlett-Packard—managing by wandering around (MBWA). In this case we'd propose that the police supervisor is "SBWA." We've seen some engage in SBWA and were astonished at the favorable results—everything from new ideas through increased job satisfaction to improved understanding and trust.

### Just Say No

The only place to get time for Category II in the beginning is from Categories III and IV. You can't ignore the urgent and important activities of Category I, although it will shrink in size as you spend more time with prevention and preparation in Category II. But the initial time for Category II has to come out of III and IV. You have to be proactive to work on Category II because Categories I and III suck you in. To say "yes" to critical Category II priorities, you have to learn to say "no" to other activities, sometimes apparently urgent things. If we expect kids to "just say no to drugs," we as adults are equally capable of just saying "no" to the time wasters.

### Time Wasters

Please turn to Structured Exercise 5-3 and complete it before reading further.

Now compare your list with those that are most commonly cited (in rank order).

**1.** Telephone interruptions
**2.** Drop-in visitors
**3.** Meetings (scheduled and unscheduled)
**4.** Crisis
**5.** Lack of objectives
**6.** Cluttered desk and personal disorganization
**7.** Ineffective delegation of responsibilities, and too much involvement in routines and details
**8.** Too much work attempted at once and unrealistic time estimates

9. Lack of or unclear communications or instructions
10. Inadequate, inaccurate, or delayed information
11. Indecision and procrastination
12. Confused responsibility and authority
13. Inability to say "no"
14. Tasks left unfinished
15. Lack of self-discipline

We are convinced that the last point (lack of self-discipline) is the principal villain and essentially allows the other fourteen wasters to surface and bug us.

### Structured Exercise 5-3

The major contributors to wasting my time at work are as follows:

1. _____
2. _____
3. _____
4. _____
5. _____
6. _____
7. _____
8. _____
9. _____
10. _____

As a group, compare the time wasters. Look for similarities. Discuss what might be done to lessen their adverse impact on you and others in the group.

## ON BECOMING A CATEGORY II POLICE SUPERVISOR

The objective of a Category II supervisor is to manage our lives effectively—from a center of sound principles, from a knowledge of our overall (career and personal) mission, with a focus on the "critical" as well as the "fast," and within the framework of maintaining a balance between increasing our actual production and increasing our capability for producing.

Category II organizing requires producing

- Individual mission statement
- Identification of roles
- Selection of your goals
- Weekly scheduling
- Taking action and being flexible

**Your Mission Statement**

When you read your agency's mission statement, or one from another police department, it is probably interesting reading and does not appear to require a formidable set of tasks.

Hold it! What you're reading is in reality a *values statement*. Moreover, if the people that represent the statement believe in it and act accordingly, you'll quickly understand where they intend to go. (Frequently the statement will convey *how* they intend to get there.)

Now it's your turn. Don't worry; your completion of the work in Responsibilities One and Two will facilitate your efforts here. If you choose not to do what is required next, then you've also chosen not to be a fourth-generation time manager.

First of all, return to Responsibility One and write down on a separate sheet of paper the top six or seven values that you identified at that point. Using those values, create a one-page mission statement for yourself. (It is likely this will take three or four drafts before you are pleased with it.)

We'll try to help you by conceiving a hypothetical: Phillip Clark, police sergeant, age twenty-seven, is married with two children. Clark's core values

---

**MISSION STATEMENT**
**PHILLIP D. CLARK**
**AGE TWENTY-SEVEN**

My mission in life is to demonstrate integrity consistently in myself and with others as follows:

- I will love and care for my wife, being certain that she is receiving top priority time.
- I will serve as an example of responsible citizenship for my children. They will be daily recipients of my love and help.
- (and so forth)

---

were, in rank order (1) integrity; (2) spouse; (3) children; (4) parents; (5) police work; (6) house; (7) financial security; and (8) physical and mental health. Here is what he might have written.

All right, once you've finished your mission statement you're ready to move to identifying your various roles in life.

## Your Roles

The first step is to record your main roles. Write down what immediately comes to mind. You have a role as an individual. You may want to list one or more roles as a family member—a husband or wife, mother or father, son or daughter, a member of the extended family of grandparents, aunts, uncles and cousins. You certainly want to list a few roles in your police job, indicating different areas in which you wish to invest time and energy on a regular basis. You may have roles in church or community affairs. (Your mission statement will coach you on what they are.)

You don't need to worry about defining the roles in a way that you will live with forever—just preview the week and write down the areas you see yourself spending time in during the next seven days. For example, our Sergeant Clark might list the following seven roles:

1. Husband
2. Father
3. Son and brother
4. Police sergeant—human relations
5. Police sergeant—production
6. Self-growth—mental and physical
7. Investor

Note how Clark's values, mission statement, and roles are integrated, systematic, and indeed logically compelling. Complete this step for yourself now, and then proceed to the next.

## Your Goals

It's late Sunday afternoon and Sergeant Clark has set aside thirty minutes for managing himself during the ensuing week. Clark lists the following:

| Role | Goals |
|---|---|
| Husband | Discuss vacation plans; review life insurance; schedule a dinner and movie; ask about her job. |
| Father | Discuss school work; play one group game; play one individual game; develop a new sport. |
| Son and brother | Phone parents; send photographs of family; write sister. |
| Police sergeant— human relations | Complete performance evaluations; counsel Officer Mead; meet with each officer for coffee (fifteen minutes each). |

| | |
|---|---|
| Police sergeant— production | Analyze called-for services; prepare a problem-oriented approach to a major need; assess assigned equipment. |
| Self-growth—mental and physical | Read assigned textbook chapters; read *Time* and fifty pages in fictional book; fifty minutes of exercise five times; read national newspaper daily. |
| Investor | Paint interior of small bathroom (first coat); read *Money* magazine, assess CDs. |

You're probably wondering how in the world Clark is going to accomplish all of the preceding goals. At this point it is straightforward, and all he has to do is *schedule*. It is now your turn to specify your goals for the next week. Stop here and do so.

## Your Schedule

Now you can look at the week ahead with your goals in mind and schedule time to achieve them. For example, if your goal is to telephone your parents you may want to set aside a fifteen-minute block of time on Sunday to do it. Sunday is often the ideal time to plan your weekly organizing.

If you set a goal to become physically fit through exercise, you may want to set aside an hour three or four days during the week, or possibly every day during the week, to accomplish that goal. There are some goals that you may only be able to accomplish during work hours or some that you can do only on Saturday when your children are home. Do you now see some of the advantages of organizing the week instead of the day? Having identified roles and set goals, you can translate each goal to a specific day of the week, either as a priority item or, even better, as a specific appointment.

Let's return to our Sergeant Clark to illustrate what must be done at this juncture. To begin with he has to (1) divide up the goals on a per-day basis and (2) at the same time assign them a priority. We'll cover Monday and Tuesday as examples of what you'll soon be doing.

| | Monday | Tuesday |
|---|---|---|
| Priorities | Complete performance evaluations | Meet with officers |
| | Meet with officers | Assess equipment |
| | Analyze called/service | Council Mead |
| | Read assigned text | Read assigned text |
| | Exercise fifty minutes | Exercise fifty minutes |
| | Schoolwork | College class |

| Time | Activity | Activity |
|---|---|---|
| 0500–0600 | Awaken 0530 | Awaken 0530 |
| 0600–0700 | Jog | Drive to work |

| | |
|---|---|
| 0700–0800 | Drive to work | Lift weights |
| | Audio tape on current affairs | |
| 0800–0900 | Briefings/roll call | Briefings/roll call |
| 0900–1000 | Meeting with officers | Meeting with officers |
| 1000–1100 | Performance evaluations | Meeting with officers |
| 1100–1200 | Performance evaluations | Review reports |
| 1200–1300 | Lunch/read text | Lunch/read text |
| 1300–1400 | Analyze called/services | Assess equipment |
| 1400–1500 | Field supervision | Council Mead |
| 1500–1600 | Field supervision | Field supervision |
| 1600–1700 | Report review | Report review |
| 1700–1800 | Drive home | Drive to college/dinner |
| 1800–1900 | Dinner | College course |
| 1900–2000 | Review schoolwork | College course |
| 2000–2100 | Games with children | College course |
| 2100–2200 | Alone time with wife | Drive home/wife |

## Structured Exercise 5-4

Take a few moments and concentrate on the key tasks that comprise your job. If with co-workers, compare the results of your analysis.

The following Job-Time Analysis Form is provided to help you assess the specific areas of time management in which you need improvement. List the individual tasks you perform on the job, and complete each column for each task.

| Job task | What percentage of my time does it consume? | What is its priority (high medium, or low)? | Do I like or dislike performing it? | Can I delegate it? | Is it discretionary or nondiscretionary |
|---|---|---|---|---|---|
| | | | | | |

After completing the Job-Time Analysis Form, review it for accuracy. Showing the analysis to colleagues at work and learning their opinion might be helpful in this respect. After ensuring the accuracy of the completed analysis, answer each of the following questions:

**1.** What unnecessary tasks am I performing?
**2.** On which tasks am I spending too much time?
**3.** On which tasks am I spending too little time?
**4.** What tasks am I performing that could be performed better by others?
**5.** What specific changes do I plan to make in the way I manage my time?

---

It's time for us to integrate another step with the preceding ones. Turn to Structured Exercise 5-5 and fill in the blanks. (Remember to prioritize your goals before scheduling the specific activities.) For future time management planning, you're welcome to copy and use the form or design one of your own. Obviously, the time frames will vary according to night- or early morning-shift work. One more reminder: Keep the Category II activities prominent in your goal setting, prioritizing, and scheduling.

### Action and Being Flexible

With Category II weekly organizing, daily action becomes more of a response to daily adaptations, of prioritizing activities and adjusting to emergent circumstances, relationships, and experiences in a systematic way. As mentioned earlier, you can analyze each incoming day and fine-tune your schedule as appropriate. (Your after-work-shift travel home or elsewhere is often a convenient time to review the immediate past and confirm your schedule for tomorrow.) You're now organizing and executing around your goals and priorities. While you actually cannot manage time, you certainly can manage yourself—if you want to.

Figure 5-1 shows five steps, in summary.

## KEY POINTS

Fourth-generation management is devoted to ensuring us that as we manage ourselves, we more effectively supervise others. It is a constant reminder that *people are always more important than things*. It has been successful because it

- Is *value laden*; it encompasses our driving forces
- Is *conscience focused*; it helps you make the correct choices about what comes first, second, and so on
- We can change our experience with time by changing what we think and feel.
- Time does not exist as an absolute.
- *Defines your individual mission* including values and goals that are prioritized

## Structured Exercise 5-5

### MANAGING PRIORITIES AND SCHEDULING

**The WEEKLY WORKSHEET** — Week of: _____

| Roles | Goals | Weekly Priorities | Sunday | Monday | Tuesday | Wednesday | Thursday | Friday | Saturday |
|-------|-------|-------------------|--------|--------|---------|-----------|----------|--------|----------|

Today's Priorities

Appointments/Commitments

| | Sunday | Monday | Tuesday | Wednesday | Thursday | Friday | Saturday |
|---|--------|--------|---------|-----------|----------|--------|----------|
| 8 | | | | | | | |
| 9 | | | | | | | |
| 10 | | | | | | | |
| 11 | | | | | | | |
| 12 | | | | | | | |
| 1 | | | | | | | |
| 2 | | | | | | | |
| 3 | | | | | | | |
| 4 | | | | | | | |
| 5 | | | | | | | |
| 6 | | | | | | | |
| 7 | | | | | | | |
| 8 | | | | | | | |
| Evening | Evening | Evening | Evening | Evening | Evening | Evening | Evening |

```
+----------------------------------------------------------------------+
|                                                                      |
|                                             Step 5                   |
|                                       Action and Flexibility         |
|                                                                      |
|                                   Step 4                             |
|                                 Plan Your Week                       |
|                                                                      |
|                            Step 3                                    |
|                         Identify Your Goals                          |
|                                                                      |
|                    Step 2                                            |
|               Identify Your Key Roles                                |
|                                                                      |
|          Step 1                                                      |
|  Develop a Personal Mission Statement                                |
|                                                                      |
+----------------------------------------------------------------------+
```

**Figure 5-1**    Fourth Generation: Five Steps to Effective Management of Priorities

- Is an *alignment of various life roles* and scheduling time accordingly
- *Provides an expanded framework for organizing* by scheduling weekly activities.

## DISCUSSION

1. If working as a group, divide into subgroups of five to six people and review your responses to Structured Exercise 5-3. Subsequently, share with one another the contents. Attempt to identify one or two common time wasters.

2. Earlier you were asked to write down the answers to two questions that we had posed. (See "A Couple of Questions for You.") First, share the responses to question one, and then do the same with the second question. What are some interesting similarities? What are some unusual considerations?

3. Review the existing overloads that individuals in the group are experiencing both at work and on a personal basis. What are some of the tactics for handling or avoiding overloads?

4. What decisions should receive a "fast response"? Conversely, what decisions can and should take more time?

5. Reevaluate the Category II activities that we listed earlier. Expand on our list by adding activities. Next, identify one or more examples of each activity.

6. Share with one another your individual successes in developing and using a fourth-generation time management form.

7. What is meant by subjective time? Have you experienced it? If so, in what way?

# PART TWO

# *Internal Partnerships*

## RESPONSIBILITIES

- Six—Motivation

- Seven—Goals

- Eight—Empowerment

- Nine—Performance

- Ten—Conflict

- Eleven—Stress

# RESPONSIBILITY SIX

# *Motivation*

The responsibility of a police supervisor is to unleash and direct an employee's motivation for higher levels of performance.

*I know of no more encouraging fact than the unquestionable ability of man to elevate his life by conscious endeavor.*

—Henry David Thoreau

**The first five supervisory responsibilities were intended to help you in understanding your staff as individuals and as a group. Such understanding positions the supervisor to motivate them in accomplishing their work. A significant part of motivation is setting goals and this is covered in R-7.**

In being responsible for understanding, predicting, and controlling individual behavior, there is probably no activity more important than worker motivation. A cursory look at any police agency shows that some personnel work harder than others. An individual with outstanding abilities may consistently be outperformed by someone with obviously inferior talents. Why do officers exert different levels of effort in different activities? Why do some employees appear to be "highly motivated," while others do not? These are some of the questions we shall attempt to answer in this chapter.

In doing so, we will explore the important distinctions between motivation and performance and between intrinsic and extrinsic motivation. We will discuss several specific theories of work motivation and bring together need theory, expectancy theory, equity theory, and procedural justice theory in an attempt to develop a full picture of motivation's central role in determining the behavior of police employees as they work toward achieving an organization's goals. An understanding of motivation by a police supervisor is of utmost importance for departmental effectiveness.

The more we examine worker motivation, we find . . .

> Motivation starts and stops with you. If you're not motivated, it is next to impossible to motivate others.

## WHY WORKER MOTIVATION?

Basically, police organizations have *three behavioral requirements* of the people who work in them. *First,* people must be attracted to join the police department and remain with it. *Second,* police personnel must dependably perform the tasks they were hired for. *Third,* employees must surpass routine tasks and engage in some form of self-initiated and innovative behavior at work. These three behavioral requirements deal squarely with the "why" of motivation. Motivational techniques must be used by the police supervisor not only to encourage police employees to join and remain with an agency, but also to perform in a dependable fashion and to think and take advantage of unique opportunities.

With respect to the ever-tightening constraints that are placed on police departments by unions, courts, and legislative bodies, agencies must find ways to improve their efficiency and effectiveness in the community. Much of the organizational slack that was tolerated in the past has diminished, requiring that all resources, especially human resources, be utilized to their maximum.

Increased attention is being devoted to motivating police employees to become resources, a sort of talent bank, from which departments can draw in the future. Examples of these efforts are seen in the increase in management development programs, work-force planning, and job redesign. The supervisor is in a key position to support this effort.

---

*Responsible supervision* plays a central role in determining an employee's *job satisfaction.*

---

From the individual's standpoint, being motivated is the key to a productive and satisfying life. Work consumes a sizable portion of our waking hours. If this time is to be meaningful and contribute toward the development of a healthy personality, the individual must be willing to devote effort toward a purpose. *Responsible supervision* plays a central role in determining an employee's *job satisfaction.*

## WHAT IS WORKER MOTIVATION?

Motivation is important because it explains why workers behave as they do. *Worker motivation* can be defined as the psychological forces within a person that determine:

- The direction of a person's behavior in an organization;
- A person's level of effort; and
- A person's level of persistence in the face of obstacles.

See Table 6-1 for further explanation about these three cornerstones of worker behavior.

**Table 6-1**  ELEMENTS OF WORKER MOTIVATION

| Element | Definition | Example |
|---|---|---|
| Direction of behavior | Which behavior does an employee choose to perform in a police organization? | Does a police officer take the time and effort to convince skeptical superiors of the need to change the specifications for a new patrol plan? |
| Level of effort | How hard does an employee work to perform a chosen behavior? | Does an officer prepare a report outlining problems with the original plan, or does the officer casually mention the issue when he or she bumps into a supervisor in the hall? |
| Level of persistence | When faced with obstacles, confusion, and conflicts, how hard does an employee keep trying to perform a chosen behavior successfully? | When the supervisor disagrees with the officer and indicates that a change in the patrol plan is a waste of time, does the officer persist in trying to get the change implemented or give up despite his or her strong belief in the need for a change? |

## THE DISTINCTION BETWEEN MOTIVATION AND PERFORMANCE

Because motivation determines what employees do and how hard and diligently they do it, you might think that a worker's motivation to do a job is the same as the worker's job performance. In fact, motivation and performance, though often confused by workers and supervisors alike, are two distinct aspects of behavior in an organization. *Performance is an evaluation of the results of a person's behavior.* It involves determining how well or how poorly a person has accomplished a task or done a job. *Motivation is only one factor among many that contributes to a worker's job performance.*

One is apt to expect a highly motivated dispatcher to perform better than one who is poorly motivated. This may not be the case, however. There are intervening influences such as an innate work ethic or lack of one; amount of training; availability of resources; working conditions; a motivated or unmotivated supervisor; a slave driver boss; and more.

———◆◆◆◆———

A high level of motivation does not always result in a high level of performance.

———◆◆◆◆———

Because motivation is only one of several factors that can affect performance, a high level of motivation does not always result in a high level of performance. Conversely, high performance does not necessarily imply that motivation is high: workers with low motivation may perform at a high level if they have a great deal of ability. Supervisors have to be careful not to automatically attribute the cause of low performance to a lack of motivation or the cause of high performance to high motivation. *If they incorrectly assume that low performance stems from low motivation, supervisors may overlook the real cause of a performance problem (such as inadequate training or a lack of resources) and fail to take appropriate actions to rectify the situation so that workers can perform at a high level. Similarly, if police supervisors assume that workers who perform at a high level are highly motivated, they may inadvertently fail to take advantage of the talents of exceptionally capable workers.* If workers perform at a high level when their motivation levels are low, they may be capable of making exceptional contributions to the department if supervisors devote their efforts to boosting their motivation.

*It ain't what you don't know that gets you into trouble.*
*It's what you know that ain't so.*

—Will Rogers

## Structured Exercise 6.1

———◆◆◆◆———

Think for a few moments about past or present jobs you've had. Which ones do you believe you were the most and least motivated to perform? Now the crucial question—why? Further, have you, or are you, working hard and doing good work but with little or no motivation to do so? Alternatively, have you, or are you, doing very little work but with a lot of motivation? In both instances—why? Share this information with your teammates. Probe for similarities and uniqueness in your discussion. What did you discover?

———◆◆◆◆———

## INTRINSIC AND EXTRINSIC MOTIVATION

Another distinction important to a discussion of motivation is the difference between the intrinsic and extrinsic sources of worker motivation. *Intrinsically motivated worker behavior* is behavior that is performed for its own sake; the source of motivation is actually a deeply personal satisfaction in performing the behavior. Police officers who are intrinsically motivated often remark that their work gives them a sense of accomplishment and that they feel that they are doing something worthwhile.

*Extrinsically motivated worker behavior* is behavior that is performed to gain material or social rewards or to avoid punishment. The behavior is not performed for its own sake but rather for its consequences. Examples of extrinsic rewards include pay, praise, and status. Both extrinsic and intrinsic rewards either promote or detract from a motivating job climate.

Intrinsic and extrinsic rewards can be likewise referred to as values (Responsibility One). Hence, if an employee is primarily extrinsically oriented, he or she will respond more quickly to salary, benefits, power and status, and job security. The job per se is not a source of motivation. The person with an intrinsic bent will relate to particular assignments, being of service to others, a feeling of full potential, and making a difference. In this case, the job itself is a motivator. The majority of us seek to attain both intrinsic and extrinsic rewards from our work. Typically, however, we tend to emphasize one set over the other.

---

It is essential that the police supervisor know on an individual basis what rewards (values), from high to low in order, each of his or her employees is seeking.

---

## Structured Exercise 6-2

The purpose of this exercise is to help you to be more perceptive and analytical about various kinds of rewards sought by police employees.

To start, set up groups of six to eight for the 45-minute exercise. The groups should be separated from each other and asked to converse only with members of their own group.

The following instrument presents a list of twelve rewards/values that relate to most jobs in police organizations. Two specific job levels are identified: (1) supervisors and (2) first-line employees.

1. Individually, group members should rank order the twelve factors on the basis of their influences on motivation from 1 (most influential) to 12 (least influential for motivation). No ties. The individual group members should provide two rank orders: (a) as they believe supervisors would respond to these factors, and (b) as they believe line employees would respond to these factors.
2. As a group, repeat the instructions presented in Step 1.
3. The group ranking should be displayed and a spokesperson should discuss the rationale for the group decision and how much variation existed in individual ranks.

**4.** A final combined ranking for the entire class should be developed. Provide a brief rationale for each one of the twelve factors.

| Factors | Supervisors | Employees |
|---|---|---|
| **1. Recognition.** Receiving recognition from peers, supervisor, or subordinates for your good work performances. | | |
| **2. Sense of achievement.** The feelings associated with successful completion of a job, finding solutions to different problems, or seeing the results of one's work. | | |
| **3. Advancement.** The opportunity for advancement or promotion based on one's ability. | | |
| **4. Status.** Being accorded various position-based aspects, such as your own nicely appointed office, selected parking place, or other prestige elements. | | |
| **5. Pay.** A wage that not only covers normal living expenses but provides additional funds for certain luxury items. | | |
| **6. Supervision.** Working for a supervisor who is both competent in doing his or her job and looks out for the welfare of subordinates. | | |
| **7. Job itself.** Having a job that is interesting challenging and provides for substantial variety and autonomy. | | |
| **8. Job security.** Feeling good about your security within the department. | | |
| **9. Co-workers.** Working with co-workers who are friendly and helpful. | | |
| **10. Personal development.** Given the opportunity in your job to develop and refine new skills and abilities.Factors Supervisors Employees | | |
| **11. Fringe benefits.** A substantial fringe benefit package covering such aspects as personal protection. | | |
| **12. Working conditions.** Safe and attractive conditions for doing your work. | | |

# THEORIES OF WORKER MOTIVATON: WHY EMPLOYEES DO WHAT THEY DO

*There is nothing so practical as a good theory.*

— Kurt Levin

From the great volume of theories and research on human motivation, we will very briefly cover two schools of thought about why we do what we do at work. Space does not permit otherwise. Please keep in mind as you progress through this subject matter that each theory is literally substantiated or refuted by several thousands of pages of theory, discourse, and scientific research. The two schools can be typed as (1) *needs* and (2) *process*. Our focus will be on how supervisors can motivate their police personnel.

All of the theories concerning worker motivation are complementary—that is, each furnishes a slightly different insight into the various spectrums of job motivation. There are still more questions than answers about what motivates us. Nevertheless, what little we have confirmed is very helpful in making employees proficient performers.

## Need Theories

The four need theories that we'll describe concentrate on a worker's requirement for *survival* and *well-being*. Basically, what's really vital to us will cause us to pursue it.

---

What's really vital to us will cause us to pursue it.

---

**MASLOW'S HIERARCHY OF NEEDS.** The most widely accepted need classification scheme was proposed by the psychologist Abraham Maslow nearly fifty years ago. His list of five needs is conveniently short, yet covers most of the dimensions that psychologists have found to be essential (see Table 6-2).

Maslow separated the five needs into higher and lower needs. Physiological and safety needs were described as lower-order needs, and love, esteem, and self-actualization as higher-order needs. As each of these needs becomes substantially satisfied, the next need becomes dominant. In essence, the individual moves up the hierarchy. From the standpoint of motivation, the theory would say that, although no need is ever fully gratified, a substantially satisfied need no longer motivates.

**ALDERFER'S ERG THEORY.** Clayton Alderfer's existence-relatedness-growth (ERG) theory is also a need theory of work motivation. Alderfer's theory builds on some of Maslow's thinking but reduces the number of universal needs from five to three and is more flexible in terms of movement between levels. Like Maslow, Alderfer also proposes that needs can be arranged in a hierarchy. The three types of needs in Alderfer's theory are described in Table 6-3.

**Table 6-2**   MASLOW'S HIERARCHY OF NEEDS

|  | Need Level | Description |
|---|---|---|
| Highest-Level Needs | Self-actualization needs | The need to realize one's full potential as a human being |
| | Esteem needs | The need to feel good about oneself and one's capabilities, to be respected by others, and to receive recognition and appreciation |
| | Belongingness needs | Need for social interaction, friendship, affection, and love |
| | Safety needs | Need for security, stability, and a safe environment |
| Lowest-Level Needs (most basic or compelling) | Physiological needs | Basic need for things such as food, water, and shelter that must be met in order for an individual to survive |

Whereas Maslow assumes that lower-level needs must be satisfied before a higher-level need is a motivator, Alderfer lifts this restriction. According to ERG theory, a higher-level need can be a motivator even if a lower-level need is not fully satisfied, and needs at more than one level can be motivators at any time. Alderfer agrees with Maslow that as lower-level needs are satisfied, a worker becomes motivated to satisfy higher-level needs. But Alderfer breaks with Maslow on the consequences of need frustration. Maslow says that once a lower-level need is satisfied it is no longer a source of motivation. Alderfer proposes that when an individual is motivated to satisfy a higher-level need but has difficulty doing so, the person's motivation to satisfy lower-level needs will increase.

**Table 6-3**   ALDERFER'S ERG THEORY

|  | Need Level | Description |
|---|---|---|
| Highest-Level Needs | Growth needs | The need for self-development and creative and productive work |
| | Relatedness needs | The need to have good inter-personal relations, to share thoughts and feelings, and to have open two-way communication |
| Lowest-Level Needs | Existence needs | Basic need for human survival such as the need for food, water, clothing, shelter, and a secure and safe environment |

**McClelland's Achievement, Power, and Affiliation Theory.** The major difference between this theory and those preceding is one's need for power (see Table 6-4).

**Table 6-4** McClelland's Achievement, Power, and Affiliation Theory

|  | Need Level | Description |
|---|---|---|
| Highest-Level Needs | Achievement needs | The drive to excel, to achieve in relation to a set of standards, to strive to succeed |
|  | Power needs | The need to make others behave in a way that they would not have behaved otherwise |
| Lowest-Level Needs | Affiliation needs | The desire for friendly and close interpersonal relationships |

**Herzberg's Motivation–Hygiene Theory.** Frederick Herzberg's research led him to conclude the opposite of satisfaction is not dissatisfaction, as was traditionally believed. Removing dissatisfying characteristics from a job does not necessarily make the job satisfying. Hygiene factors in the workplace provide the necessary foundation for the motivator factors to function, because they bring motivation to a "zero point" by preventing negative behavior. By themselves, hygiene factors do not motivate individuals to better performance. The motivators, or satisfiers, are higher-level needs. These are the job-content factors that motivate people to perform. According to Herzberg, only such aspects as a challenging job, recognition for doing a good job, and opportunities for advancement, personal growth, and development will function to provide a situation for improved worker performance (see Table 6-5).

**Research Findings and Applications.** Of the four need theories covered, Maslow's is the most widely known. However, it and the three others have tended not to receive support from scientific research. The "power need" in McClelland's work has attained scientific merit, and Herzberg's theory stands up reasonably well. Even though the theories have not achieved high validity when studied, police supervisors can still apply some valuable lessons thanks to Maslow and his colleagues. Consider the following:

- Do not assume that all police employees are motivated by the same needs or values. (See again Responsibility One.)
- To determine what will motivate any given worker, determine what needs that individual is trying to satisfy on the job.

**Table 6-5**  HERZBERG'S MOTIVATION–HYGIENE THEORY

|  | Need Sources | Description |
|---|---|---|
| Motivating Needs | Intrinsic (Potential satisfiers) | Achievement<br>Work itself<br>Empowerment<br>Responsibility<br>Advancement<br>Personal growth and development |
|  | Extrinsic (Potential dissatisfiers) | Job security<br>Salary<br>Working conditions<br>Status<br>Company policies<br>Quality of technical supervision<br>Quality of interpersonal relations among peers, supervisors, and subordinates |
| Hygiene Needs |  | Fringe benefits |

- Make sure you have the authority and power to administer or withhold consequences that will satisfy a person's needs.
- Design job situations so that the officers and civilians can satisfy their needs by performing behaviors that enable the department to achieve its mission.

### Process Theories

In this section, three process theories of motivation are explained: expectancy, equity, and procedural justice.

**EXPECTANCY THEORY.**  This theory was originally conceived by Victor Vroom and assumes that employees are motivated to receive positive outcomes. Presently, it is the most accepted theory on *how* we decide which behavior to perform and *how* much effort to exert. (Need theories concentrate on *what* motivates us.)

In order for a police employee to be motivated to perform desired behaviors and to perform them at a high level, the following conditions are necessary:

- *Valence* must be high: The worker desires outcomes the organization has to offer.
- *Instrumentality* must be high: The worker perceives that she or he must perform desired behaviors at a high level to obtain these outcomes.
- *Expectancy* must be high: The worker thinks that trying hard will lead to performance at a high level.

If just one of these three factors—valence, instrumentality, or expectancy—is zero, motivation will be zero. High performance in a police organization depends on what a worker does and how hard he or she does it. According to expectancy theory, in trying to decide what to do and how hard to do it, police employees ask themselves questions such as these:

- Will I be able to obtain outcomes I desire? (In expectancy theory terms: Is the valence of outcomes that the police agency provides high?)
- Do I need to perform at a high level to obtain these outcomes? (In expectancy theory terms: Is high performance instrumental for obtaining these outcomes?)
- If I try hard, will I be able to perform at a high level? (In expectancy theory terms: Is expectancy high?)

*Research findings and applications.* Expectancy theory is a popular theory of motivation and has received extensive attention from researchers. Some studies support the theory and others do not, but by and large the theory has been supported. A supervisor should apply its precepts as follows:

- Determine what outcomes your employees desire. More specifically, identify outcomes that have high positive valence (values) for your crew in order to motivate them to perform at a high level. Clearly communicate to the group what behaviors or performance levels must be obtained for them to receive the valent outcomes.
- Once you have identified desired outcomes, make sure that you have control over them and can give them to employees or take them away when warranted.
- Let your staff know that obtaining their desired outcomes depends on their performing at a high level (raise instrumentalities). Administer the highly valent outcomes only when they perform at a high level (or engage in desired organizational behaviors).
- Do whatever you can to encourage workers to have high expectancies: Express confidence in their abilities, let them know that others like themselves have been able to perform at a high level, and give them guidance in terms of how to perform at a high level (for example, by being better organized, setting priorities, or managing time better).
- Periodically assess workers' beliefs concerning expectancies and instrumentalities and their valences for different outcomes by directly asking them or administering a survey.

### Structured Exercise 6-3

To illustrate valence, instrumentality, and expectancy, as a group or individually, ask yourself these questions: How critical is it for each of you to get an "A" in this class or be rated as an outstanding line employee, supervisor, and so forth? What effort are you willing to make to cause this to happen? What is your probability of success?

———————

**EQUITY THEORY.**    Equity theory states that, if one *perceives* a discrepancy between the amount of rewards received and one's efforts, one is motivated to reduce efforts; furthermore, the greater the discrepancy, the more one is motivated to reduce it. Discrepancy refers to the perceived difference that may exist between two or more people.

J. Stacy Adams has been associated with the initial development and testing of the equity theory. He defined a discrepancy, or inequity, as existing whenever a person perceives that the ratio of his or her job outcomes to job inputs is unequal in comparison to a reference person's job outcomes to job inputs. The reference person may be someone in an individual's group, in another group, or outside the organization. In equity theory, *inputs* are aspects such as efforts, skills, education, and task performance that one brings to or puts into a job. *Outcomes* are those rewards that result from task accomplishment, such as pay, promotion, recognition, achievement, and status.

The equity theory provides the following for police supervisors to consider.

***Research findings and applications.***    The research to date tends to confirm the major ideas in equity theory. Consequently, a supervisor should apply equity theory as follows:

- Because inputs (including effort and behaviors) are likely to vary among police employees, outcomes should also vary. Do not give all workers at a given level the same level of outcomes (such as performance ratings) unless their inputs are identical.

- Distribute outcomes to workers based on their inputs to their jobs and the organization.

- Because it is the perception of equity or inequity that drives motivation, frequently monitor and assess workers' perceptions about relevant outcomes and inputs and about their perceptions of their own standing on these outcomes and inputs. Then correct inaccurate perceptions by presenting the facts.

- Realize that failure to recognize above-average levels of inputs (especially performance) has major motivational implications. It might decrease performance.

### *Structured Exercise 6-4*

———————

The crux of equity theory lies in the word "perceived." In your job right now, what do you think is fair? What is your basis for such an opinion? How might this unequitable situation be corrected? Is your opinion substantiated by facts or feelings?

———————

**PROCEDURAL JUSTICE THEORY.** Equity theory focuses on the fair distribution of outcomes; hence, it is often called a theory of *distributive justice*. As another dimension of fairness in organizations, *procedural justice* is also crucial for understanding worker motivation. *Procedural justice theory*, a fairly new approach to motivation, is concerned with the perceived fairness of procedures used to make decisions about the distribution of outcomes (it is not concerned about the actual distribution of outcomes). Procedural decisions pertain to how performance levels are evaluated, how grievances or disputes are handled, and how outcomes (such as raises) are distributed among employees. In procedural justice theory, as in equity theory, workers' *perceptions* are key.

Procedural justice theory holds that workers are going to be more motivated to perform at a high level when they perceive the procedures used to make decisions about the distribution of outcomes as fair. Police employees will be more motivated, for example, if they think that their performance will be accurately assessed. Conversely, if they think that their performance will not be accurately assessed because the police supervisor is not aware of their contributions to the organization or because the supervisor lets personal feelings affect performance appraisals, they will not be as strongly motivated to perform at a high level. Procedural justice theory seeks to explain what causes workers to perceive procedures as fair or unfair and the consequences of these perceptions.

***Research findings and applications.*** Although a lot of work still needs to be done in the area of procedural justice, it nevertheless appears to be of consequence when attempting to understand motivation in organizations.

A police supervisor should:

- Be candid. No matter how unpleasant it may be, diplomatically inform the person or group of the reasons for a decision.

- Encourage the employees to contribute their thoughts about the decision-making process.

- Explain how a performance rating was derived.

- Justify the ethical basis for your decisions and solicit input on how it is perceived.

## QUESTIONS AND ANSWERS

Being able to ask the right questions means that the police supervisor has advanced two-thirds the distance toward answering the question of worker motivation—either for a group of workers or for an individual employee. Together the theories that we've explored afford us a series of questions for the supervisor to ask of himself or herself and others. (As mentioned earlier, the theories are complementary—each one provides different but relevant perspectives and questions.) A prudent assessment of the responses enables the supervisor to formulate a strategy for motivating employees (see Table 6-6).

**Table 6-6** QUESTIONS POSED BY THE THEORIES OF MOTIVATION

| | |
|---|---|
| Need theories | What outcomes are individuals motivated to obtain in the workplace? |
| Expectancy theory | Do individuals believe that their inputs will result in a given level of performance? |
| | Do individuals believe that performance at this level will lead to obtaining outcomes they desire? |
| Equity theory | Are outcomes perceived as being at an appropriate level in comparison to inputs? |
| Procedural justice theory | Are the procedures used to assess inputs and performance and to distribute outcomes perceived as fair? |

### *Structured Exercise 6-5*

**OBJECTIVE.** Your objective is to gain experience in confronting the challenges of (1) maintaining high levels of motivation when resources are shrinking and (2) developing an effective motivation program.

**PROCEDURE.** The class divides into groups of from six to eight people, and each group appoints one member as spokesperson, to present the group's recommendations to the whole class. Here is the scenario:

Each group plays the role of a team of police supervisors in a police department that has recently downsized. Now that the layoff is complete, police management is trying to devise a program to motivate the remaining police employees.

As a result of the downsizing, the workloads of most employees have been increased by about 30 percent. In addition, resources are tight. A very limited amount of money is available for things such as pay raises and benefits. Nevertheless, management thinks that the agency has real potential and that its misfortune will turn around if employees could be motivated to perform at a high level, be innovative, and work together.

Your group of supervisors has been asked by management to answer the following questions.

1. What specific steps will you take to develop a motivation program based on the knowledge of motivation you have gained from this chapter?
2. What key features will your motivation program include?
3. What will you do if the program you develop and implement does not seem to be working—if motivation not only does not increase but also sinks to an all-time low?

When your group has completed those activities, the spokesperson will present the group's plans and proposed actions to the whole class.

# JOB SATISFACTION

*It is important to acknowledge the kind of work we do because we are what we do, and what we do shapes society.*

—John Naisbett

Job satisfaction and job performance are related to one another. Both provide an indication of what motivates us. When we measure individual job satisfaction and combine the results, it spells out group morale. Low job satisfaction or low morale typically produces poor work performance.

---

Low job satisfaction or low morale typically produces poor work performance.

---

A number of causal factors from the earlier theories of motivation have been grouped into four categories as shown in Table 6-7.

**Table 6-7**  PRIMARY CAUSAL FACTORS INFLUENCING JOB SATISFACTION

| Organization-wide factors | Job-content factors |
|---|---|
| Pay system | Training |
| Promotional opportunities | Job scope |
| Departmental policies and procedures | Role clarify and conflict |
| Organization structure | Challenge and opportunities |
| Communications | |
| **Immediate work-environment factors** | **Personal factors** |
| Supervisory style | Age |
| Participation in decision making | Tenure |
| Work-group size | Personality |
| Co-worker relations | Past experiences |
| Working conditions | Health |
| Recognition | |
| Trust | |

## *Structured Exercise 6-6*

---

On an individual basis, self-administer the following questionnaire. Add up your scores when finished and compare them to the ending scale. As either a work group or a class, compare your scores and calculate an arithmetic mean and top to bottom ranges. Do you see any patterns or unusual findings? Discuss what can be done to elevate your job satisfaction. (Keep in mind that the group score equals morale.)

1.  How satisfied are you with the sort of work you are doing?

    1        2        3        4        5
    Very dissatisfied                Very satisfied

2.  What value do you think the community puts in your service?

    1        2        3        4        5
    None                             Very great

3.  In your daily work, how free are you to make decisions and act on them?

    1        2        3        4        5
    Not at all                       Very free

4.  How much recognition does your supervisor show for a job well done?

    1        2        3        4        5
    None                             Great deal

5.  How satisfied are you with the type of leadership you have been getting from your supervisor?

    1        2        3        4        5
    Very dissatisfied                Very satisfied

6.  To what extent do you get to participate in the supervisory decisions that affect your job?

    1        2        3        4        5
    None                             Great deal

7.  How closely do you feel you are observed by your supervisor?

    1        2        3        4        5
    About right                      Too closely

8.  Are you satisfied with the department as it now stands?

    1        2        3        4        5
    Very dissatisfied                Very satisfied

9.  How satisfied are you with your prestige within the city government?

    1                2        3        4        5
    Very dissatisfied                Very satisfied

**10.** How satisfied are you with your possibilities of being promoted to a better position?

| 1 | 2 | 3 | 4 | 5 |
|---|---|---|---|---|
| Very dissatisfied | | | | Very satisfied |

**11.** How satisfied are you with your present salary?

| 1 | 2 | 3 | 4 | 5 |
|---|---|---|---|---|
| Very dissatisfied | | | | Very satisfied |

**12.** How satisfied are you with your status in the community?

| 1 | 2 | 3 | 4 | 5 |
|---|---|---|---|---|
| Very dissatisfied | | | | Very satisfied |

**13.** Would you advise a friend to join this department?

| 1 | 2 | 3 | 4 | 5 |
|---|---|---|---|---|
| No | | | | Yes |

**14.** Do you receive a feeling of accomplishment from the work you are doing?

| 1 | 2 | 3 | 4 | 5 |
|---|---|---|---|---|
| Very dissatisfied | | | | Very satisfied |

**15.** Rate the amount of pressure you feel in meeting the work demands of your job.

| 1 | 2 | 3 | 4 | 5 |
|---|---|---|---|---|
| Very dissatisfied | | | | Very satisfied |

The higher the total score, the greater is your job satisfaction. A general rule of thumb is:

| 55+ | Very high |
|-----|-----------|
| 50–54 | High |
| 45–49 | Above average |
| 40–45 | Average |
| 35–39 | Below average |
| 34– | Take this job and shove it |

Assuming you've discussed what might be done to increase one's job satisfaction, let's inspect some practices that have proven to be successful in both governmental and business organizations. (Many of the suggestions below are drawn from the prior theories.)

### Winning Environment

Excellent organizations have a deeply ingrained philosophy that says, in effect, "respect the individual," "make people winners," "let them stand out," "empower our staff," "treat people as adults." More significant, both for society and these organizations, they create environments in which people can blossom, develop self-esteem, and otherwise be excited participants in the career and society as a whole. Clearly, this thinking and *practice* tend to motivate employees to become winners.

### Intrinsic Rewards

People work primarily for money—and what money can buy. The trouble is that today, give or take a few cents, most police agencies pay about the same wages for the same kind of work. To make a job with your department more attractive to an individual than a job with another agency, you've got to look far beyond the paycheck. Remember the famous salesman Elmer Wheeler who sells the sizzle, not the steak? Selling jobs to employees is a lot like that. You must show them how their job as a police officer with a particular agency brings them prestige among their friends, skills that represent security for them, and a feeling of accomplishment. Basically, they find joy in their work.

### Extrinsic Rewards

The allocation of performance-based wage increases and other pay incentives is important in determining job satisfaction. Likewise, job security, a solid retirement program, comprehensive health and dental benefits, child care, family leave, modified workweek (4 days/40 hours), and telecommuting all serve to make the job appealing.

### Allow for Individual Differences

Almost every motivation theory recognizes that employees are not homogeneous. People have different needs. They also differ in terms of attitudes, personalities, and human capacities. A "winning" environment will not only permit but also encourage us to respect one another's unique individuality.

### Matchmaking

Motivational benefits accrue from carefully matching people to jobs. For example, don't put a high achiever into a job that is inconsistent with his or her needs. Achievers will do best where the job provides opportunities to participate in goal setting and where there is autonomy and feedback. Remember that not every police officer will be motivated by assignments with increased autonomy, variety, and responsibility.

## Goal Setting

Supervisors should ensure that officers have firm and specific goals, as well as feedback on how well they are doing in pursuit of those goals. For those with high achievement needs, typically a minority in any organization, the existence of external goals is of less importance because these people are already internally motivated.

- *Usually* the officer should participate in setting the goals.
- *Always* be certain that the goals are *perceived* as attainable.
- *Consistently* use an appraisal process by which performance and goal attainment will be reliably evaluated.

## Rewards

Supervisors should seek to

- Use their knowledge of the officer to individualize rewards over which they have control. Scheduling and assignments are two examples.
- Link the reward to performance. Consistent with maximizing the impact of the reward contingency, supervisors should look for ways to increase the visibility of rewards.
- Ensure that rewards or outcomes are perceived by police employees as equitable with the effort and results they produce.
- Say thank you—yes, *thank you.*
- Actively *listen* to others—on occasion emphatically listen to others.
- *Smile!*

———◆•◆◆•◆———

People who thank us for our efforts, listen to us when we voice a need or an opinion and smile at us tend to motivate us.

———◆•◆◆•◆———

The latter three rewards may seem rather dull or impotent. They're not for most of us. *People who thank us for our efforts, listen to us when we voice a need or an opinion, and smile at us tend to motivate us.* They are simple rewards—but they tend to motivate. If you disagree with us, we'd ask whether you have ever worked for a supervisor who never or rarely said thanks, ignored you when you spoke, and seldom smiled. Did this person seem motivated? Did he or she motivate you?

## Inspiration and Perspiration

Responsibility One showed that our value system served, among others, as a motivating force. Our work ethic may include such values as integrity, loyalty, accountability, caring, and more. Or, is our work ethic one of lying, greed, irresponsibility, and not caring? Are you inspired to set an example, create a positive work culture, get results? Are you willing to exert yourself, perspire if necessary, to get your job done as a supervisor?

If you're not inspired, if you're not burning energy as a supervisor—how in the world can you expect it from others? *Motivation starts with you.*

We hear a lot about "burnout," and at times see it in ourselves and others. We would be the first to acknowledge that constant inspiration, 100 percent perspiration, is unrealistic. Nevertheless, with the proper mix of commitment, technical skills, positive attitude, and a willingness to try, you'll evidence motivation—you'll motivate others. For one, I want to be the lead mule. Will Rogers put it this way, "Only the lead mule gets a change of scenery."

As far as burnout is concerned, we'd rather burn out than rust out. Inspiration and perspiration— high octane motivational fuel for top performance.

## KEY POINTS

- Motivation starts with you.
- The police supervisor is in a vital position to motivate others.
- One school of motivational thought centers on our needs.
- Another school of motivational thought concentrates on the human process.
- Basically, both our fundamental needs and human processes drive and guide us.
- Job satisfaction does not guarantee good performance.
- The link between job satisfaction and good performance is the police supervisor.
- Individual job satisfaction, when calculated for a work group, indicates its morale.
- The causes of job satisfaction stem from the organization, work environment, job content, and person.
- The efforts that a supervisor can make to increase job satisfaction involve work climate, intrinsic and monetary rewards, tolerance for uniqueness, matchmaking, goal setting, and use of rewards.

## DISCUSSION

**1.** Why might a person with a very high level of motivation perform poorly?

**2.** Why might a person with a very low level of motivation be a top performer?

**3.** What are the distinguishing features of the needs theories?

**4.** Similarly, what are the unique aspects of the process theories?

**5.** What are the important differences between the two schools of motivational thinking? Are there any points of agreement?

**6.** How does one's motivation and job satisfaction relate to one another?

**7.** Attempt to expand the list of causes of job satisfaction.

**8.** Also, endeavor to increase the list of consequences of poor job satisfaction.

**9.** If you're supervised by an unmotivated person, what might you do (besides transferring or quitting) to change that?

# RESPONSIBILITY SEVEN

---

# *Goals*

The police supervisor is responsible for collaboratively establishing performance goals; and then leading the employees toward their accomplishment. In practice, this is known as "supervising by objectives."

*I'm a great believer in luck, and I find the harder I work, the more I have of it.*

—Thomas Jefferson

The setting of goals is a pivotal and motivating (R-6) force for your work unit. It increases the likelihood of your unit's peak performance (R-9).

---

Our beginning should be with an end in mind. In other words, before we start our journey, we should have a destination or goal set for ourselves.

By keeping the end clearly in mind, you can make certain that whatever you do on any particular day does not stray from the goal you have set as supremely important, and that each day of your life contributes in a logical way to the vision you have of your life as a whole.

*Organizations share the same urgent need for beginning with an end in mind.* The "end" is typically referred to as a "mission statement." And, within the mission statement, you'll find the "ends" or goals of the organization—in our case, a *police organization*. Police organizations should have a clear understanding of their goals. It means that they are *conscious* of where they're going so that they better comprehend where they are now and so that their efforts are always pointed in the right direction.

A while ago, one of us conducted a three-day team-building workshop for a large, full-service sheriff's department. The sheriff is a tall, rugged, red-headed, affable guy. At that time, he'd been the sheriff of the 1,800-person organization for twelve years. The workshop was comprised of an undersheriff, four assistant sheriffs, a coroner, and fifteen captains. The second day started with a discussion of a pending shift in the allocation of sworn personnel. Within a few minutes, the fifteen captains were adamantly defending their assigned turfs. The sheriff sensed this and asked, "Hey, what are our goals?" No one said a word. We saw his face start to match the color of his hair. In a louder voice he stated, "I guess there's no reason to ask you: What are our priorities?" Then there was silence—perhaps sixty seconds, which seemed like an hour.

Finally, one brave captain ventured out with, "Sheriff, in my opinion, our number one priority and goal is corrections. After all, about one-half of our personnel are assigned to it." In a second the sheriff's obvious anger switched to puzzlement. He dropped his head and then looked up and scanned the group. He proceeded to surprise us by saying, "I apologize. I thought you knew. It's my mistake for not telling you, and then retelling you. Our goals, in order of their priority are (1) drug abuse enforcement; (2) contract cities; (3) corrections; (4) county patrol areas; and (5), the coroner's office. Now, don't forget them." We're confident no one has—we certainly haven't.

It is very easy to get in an "activity trap," in the business of police work, to work harder and harder at producing results only to discover that they're unnecessary. A police organization without goals can be highly efficient and very ineffective. *The police organization that lives without goals will spend its future in the present.*

---

The primary responsibility of a police supervisor is to get results through people.

---

The crux of this book bears repeating here—the primary responsibility of a police supervisor is to get results through people. The first step is to set the requisite goals for doing so. Second, the supervisor must generate plans that propel him or her in the direction of *goal fulfillment*. Finally, the police supervisor must construct a method for combining *goals* and *plans* to attain them. Finally, we conclude with an argument for the use of MBO.

The effective police supervisor will set goals, plan for their execution, and apply MBO to connect goals with plans and ultimately performance. Hence, the police supervisor is a goal setter, planner, and monitor.

## GOAL SETTING

*Trenell began to explain: "Once he has told me what needs to be done or we have agreed on what needs to be done, then each goal is recorded on no more than a single page. The One Minute Manager feels that a goal, and its performance standard, should take no more than 250 words to express. He insists that anyone be able to read it within a minute. He keeps a copy and I keep a copy so everything is clear and so we can both periodically check the progress."*

—Kenneth Blanchard and Spencer Johnson
*The One Minute Manager* (New York: William Morrow and Co., Inc., 1982), p. 37

A goal is something we desire, we hope for in the future. An *objective* is a goal, only it is more finite and time certain. For example, a police supervisor may set a goal of developing his or her assigned personnel to the maximum of their innate strengths. An objective that would support fulfillment of this goal could be: All personnel within my purview will have attended an officer survival course within the next six months. Note that the goal is more broad in scope, while an objective is specific, with an assigned time frame.

## Multiplicity of Goals

At first glance, it might appear that organizations have a singular objective: for police departments to apprehend criminals. But closer analysis demonstrates that all organizations have multiple objectives. Police agencies also seek to increase public safety and provide general government services. No one measure can effectively evaluate whether an organization is performing successfully. Emphasis on one goal, such as crime, ignores other goals that must also be achieved if long-term safety is to be achieved. Additionally, the use of a single objective almost certainly will result in undesirable practices, since supervisors will ignore important parts of their job in order to look good on the single measure.

## Real versus Stated Goals

Stated goals are official statements of what an organization says and what it wants various publics to believe are its objectives. But stated objectives, which can be pulled from the organization's charter, annual report, public relations announcements, or from public statements made by a police chief, are often conflicting and excessively influenced by what society believes police organizations *should* do.

The conflict in stated goals exists because organizations respond to a vast array of constituencies. Unfortunately, these constituencies frequently evaluate the organization by different criteria. As a result, police management is forced to say different things to different audiences.

Given the diverse constituencies to which police management is required to respond, it would be a surprise to find a department with a set of objectives stated to everyone that actually describes what the organization seeks to achieve.

There is visible evidence to support, for example, the idea that police managers give much attention to their social responsibilities in the decisions they make and the actions they take. The overall goals that top management states can be the actual or real, or fiction. If you want to know what a police department's *real objectives* are, closely observe what members of the organization actually do. It is behavior that counts.

If we are to develop comprehensive and consistent plans, it is important to differentiate between stated and real objectives. An understanding of the latter's existence can assist in explaining what otherwise may seem like management inconsistencies.

## What Business Are We Really In?

*An old story tells of three stonecutters who were asked what they were doing. The first replied, "I am making a living." The second kept on hammering while he said, "I am doing the best job of stonecutting in the entire country." The third one looked up with a visionary gleam in his eyes and said, "I am building a cathedral."*

The third man is, of course, the true supervisor. The first man knows what he wants to get out of the work and manages to do so. He is likely to give a "fair day's work for a fair day's pay." But he is not a supervisor and will never be one. The second man is a problem. Workmanship is essential; in fact, an organization demoralizes if it does not demand of its members the highest workmanship they are capable of. But there is always a danger that the true workman, the true police professional, will believe that he is accomplishing something when in effect he is just polishing stones or collecting footnotes. Workmanship must be encouraged in the police enterprise. But it must always be related to the needs of the whole.

———————

The effective police supervisor will quickly and easily be able to assert the real goals of the department.

———————

The effective police supervisor will quickly and easily be able to assert the real goals of the department. Hence, he or she understands existing values and possesses a clear vision of the incoming future.

### *Structured Exercise 7-1*

———————

This is a simple but powerful exercise to help you understand the significance of goal substitution.

- Imagine learning that you have to retire in one year. List three things you'd like to accomplish during this last year.
- Assume eleven months have passed, and you have one month left. Again, list three things you would like to do.
- Make a new list assuming you have one week left and another assuming that you have only forty-eight hours left.
- Examine what you've written. If your list includes activities you're not currently pursuing, what's stopping you from pursuing them now? *Get on track!*

(*Note:* This exercise can be easily modified to focus on your personal life. Merely assume that you have one year to live. List three things you'd want to do within the year and so on to forty-eight hours.)

———————

## From Goal Setting to Planning

*The whole of life should be spent thinking about how to find the right course of action to follow. Thought and forethought give counsel both on living and achieving success.*

—Baltsar Gracian, S.J.C.

In a police enterprise, supervisors are not automatically directed toward a common goal. On the contrary, organization, by its very nature, contains four powerful factors of misdirection: (1) the specialized work of most supervisors, (2) the hierarchical structure of management, (3) the differences in vision and work and the resultant insulation of various levels of supervision and management, and (4) the compensation structure of the management group. To overcome these obstacles requires more than good intentions, sermons, and exhortations. It requires policy and structure. It requires that planning be purposefully organized and be made the living law of the entire supervisory cadre.

### Planning Defined

Planning is the process of implementing objectives. It is concerned, then, with means (how it is to be done), as well as with ends (what is to be done). Planning can be further defined in terms of whether it is informal or formal. All police supervisors engage in planning, but it may be only the informal variety. Nothing is written down, and there is little or no sharing of objectives with others in the organization.

When we use the term "planning," we are implying formal planning. There exist specific objectives. These objectives are typically committed to writing and available to organization members. They cover a period of months or years. Finally, specific action programs exist for the achievement of these objectives; that is, supervision and management have clearly defined the path that they want to take from getting where they are to where they want to be.

### Why Planning?

Why should police supervisors engage in planning? Because it gives direction, reduces the impact of change, minimizes waste and redundancy, sets the standards to facilitate control, and increases performance.

First, planning establishes coordinated effort. It gives directions to supervisors and officers alike. When everyone knows where the agency is going and what they are expected to contribute toward achieving the objectives, there should be increased coordination, cooperation, and teamwork. A lack of planning can foster "zigzagging" and thus prevent a department from efficiently moving toward its objectives. Second, planning is a way to reduce uncertainty through anticipated change. It also clarifies the consequences of the actions supervision might take in response to change. Planning forces supervisors to look ahead, anticipate changes, consider the impact of these changes, and develop appropriate responses.

Planning gives direction, reduces the impact of change, minimizes waste and redundancy, sets the standards to facilitate control, and increases performance.

Third, planning can also reduce overlapping and wasteful activities. Coordination before the fact is likely to uncover waste and redundancy. Additionally, when means and ends are clear, inefficiencies become more obvious. Fourth, planning reinforces the objectives or standards that are to be used to facilitate control. If we are unsure of what we are trying to achieve, how can we determine if we have achieved it? In planning, we implement the objectives. In the controlling function, we compare actual performance against the objectives, identify any significant deviations, and take the necessary corrective action. Without planning, there can be no control.

Finally, there is considerable evidence that supervisors and organizations that plan outperform those that do not. Although the evidence is strong, do not assume that all efforts require planning. After all, planning can be time-consuming and costly. The key question is: Does the planning effort appear to be justified in view of the expected gains or outcomes?

## Types of Planning

The most popular way to describe plans is by their breadth. Plans that are organization-wide, that establish the organization's overall objectives, and that seek to position the police organization in terms of its environment are called *strategic* plans. Plans that specify the details on how the overall objectives are to be achieved are called *operational* plans.

STRATEGIC PLANS. Strategic planning typically encompasses a long-term time frame (three to five years or more), has an open-ended perspective, and attempts to predict emerging "driving forces." This form of planning is just now being introduced into police organizations. Since this process is usually executed by top management, we will provide a benchmark reference for those of you who want to learn more about this vital method: George A. Steiner, *Strategic Planning: What Every Manager MUST Know* (New York: Free Press, 1979).

OPERATIONAL PLANS. There are two categories of operational plans, *single use* and *standing*. The first is nonrecurring, such as multiagency police planning for the 2000 Olympic Games. In other words, any plan that identifies how the organization's primary objectives are to be achieved, is developed for a specific purpose, and dissolves after this purpose is accomplished, is a single-use plan.

The two main single-use plans are *programs* and *budgets*. A program is a complex of miniplans for achieving an objective. Administrators in a police agency develop a program to respond to the acts of a terrorist or other unexpected disaster. The plan is designed for the particular requirements of the occurrence. Once the victims have been helped, the plan is assessed, updated, and stored for future application.

The most familiar single-use plan is the numerical budget. Police management typically prepares budgets for revenues, expenses, and capital expenditure needs such as personnel and equipment. It's not unusual, though, for budgets to be used for improving time, space, and human resource utilization.

Police supervisors are not planning for future decisions. Rather, they are planning for the future impact of those decisions that they currently make. Decisions made today become a commitment to some future action or expenditure.

## FROM PLANNING TO MBO

Management by objectives (MBO) is essentially a threefold process that

**1.** Sets a course of desired direction—the objective
**2.** Motivates the person to proceed in that direction—the result
**3.** Ensures self-control via feedback—the managing/supervising

MBO necessitates participatively set goals that are tangible, verifiable, and measurable. Rather than using goals to control, MBO seeks to use them to motivate. The remainder of this section concentrates on the development and use of MBO in police organizations. The practice of MBO by police supervisors has enormous positive payoffs for the overall organization. In the material that follows, *mentally translate the M in MBO into that all-important S for supervisor.*

### What is MBO?

Management by objectives is not new. The concept dates back over forty years. Its appeal undoubtedly lies in its emphasis on converting overall organizational objectives into specific objectives for organizational units and individual members. MBO operationalizes the concept of objectives by devising a process by which objectives cascade down through the organization. As depicted in Figure 7–1, the organization's overall goals are translated into specific objectives for each succeeding level (i.e., division, bureau) in the police department. This linking ensures that the objectives for each unit are compatible with and supportive of the unit just above it. At the individual level, MBO provides specific personal performance objectives. All police personnel, therefore, have an identified specific contribution to make to their unit's performance. If all the individuals achieve their objectives, then their unit's objectives will be attained and the organization's basic goals are pursued:

- Crime control
- Crime prevention
- Order maintenance
- Human services

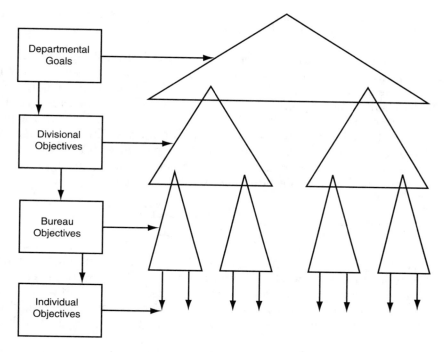

**Figure 7–1**　From Goals into Objectives

## Goals and Objectives

For our purposes, a *goal* is comprised of one or more objectives. An *objective* is a more precise statement of what an organization or individual seeks to accomplish. Also, it typically has a shorter time frame, ranging from a few months to a few years. The following quotation is probably best defined as a goal. The concrete steps specified as necessary to accomplish the goal are objectives.

A goal is comprised of one or more objectives.

### Need for Local Objectives and Priorities

*While the scope and objectives of the exercise of the government's police power are properly determined in the first instance by state and local legislative bodies within the limits fixed by the Constitution and by court decisions, it should be recognized there is considerable latitude remaining with local government to develop an overall direction for police services. Within these limits, each local jurisdiction should decide upon objectives and priorities. Decisions regarding police resources, police personnel needs, police organization, and relations with other government agencies should then be made in a way which will best achieve the objectives and priorities of the particular locality.*[1]

Once the goals and the more specific objectives have been decided, we find ourselves in a position to manage—in this case supervise—by them. While the literature on MBO is extensive and covers both public and private organizations, the term still remains subject to varying definitions. Peter Drucker first coined the term in 1954 and describes MBO as a mutual understanding between the manager and his or her subordinates of what their contribution will be for the organization over a given period of time. It thus establishes parameters of *self-control* and *common direction*.[2] Moreover, it establishes parameters that target the individual and the agency, both in the direction of accomplishing the much to be desired goals.

### *Structured Exercise 7-2*

As a newly promoted police sergeant, you recently attended a mandatory and state-certified two-week "Supervisors' Course." You were an enthusiastic and active learner, graduating number three in a class of eighty-two sergeants. Not everything you heard during the course seemed potentially useful on the job. Nonetheless, you vowed to apply the ideas that appeared plausible, the foremost being MBO.

Presently you are one of three field sergeants assigned to the uniform patrol evening watch (1600–2400). Your span of control and responsibility includes seven patrol officers. All are deployed in single-person patrol cars. Their experience ranges from one to fourteen years, with an average of five years. One is a white female, and one is a black male. The others are white males. Three of the seven you know well, having worked with them in the past. Your police experience includes two years as a cadet, three years in patrol, and one year as a detective. During that period of time you acquired a bachelor's degree in Criminal Justice with a grade point average of 3.96.

You consider yourself to be fair, practical, goal-oriented, intelligent, and approachable. Among your weaknesses you include impatience, stubbornness, and a lack of affability. In knowing your weaknesses, you constantly guard against them.

After one month of supervising your officers, you asked for feedback on your style and tactics. The comments were generally favorable (e.g., "I have no problems with you," "You're OK so far," "I'm glad you're our boss").

For one week you lectured your officers on the merits of MBO and alerted them to the eventual use of it in your work unit. Simultaneously, you secured the tentative approval of your superior, Lieutenant Lance, for its implementation. He commented, "OK, it's your crew. But don't make any waves."

[1]Advisory Committee on the Police Function, *The Urban Police Function* (Washington, D.C.: American Bar Association, 1973), p. 4.

[2]Peter F. Drucker, *Management: Tasks, Responsibilities, Practices* (New York: Harper & Row, 1973), p. 438.

You carefully set a number of objectives for the entire group as well as each individual officer. The objectives are, in your opinion, clear, precise, practical, and attainable. The objectives for the work group are:

1. Reduce residential burglaries by 5 percent within six months.

2. Increase the number of traffic citations (nonparking) by 3 percent in three months

3. Reduce citizen complaints from two per month to one per month within three months

4. Improve the service response time from an average of 4.6 minutes per call to 4.0 minutes per call.

Your first MBO conference is scheduled today with Officer Mike D. Nadler. The officer uses the *D* as his middle initial to denote "Dynamo," a hard-working street cop with eleven years' experience in patrol. His performance ratings have rarely been "outstanding"; however, he has always been rated above average. He is highly dependable, prone to light-hearted sarcasm, and has completed fifteen units of college courses.

After the usual social amenities, you hand Mike a written copy of the MBO agreement. Besides the group's objectives, you listed for him (1) to seek an assignment in another function within one year in order to broaden his experience, (2) to bring his ratings up to the "outstanding" category within six months, and (3) to enter college and complete a minimum of three units per semester starting with the next semester.

Mike appeared to like what he was reading in that his facial expression gradually developed into a relaxed smile. He finished his reading, handed the form back to you, and candidly remarked, "Very amusing, Sergeant. But unless you order me to do so, I'm not signing this form. Why should I? It could be used against me. After all, I work hard. I'm proud to be a patrol officer; why should I become a detective? Also, I have three young kids and all my spare time is devoted to them. I'll be damned if I'll commit any of it to a college course. Are you ordering me to sign the form or not, Sergeant?"

1. How should you respond to Officer Nadler?
2. Define the problem.
3. How can you correct this situation?
4. What will be your future approach to MBO, if any?

## Dynamics of MBO

MBO is not a simple or undemanding chore. It requires a major commitment and effort, for workers seldom automatically cooperate, and even more rarely do they cooperate in the pursuit of a common goal. Regretfully, there are many distorting influences. First, the top or middle managers can create dysfunctional situations by egoism or ingrained biases. Also, by merely filtering information up, down, and laterally within the hierarchy, one finds excessive differences in interpretations of the subject matter at hand. Finally, status differentials—whether they be rank, pay, or position based—cause errant decisions on what to do, when, and where.

## Specific Objectives

Are we not at a point where one should ask, "What are the objectives of the police supervisor?" Each manager, from the chief down to the supervisor, needs clearly spelled objectives. Otherwise, confusion can be guaranteed. These objectives should specify what performance a supervisoral unit is supposed to achieve. They should indicate what contribution the supervisor and his or her unit are expected to make to help other units attain their objectives. Finally, they should detail what contribution the supervisor can expect from other units toward the attainment of his or her own objectives. Right from the start, in other words, emphasis should be on *teamwork* and *team* results. These objectives should always derive from the goals of the police agency.

---

Emphasis should be on teamwork and team results.

---

The objectives of every supervisor should spell out his or her contribution to the attainment of agency goals in all areas of the police service. Obviously, not every supervisor has a direct contribution to make in every area. To obtain balanced efforts, the objectives of all police supervisors on all levels and in all areas should also be keyed to both short- and long-range considerations. And, of course, all objectives should always contain both the tangible police objectives and such "intangible" objectives as supervisory development, worker performance and attitude, and public responsibility. *Anything else is short-sighted and inappropriate.*

## Who Sets Objectives?

Another critical consideration about MBO deals with the question of how the supervisor's objectives ought to be set and by whom. Most basically, the supervisor's objectives should be established by the supervisor in light of (1) his or her expected contribution to the agency, (2) the expectation of his or her subordinates, and (3) the expectation of his or her manager. The supervisor's manager has, as the supervisor should have, the ultimate purview for approval or rejection.

To accomplish all three, a sizable amount of information exchange must occur. Thus, managing supervisors, or supervising police employees, requires special efforts not only to establish common direction but to eliminate misdirection. Mutual understanding can never be attained by "communications down," can never be created by talking. It can result only from "communications down, up, and across." It requires both the superior's willingness to listen and a tool especially designed to make the employee not only heard but understood.

## Measuring Performance

To be able to control his or her own performance, a police supervisor needs to know more than what the objectives are. The supervisor must be able to measure his or her performance and results against the expressed objectives. It should be an axiomatic practice to supply supervisors with clear and universal measurements in all areas of activity. These measurements need not be rigidly quantitative; nor need they be precise. But they have to be *clear, simple,* and *rational.* They have to be germane and direct attention and efforts to where they should go. They have to be reliable—at least to the point where their margin of error is acknowledged and understood. Supervisory control is best manifested by directives explicit in an MBO program that concentrates on one's performance, which is constantly measured in relation to the expressed objectives.

Each police supervisor should have the information she or he needs to measure her or his own performance and that of subordinates and should receive it soon enough to make any changes necessary for the desired results. And this information should go to the supervisor as well as her or his manager. It should also be reported to the police employee. More and accurate information can result in a blessing or a curse, depending on how it is used. For the new capability to produce, measuring information will make possible effective self-control; and if so used, it will lead to a tremendous improvement in the effectiveness and performance of supervision. But if this new capability is abused to impose rigid or excessive control on supervision from above, the new technology will cause incalculable harm by demoralizing supervisors and police officers, which in turn tends to reduce their effectiveness.

## Your Assumptions

MBO forces the supervisor and the police officer to exert self-discipline in light of meeting the stated objectives. Indeed, it may well lead to demanding too much rather than too little. This has been the main criticism leveled against the concept. Yet it remains that MBO is linked to one's ability to accept self-discipline. A supervisor must assume that the vast majority of subordinates are capable of doing so. If not, then MBO will fail. A supervisor who starts out with the assumption that people are weak, irresponsible, and lazy will get weakness, irresponsibility, and laziness. He or she corrupts. A supervisor who assumes strength, responsibility, and desire to contribute may experience a few disappointments. But the supervisor's first task is to make effective the strengths of people, and this can be done if he or she starts out with the assumption that people—and especially supervisors and professional police officers—want to achieve. Above all, the police supervisor must make this assumption with regard to the young educated people of today who will be tomorrow's police officers. They may not know what they mean when they demand to be allowed to "make a contribution." But their demand is the right demand. And they are right also that supervision, as it has been practiced so far in most police agencies, does not act on the assumption that the young educated people want to make a contribution. Police supervisors need to subject others—and to subject themselves—to the discipline and the demands of MBO.

---◆●◆◆●◆---

Police supervisors need to subject others—and to subject themselves—to the discipline and demands of MBO.

---◆●◆◆●◆---

## A Philosophy

The police organization is in need of a philosophy of management and supervision that will give full scope to individual strength and responsibility, as well as common direction to vision and effort; establish teamwork; and harmonize the desires of the individual with the goals of the agency. MBO substitutes for control from outside the stricter, more exacting, and more effective control from inside. It motivates the supervisor and subordinates to action, not because somebody tells them to do something or talks them into doing it, but because the objective task demands it. They act, not because somebody wants them to, but because they decide that they have to. Finally, this philosophy must permeate the entire hierarchy of the agency. It must apply to every manager, every supervisor, and every employee, whatever the level or assignment.

## SUPERVISING BY OBJECTIVES

*Policy making for the police is complicated by the fact that, at least in large cities, the police department is an organization with at least two objectives, one of which produces conflict and the other of which cannot be obtained.*

—James Q. Wilson
*Varieties of Police Behavior* (New York: Basic Books, 1968), p. 135

The decision to set objectives on the part of a police agency automatically presents a major challenge to its entire decision-making process. MBO first requires a series of decisions on what objectives ought to be pursued. Second, an infinite number of decisions are needed to accomplish them. Odiorne's book provides testimony to this thinking in its title, *Management Decisions by Objectives*.[3] He states that three steps of objectives should be rank ordered according to the level of difficulty in their achievement. In order of ascendancy, they are

**1.** Regular or routine: measured by exceptions from standards objectives
**2.** Problem solving: measured by solutions and time established as objectives

---

[3]George S. Odiorne, *Management Decisions by Objectives* (Englewood Cliffs, N.J.: Prentice Hall, 1969), see Chapter 7.

**3.** Innovative goals: measured by productive changes sought and achieved in time

Regardless of the type of objective, a singular and common process can be used to set them. Again, the complexity, the challenge, the certainty, and the time frame will vary based on the type of objective involved. The objective-setting process consists of seven interrelated steps.

**1.** Identification of the problem
**2.** Definition of the problem in specific, operational terms
**3.** Development of alternative strategies to deal with the problem
**4.** Selection of the appropriate alternative
**5.** Implementation
**6.** Evaluation
**7.** Feedback

## Identification of the Problem

At first glance this might appear to be an oversimplification, but experience has shown that this step is often the most difficult part of the entire process. For example, let us assume that a sergeant in a medium-sized police department has the responsibility for supervising a team of fourteen police officers. In addition to this overall responsibility, he is responsible for the division's in-service training program and supply requisitioning. He is actively pursuing his own formal education and will soon be awarded his associate of arts degree from the local college. The chief of police is interested in converting the traditional patrol patterns and assignments to a team-policing program. The agency has never experienced such an ambitious undertaking and, in fact, is understrength by approximately four personnel. Because the department uses a formal hierarchy, the sergeant's immediate supervisor is a lieutenant (of which the agency has four). The chief has selected the sergeant to research, develop, and present to him a position paper exploring the team-policing concept for their agency.

In reviewing this example and placing yourself in our sergeant's shoes, what would you say is the real problem—the one to which meaningful objectives must ultimately be addressed? Is it time, personnel, converting the attitudes of the department to accept the change, or training, or is it a combination of all these? If you selected the last alternative, then our description of the difficulty of adequately defining the problem is becoming clear.

Various techniques can assist the supervisor in this step. These include reflective thinking, analyzing available data, generating new data about the problem, brainstorming, paper slip techniques, personal observation, or asking someone internal or external to the agency who may have had more experience with such problems. The critical part, however, remains thinking clearly about the problem and then writing it down in the most specific terms possible. This might require several attempts, and the supervisor is encouraged to keep at the task until he or she is satisfied that what he or she has written is an accurate statement about the problem—and that it is the *real* problem.

## Specific Statement

This step of the process is somewhat similar to the identification step; however, it is separated due to its importance. In addition to the advice and cautions offered previously, the supervisor should reflect on the "objective statement" he or she has developed about the problem. It is often productive to use colleagues and a work group as a sounding board to modify, correct, or reinforce the objective statement and to assure himself or herself that what has been written is in fact a specific problem statement amenable to solution and measurement.

## Alternative Strategies

In this step of the process, the supervisor is to develop as *many* alternatives as possible to solve the problem. In the first phase of the exercise, the supervisor should not disregard any possible alternative. The same techniques as indicated before can be utilized to do this—ranging from individual thinking to group thinking. After all the possible alternatives have been identified, the supervisor can then proceed to reduce the list to the handful that hold the most promise. Factors that affect the decision to leave an alternative on the list or remove it are almost limitless. A few of the more outstanding include

- Time
- Money
- Personnel
- Political ramifications
- Tradition and custom
- Attitudes
- Skill of the participants

The skill and expertise of the individual and the size of the problem also influence the choice of techniques used to evaluate each alternative. These range from a simple weighing system to complex mathematical formulas and system techniques.

## Selection of an Alternative

This step is what the supervisor has been aiming toward from the start of the process. After following the preceding steps, the supervisor is finally ready to select the paramount one and implement it. One caution deserves to be reinforced here; that is, the best alternative is not always the most feasible one. The supervisor should be aware of this and should not become disillusioned when the "number one" alternative cannot be implemented. This is caused by a variety of reasons ranging from money to politics.

## Implementation

Following the selection step, we are ready for implementation. In preparing to implement the selected alternative, the supervisor should have thought through the alternative to the point where he or she knows which individuals are going to be impacted, how they will be affected, and where the alternative will be exercised. In effect, the supervisor has a "battle plan" for following through with the selected alternative. This also proves useful in the last two steps, evaluation and feedback.

## Evaluation

There is a growing awareness in the police community of the worth of evaluation. The benefit accrues from such things as being able to explain and justify action taken, fend off criticism of the approach to the problem that was taken, demonstrate the cost-effectiveness of the objective, and reinforce the value of introducing new techniques and methodologies into the police profession. Here, again, a host of techniques can help the supervisor evaluate the program. These range from simple statistical review to esoteric schemes developed by the aerospace industry to evaluate spaceflights. The selection of the correct technique depends on such factors as the size of the program, number of people involved, cost, geographical area involved, and number of interrelated components in the program.

## Feedback

Finally, in the context of this process we are using the term "feedback" to mean communicating the results of our objective-setting process back to those above *and* below us in the hierarchy. Whether or not the results are favorable or unfavorable, it is imperative that we communicate the results back into our system. This is done for the following reasons:

- It keeps people informed of results.
- It leads to refined objectives, one building on the results of the last.
- It continues the process of constantly refining our ability to affect problems in our work group.
- It builds a database on which to build future objectives and decisions.

In reviewing the theme of this section, the *objective-setting process is critical in the supervisor's role of problem solving,* the following series of questions should be asked of each objective:

- Is the objective a guide to action?
- Is it explicit enough to suggest certain types of action (alternatives)?
- Does it suggest tools to measure and control effectiveness?
- Is it challenging?
- Does it show cognizance of internal and external constraints?

## Structured Exercise 7-3

This exercise is intended to build your skill as a supervisor in the use of MBO. Based on the agency for which you work, select one of the following subjects, or generate one of your own. Write a goal (objective) statement related to the subject using no more than 250 words. Be certain that the goal statement complies with the guidelines expressed earlier in this chapter (e.g., clear, specific, attainable, etc.). A few subjects of concern might be:

- Residential burglary rate
- Commercial burglary rate
- Commercial robbery rate
- Officer-involved traffic accidents
- Citizen complaints
- Response times
- Care and maintenance of equipment
- In-service training

If in a group setting, then divide into teams of five to seven individuals. Each person reads aloud his or her goal statement. Then collaborate to refine the statement into a highly practical objective worthy of implementation in a police department. This process should be repeated at least once or twice. Practice ensures your successful use of this powerful supervisor's tool.

## OBSTACLES TO MBO

Much like the "I've got good news and bad news for you, which do you want first?" jokes, I have discussed but one side of MBO—the good news. Now for some bad news. MBO is not without obstacles. As expressed thus far, the advantages are that police managers and supervisors are encouraged to think seriously about their objectives and to try to get them into meaningful and also measurable terms; also, it encourages forecasting, planning, and dialogues between all administrative levels. The disadvantages are that the system is basically foreign to those systems that have developed in both industry and government.

Common obstacles include dilution of efforts, crisis management, employer–employee goal divergence, organizational structure, cost inflation, and macro-personal problems. In addition, limitations to MBO particular to police agencies include organizational structure and basic goals, processes, and economic rewards largely set by statute.

We can conclude our discussion of MBO by suggesting three contingency variables that may determine whether it succeeds or fails: organization culture, top management commitment, and organizational type. It's very likely that those instances when MBO has not succeeded can be explained by an unsupportive culture, lack of top management commitment, or organizational constraints that undermine MBO ideology.

## KEY POINTS

- The supervisor is responsible for (1) setting goals, (2) creating plans for their accomplishment, and (3) linking goals and plans via MBO.
- A goal is a desired future. An Objective is one form of a goal, only it includes a more specific and time-limited dimension.
- Police organizations have multiple goals and objectives.
- Real goals and stated goals may differ from one another.
- Planning is a process for implementing goals and objectives.
- Police supervisors who plan their work typically outperform others who do not.
- In MBO, the objectives must be specific, set in collaboration with the employee, and used to measure performance.
- MBO is comprised of seven sequential steps: (1) identify the problem(s), (2) create a specific statement, (3) develop alternative strategies, (4) select a strategy, (5) design an implementation plan, (6) evaluate the results, and (7) provide feedback to the police employee.
- The three main obstacles to MBO are (1) a resistive working culture, (2) lack of top management backing, and (3) departmental constraints.

## DISCUSSION

1. Is the phrase "to protect and serve" a goal or an objective? Why?
2. Convert the statement, "We had best reduce our burglary rate," into an objective.
3. In your opinion, what are the *real goals* of a police agency?
4. Besides the budget, can you identify one or more plans in your agency? (or, if not your department, then someone else's.)
5. "Rather than using goals to control, MBO seeks to use them to motivate." Explain this assumption.
6. Earlier we covered the *assumptions* and *philosophy* we hold about people as workers. What are your assumptions and philosophy about police employees? Is there any need to make adjustments so as to increase your effectiveness as a supervisor?

# RESPONSIBILITY EIGHT

# *Empowerment*

The police supervisor is responsible for creating a partnership with his or her work team that is centered in empowerment and results in enhanced commitment, better decisions, and good police work.

*The best executive is the one who has enough sense to pick good people to do what he wants done, and self-restraint enough to keep from meddling with them while they do it.*

—Theodore Roosevelt

With the work unit motivated (R-6) and with its goals in place (R-7), it is essential that each person be empowered (R-8) as a full partner in their accomplishment. Empowered employees are a prerequisite of community-oriented policing (R-14).

---

The supervisory word of the moment is "empowerment." It is alleged to be the cure-all for job dissatisfaction, low morale, employee inefficiency, poor performance, and risk avoidance. Everyone seems to be hailing its virtues and scorning any detractors.

*Empowerment works!* The advantages far exceed any downside. Our *concern* is for those who seek to wave a magic wand and "bang" it happens. Our *hope* is for those sworn and civilian supervisors who choose to nurture and carefully unleash the full potentiality of their staff.

If you want community-oriented policing (COP), then you must empower your staff.

If you want community-oriented policing (COP), then you must empower your staff. Without their empowerment, COP will be a success on paper and a failure in reality. There are several other benefits associated with empowerment. Before discussing them, we believe it best to disclose some of the issues and pitfalls that could jump up and surprise you when empowering others.

## WE DON'T ACT ON WHAT WE KNOW

What is beguiling about our situation is that we already know a lot about service and about empowerment. The books have been written, the experiments have been conducted, and the results are in. We know, intellectually and empirically, that empowerment is a leadership strategy for creating high-performance workplaces. Virtually every police organization showcases the success it has had with empowerment, quality improvement efforts, community-efficient operations, and giving superior service to customers.

### What's the Problem?

So what's the problem? The problem is that despite this load of knowledge and evidence, there has been disturbingly little fundamental change in the way police departments manage themselves. Even the organizations that are out telling their stories about COP and empowered police personnel have enormous difficulty in capitalizing on their experience. This overall problem is comprised of barriers as follows:

**1.** *Really opening up.* What remains untouched is the belief that power, purpose, and decision making can reside at the top and the police organization can still learn how to better serve its customers via COP. When an innovative program such as COP challenges this fundamental belief about how to govern, one of two things usually occurs. Either police management rejects it and it is power and decision making as usual, or an effort is made to drive new programs across the bottom layers of the department, never really touching the real centers of control.

    In essence, *empowerment is enabling decision making in others.* Since empowerment is cutting-edge stuff today, most police managers and supervisors are espousing its magic. But, in fact, they are adverse to really opening up and sharing their decision-making authority.

---

Empowerment is enabling decision making in others.

---

**2.** *Ducking.* When you empower your staff, you share with them successes and failures. Everyone is in the same boat. You can't sign on only for the victories and duck the failures. There are some people that do not want to be empowered! They do not, or cannot, make the commitment to be held accountable.

They prefer to gripe about decisions and, when asked for theirs, respond with, "Whatever you say. You're the boss."

**3.** *Believing.* Empowerment necessitates a strong belief in the integrity of the employees' work ethic. If a supervisor does not truly believe that the staff wants to do a good job and enjoy their work, then empowering them is impractical.

**4.** *Rightness.* Empowering others is stressful when you lack faith in them being able to make the right decision. Whether unprepared, unskilled, or unanalytical, it matters not. A supervisor would be foolish to chance a set of no-brainer decisions in order to be recognized as an empowerer. Taking a risk and being a fool are not synonymous.

**5.** *Misunderstanding.* A few moments ago, you read that "empowerment is enabling decision making in others." Those being empowered could erroneously assume that they own the ultimate decision, that the supervisor abdicated the rights and responsibilities of his or her rank. Empowerment is not giving away the decision; it is permitting those who are affected by it to input their ideas and aspirations. While empowerment is akin to a partnership, the supervisor is the senior partner. The senior partner retains the final authority for saying "yes" or "no." *Some see empowerment as a vote on what to do, when it is a voice on what to do.* Those who consider empowerment as the "majority rules" will experience frustration and confusion. Those who accept empowerment as a vehicle for expressing, even arguing, one's point of view will be grateful for the opportunity and supportive of the final decision. The final decision can be the result of collective thinking. The accountability for its results sticks with the supervisor.

---

Empowerment is not giving away the decision; it is permitting those who are affected by it to input their ideas and aspirations.

---

**6.** *All or none.* The "all or none" approach to empowerment can be mistakenly adopted by a police supervisor. Behind such thinking is equal treatment. While well intentioned, the underlying reasoning is faulty. For example, if supervisor has a staff of six people, and five are ready and willing to share in decisions that affect them, while one is not, then no empowerment. Thus, all experience equal treatment—all or none. If equality really counted, then all of us should have the same salary, same rewards, and so on. What really counts is being fair with everyone. Clearly, it is fair to empower those that are ready, while denying it to those who are incapable of handling expanded decision-making authority.

**7.** *At the core.* The core of COP is a police-customer partnership. This partnership seeks to empower the public in making decisions about the quantity and quality of police services they experience. Empowering the citizenry without empowering the staff is not only ridiculous and confusing but also counterproductive. An empowered public, combined with an empowered police, spells "COP"—real COP!

## EM-POWER-MENT

Many of us approach some of our most vital ideas and emotions as if they were finite—limited. For example, there is only so much beauty to go around. Fairness can be counted up to 100 percent. Love is like a pie; there are only so many pieces to serve. The same can be thought of in terms of loyalty, trust, integrity, and power. All of these concepts are unlimited in mind and deed.

Some would agree, as we do, that the more you give away, the more you're likely to possess. Rogers and Hammerstein wrote in lyric, "A bell is not a bell until it is rung, a song is not a song until it is sung, and love is not love until you give it away." Similarly, *power is not power until you give it away.*

It stands to reason that the police supervisor who opts to give a share of his or her power to others automatically expands his or her sphere of influence. Basically, the supervisor has empowered others and is, in turn, in a much better position to accomplish his or her assigned tasks.

By now you may see the link between empowerment and delegation. *Delegation means sharing power, sharing power leads to empowerment, and empowerment means that employees experience ownership of their job.* In essence, they are given the opportunity to become 100 percent responsible.

Next we'll cover delegation in detail and then later on its partner in empowering others—participation. Remember the following simple but proven formula:

Delegation + Participation = Empowerment

## *Structured Exercise 8-1*

**INSTRUCTIONS.** Twenty-seven statements follow. They are statements about your job environment. If you feel the statement is *true* or *mostly true* of your job environment, mark it T. Conversely, if you believe the statement is *false* or *mostly false*, mark it F.

1. The work is really challenging.
2. Few employees have any important responsibilities.
3. Doing things in a different way is valued.
4. There's not much group spirit.
5. There is a fresh, novel atmosphere about the place.
6. Employees have a great deal of freedom to do as they like.
7. New and different ideas are always being tried out.

8. A lot of people seem to be just putting in time.
9. This place would be one of the first to try out a new idea.
10. Employees are encouraged to make their own decisions.
11. People seem to take pride in the organization.
12. People can use their own initiative to do things.
13. People put quite a lot of effort into what they do.
14. Variety and change are not particularly important.
15. The same methods have been used for quite a long time.
16. Supervisors encourage employees to rely on themselves when a problem arises.
17. Few people ever volunteer.
18. Employees generally do not try to be unique and different.
19. It is quite a lively place.
20. Employees are encouraged to learn things even if they are not directly related to the job.
21. It's hard to get people to do their work.
22. New approaches to things are rarely tried.
23. The work is usually very interesting.
24. Things tend to stay just about the same.
25. Supervisors meet with employees regularly to discuss their future work goals.
26. Things always seem to be changing.
27. Employees function fairly independently of supervisors.

SCORING.    This awareness is comprised of three dimensions: involvement, independence, and innovation ($I^3$). We believe that a high $I^3$ score for you means high empowerment. The lower the $I^3$ score, the greater the likelihood that you're not experiencing much if any empowerment at work.

Give yourself one point if you've marked the following statements as follows: 1 = $T$; 4 = $F$; 8 = $F$; 13 = $T$; 17 = $F$; 19 = $T$; 21 = $F$; and 23 = $T$. Your score for *involvement* is_____.

Give yourself one point if you've marked the following statements as follows: 2 = $F$; 6 = $T$; 10 = $T$; 12 = $T$; 16 = $T$; 18 = $F$; 20 = $T$; 25 = $T$; and 27 = $T$. Your score for *independence* is _____.

Following the same pattern: 3 = $T$; 5 = $T$; 7 = $T$; 9 = $T$; 14 = $F$; 15 = $F$; 22 = $F$; 24 = $F$; and 26 = $T$. Your score for *innovation* is _____.

If your scores were 0 to 3, that particular dimension is very low; 4 to 5 is below average; 6 is average; 7 is above average; 8 is well above average; and 9 is very high.

Obviously we're hoping that you are looking at scores from 6 on up. An understanding of your job environment can help you deal with both the positive and negative aspects of your work. This information may help you in improving the various aspects of empowerment.

---

## DELEGATION

Delegation of responsibility has been a central topic in supervisory and management texts through the ages. But today's demands on police employees to initiate far-reaching actions and think creatively propels the subject toward the top of the list.

Delegation frees up the police organization to work faster and with less traditional hierarchy (e.g., strict adherence to chain of command, rules and regulations for everything, established routines, etc.). Much more delegation is required now than ever before in meeting the challenges of police work.

### Yes, But

A very bright trainer once commented, "When you delegate you are always delegating one thing for certain—uncertainty!" In other words, will the person who now possesses the responsibility come through? Will the empowered individual perform the task, and, if so, will it be done correctly?

The media is quick to expose police corruption. It makes exciting news. In many instances the newspaper article will implicitly point out that someone or a group of officers failed to execute their duties correctly or faithfully. The officers may have been delegated certain responsibilities and either accidentally or willfully violated the trust placed in them.

Is it any wonder why many police supervisors are fearful of delegating? After all, when something goes sideways, they're accountable. They must answer for their decision to delegate. At the same time, how would police work ever get done if delegation did not occur? The "yes, but" syndrome is often voiced like this, "Yes, but if I delegate this task it may not get done, or at least done to my satisfaction." This leads us to not really "letting go."

### Really Letting Go

The plain fact is that nine out of ten police supervisors are not delegating enough. They think they are. They hand over tasks and pass out assignments routinely. But rarely does the officer really become empowered with true ownership—and its parallel, the sense of being 100 percent responsible.

---

Nine out of ten police supervisors are not delegating enough.

---

What goes wrong? First of all, there is a distinction between "letting go" and "really letting go." However, does really letting go mean chaos, confusion, and substandard performance? Perhaps but not necessarily so. Steps can be taken to avoid the pitfalls of delegation, all the while assuring that its advantages are secured for the police agency. Before we review these steps it's important that we consider the benefits of delegation.

## Who Benefits

First of all many police organizations would cease to function, or at minimum be highly dysfunctional, if delegation did not occur. After all, the chief or the sheriff cannot effectively administer the department and conduct criminal investigations. Watch commanders cannot *effectively* supervise their crew if they're responding to police radio calls. The key word here is "effectively." Yes, they can engage in police work if they choose to do so. Unfortunately, there are some police managers and supervisors that just can't let go, let alone really let go.

A police officer or deputy sheriff is expected to produce a service—get desired results. With each role we play in life (spouse, parent, friend, etc.) are attached expectations (see Responsibility Five). But when we are expected to work with and through people and systems to produce results, we become a supervisor or manager. Many of our other life roles involve working with and through people such as family and friends.

We can (assuming no loss of efficiency) generate one hour of effort and produce one unit of results or police services.

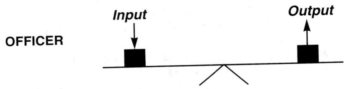

A supervisor, conversely, can invest one hour of energy and create ten or fifty or a hundred units of services through effective delegation. Police supervision, after all, is shifting the fulcrum over to achieve 1 : 10 or 1 : 50 or 1 : 100. *Effective supervision is effective delegation.*

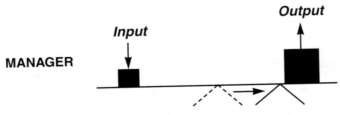

There are four parties that benefit from appropriate delegation. First, there is the community—you and me. Empowered police employees are typically more skillful and dedicated. Hence we get better, less costly services. We in turn are more likely to respect and support our police department.

Second, the organization itself harvests the wealth of brainpower that exists within its sworn and civilian ranks. Everyone takes on the mantel of "I'm 100 percent responsible!" Everyone sets his or her sights on *excellence.*

Third, you benefit as a supervisor because you're

- Building *commitment* for getting the job done
- Increasing *mutual trust* between yourself and your officers
- Enhancing the officers' *job skills and knowledge*
- Encouraging a feeling of *ownership* and
- Leveraging *your power to provide quality police services* (most important)

Fourth, your staff benefits by becoming more

- *Committed* to their work
- *Trusting* and *trustworthy*
- *Professional*
- *Competent*
- *Self-confident*
- *Capable of producing top-notch police work* (most important)

Obviously everyone stands to benefit from really letting go. Again, far too many of us are unwilling to take the risk, and resort to the "yes, but" tactic. The "yes, but" game that some of us play today cannot be tolerated any longer. Empowerment is the game, and being 100 percent responsible is the price you pay to play it.

## Setting the Context

Eight forces must be at work when you delegate. Without them you're taking a big risk. With them in place and functioning, you are apt to achieve superb performance.

- Those being delegated to must be *well trained* in doing their job.
- The training must be ongoing, reliable, and pertinent.
- You should project *high standards*, which you live and demand of everyone uniformly—including yourself.
- You should understand the *values and needs* of each employee.
- From the preceding, establish and maintain a conduit for *open and candid communications*.
- Known anticipations should exist for those who fulfill their duties—*rewards*.
- Known anticipations should exist for those who do not fulfill their duties—*reprimands*.
- Create *feedback* systems. The new employee should receive feedback more often because he or she is earning your trust. The established officer should receive feedback less frequently because he or she has gained your faith.

When delegating, therefore, you must set a context that imposes training, standards, values and needs, communications, rewards, reprimands, and feedback. With such a context operating for you, you'll reap the benefits of being a delegator—you'll like it, and so will those who work for you.

## Lonership–Ownership

Have you heard about the mushroom theory of delegation? You put the police employees into a dark, damp closet and feed them fertilizer. We doubt many supervisors would subscribe to such a theory let alone practice it.

Let us assume that you: (1) understand the virtues; (2) are not a "yes, but" supervisor; (3) are really willing to let go; and (4) have developed the proper context for successful delegation. The next consideration centers on just what should you delegate. Will the responsibility result in empowering ownership or mere lonership? Will the responsibility produce meaningful individual growth or monotonous routine? Such a matrix looks like the one that follows.

|  | OWNERSHIP | LONERSHIP |
|---|---|---|
| | 100% | Interesting |
| | Boring | Gofer |

EMPOWERMENT ←

GROWTH ROUTINE ↑

Remember, we accomplish all that we do through delegation—either to time or to other people. If we delegate to time, we manifest *efficiency*. If we delegate to other people, we generate *effectiveness*. *Delegating to others is the single most powerful high-leverage activity there is.*

There are two polar types of delegation—lonership and ownership. Both contain opportunities for growth as well as humdrum, non-learning experiences.

**LONERSHIP DELEGATION.** Lonership delegation occurs when I give you something to do and then very closely direct it. It may also be referred to as "oversupervision." Although I may consider myself as having delegated something to you, you'll likely not think of it as delegation. In fact, you're more apt to look on it as unnecessary meddling. You're apt to feel like a "gofer."

Gofer delegation is a form of lonership wherein you go for this, go for that. You're not encouraged to think of the task as being a part of *your job*. Indeed, you're probably not encouraged to think at all. Some police supervisors suffer from this practice. In most instances, they're afraid that if they do not direct you each and every moment the work won't be done right. How much does gofer delegation really accomplish? How many people is it possible to supervise when you oversupervise? The answers are, respectively: "not much" and "very few." Gofer delegation is a turnoff for police employees. Ask them—they'll tell you it is. Some may open up and respond with, "Why don't you just do the job yourself? I'm merely an errand boy."

Lonership delegation can be interesting—even with oversupervision. Let us say you're being trained to work in a new assignment such as vice operations. It's different and requires additional police skills and knowledge. The sergeant loans you some responsibility and then carefully monitors how you perform. He trains you along the path to becoming a proficient vice officer. Each day he loans you more responsibility. Eventually you'll reach a point of being able to assume responsibility for the assigned tasks.

When an officer is ready for 100 percent responsibility and ownership, then it is up to the supervisor to really let go. If the supervisor fails eventually to transfer the lonership into ownership, then regression to a gofer situation will occur. In essence, the training and growth phase devolves into one of oversupervision. Skill development is substituted with ill will.

**OWNERSHIP.** Ownership delegation concentrates on results instead of methods. It affords police personnel with a choice of method but, more important, makes them 100 percent responsible for results. Admittedly it takes more time in the beginning. But it's time wisely invested. Ownership delegation moves the production fulcrum way over, thereby *increasing your empowerment leverage*. This holds for both *growth* and *routine* activities.

In addition to the eight forces that should be operational before you delegate (see earlier), ownership delegation involves

- Clear, up-front mutual understanding
- Commitment regarding expectations in five areas

*Desired results.* Generate a mutual understanding of what needs to be accomplished, focusing on *what*, not how, and *results* not methods. Spend time. Visualize the needed outcome. Have the officer describe for you how the results will look and when they will be achieved.

*Guidelines.* Carefully identify the boundaries within which the person must function. These should be as few and inflexible as possible. If you know of any land mines, be certain to reveal them. In other words, instruct them in what *not* to do but do tell them what *to* do. Keep the responsibility for their performance with them—*to do whatever is essential but within the guidelines*.

*Resources.* Identify the various resources that the person can elicit to obtain the preferred outcomes.

*Accountability.* Establish minimum standards that will be applied in evaluating the work effort and when it will occur.

*Consequences.* Indicate what will happen, both positive and negative, as an outcome of the evaluation. This involves rewards and reprimands.

Ownership delegation on occasion may include some highly routine processes. Writing crime reports after a while can become monotonous. Routine work is unavoidable. It happens to all of us. We can choose to insert some change at times. Write the report differently, drive a new route to work, whatever. The saving grace is that at least it's our routine and not someone else's. We own it and can even change it within the guidelines.

Ownership delegation means no nagging on your part. Within the guidelines and standards *you* set, the other person becomes the boss.

## Delegation and Trust

Trust brings out the very best in us. But it takes time and persistence, which includes constant training and consistent encouragement for people to enhance their competencies. Ownership delegation changes the nature of a supervisor–police employee relationship. The police officer, civilian dispatcher, or criminal investigator becomes his or her own boss, governed by a conscience that lives commitment to agreed-on, desired outcomes. It also frees creative forces for conduct that is in harmony with the mission of the department.

With mature employees you provide more challenging expectations, fewer guidelines, less frequent accountability, and less measurable criteria. With the immature employee (we define maturity as emotional wisdom) it is the exact opposite—fewer challenging expectations and so on.

Ownership delegation is perhaps the best indicator of effective supervision because it is so fundamental to both professional and personal growth.

## How Do I Know?

Are you really letting go? Here is a checklist of questions that will help you know if you are or not.

- Have you transmitted the overarching vision with clarity? Does the officer, through demonstrated behavior, clearly "buy in"?
- Is the person aware of the level of performance standards?
- Do you trust the person and have you conveyed it?
- Are you known for butting in at the last minute to handle a problem that someone is experiencing with his or her assignment?
- Do you hold your tongue on asking questions about someone's work efforts?
- Have you avoided excessive reporting?
- When the officer stops by, do you avoid giving direct orders or implying that such and such may be a better approach?

## Common Chord

We would be sorely remiss if we failed to mention Napoleon, Moshe Dayan, and coaches Vince Lombardi and Bear Bryant. They furnish us with a final and highly valuable message about delegation. All four were tough task masters. In word and deed they expected the ultimate from their personnel/players—and got it. Beneath their incessant drive, however, was abiding love and respect for their people. And the people knew it!

---

Confidence and caring are twin pillars of successful delegation.

---

Most treatments of delegation focus exclusively on letting go, with a bit on formal feedback for keeping track. Few discussions of delegation emphasize the place of faith, belief, vision, caring, intensity, and the psychological contract that the effective police supervisor sets up with his or her staff. Small things enhance delegation. Even smaller things destroy it.

*Confidence* and *caring* are twin pillars of successful delegation. Without them everything expressed thus far on the subject of delegation is senseless.

### *Structured Exercise 8-2*

---

Make a list of responsibilities you could delegate, and the police personnel you could delegate to or train to be responsible in these areas. Determine what is needed to start the process of delegation or training.

_____

_____

_____

_____

_____

_____

_____

_____

_____

_____

_____

---

## PARTICIPATION

We have seen on the desks of a couple of police supervisors the epigram, "When I want your opinion, I'll give it to you." Unfortunately, we discovered that they weren't kidding. A few years ago a police chief told us, "I'm a great believer in participative management. I'm going to manage, and you'd damn well better participate." How do you feel about working for such a person? Are you working for that person right now? (Are you that type of a supervisor?) What's delegation like in your organization? How about empowerment?

### Misconceptions about Participation

Allowing others to have an opportunity to express their ideas, needs, and hope about an issue or pending decision that affects them is what we mean by participation.

We've heard some police supervisors voice irritation with, and resistance to, participation as follows, "We're not running a democratic vote here. I'll make the decision, and they're expected to get with it." In part we agree. A police organization cannot be effective if the majority rules. Can you imagine a police sergeant, during roll call briefing, asking his officers to vote on whether they want to patrol or stay in the station? The sergeant is being paid to make such decisions.

Our proposition is rather simple but extraordinarily compelling—when a decision is going to affect others, let them have a chance to express their ideas. Do you wonder why people reject an idea, general order, new policy? Often it is because they had no input—"No one asked me!"

*Letting others participate in decisions that may affect them does not surrender your authority or responsibility for the ultimate decision.* It's yours; you got it when you decided to become a supervisor. You can give it away, but no one can take it away from you. Through the participation of others you listen, you learn, and then you're likely to make a much more reliable decision.

### Why, and Why Not, Allow Others to Participate?

Let us rephrase the preceding heading—why, and why not, *encourage* others to participate in decisions that (will or might) affect their ability to do their job? Here are some reasons that you will want to review.

The best means for getting a good idea is to generate a lot of ideas.

- It builds others' faith that you really care about their welfare and workfare.
- Others' inclusion in a decision-making process usually increases their commitment to its eventual implementation.
- Increased commitment often causes increased productivity.
- A sense if *teamwork* is fostered.
- Teamwork leads to *synergy* wherein the mental energy of a few people multiplies into what hundreds are capable of contributing.

Let's now examine some reasons not to encourage your staff to get involved in the decision process.

- Participation takes time—you have to listen to others (eight, nine, or more people).
- You may experience a sense of frustration or insecurity when confronted with ideas that refute yours.
- You may be convinced of the correctness of their approach—the easy route—and thus opt for group consensus.
- Some may accuse you of manipulation, being conned. "The sergeant asked me for my opinion. She then proceeded to do the exact opposite of what I suggested." (This can be corrected by simply providing feedback on the reasons for your decision. It may be so candid as, "My guts told me so.")

The preceding list of reasons for and against participation is a starter list. Please add to it as you deem appropriate. Albeit, if you've decided to empower yourself and those who work for you, then participation is *in*.

## Structured Exercise 8-3

———◆•✺•◆———

**ALPHA II SUGGESTED REGULATIONS SHEET.** The following group exercises will assist you and your associates to identify the key variables in group dynamics, decision making, consensus, and conflict resolution. Enjoy your journey to Alpha II.

**BACKGROUND.** Scientists have discovered that the second planet orbiting Alpha Centauri is almost an exact duplicate of Earth, except there are no intelligent life forms. A colonization party, including you and your group, has been formed to settle on Alpha II. The five hundred members of the colonization party come from many different regions and cultures with many differing customs and mores.

**INSTRUCTIONS.** Your group has been asked to recommend a list of the five most important rules from the following list to govern social conduct and relationships both on the space journey and on Alpha II. You need not concern yourself with questions of enforcement; assume that all rules can be enforced.

**RULES RECOMMENDED BY THE INTERNATIONAL SOCIAL CONTROL COMMISSION (CAN BE REVISED)**

**1.** The social control process shall be governed by a three-member body representing the police, courts, and corrections.
**2.** There will be no plea bargaining in the court system.
**3.** The Bill of Rights will apply in total on Alpha II.
**4.** There will be no death penalty.

5. The police will not carry guns.

6. No juvenile, regardless of the offense, will be incarcerated in an institution.

7. The social control mechanism (police, courts, and corrections) will be at the national level of government.

8. All social control personnel will not be under civil service but serve at the pleasure of the community.

9. No harmful or addictive drugs will be permitted in Alpha II.

10. There shall be no public displays of sexual behavior, but sexually explicit literature will be available privately as desired.

11. No individual shall be discriminated against or be guilty of any sexual act because of his or her sexual preferences.

12. All police officers will possess a bachelor's degree.

---

### Why Is Participation So Effective?

Perhaps you've heard about the benefits of employee participation. Most of what you've heard is accurate. In today's employer–employee relations, few practices have been so successful in developing consensus and the attainment of common goals as the development of participation by the police supervisor.

- Participation is an amazingly simple way to inspire police employees. And its simplicity lies in the definition of the word: "To share in common with others."

- *Sharing*, then, is the secret. You must share knowledge and information with others to gain their cooperation. You must share your own experience so that officers will gain from it. You must share the decision-making process itself so that personnel can do some things the way they'd like to. And you must share credit for achievement.

Participation or sharing may not come easy for you. However, once you've learned how to share, participation is self-perpetuating. Supervision becomes easier when police employees begin to share responsibility with you. No longer do you alone have to watch for every problem. An employee won't wait for you to say what to do in an emergency. You'll find the officers using their own initiative to keep crime down. So sharing pays off as employees share your decision and their work accomplishments with you.

### Three Rules

There are three fundamental rules to abide by. First, recognize that without group support your chance of achievement is slim. Second, your best chance for winning group support is by allowing the forces within the group to formulate a decision with minimum interference from you. But you must not stand by while your "team" strikes off in the wrong direction. You can offer sound coaching by providing facts that might be overlooked and by asking the group to weigh pros and cons of various options. Third, be honest with yourself. Are you using participation to motivate or manipulate? If it is the former—congratulations. If it is the latter, eventually the officers will discover that they are being conned. When this happens, kiss both your supervisory power and leadership goodbye.

## KEY POINTS

- Delegation plus participation leads to *empowerment* of personnel.
- There are four parties that benefit from proper delegation: the community, the department, the supervisor, and the staff.
- If we delegate to *time* we create efficiency. If we delegate to other *people* we produce effectiveness.
- Confidence and caring are time pillars of successful delegation.
- Letting others participate in decisions that are going to affect them *does not* surrender a supervisor's authority or responsibility for the final decision.
- Teamwork is participative supervision.
- The key to participation is sharing.

## DISCUSSION

1. What is meant by "really letting go" when one delegates? What are the advantages in doing so? Are there any risks involved?
2. There are eight forces that must be functioning when you delegate (see "Setting the Context"). Rank order the eight forces in terms of their importance.
3. How can a supervisor engage in ownership delegation as compared with lonership?
4. What are the reasons for others to participate in decisions that are going to affect them? What are the reasons not to?
5. What is the key or secret of participation? Why is it effective?

# RESPONSIBILITY NINE

# *Performance*

The supervisor's responsibilities for measuring performance serves as compass, rudder, and thermostat for the employee's work efforts and attitudes.

*The wise leader does not protect people from themselves. The light of awareness shines equally on what is pleasant and what is not.*

—Tao Te Ching

Once the goals of the work unit have been agreed upon (R-7) and the staff has been empowered (R-8) to achieve them, then the supervisor must concentrate on measuring success and avoiding conflict (R-10).

Police supervisors accomplish things by working through other people. They need and depend on police personnel to achieve their unit goals. It's important, therefore, for supervisors to get their employees to behave in ways that police management considers desirable. But how do supervisors ensure that police employees are performing as they are supposed to?

Basically, the police supervisor uses two methods. The first method occurs on a day-to-day basis. Using MBO, the supervisors oversee employees' work and make corrections as they occur. The supervisor who spots a police officer taking an unnecessary risk when operating his or her radio car will point out the correct way and tell the employee to do it this way in the future.

The second method is a formal process whereby supervisors assess the work of their employees through systematic performance evaluations. An employee's recent performance is appraised. Based on that appraisal, sanctions follow. If performance is positive, the employee's behavior is typically reinforced with a reward, such as a new assignment. If performance is below standard, supervisors seek to correct it or, depending on the nature of the deviation, may discipline the employee. Both performance evaluation methods (informal daily and formal periodic) are best supported by an MBO program.

It is ironic that much of what is expected of us at work is rarely evaluated but commonly emphasized—such is the case of teamwork. Most performance appraisal systems ignore or marginally touch on one's commitment to a team effort. Later, you will find that the Arvada Police Department's rating process has such a focus. If something is really important to the success of an organization, then it must be measured. Teamwork is critical for success, and thus it must be constantly reinforced and periodically evaluated on an individual and team basis.

---

> Teamwork is critical for success, and thus it must be constantly reinforced and periodically evaluated on an individual and team basis.

---

## RESPONSIBILITY OF THE POLICE SUPERVISOR

*Take a Minute:*
*Look at Your Goals*
*Look at Your Performance*
*See If Your Behavior Matches Your Goals*

—Kenneth Blanchard and Spencer Johnson
*The One Minute Manager* (New York: William Morrow, 1982), p. 97

The bottom-line test of a police organization is the spirit of performance, and it is the very cornerstone of a supervisor's responsibility to evoke this spirit. To manifest this spirit, you must not fall prey to mere exhortations, lofty sermons, or well-meaning intentions. *It must be practices.* Specifically, there are four required practices:

1. The focus of the police agency must be on *performance.* The first requirement of the spirit of organization is high performance standards, for the group as well as for each officer. The department must establish a habit of achievement. However, performance does not mean "success every time." Performance is rather a "batting average." It will, indeed it must, have room for mistakes and even for failures. What performance has no room for is complacency and low standards.

2. The focus of a successful police agency must be on *opportunities* rather than on problems.

3. The decisions that affect people, their placement, pay, promotion, demotion, and severance, must express the values of the organization. They are the true controls of an organization. (See Responsibility One on values.)

4. In its people decisions, supervision must demonstrate that it realizes that *integrity* is one absolute requirement of an effective supervisor. It is the one quality that you have to bring with you and cannot be expected to acquire later.

---

> The bottom-line test of a police organization is the spirit of performance, and it is the very cornerstone of a supervisor's responsibility to evoke this spirit.

---

Hence, your role as a police supervisor requires you to think and act in such a fashion that you

- Emphasize performance
- Create opportunities
- Promote values
- Evidence integrity
- Provide feedback

## PERFORMANCE EVALUATION DEFINED

Most simply, performance evaluation is a complex process with three key purposes: behavioral motivation, control, and feedback. You are destined to learn that, to a large extent your success as a supervisor is directly related to your ability to appraise the performance of your assigned personnel.

Performance evaluation (or performance appraisal or rating) can be defined as both a process and a method by which a police agency obtains feedback on and provides guidelines for the effectiveness of its personnel—feedback, in the sense that past work effort is evaluated, and guidelines, to the extent that performance objectives are specified for the immediate future. Traditionally, the evaluation process and methods were designed with feedback as an end in mind; having guidelines as part of the evaluation system is more recent. An evaluation system that uses both feedback *and* guidelines is commonly referred to as MBO.

In general, the process and method serve an auditing and feedback function by generating information upon which many departmental decisions are made. In practice, performance evaluation is very challenging for several reasons.

First, it must serve many purposes, from evaluating the success of selection decisions, to assessing the effectiveness of a leader, to evaluating training efforts, to determining the quantity and quality of individual work effort. Second, the assessment of performance itself is a difficult measurement task because so many factors influence performance, including environmental, organizational, and individual factors. Finally, a great number of ethical and emotionally charged issues arise when performance is evaluated. The results of the process can have profound influences on the jobs, careers, attitudes, personal self-concepts, and general sense of well-being of police employees.

## COMPLEX PROCESS

Imagine for a moment that you are a supervisor in command of a criminal investigations unit. Because of the retirement of one of your detectives, it has become necessary to select a new investigator from the ranks of the patrol operation or administrative services. You review the performance evaluation forms of police personnel with two or more years of service with the agency. A patrol officer and a training officer have received outstanding ratings over the past three years. However, the training officer is three percentage points higher than the patrol officer. As a result, you decide to request that the chief of police transfer the training officer to your division. When you announce your decision, the patrol officer asks to confer with you.

The patrol officer makes five points: (1) The officer questions the adequacy of the performance evaluation form used to make six-month performance reviews, arguing that how well one scores on the form depends upon who is doing the evaluation and that the form does not rate the truly proper aspects of the job. (2) The officer charges that those in patrol are rated more strictly than are those in administrative assignments. (3) The officer indicates that it appeared you made your decision based on a single trait: that of the training officer's friendly disposition. (4) The officer argues that the ratings reflect past performance without in any way predicting one's success as a detective. (5) The officer asserts that his last performance appraisal was mainly drawn from the three weeks prior to the actual rating, and that most of his fine accomplishments during the entire six months were ignored.

This situation raises a number of prominent issues, all of which cause or can cause major problems for police management. Performance evaluation is linked to personnel decisions that determine assignments, salary adjustments, promotions, training, affirmative action, discipline, and individual self-worth and job satisfaction. This chapter addresses these issues in the way of offering practical advice and proven recommendations that are intended to eradicate the "damned if we do" possibilities in assessing an employee's performance.

## VARIETY OF PURPOSES

Personnel decisions can be made without performance evaluation systems. They can be made by drawing random numbers, by choosing whomever you like best, by choosing the person you owe a favor to, or by choosing someone who wears the best-smelling aftershave lotion or perfume, and so on. Clearly, an effective organization requires a proficient process and method for assessing the past performances and the future potentials of its most valuable asset: human resources.

Performance evaluation plays an important role in control because it serves as an audit, which facilitates feedback and motivation. Performance evaluation, then, is an auditing procedure that generates the information necessary to control and direct the process of an organization. The review procedure would usually start at the first level of operations, with each employee's performance being reviewed by immediate supervisors in each division. Entire departmental performance would be reviewed at the next level of analysis. Finally, the city manager, city council, or sheriff would evaluate the overall performance of the entire agency.

Control and motivation can take many forms, all involving supervisory decisions. One way of controlling and motivating performance is through selection, job placement, and promotion. The kind of person who is selected for employment and the type of assignment in which he or she is placed will have a direct influence on level of job performance. Another set of decisions that is intended to control performance involves job and organizational design. Performance results may be used to suggest ways of redistributing tasks and responsibilities in the police organization. In addition, when management wants to tie rewards and performance together, performance evaluation is a critical basis for making differential reward decisions. Furthermore, any decisions that a police agency makes with regard to improving performance through training and other forms of organizational change and development must be based on appraisals of skill deficiencies made during performance evaluations. Decisions on individual performance objectives (MBO) serve to direct the individual police employee *and* the police organization toward desired ends or goals. As a consequence, one can see that performance evaluation serves at least the following purposes:

1. Promotion, separation, and transfer decisions
2. Feedback for each employee regarding how the organization views his or her performance
3. Evaluations of relative contributions made by individuals and entire departments in achieving higher-level organizational goals
4. Reward decisions, including merit increases, promotions, and other rewards
5. Criteria for evaluating the effectiveness of selection and placement decisions, including the relevance of the information used in those decisions
6. Ascertaining and diagnosing training and developmental needs for individual employees and entire divisions within the organization
7. Criteria for evaluating the success of training and development decisions
8. Information upon which work-scheduling plans, budgeting, and human resources planning can be based
9. Specification of new performance objectives (MBO) for the ensuing time period

## Performance Evaluation Must Be Job Related

All the problems to which police supervisors and employees point when performance is reviewed can be summarized by two terms: *reliability* and *validity*. Both terms are qualities of the entire evaluation process and refer to the adequacy of the information that is generated and employed in subsequent decisions about employees.

❖◆❖◆❖

All of the problems to which police supervisors and employees point when performance is reviewed can be summarized by two terms: *reliability* and *validity*.

❖◆❖◆❖

**RELIABILITY.** The first demand that must be made of a performance appraisal procedure is that it be reliable. Reliability actually refers to two major characteristics of the method by which performance information is collected: consistency and stability. *Consistency* demands that two alternative ways of gathering the same data should substantially agree in their results. For example, when two items are used on the same rating form to measure the same aspect of job performance, the supervisor's responses to them should agree with each other when evaluating the same subordinate. Similarly, two interviewers who evaluate the same employee should substantially agree in their findings. *Stability* demands that the same measuring device give the same results several times in a row if the characteristic it is supposed to be assessing has not changed. Thus, if the way in which a patrol officer treats citizens has not changed between Monday and Tuesday, we would expect a rating form to yield the same information about this aspect of performance on both days.

In actual practice, a variety of situational and personal factors can lead to either form of unreliability—inconsistency and instability—when police employees are evaluated. The most common error sources are illustrated in Figure 9-1.

One must recognize that *no specific appraisal forms or methods are universally reliable across police functions and across police agencies.* Indeed, the burden of reliable assessment rests on those who are going to *use* performance appraisal. A form or a technique that is reliable in one police organization may very well be totally inadequate in a different one.

**VALIDITY.** Although reliability is a necessary precondition for validity or relevance, it does not alone ensure that a measure will actually be valid. For a method of appraisal to be relevant, three considerations must be taken into account: performance dimensions, the level of abstraction, and time. The single most important problem in designing an appraisal system is to take all three fully into account.

**1.** *Performance dimensions.* The validity problem, with respect to performance dimensions, is to adequately determine the different aspects of work behavior and performance to be evaluated. Very rarely is there a job that is unidimensional: For example, the job of a patrol officer must at least include the accuracy of social judgments, quality of direct citizen assistance, management of paraprofessionals, and interaction with peers. One of the first major steps in performance appraisal research in an organization is to empirically determine how many dimensions of performance must be assessed in order to validly appraise an employee's job performance—that is, job analysis.

Performance measures that do not define and assess all relevant dimensions of the job will be deficient and therefore not completely valid. However, measures that include dimensions that are not properly part of the job will be seen as invalid.

**2.** *Level of abstraction.* In addition to static performance dimensions, the validity of a performance measure depends on using the proper level of

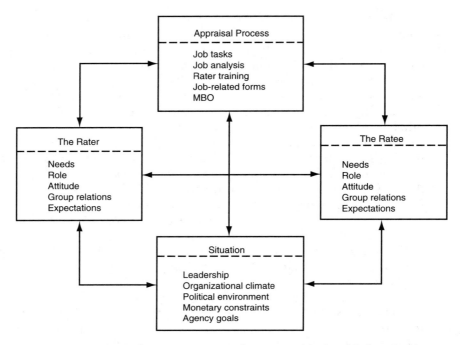

**Figure 9-1** Performance Appraisal Process (Paul Whisenand, *The Effective Police Manager*, © 1981, p. 200. Reprinted by permission of Prentice Hall, Inc., Englewood Cliffs, N.J.)

organizational analysis. We have pointed out that there are many models of organizational effectiveness, many of which differ in the level at which they conceptualize effectiveness (organizational, group, or individual). In practice, an evaluation system must incorporate and deal with all three levels of analysis. This problem is indicated in Figure 9-2, which also illustrates three possible levels of analysis or abstraction in performance appraisal.

**3.** *Time.* Time is the third critical dimension influencing the validity of performance appraisal; it operates in two major ways as an influence. First, immediate, intermediate, and ultimate criteria have a short-run and a long-run orientation. Specific and immediate criteria (such as job behaviors) are appropriately measured in the short run, at the time the work is being done. Less immediate outcomes (such as group task performance) and organizational outcomes (such as crime prevention and efficiency) may require months and perhaps years to become apparent. Assessing various criteria at too early or too late a time may seriously limit the validity of performance appraisal. Moreover, not collecting facts over a protracted period of time can cause considerable distortions in any performance review. Human nature unfortunately emphasizes the most recent past in recollections. Thus, one's being "good" or "bad" in the past month is likely to strongly bias the appraisal. (One way to offset this effect is to employ the "significant incident" technique; more will be said about this technique later.)

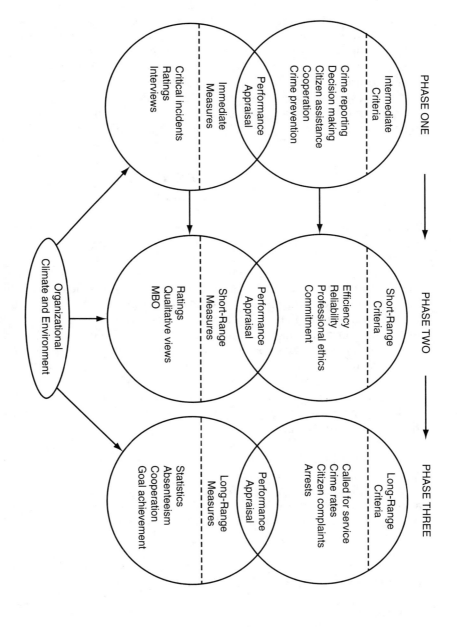

**Figure 9-2** Performance Appraisal: Criteria and Measures (Paul Whisenand, *The Effective Police Manager*, © 1981, p. 203. Reprinted by permission of Prentice Hall, Inc., Englewood Cliffs, N.J.)

PHASE ONE

PHASE TWO

PHASE THREE

Intermediate Criteria

Crime reporting
Decision making
Citizen assistance
Cooperation
Crime prevention

Performance Appraisal

Immediate Measures

Critical incidents
Ratings
Interviews

Organizational Climate and Environment

Short-Range Criteria

Efficiency
Reliability
Professional ethics
Commitment

Performance Appraisal

Short-Range Measures

Ratings
Qualitative views
MBO

Long-Range Criteria

Called for service
Crime rates
Citizen complaints
Arrests

Performance Appraisal

Long-Range Measures

Statistics
Absenteeism
Cooperation
Goal achievement

### Job Analysis Leads to Reliability and Validity

The prime means for a police agency to ensure the job relatedness (reliability and validity) of a performance evaluation system is *job analysis*. A *job* is a relatively homogeneous cluster of work tasks carried out to achieve some essential and enduring purpose in an organization; *job analysis* consists of defining the job and discovering what the job calls for in employee behaviors. Job analysis. then, is a procedure for gathering the judgment of people who are knowledgeable about the organization, the positions within it, and the specific content of a job. Furthermore, the *content* of the job is defined to be specific work activities or tasks. In effect, job analysis is a broad term describing an entire series of judgments that are made in the design of an organization. Figure 9-3 illustrates the purposes served in job analysis.

### *Structured Exercise 9-1*

As a new police supervisor, you take your job most seriously, especially performance rating. During your recent two-week Supervisor's Training Course, eight hours (10 percent) was devoted to the do's and don'ts of rating.

Your agency uses a global rating scale (see Figure 9-4), which it applies once a year in the month of March. Your lieutenant instructed you and the other field sergeant to administer the scales. He went on to add, "In the next few months a number of critical personnel decisions will be made. Your ratings are likely to determine the outcome of some of these spending decisions."

You have a fairly good feel for the police personnel in your unit as compared to the other sergeant's. If anything, your group is a slight cut above the other crew. Nonetheless, you recognize that your staff is not perfect. The results of your first rating are (1) two "improvement needed," (2) four "competent," and (3) one "outstanding." All seven officers read, discussed with you, and signed the form. No problem!

Three days later it was revealed that your colleague sergeant rated all seven of his personnel "outstanding." Rumors and complaints quickly surfaced among your team of officers.

The lieutenant has asked to see you and the other sergeant about this situation. What is on your mind? What are you planning to say? What is your position(s) on this matter? How might it be resolved?

## THREE METHODS OF PERFORMANCE EVALUATION

Performance appraisal may serve many purposes; because of this, there can be no general method that is appropriate for all purposes. The problem for police supervisors is to determine what kind of performance appraisal method is adequate, given the purpose to be served.

Specifically, the problem for you is to select a performance appraisal method that is appropriate given the following considerations:

1. Specific *organizational and environmental properties*, such as technology, the design of the agency, the firm's industry, and other factors indicated in Figure 9-4
2. Unique *individual characteristics* that influence police performance including specific skills and abilities and motivation levels
3. The mix of specific *work behaviors* that are appropriate, given departmental and individual officer considerations
4. The mix of *relevant performance dimension*, given a consideration of the agency and personnel involved
5. The specific set of *goals* to be achieved at divisional and departmental levels

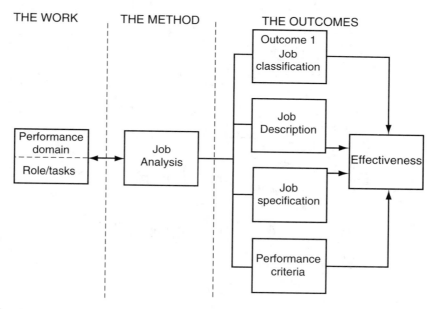

**Figure 9-3** Job Analysis (Paul Whisenand, *The Effective Police Manager,* © 1981, p. 205. Reprinted by permission of Prentice Hall, Inc., Englewood Cliffs, N.J.)

We will now examine three methods or forms for assessing an officer's performance: the traditional method and two advanced methods.

**TRADITIONAL METHOD: THE GLOBAL RATING SCALE.** The most frequently used forms of appraisal today by police agencies are still based on traditional methods, and usually take one of two basic forms: rating or ranking. Both kinds of appraisal methods are based on traditional, descriptive forms of job analysis: Observers make a very brief study of the job, focusing on several major task dimensions; they note these in broad, descriptive language and use these

```
                SHERIFF'S DEPARTMENT - COUNTY OF LOS ANGELES

     NAME _____  DATE _____
                                                      |
                                                      |      NARRATIVE
     RATE EACH      OUTSTANDING-----------------.      |_____
     FACTOR         VERY GOOD----------------.  |      |
                    COMPETENT-------------.  |  |      |_____
                    IMPROVEMENT NEEDED--. |  |  |      |   SEE ATTACHED PAGE
                    UNSATISFACTORY---. | |  |  |      |_____
                                     | | |  |  |      |
     QUANTITY                       [ ][ ][ ][ ][ ]   |_____
     AMOUNT OF WORK PERFORMED........[ ][ ][ ][ ][ ]  |_____
     COMPLETION OF WORK ON SCHEDULE..[ ][ ][ ][ ][ ]  |_____

     QUALITY                        [ ][ ][ ][ ][ ]   |_____
     ACCURACY........................[ ][ ][ ][ ][ ]  |_____
     NEATNESS OF WORK PRODUCT........[ ][ ][ ][ ][ ]  |_____
     THOROUGHNESS....................[ ][ ][ ][ ][ ]  |_____
     ORAL EXPRESSION.................[ ][ ][ ][ ][ ]  |_____
     WRITTEN EXPRESSION..............[ ][ ][ ][ ][ ]  |_____

     WORK HABITS                    [ ][ ][ ][ ][ ]   |_____
     OBSERVANCE OF WORKING HOURS.....[ ][ ][ ][ ][ ]  |_____
     ATTENDANCE......................[ ][ ][ ][ ][ ]  |_____
     OBSERVANCE OF RULES AND
       REGULATIONS...................[ ][ ][ ][ ][ ]  |_____
     OBSERVANCE OF SAFETY RULES......[ ][ ][ ][ ][ ]  |_____
     ORDERLINESS IN WORK.............[ ][ ][ ][ ][ ]  |_____
     COMPLIANCE WITH WORK
       INSTRUCTIONS..................[ ][ ][ ][ ][ ]  |_____
     APPLICATION TO DUTIES...........[ ][ ][ ][ ][ ]  |_____
     POSSESSION, USE, AND MAINTENANCE
       OF WORK EQUIPMENT.............[ ][ ][ ][ ][ ]  |_____

     PERSONAL RELATIONS             [ ][ ][ ][ ][ ]   |_____
     GETTING ALONG WITH FELLOW
       EMPLOYEES.....................[ ][ ][ ][ ][ ]  |_____
     MEETING AND HANDLING THE PUBLIC.[ ][ ][ ][ ][ ]  |_____
     PERSONAL APPEARANCE.............[ ][ ][ ][ ][ ]  |_____

     ADAPTABILITY                   [ ][ ][ ][ ][ ]   |_____
     PERFORMANCE IN NEW SITUATIONS...[ ][ ][ ][ ][ ]  |_____
     PERFORMANCE IN EMERGENCIES......[ ][ ][ ][ ][ ]  |_____
     PERFORMANCE WITH MINIMUM
       INSTRUCTIONS..................[ ][ ][ ][ ][ ]  |_____

     OTHER                          [ ][ ][ ][ ][ ]   |_____
                    (SUPERVISORS)
     SUPERVISORY ABILITY(   ONLY   )[ ][ ][ ][ ][ ]   |_____
     PLANNING AND ASSIGNING..........[ ][ ][ ][ ][ ]  |_____
     TRAINING AND INSTRUCTING........[ ][ ][ ][ ][ ]  |_____
     DISCIPLINARY CONTROL............[ ][ ][ ][ ][ ]  |_____
     EVALUATING PERFORMANCE..........[ ][ ][ ][ ][ ]  |_____
     LEADERSHIP......................[ ][ ][ ][ ][ ]  |_____
     MAKING DECISIONS................[ ][ ][ ][ ][ ]  |_____
     FAIRNESS AND IMPARTIALITY.......[ ][ ][ ][ ][ ]  |_____
     APPROACHABILITY.................[ ][ ][ ][ ][ ]  |_____
     MAINTAINING AN EFFECTIVE SAFETY
       PROGRAM.......................[ ][ ][ ][ ][ ]  |_____
     AFFIRMATIVE ACTION..............[ ][ ][ ][ ][ ]  |_____
```

**Figure 9-4**   Deputy Evaluation Form of the Los Angeles County Sheriff's Department (Courtesy of the Los Angeles County Sheriff's Department)

dimensions as a basis for designing ad hoc rating scales or ranking forms. The police sergeant applies this form once or twice a year to rate or rank his or her subordinates.

Figure 9-4 displays a traditional form. Forms or scales of this sort are known as *global rating scales* (GRS), because they define the qualities to be assessed and levels of such qualities in broad, global terms. As such, they are

```
                    SHERIFF'S DEPARTMENT - COUNTY OF LOS ANGELES

                        REPORT ON PERFORMANCE EVALUATION

NAME _____ DATE _____

TYPE OF EVALUATION:  ANNUAL [ ]    TRANSFER [ ]    FROM _____ TO _____

                     OTHER _____

EMPLOYEE'S RANK/TITLE _____ EMPLOYEE NO. _____

ITEM NO. _____ DEPT. 770   DIVISION _____ UNIT _____

EMPLOYEE'S DRIVER'S LICENSE NO. _____ CLASS ____ EXPIRATION DATE _____

MAJOR ASSIGNMENTS

     SPECIFIC JOB(S) DURING EVALUATION PERIOD: _____ ( ) MONTHS

          _____ ( ) MONTHS          _____ ( ) MONTHS

          _____ ( ) MONTHS          _____ ( ) MONTHS

SUPERVISED BY, AND/OR PROVIDED DOCUMENTED INPUT TO EVALUATION:

     _____          _____

     _____          _____
```

| OVERALL EVALUATION | | | | |
|---|---|---|---|---|
| UNSATISFACTORY | IMPROVEMENT NEEDED | COMPETENT | VERY GOOD | OUTSTANDING |
| | | | | |

```
NAME AND SIGNATURES OF REPORTING      SUCCESSFUL COMPLETION OF CUSTODY
OFFICERS:  THIS REPORT IS BASED ON    DEPUTY TRAINING PROGRAM:
OBSERVATION AND/OR KNOWLEDGE.  IT     DATE _____
REPRESENTS MY BEST JUDGMENT OF THE    SUCCESSFUL COMPLETION OF PATROL
EMPLOYEE'S PERFORMANCE.               DEPUTY TRAINING PROGRAM:
                                      DATE _____


RATER: _____     COPY OF REPORT GIVEN TO EMPLOYEE:
          PRINT/TYPE/NAME/JOB TITLE   EMPLOYEE'S
                                      SIGNATURE _____ DATE _____
_____ DATE _____
        SIGNATURE                     COPY OF REPORT MAILED TO EMPLOYEE:
I HAVE REVIEWED THIS REPORT           ADDRESS _____ DATE _____

REVIEWER _____     REPORT DISCUSSED WITH EMPLOYEE:
         PRINT/TYPE NAME/JOB TITLE    BY: _____ DATE _____
_____ DATE _____
        SIGNATURE

                                      THIS REPORT HAS BEEN DISCUSSED WITH
_____       ME:
I CONCUR IN AND APPROVE THIS REPORT.  EMPLOYEE'S
DEPT. HEAD _____ DATE _____     SIGNATURE _____ DATE _____
   (OR AUTHORIZED REPRESENTATIVE)
```

**Figure 9-4**  *(Continued)*

extremely vulnerable to a variety of errors that reduce their reliability and validity. The most common errors of GRS can be summarized as follows: halo errors, strictness errors, leniency errors, and central-tendency errors.

*Halo errors* occur when an evaluator incorrectly treats two or more dimensions of performance as if they were identical or highly correlated. For example, the evaluator making this error might believe that, if a police employee's work performance

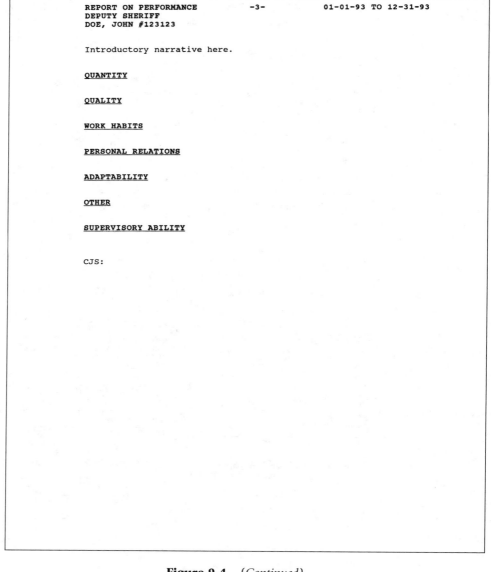

```
REPORT ON PERFORMANCE          -3-          01-01-93 TO 12-31-93
DEPUTY SHERIFF
DOE, JOHN #123123

Introductory narrative here.

QUANTITY

QUALITY

WORK HABITS

PERSONAL RELATIONS

ADAPTABILITY

OTHER

SUPERVISORY ABILITY


CJS:
```

**Figure 9-4** *(Continued)*

deserves a high rating on quality, it should also merit a high rating on cooperation. The result is that employees show no variation in ratings across dimensions; they are rated consistently high, medium, or low on all performance dimensions.

*Strictness errors* occur when an evaluator rates all employees as very poor performers. Ratings given by this type of evaluator tend to cluster closely toward the low end of the rating scale.

*Leniency errors* are the opposite of strictness errors; with leniency errors the evaluator mistakenly gives all employees uniformly high ratings. Ratings given by this type of evaluator cluster together at the high end of the scale.

*Central-tendency errors* are similar to leniency and strictness errors, except that in this case the ratings made by the evaluator cluster artificially at the middle of the scale.

The traditional method of appraising a police employee is full of validity and reliability holes. It is clearly wise to avoid the use of a GRS.

**ADVANCED METHOD: THE PERFORMANCE DOMAIN RATING SCALE.** Some police agencies have recognized the urgent need for making their evaluation method more relevant to the operating task environment of a police officer. To this end, they have often succeeded in designing highly valid and reliable rating scales. These scales are produced in conjunction with the performance domain; that is, what the officer should be doing in his or her work assignment is what is appraised. This can be referred to as a *performance domain rating scale* (PDRS). A PDRS is job related and thus does not fall prey to the inadequacies of a GRS. Figure 9-5 presents a PDRS that (with necessary modifications) may improve the effectiveness of your overall rating system. (Keep in mind that this particular PDRS does *not* apply to other performance domains, such as nonsworn, supervisory, and so on.) Depending on the unique characteristics of each agency, three to six PDRSs may be required to ensure and maintain job-related personnel evaluations. One final comment: A key feature of a PDRS that is often overlooked is that it elicits narrative comments. Without written comments, the PDRS starts to show some signs of the deficiencies of the GRS, expressed earlier. Although it is obviously not a panacea, a PDRS is certainly a far superior method for employee evaluation than is a GRS.

Of the many available examples of a PDRS, we chose to include here the Arvada Police Department's (Colorado). On behalf of Chief Ahlstrom, Commander Scott wrote a letter of explanation as follows. (His letter is one of the reasons that we decided to present their PDRS.)

————◆✦◆————

Since time immemorial, supervisors and officers within the department have complained about a variety of concerns with the previous evaluation formats.

————◆✦◆————

*In order for you to better understand these evaluations, I would like to provide you with some background information on the process used to arrive at the content and format of these evaluations. Since time immemorial, supervisors and officers within the department have complained about a variety of concerns with the previous evaluation formats. Supervisors expressed the desire to have a check-off type of evaluation form. At the same time, officers and supervisors were concerned with the*

# City of Arvada

### POLICE DEPARTMENT
### OPERATIONS BUREAU POLICE OFFICER

## E V A L U A T I O N   O F   P E R F O R M A N C E

| | |
|---|---|
| **Employee Name:**  • | **Employment Date:**  • |
| **Position:**       • | **Div./Dept.:**      Patrol/Public Safety |
| **Appraisal Period from:**  • | **Time in Position:**  • |
| **Appraised By:**    • | **Title:**        • |

**PART I. EVALUATION OF PAST YEAR'S PERFORMANCE:**

A. Accomplishment of Objectives

During the past year, what were results of the employee's work?  The purpose is to compare the objectives agreed upon in the previous evaluation with actual performance.

| OBJECTIVES | COMMENTS ON ACCOMPLISHMENTS |
|---|---|
| • | |

**Figure 9-5** Police Department Evaluation of Performance (Courtesy Arvada Police Department, Arvada, Colorado.)

## PART II. PERFORMANCE STANDARDS

Evaluators are to review each and every item of performance under each of the Standards. The degree to which an employee is <u>capable</u> of engaging in a specific item may vary with the shift or assignment.

When evaluating the employee, the evaluator is to check off the appropriate rating for each element of an evaluation category. Each rating is given a value as follows:

| | |
|---|---|
| Unsatisfactory | = 1 |
| Below Expectations | = 2 |
| Meets Expectations | = 3 |
| Exceeds Expectations | = 4 |
| Distinguished Performance | = 5 |

After completing the evaluation of each element of a category (i.e., Customer Service - Community Problem Solving), the evaluator is to total the rating scores in that category and multiply by the <u>Weight</u> for that category. This provides a score for that category. At the conclusion of the evaluation, all category scores are totalled to yield a final evaluation <u>total</u> which is divided by the possible total score of 935 to give the percentage score which can be used (as can the point score) to determine the overall performance rating of the employee.

The supervisor must be able to articulate, in detail, the justification for a specific performance category (element) score. "Description of Performance Guidelines" as found in the <u>Supervisor's Guide to Performance Evaluations</u> is to be used when assigning one of the 5 performance levels to a given Standard of performance. A narrative explanation <u>must</u> accompany any score which is either a "Distinguished" or below the "Meets Expectations" level. This narrative must detail the reasons for the score and, in the case of "Below Expectations" and "Unsatisfactory", there must be a plan explaining what is necessary to improve performance to a "Meets Expectations" level. These comments are to be done by listing the letter (a, b, c, etc.) of the corresponding element in the "Comments" section of the page, followed by the brief explanation.

When a general category (i.e., Customer Service) contains a series of "4" (Exceeds Expectatons) ratings, the evaluator must justify that rating, but may provide that justification in the "Comments" area with detailing each sub-section (i.e., a, b, f, i).

**Figure 9-5** *(Continued)*

| 1. CUSTOMER SERVICE/COMMUNITY PROBLEM SOLVING - WEIGHT 3 | 1 | 2 | 3 | 4 | 5 |
|---|---|---|---|---|---|
| a. Responsive to service requests | • | | | | |
| b. Displays helpful, cooperative attitude | | | | | |
| c. Sensitive to citizen needs | | | | | |
| d. Participates in community programs including Neighborhood Watch Meetings, D.A.R.E. classes/graduations, community meetings | | | | | |
| e. Actively identifies and recognizes the origins of community problems, evaluates issues and develops possible solutions to problems | | | | | |
| f. Awareness of and use of community/citizen/city government resources | | | | | |
| g. Appropriate use of citizen contacts | | | | | |
| h. Achieves a positive community image | | | | | |
| i. Effective initiation of and follow-up on Police Service Requests | | | | | |
| TOTAL (Element Score) | | | | | |

Weight 3 x Total of All Element Scores ____•____ = Performance Standard Score ___•___

COMMENTS:

•

| 2. TEAMWORK/INTERPERSONAL ACTIONS - WEIGHT 2 | 1 | 2 | 3 | 4 | 5 |
|---|---|---|---|---|---|
| a. Takes steps to eliminate bias in the department when observed | • | | | | |
| b. Cooperates with others in establishing reasonable objectives and achieving desired results | | | | | |
| c. Displays behavior which builds trust and mutual respect and cooperation among fellow workers | | | | | |
| d. Has a positive approach when participating in routine activities, assignments, and problem solving | | | | | |
| e. Avoids unnecessary confrontation and adequately resolves conflicts when necessary | | | | | |
| f. Shares information with other members of the organization | | | | | |
| g. Respectful when interacting with co-workers and supervisors | | | | | |
| h. Actively seeks the opportunity to assist peers with their work performance | | | | | |
| i. Displays an awareness of shift/department workload and makes himself/herself available to assist fellow workers | | | | | |
| j. Makes comments and takes action to constructively enhance a team environment | | | | | |
| TOTAL (Element Score) | | | | | |

Weight 2 x Total of All Element Scores ____•____ = Performance Standard Score ___•___

COMMENTS:

•

**Figure 9-5**  *(Continued)*

| 3. COMMUNICATIONS - WEIGHT 3 | 1 | 2 | 3 | 4 | 5 |
|---|---|---|---|---|---|
| a. Radio transmissions are clear, concise and follow procedures | • | | | | |
| b. Expresses thoughts in writing and orally in a clear, concise, and well organized manner | | | | | |
| c. Displays good penmanship, grammar, and spelling in written reports | | | | | |
| d. Courtroom testimony is clear, accurate, and prepared | | | | | |
| e. Demonstrates ability and willingness to listen | | | | | |
| f. Understands and properly carries out instructions and orders | | | | | |
| g. Able to give and receive constructive feedback | | | | | |
| h. Ability to adjust communicative style for differing groups and situations | | | | | |
| i. Follows chain of command | | | | | |
| j. Comments, suggestions, and criticisms are presented in a constructive manner | | | | | |
| k. Written reports are grammatically correct and clearly understandable | | | | | |
| TOTAL (Element Score) | | | | | |

Weight 3 x Total of All Element Scores ____•____ = Performance Standard Score ___•___

COMMENTS:

•

| 4. INITIATIVE - WEIGHT 3 | 1 | 2 | 3 | 4 | 5 |
|---|---|---|---|---|---|
| a. Accepts direct responsibility for District/assignment | • | | | | |
| b. Shows initiative in everyday work activity - identifies and addresses community problems - initiates PSR's based upon knowledge of problems | | | | | |
| c. Ability to adapt to change | | | | | |
| d. Strives to improve the work product | | | | | |
| e. Serves as a role model for peers | | | | | |
| f. Ability to work constructively with a minimum of supervision | | | | | |
| g. Volunteers to direct or manage tough assignments | | | | | |
| h. Demonstrates ability to organize and coordinate various activities/operations | | | | | |
| i. Generates ideas and approaches to improve Police Department/City performance and the operation of the organization | | | | | |
| j. Maintains activity and productivity levels consistent with shift averages and expectations of supervisors and the community | | | | | |
| k. Looks for, and engages in, non-assigned productive activities which try to fulfill the community's needs. | | | | | |
| l. Looks for opportunities to conduct follow-up investigation on own initiative | | | | | |
| TOTAL (Element Score) | | | | | |

Weight 3 x Total of All Element Scores ____•____ = Performance Standard Score ___•___

COMMENTS:

**Figure 9-5** *(Continued)*

| 5. PROFESSIONAL JUDGEMENT - WEIGHT 3 | 1 | 2 | 3 | 4 | 5 |
|---|---|---|---|---|---|
| a. Demonstrated awareness of impacts of decisions | • | | | | |
| b. Ability and willingness to make sound decisions based on available information without the assistance of supervisors | | | | | |
| c. Willing to take acceptable risks, but not recklessly | | | | | |
| d. Accepts responsibility for decisions and the subsequent results | | | | | |
| e. Proper use of police discretion | | | | | |
| f. Sensitive to needs of community or individuals | | | | | |
| g. Alert to surroundings and able to understand and react quickly and appropriately | | | | | |
| h. Has full understanding and application of the laws, rules and procedures governing the use of force, pursuit policy, search and seizure, arrest, and domestic violence | | | | | |
| i. Exercises proper degree of assertiveness when needed | | | | | |
| TOTAL (Element Score) | | | | | |

Weight 3 x Total of All Element Scores ____•____ = Performance Standard Score ___•___

COMMENTS:

•

| 6. WORK PERFORMANCE/QUALITY - WEIGHT 3 | 1 | 2 | 3 | 4 | 5 |
|---|---|---|---|---|---|
| a. Keeps current with legal changes and changes in Rules and Procedures Manual | • | | | | |
| b. Proper recognition, collection and preservation of evidence | | | | | |
| c. Demonstrated understanding and application of State/Federal Laws, Municipal Ordinances, Departmental Rules and Procedures, Rules of Criminal Procedure, legal decisions, and directives | | | | | |
| d. Knowledge of and proper use of equipment and investigative techniques: Radar, Intoxilyzer, camera equipment, crime scene equipment (fingerprinting), computers, Nystagmus, firearms, to include follow-up activities when appropriate | | | | | |
| e. Assignments/investigative reports are properly carried out and completed in a timely manner | | | | | |
| f. Knowledge of police patrol districts | | | | | |
| g. Continuous adherence to the RPM and other procedural guidelines | | | | | |
| h. Work product is consistently completed in a professional, thorough manner | | | | | |
| i. Documentation is an accurate reflection of a thorough investigation to include the elements of the crime, proper classification, correct report formatting, complete witness information, MO, and suspect information | | | | | |
| TOTAL (Element Score) | | | | | |

Weight 3 x Total of All Element Scores ____•____ = Performance Standard Score ___•___

COMMENTS:

•

**Figure 9-5** *(Continued)*

| 7. PERSONAL APPEARANCE, GENERAL SAFETY PRACTICES AND PRIDE IN WORKING ENVIRONMENT - WEIGHT 1 | 1 | 2 | 3 | 4 | 5 |
|---|---|---|---|---|---|
| a. Cares for uniform, equipment, police facility, vehicle, and weapons as required | • | | | | |
| b. Cognizant of personal health and keeps physically fit | | | | | |
| c. Maintains positive image in appearance and demeanor at all times among peers and members of the public | | | | | |
| d. Exercises proper field survival practices | | | | | |
| e. Operates motor vehicles in a safe and prudent manner - obeys traffic laws | | | | | |
| TOTAL (Element Score) | | | | | |

Weight 1 x Total of All Element Scores ____•____ = Performance Standard Score ___•___

COMMENTS:

•

| 8. PROFESSIONAL AND ORGANIZATIONAL COMMITMENT - WEIGHT 2 | 1 | 2 | 3 | 4 | 5 |
|---|---|---|---|---|---|
| a. Is a positive role model for others to emulate | • | | | | |
| b. Demonstrates loyalty and commitment to department and profession | | | | | |
| c. Continually strives to improve the image of the Arvada Police Department in the eyes of the public | | | | | |
| d. Demonstrates pride in the performance of others as well as self | | | | | |
| e. Demonstrates understanding of and commitment to Accreditation Standards | | | | | |
| f. Takes overt steps to overcome and combat bias in the community | | | | | |
| TOTAL (Element Score) | | | | | |

Weight 2 x Total of All Element Scores ____•____ = Performance Standard Score ___•___

COMMENTS:

•

**Figure 9-5**  *(Continued)*

**PART III. Overall Rating**

1. Customer Service/Community Problem Solving _____
2. Teamwork/Interpersonal Actions _____
3. Communications _____
4. Initiative _____
5. Professional Judgement _____
6. Work Performance/Quality _____
7. Personal Appearance, General Safety Practices, and Pride in Work Environment _____
8. Professional and Organizational Commitment _____

TOTAL POINT SCORE _____

Total $\dfrac{\text{Point Score}}{935 \text{ Points}}$ = _•_ %

OVERALL RATING SCORE = ___•___

| Unsatisfactory [_] (20-34) | Below Expectations [_] (35-54) | Meets Expectations [_] (55-71) | Exceeds Expectations [_] (72-91) | Distinguished Performance [_] (92-100) |
|---|---|---|---|---|

Relative to this employee's overall work record during this evaluation period, I recommend: (Include status and salary recommendations within the parameters listed in the "City of Arvada Supervisor's Guide to Performance Evaluations")

• 

**PART IV. EMPLOYEE ASSESSMENT**

Based upon current performance, what are the current employee strengths and development needs?

A. Employee Strengths:

• 

B. Development Needs:

• 

**Figure 9-5** *(Continued)*

C. Enter other comments relevant to the employee's performance.

&bull;

PART V. ESTABLISHMENT OF OBJECTIVES FROM &bull; TO &bull;

This section establishes the objectives to be accomplished during the next evaluation period. Objectives should be as specific as possible, including where appropriate, completion date. The supervisor's objectives for the employee <u>and</u> the employee's objectives for her/himself are to be included.

| OBJECTIVES | PLANS TO MEET THE OBJECTIVE | PROPOSED COMPLETION DATE |
|---|---|---|
| &bull; | | |

**Figure 9-5** *(Continued)*

**PART VI.**

Comments:

_____   _____   _____
Supervisor's Signature     Title                      Date

Comments:

_____   _____   _____
Lieutenant's Signature     Title                      Date

Comments:

_____   _____   _____
Bureau Commander's Signature   Title                  Date

Comments:

_____   _____   _____
Chief of Police's Signature    Title                  Date

Comments:

_____   _____   _____
Admin. Ass't. Signature    Title                      Date

Comments:

_____   _____   _____
Personnel Signature        Title                      Date

**Figure 9-5**   _(Continued)_

**PART VII.**

Any comments which the employee would like to make, or modifications of performance evaluation by the Supervisor due to the discussion of this evaluation, should be noted here.

My Supervisor reviewed and discussed the contents of the Performance Evaluation with me. My signature below does not indicate whether I agree or disagree with this evaluation.

_____     _____
Employee's Signature                                              Date

Employee Comments Reviewed By:

_____     _____     _____     _____     _____
Supv. Init.              Div.Hd. (Lt.)           Bur.Cmdr.            C.O.P.                  Admin.
                             Init.                      Init.                   Init.                   Asst. Init.

_____
Personnel
Init.

**Figure 9-5**   _(Continued)_

Police Officer Performance

935 Possible Points

|  | Percentage Spread | Point Spread | Salary Adj.-*Scale |
|---|---|---|---|
| Distinguished | 97-100 | 906-935 | 10% |
|  | 92-96 | 860-905 | 9% |
| Exceeds | 87-91 | 813-859 | 8.5% |
|  | 82-86 | 766-812 | 8% |
|  | 77-81 | 720-765 | 7.5% |
|  | 72-76 | 673-719 | 7% |
| Meets | 67-71 | 626-672 | 6% |
|  | 60-66 | 561-625 | 5% |
|  | 55-59 | 514-560 | 4% |
| Below | 50-54 | 467-513 | 2% |
|  | 40-49 | 374-466 | 0 |
|  | 35-39 | 327-373 | -2% |
| Unsatisfactory | 30-34 | 280-326 | -3% |
|  | 25-29 | 233-279 | -4% |
|  | 20-24 | 187-232 | -5% |

*Non-top step employees - Increases are only possible up to the maximum top step.

**Figure 9-5** *(Continued)*

fact that a generic evaluation for a given rank did not address the specifics found within particular job assignments; i.e., the difference between detective, patrol officer, traffic officer, narcotics officer, etc.

In the interim, the city Personnel Department and the City Manager's Office came down with a mandate that the various city departments would develop evaluations which would have weighted values for various performance categories and would also be utilized, based upon overall score, to determine salary increases or decreases. When the original mandate came down from the City Manager and Personnel Department, performance categories were examined for content and revised to a greater or lesser degree to more accurately reflect the expectations of various assignments within the department. Nevertheless, the final forms were still somewhat generic and really did not address the specific expectations of particular assignments.

. . . I began the revision process for the performance evaluations within the Operations Bureau. I took the previous evaluation format which, in essence, consisted of a series of performance categories which were then explained by a paragraph of narrative detail. These performance categories were then broken down by myself into particular elements within a category with a point rating of 1 to 5 for the level of performance for each of those particular elements within a category. The category was then weighted based upon input from supervisors and the personnel to be evaluated. This weight value was then multiplied times the raw score to give an overall score for that performance category. At the end of the evaluation, the supervisors are to tabulate all of the calculated scores (raw score times weight value) to calculate a final raw score. This raw score is then divided by the total possible points for that particular evaluation to determine a percentage score, which is then used to determine the overall quality of performance and which can then be correlated with the City's breakdowns for salary increase or decrease.

I have instructed each of the elements and units within the Operations Bureau to critically evaluate and review the performance evaluation for each of their units. They are then authorized as a unit to revise the performance evaluation . . . based upon what they perceive as those elements which specifically address the performance and expectations in their particular unit. For example, the undercover officers, while they are still police officers, have very specific performance criteria that are much different than the detectives (police officers) and street officers (police officers). In this way, each unit can develop a customized evaluation for the members of that unit. They are free to add, delete, and revise the elements within the performance criteria for that unit, based upon their specific expectations and job duties. This will allow for the customization of evaluation forms for specific ranks and assignments within the Operations Bureau. This allows the evaluation process to be dynamic and changeable through the years as programs and priorities change with time. In the end, the total possible points will vary, depending upon the degree of customization for that particular form, but the percentage utilized by personnel for determination of salary increase or decrease will still be available by dividing the total possible points into the performance points totaled at the end of the form.

While this all may seem fairly complex and confusing, it is being done in a systematic manner in an attempt to reduce the amount of confusion felt by the supervisors and employees. I would like to call your attention to page 2 of each of the performance evaluations, making special note of the areas which state that documentation must be provided to varying degrees depending upon the evaluation score for each of the elements within an evaluation category. This is to insure that supervisors are, in fact, able to justify the scores given to their personnel and be able to provide feedback, and in the case of the low expectations performance, a program for improvement, to both the employee being evaluated and the individuals reviewing all performance evaluations.

ADVANCED METHOD: THE BEHAVIORALLY ANCHORED RATING SCALE. In recent years, a series of techniques has been developed that show promise of overcoming the problems of reliability and validity. These are called *behaviorally anchored rating scales* (BARS) of job performance, because they focus on detailed evaluation of specific acts or behaviors, rather than on global aspects of performance. By design, they treat job performance as multidimensional and use actual instances of behavior to illustrate effective and ineffective performance on these dimensions.

Figure 9-6 depicts a BARS that is designed to assess the performance of a police officer. Similarly to the PDRS, it should significantly increase the validity and reliability of your personnel system.

A BARS incorporates all the important benchmarks of an effectiveness measure. For example, it (1) is derived from experienced observers' reports of actual behavioral episodes regarded as illustrative of actions that are instrumental to continued organizational functioning; (2) samples behavior over the long term, as opposed to short-range judgments or impressions; (3) specifies with precision the myriad information-processing activities that constitute the multiple facets of effective police behavior; (4) implies many possible configurations or patterns of effective officer behavior, rather than just one presumed best mode; (5) forces attention on what the employee does on the job, thereby guarding against defining his or her level of success in terms of other causal agents; and (6) takes account of an employee's membership in several organizational units, and of his or her potential impact on their continued functioning.

There are other patrol officer job categories such as "The Use of Physical Force." Space does not allow us to include them. Clearly, they are worth your time to review. Additionally, this document contains BARS for a number of other police positions (e.g., investigator) and ranks (e.g., sergeant).

## Recommendations for the Design and Implementation of a Personnel Evaluation System

It is time to coalesce our thinking and to travel from a method to a single system of evaluation—in this case, the job of performance evaluation. Remember the common precept of this entire book: that there is no *one* best way to do anything, organizationally speaking. However, there are *better* ways of doing things. The ten-step system to be described here seeks to proffer a *better* (not perfect) way to assess police personnel.

**1.** *Job analysis: What is to be evaluated?* The first step to be taken in building a reliable and valid evaluation process is to conduct a comprehensive, in-depth job analysis. A prior section dealt with this subject. The point to be made here is that job analysis is a start, and a must for successful performance evaluation. Without it, the remainder of the recommended steps are likely to fail.

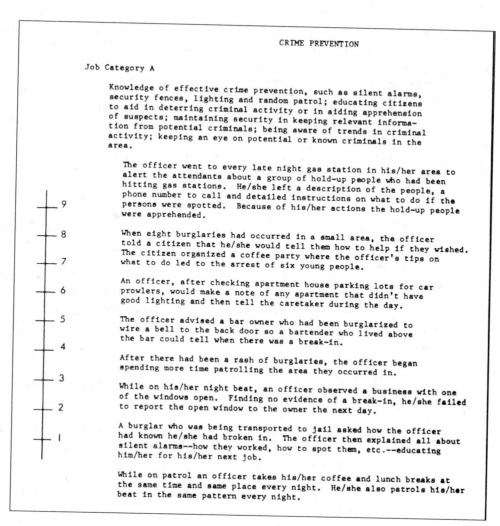

CRIME PREVENTION

Job Category A

Knowledge of effective crime prevention, such as silent alarms, security fences, lighting and random patrol; educating citizens to aid in deterring criminal activity or in aiding apprehension of suspects; maintaining security in keeping relevant information from potential criminals; being aware of trends in criminal activity; keeping an eye on potential or known criminals in the area.

9 — The officer went to every late night gas station in his/her area to alert the attendants about a group of hold-up people who had been hitting gas stations. He/she left a description of the people, a phone number to call and detailed instructions on what to do if the persons were spotted. Because of his/her actions the hold-up people were apprehended.

8 — When eight burglaries had occurred in a small area, the officer told a citizen that he/she would tell them how to help if they wished. The citizen organized a coffee party where the officer's tips on what to do led to the arrest of six young people.
7 —

6 — An officer, after checking apartment house parking lots for car prowlers, would make a note of any apartment that didn't have good lighting and then tell the caretaker during the day.

5 — The officer advised a bar owner who had been burglarized to wire a bell to the back door so a bartender who lived above the bar could tell when there was a break-in.
4 —

3 — After there had been a rash of burglaries, the officer began spending more time patrolling the area they occurred in.

2 — While on his/her night beat, an officer observed a business with one of the windows open. Finding no evidence of a break-in, he/she failed to report the open window to the owner the next day.

1 — A burglar who was being transported to jail asked how the officer had known he/she had broken in. The officer then explained all about silent alarms--how they worked, how to spot them, etc.--educating him/her for his/her next job.

While on patrol an officer takes his/her coffee and lunch breaks at the same time and same place every night. He/she also patrols his/her beat in the same pattern every night.

**Figure 9-6** Patrol Officer Evaluation Form

**2.** *A method: PDRS or BARS?* As a step, we would recommend that one of the two advanced methods (PDRS or BARS) be adopted for implementation. Now that a method of rating has been identified, we will proceed to a discussion of who will do the rating.

**3.** *The raters.* There are five possible sources of performance appraisal: (a) supervisors, (b) peers, (c) the appraisee himself or herself, (d) subordinates of the person to be appraised, and (e) people outside the immediate organization, such as citizens. Who the best person is to make the appraisal depends on the purpose of the appraisal and the level of the criteria being evaluated (immediate behavior versus intermediate and ultimate outcomes). Most performance appraisals are made by an officer's immediate superior. This is particularly true when the major purpose of the appraisal is for evaluation rather than for employee development. To overcome problems of stress and perceived threat, a few police agencies have tried to introduce evaluation by peers and self-evaluation, pointing out that these two methods work best under conditions of high interpersonal trust, highly specialized skills, high visibility among peers, and when development rather than evaluation is the major purpose to be served by the appraisal.

Since the primary goal in this instance is to assess an officer's performance, the immediate supervisor should have the fundamental responsibility for conducting the appraisal; however, a couple of significant alterations should be made.

First, it is recommended that multiple raters be used in completing the form: for example, the current supervisor, most recent past supervisor, and a supervisor who is on the same work shift. The present supervisor would be responsible for coordinating efforts and conducting the one-on-one interview with the officer. There are many advantages to the use of more than one rater, such as enhanced objectivity, improved clarity, more information, greater acceptance on the part of the ratee, and others. The only disadvantage that has been voiced deals with the amount of time that is consumed. The response to this concern resides in a question, "Where is the largest percentage of the agency's budgeted dollars allocated?" The majority responding would answer that it is to personnel (80 percent to 90 percent). Thus, is it not sensible to expend considerable time and effort in assessing their effectiveness?

The second feature involves self-appraisal, which will be covered in the MBO section that appears later.

**4.** *Trained raters.* We have frequently asked police supervisors and managers if they are required to assess the performance of their subordinates' work activities, and the majority say yes. However, when we ask the same group of people if they received any training on rating, the most common answer is no! As a result, it is strongly recommended that *those responsible for rating should be trained as raters.*

**5.** *Rating the raters.* We have also perceived that, although rating is acknowledged to be a highly fundamental and critical task of a police supervisor, in many cases the raters are *not* rated on their own willingness or ability to rate. In other words, a paramount dimension is being missed in terms of assessing a supervisor or manager's performance, which would be analogous to expecting patrol officers to behave with proper attitudes toward the public, but not rating them on their citizen contacts. *Raters should be evaluated on their rating skills.*

**6.** *A rating manual.* All performance-evaluation systems need a guide or a manual. Without a set of common definitions (such as the meaning of "community and human relations"), instructions, and procedures, the entire process is apt to suffer severe problems of ambiguity and integrity. A pertinent rating manual should address the obligations and concerns of the police agency, the police rater, and those to be assessed. *A manual is a must.*

**7.** *Significant (critical) incidents: A database.* We are prone to have a better recall of the immediate past, which is human nature. Thus, when rating, a rater normally has a clearer remembrance of those events that occurred over the preceding few weeks than of those that occurred months ago. Indeed, by being "officer perfect" shortly before evaluation, one can probably receive a fairly high evaluation. Regrettably, though, if one's performance had been good for eleven months but during the last four weeks one's luck turned (such as getting citizen complaints, damaging the radio car, or arguing with one's supervisor over the vacation schedule), then the rating would probably be poor.

This phenomenon cannot be totally eliminated, but fortunately it can be guarded against through the use of the significant (critical) incident technique (SIT). The critical-incident technique (CIT) was first introduced in a business setting as a single method for evaluating a person's performance. We see it as a most helpful technique in a performance evaluation system. (We prefer to substitute the term "significant" for "critical" to avoid the negative connotations of the latter term.)

The SIT involves the recording of what can be termed significant or highly important behavior on the part of a police officer, which can be of either a positive or negative nature. Over the course of the evaluation period, the rater documents the significant behavior of his or her ratees (typically, two to three are generated per week). At the time of rating, the supervisor should utilize this database for purposes of completing the rating form and the interpersonal interview. Also, the SIT is most useful in executing the activity that follows next.

**8.** *Feedback: Event and time triggered.* Police employee–supervisor feedback is a clear-cut must. It can be event feedback, time-triggered feedback, or preferably both. In event feedback, as favorable conduct is observed it should be positively reinforced (such as "Good job, officer. Let's discuss it for a few minutes"); and as misconduct is witnessed, it should be corrected ("Hey, officer, you really fouled up! Let's discuss it for a few minutes"). Most of us want to know when we are doing right or wrong—not once every six to twelve months, but at that moment in time, so that we can continue or abandon a particular behavior. Such events are best made a part of a SIT. Feedback is the breakfast of champions!

**9.** *Management by objectives.* You should recall from Responsibility Seven that MBO is the setting of performance objectives, tracking progress (or lack of progress), and evaluating results. While you as a supervisor should initiate the MBO process, it is best structured as a two-way channel. As a type of a contract, both parties ought to be included in drafting and approving the agreement. Because an MBO statement acts as a basis for both *past and future performance rating*, it should encompass the thinking of both the rater and the ratee. All police supervisors should separately produce a *tentative* MBO contract for employees. Concurrently, employees should be requested to independently generate their own contracts. Once both contracts have been finished, the two should confer and negotiate a final form.

Both event and time-triggered feedback are necessary. Monitoring an employee's performance assists in determining when which type should be applied. Time-triggered feedback is especially relevant for MBO in that set time periods or milestones should be reviewed according to schedule on a one-to-one basis (supervisor–subordinate). This is where SITs and counseling merge to act as a reinforcer or corrective motivator for getting the needed performance. See again Figure 9-5, which has MBO built-in.

**10.** *Making mission statements happen.* In Responsibility Four we underscored the importance of a leader projecting a vision on where the department is headed and why. Regretfully, many mission statements are given lip service with little follow-through in actual practice. Yet some agencies have put muscle into their mission statements by expanding them into performance rating systems. In other words, the values and standards comprising the department's mission are being looked for in an employee's daily work effort. Connecting performance appraisal to a mission statement increases the likelihood that it will be *practiced* and not just preached.

This system is not a panacea, but it *is* the least-imperfect set of methods for *effectively* appraising an employee's performance.

————◆◆◆◆————

A well-designed evaluation process is only as effective as the boss who is responsible for administering it.

————◆◆◆◆————

Organizational effectiveness is derived from individual effectiveness; individual effectiveness is heavily dependent on an accurate and valid personnel evaluation process. Also, a well-designed evaluation process is only as effective as the boss who is responsible for administering it.

## Structured Exercise 9-2

————◆◆◆◆————

The goals of this exercise are to (1) give participants an opportunity to create agenda for performance appraisals; (2) allow participants to experience the roles of supervisor, subordinate, and observer in a performance appraisal; and (3) provide participants with an opportunity to give and receive feedback on performance-appraisal techniques.

Any number of triads can engage in this exercise. The time required is approximately one hour.

The materials needed are

- One copy of the Performance Appraisal Supervisor's Role Sheet for every participant
- One copy of the Performance Appraisal Subordinate's Role Sheet for every participant

- One copy of the Performance Appraisal Observer's Role Sheet for every participant
- Blank paper and a pencil for each participant
- A portable writing surface for each participant
- A newsprint flip chart and a felt-tipped marker
- Masking tape for posting newsprint

The participants are assembled into triads. One member of each triad is given a copy of the supervisor's role sheet; another member is given a copy of the subordinate's role sheet; and the third member is given a copy of the observer's role sheet.

The facilitator asks the participants who have the supervisor's role sheets to interview the person playing the role of subordinate according to the instructions on their role sheets. The observer takes notes about the nature of the subordinate's job. The facilitator then interrupts the interviews and asks each supervisor and subordinate to create and prioritize agenda for the performance appraisal as instructed on the role sheets. The observers take notes on the agreed-on agenda.

The facilitator instructs the triads to begin the performance-appraisal process. At the end of ten minutes, the facilitator stops the appraisal. The facilitator next instructs each supervisor and his or her subordinate to continue the conversation just long enough to summarize what they have already discussed. The subordinate is instructed to make notes that could be used later to write a summary. Each observer is instructed to give feedback to the other two members of the triad and to allow them to ask for clarification and suggestions at the end of the feedback.

Each subordinate is given a copy of the supervisory role sheet; each observer is given a copy of the subordinate's role sheet; and each supervisor is given a copy of the observer's role sheet. The facilitator announces that each participant will play the role that corresponds to the new sheet. Subsequently, the preceding steps are repeated.

The total group is reassembled, and the facilitator leads a discussion on the following questions:

1. How did you feel when you played the role of supervisor? Subordinate? Observer?
2. What did you like/dislike about each role?
3. Which role was most helpful to you in understanding the performance appraisal process? How?
4. In what ways were the agenda helpful? In what ways were they a hindrance?
5. In what ways were the summaries helpful?
6. What types of statements or topics caused problems during the appraisal? How?
7. What topics, phrases, statements, or behaviors enhanced the process? How?
8. What discoveries have you made about the performance appraisal process?
9. How can this experience benefit you and your organization in the future?

**PERFORMANCE APPRAISAL SUPERVISOR'S ROLE SHEET.** You will play the role of the supervisor during a performance appraisal. Before the appraisal process begins, you will interview the person who is playing the role of your subordinate to find out what type of organization he or she works for, what kind of work he or she does, and other details that would help you appraise the subordinate's performance.

The facilitator will interrupt your interview and ask you and your subordinate to create agenda for the performance appraisal. You will write down topics that you want to discuss while your subordinate is writing down topics that he or she wants to discuss. When you finish, you and your subordinate will exchange agenda and discuss them, and come to an agreement about which items will remain on the final agenda.

Because time is limited for this activity, you will not be able to cover every agendum. Therefore, you and your subordinate will prioritize the items on the final agenda.

Some items that you may want to include on the agenda are listed subsequently.

**1.** Things that the subordinate has done well

**2.** Things that the subordinate needs to improve

**3.** Progress on previously set goals

**4.** Goals toward which the subordinate might work

**5.** Things that the supervisor does that help or hinder the subordinate's work

After you have completed the agenda, the facilitator will tell you to begin the performance appraisal.

When giving feedback to your subordinate, cite specific behavior. For example, say, "Your weekly reports were late twice last month," or "Your errors dropped from six in January to only two in February," not "Your work is always lagging behind," or "Your accuracy seems to be improving."

Resist the temptation to sandwich negative criticism in between compliments. For example, do not say, "Your investigative work is excellent, you make too many mistakes on the crime reports, and I think you are a very good organizer." Instead, remind the subordinate that you had to return six crime reports for corrections last week, and that one of his or her goals should be to proofread typed material carefully before giving it to you. Make sure the subordinate understands your complaint before proceeding further.

The facilitator will interrupt the performance appraisal and instruct you and your subordinate to summarize jointly what you discussed during the appraisal. Your subordinate will be instructed to take notes. (In a real situation, the subordinate is sometimes asked to write a summary of the appraisal and to present it the following day to the supervisor for discussion.)

**PERFORMANCE APPRAISAL SUBORDINATE'S ROLE SHEET.** You will play the role of the subordinate during a performance appraisal. Before the appraisal process begins, you will be interviewed by the person who is playing the role of your supervisor. Expect that person to ask you about where you work, what kind of work you do, and other details that would help in giving a performance appraisal.

The facilitator will interrupt the interview and ask you and your supervisor to create agenda for the performance appraisal. While your supervisor is writing down topics that he or she wants to discuss with you, you should also write down topics that you want discussed. When you finish you will exchange agenda with your supervisor and will discuss them and come to an agreement about which items will remain on the final agenda.

Because time is limited for this activity, you will not be able to cover every agendum. Therefore, you and your supervisor will prioritize the items on the final agenda.

Some items you may want to include on your agenda are listed subsequently.

**1.** Things that I do well
**2.** Things that I need to improve
**3.** Progress on previously set goals
**4.** Goals for the future

After you have completed the agenda, wait for the facilitator to tell you to begin the performance appraisal.

If your supervisor asks you for feedback on his or her performance, cite specific behavior. For example, say, "You missed a meeting we scheduled for last Thursday," not "You're never around," or say "The note you wrote me about my crime statistics report inspired me to try to finish on time every month," not "You are always giving me encouragement."

The performance appraisal will be interrupted by the facilitator, who will instruct you and your supervisor to summarize jointly what you discussed. At this point, you will be asked to make notes so that you would be able to write a summary later. (In a real situation, the subordinate is sometimes required to write a summary of the performance appraisal and to present it to the supervisor the following day for discussion.)

**PERFORMANCE APPRAISAL OBSERVER'S ROLE SHEET.**    You will play the role of the observer during a performance appraisal. When real performance appraisals are conducted, the supervisor's supervisor sometimes observes the process and gives feedback to the person performing the appraisal. Your task will be to give feedback to *both* parties.

Before the performance appraisal, the person playing the role of supervisor will interview the person playing the role of subordinate to obtain information about the person's job. The supervisor and subordinate will also plan the agenda.

During the interview, agenda setting, and performance appraisal, take notes but do not interrupt or join the conversation. The other two members of your triad will probably become so involved in their conversation that they will not even be aware of your presence.

You should not give feedback on the performance appraisal until the facilitator instructs you to do so. When you have finished giving feedback, you should allow the other members of your triad to ask you for clarification and suggestions.

If you play another role after being an observer, try to benefit from the feedback you gave the other members of your triad.

The following items provide a checklist that may be helpful as you observe the supervisor and subordinate:

1. The supervisor and subordinate created the agenda jointly.
2. The supervisor and subordinate followed the agenda they created.
3. The supervisor was in control of the process.
4. The supervisor used concrete examples to describe performance.
5. The subordinate reacted to the supervisor's feedback nondefensively.
6. The supervisor and subordinate set goals jointly.
7. The supervisor solicited feedback about his or her performance.
8. The subordinate used concrete examples to describe the supervisor's performance.
9. The supervisor reacted to the subordinate's feedback nondefensively.
10. The supervisor and subordinate shared the discussion.
11. The supervisor and subordinate summarized the discussion jointly.
12. The subordinate took notes on the summary.

## KEY POINTS

- The police supervisor has two interrelated performance appraisal methods; informal daily and formal periodic.
- The most reliable test of a police department is its spirit of performance.
- The three key reasons for assessing a person's performance are behavioral: control, motivation, and feedback.
- Performance evaluation serves a large number of purposes, ranging from decisions about promotions through dealing with MBO contracts.
- For a performance evaluation system to be reliable *and* valid, it must be job related.
- Job-related performance appraisal systems are based on a *job analysis*.
- Basically, there are three performance evaluation methods: (1) global rating scales, (2) performance domain rating scale, and (3) behaviorally anchored rating scale.
- An internally and externally sound performance rating system must include (1) a job analysis, (2) a rating method, (3) more than one rater, (4) trained raters, (5) raters who are rated for their rating skills, (6) a rating manual, (7) the recording of significant incidents, (8) feedback, (9) MBO, and (10) making mission statements happen.

# DISCUSSION

1. One of four ways to develop a "spirit of performance" is via *establishing a habit of achievement*. How does a supervisor create such a habit?

2. Return to the section entitled, "Complex Process." Imagine for a moment that you are the supervisor of the patrol officer who did not receive the desired assignment. After hearing his fine points, what are your (1) thoughts and (2) verbal reactions?

3. What do *reliability* and *validity* mean? How do they differ? What is the best tool for ensuring that they exist in a rating process?

4. Review the three rating scales presented earlier. Which would you, as a supervisor, prefer to use and why?

5. It is underscored that the raters must be trained to ensure the integrity of a performance appraisal process. What are some of the ways to train police supervisors as raters?

6. How might individual feedback on performance enhance teamwork? How might it hinder it?

# Responsibility Ten

# *Conflict*

The police supervisor is responsible for anticipating, defining, and solving personnel, interpersonal, and group conflicts with certainty and compassion.

*When elephants fight, it is the grass that suffers.*

—Kikuya Proverb

By now, the work force is motivated (R-6) to achieve specified goals (R-7) by being empowered (R-8) to do so. Nevertheless, conflicts (R-10) will occur and must be solved based on nonnegotiable principles.

Most police officers are honest, hardworking, and helpful human beings. They project a *positive mental attitude* (PMA) and will make your job as a supervisor a rewarding one. Similarly, the majority of police work groups possess one or two individuals who are seemingly dedicated to making you miserable. As their supervisor, however, you can master their fate.

We heard one supervisor comment with chagrin, "Being a sergeant could be relatively easy, if it weren't for those miserable ——s that I have to supervise." Supervision is a people process. A select few people will command more of your thinking and attention than others. People problems can occur on an individual basis (malingering) or on a group basis (the whole crew is malingering). People problems—singular or plural—are a major job responsibility for you.

Problem police employees come in a variety of symptomatic packages. Basically, they can be categorized as either honest (mistakes of the mind) or dishonest (mistakes of the heart). Oddly, the honest problem employee, for example, the "whining, sniveling, malcontent" (WSM) is frequently more difficult to handle. The dishonest officer is detected, apprehended, discharged, and probably prosecuted. The WSM requires considerably different treatment.

As a supervisor, you are destined to expend a large portion of your energy on the handling of problem employees. They will tax your patience, at times push your anger control, and test your ability to develop a creative response. Alternatively, you must not lose sight and contact with the PMAS, the productive and team-spirited employees. Concentrate on, reinforce, and reward the productive officer. The strength of your work team is centered here. Nobody said supervising was easy. If it were easy, everyone would be doing it.

---

Nobody said supervising was easy. If it were easy, everyone would be doing it.

---

## RESPONSIBILITY OF THE POLICE SUPERVISOR

*All that a man achieves and all that he fails to achieve is the direct result of his own thoughts.*

—James Allen
*As a Man Thinketh* (New York: Grosset and Dunlap, 1983), p. 49

Supervision is nothing more than motivating other people. First, however, you must be motivated. If you're not a "turned-on" supervisor, the likelihood of your "constructing an environment in which they motivate themselves" is very low. Remember, the first person to motivate is yourself.

The second ingredient for building a motivating environment is listening. Yes, listen. If you're not listening (ears, eyes, and intuition), then you'll not know who is responding to the opportunity to participate together as a team. Vince Lombardi, the legendary football coach, once commented, "Most people call it team spirit. When the players are imbued with that special feeling, you know you've got yourself a winning team."[1]

For a variety of reasons, there are at times a few employees who either cannot or will not make a team commitment. Through either professional or personal difficulties, or both, they march to a different drummer. Your role as a police supervisor, very simply stated, although not easily fulfilled is: All problem employees have a different drummer, one that is causing him or her to conflict with the pace and direction of the work unit. This drummer should be discovered and brought into line.

The remainder of this chapter examines conflict as potentially both a positive and negative human force.

---

[1]As quoted by Lee Iacocca, *Iacocca: An Autobiography* (New York: Bantam Books, 1984), pp. 56–57.

## Structured Exercise 10-1

There are numerous creative and positive ways of resolving conflict. An unusual one is described below. In a group setting, think about a variety of methods for handling conflicts. Apply your imagination and have fun while completing this exercise.

> *An Inupiat Eskimo, when felt wronged by another person, would challenge that individual to an exchange of belittling songs. The entire tribe would gather to witness the duel. The disputing parties would take turns singing songs which via wit and derision described the wrongdoing or perversity of the other person. The tribe would respond with laughter to each song and the duel would continue until one person withdrew in shame. The issue was expected to be resolved and closed with the ending of the song duel.*

## CONFLICT: THE INTERNAL CONSEQUENCES

*Having thought about your interests, you should go into a meeting not only with one or more specific options that would meet your legitimate interests but also with an open mind. An open mind is not an empty one.*

—Roger Fisher and William Ury
*Getting to Yes* (Boston: Houghton Mifflin, 1981), p. 55

Human conflict is to be expected; indeed a certain amount of internal conflict can be considered healthy. An analogy would be the necessity for tension on the mainspring of a watch. At the same time, however, too much tension will cause it to break. In an organizational setting, too much conflict is counterproductive to goal attainment. The police supervisor is in a unique position to control the degree of conflict in an agency.

A certain amount of internal conflict can be considered healthy.

When we use the term "conflict," we are referring to perceived incompatible differences resulting in some form of interference or opposition. Whether the differences are real or not is irrelevant. If people perceive the differences exist, then a conflict state exists. Additionally, our definition covers a range that includes the extremes, from subtle, indirect, and highly controlled forms of differences to overt acts, such as physical altercations, job terminations, and criminal acts.

Competition is different from conflict. Conflict is directed against another party, whereas competition is aimed at obtaining a goal without interference from another party. Of course, competition can lead to conflict. If three police supervisors in a patrol watch are competing for the number one performance rating, the scarceness created by availability of only one top position can result in conflict.

## Conflict: A Plus or a Minus?

The response to the question of conflict being either a plus or a minus in a work group is, "It all depends."

Some conflicts support the goals of the organization; These are functional conflicts of a constructive form. Additionally, there are conflicts that hinder an organization in achieving its goals; these are dysfunctional conflicts and are destructive forms.

Of course, it is one thing to argue that conflict can be valuable, but how do you tell if a conflict is functional or dysfunctional? Unfortunately, the demarcation is neither clear nor precise. No one level of conflict can be adopted as acceptable or unacceptable under all conditions. The type and level of conflict that create healthy and positive involvement toward one department's goals may, in another department or in the same department at another time, be highly dysfunctional. Functionality or dysfunctionality, therefore, is a judgment call on your part. Hence, it remains for you to make intelligent judgments concerning whether conflict levels in your unit are appropriate, too high, or too low.

## Value of Conflict

If harnessed and channeled, conflict can produce the following results for you and your team officers:

- Major stimulant for change
- Fosters creativity and innovation
- Clarifies issues and goals
- Encourages individuality
- Enhances communication
- Increases energy within a unit
- Promotes cohesiveness
- Psychologically healthy

It is vital that you, as a supervisor, not only tolerate but respect an officer's individuality and preferences as long as they do not detract from getting police work done in a professional and legally accepted manner. If you as a supervisor push for uniformity and ignore individual strengths and styles, you are promoting the negative aspects of conflict.

Because conflict has positive attributes, you can, as appropriate, stimulate it. In fact, Bill Gates of Microsoft fame has repeatedly cited conflict as the primary reason his company has been so successful.

## Sources of Conflict

Conflict can emanate from one of four sources: (1) existing conditions (especially novel ones), (2) our attitudes, (3) our thoughts, (4) our behavior. Typically, all four combine to produce the conflict.

Fortunately most conflicts are of minor importance. Few police officers are likely to be psychologically crippled by trying to decide between two patrol routes. Few of us encounter daily conflicts that we cannot respond to in a routine or "programmed" manner. The police officer, however, generally experiences the unusual. He or she is more often than not faced with highly diverse nonprogrammable choices. Briefly stated, the police officer typically deals with novelty rather than familiar and precedented problems. Today there is a hidden conflict in our lives between the pressures of acceleration and those of novelty. One forces us to make faster decisions while the other compels us to make the hardest, most time-consuming type of decisions.

## Conflict Resolution

Fundamentally, there are seven tactical routes for resolving conflict. They can be applied singularly or in various mixes. Be certain to accurately comprehend the source of a conflict before you use a particular tactic. If the tactic you select does not fit the situation, you will regretfully exacerbate the problem at hand.

SUPERORDINATE GOALS.    Common goals that two or more conflicting parties each desire and that cannot be reached without the cooperation of those involved are called *superordinate goals*. These goals must be highly valued, unattainable without the help of all parties involved in the conflict, and commonly sought. Evidence supports the fact that, when used cumulatively, superordinate goals develop long-term "peacemaking" potential, thereby reinforcing dependency and developing collaboration.

EXPANSION OF RESOURCES.    Police officers are usually competitive by nature and seek opportunities to advance professionally. Some agencies have responded to this need by creating corporal senior officer or field training officer positions. Others have established sergeant one and two positions, lieutenant one and two positions, and so on. This technique is extremely successful because it leaves the competitive parties satisfied. However, its use is obviously restricted by the nature of its inherent limitation; that is, resources rarely exist in such quantities so that they can be easily expanded.

AVOIDANCE.    One method of dealing with conflict is simply to avoid it. Avoidance does not offer a permanent way of resolving conflict, but it is an extremely popular short-term solution. In our day-to-day relations, each of us frequently withdraws from the arena of confrontation or suppresses a particular conflict. The method has obvious limitations, but it has nonetheless been described as "society's chief instrument for handling conflict."

SMOOTHING.    Smoothing can be described as the process of playing down differences that exist between individuals or groups while emphasizing common interests. Differences are suppressed in smoothing and similarities are accentuated. When we recognize that *all* conflict situations have common points of interest or agreement, we see smoothing represents a way in which one minimizes differences.

COMPROMISE.    Compromise techniques make up a major portion of resolution methods. Included here are external or third-party interventions, plus internal compromise between conflicting parties through both total-group and representative negotiation and voting. What differentiates compromise from the other techniques is that in a compromise solution each party must give up something of value. While there is no clear winner, there is also no clear loser. In our democratic society and in many police agencies, compromise is the classic method by which conflicts can be resolved.

FORCING.    In police organizations, probably the most frequently used method for formally resolving opposing interactions is the use of forcing or formal authority. Members of the police departments, with rare exception, recognize and accept the authority of their superiors, and even though they may not be in agreement with their decisions, they will almost always abide by them. Thus, forcing is highly successful in achieving short-term reduced conflict levels. As a supervisor, constantly remember that its major weakness is the same as that of avoidance, smoothing, and compromise; that is, the cause of the conflict is not treated, but only its effects.

REORGANIZE.    If a conflict's source is the police organization's structure, it seems only reasonable to look again at structure for the solution. You might, for instance, transfer or exchange members between departments, create coordinating or buffer positions, develop an appeals system, realign department boundaries, or change individual responsibilities.

## PROBLEM EMPLOYEES: WORKER RELATIONS

Problem employees are the chronic absentee, the rule breaker, the boss hater, the psychosomatic, the malingerer, the person who's lost his confidence, the heavy drinker, the alcoholic, the WSM, and, yes, even the workaholic. Problem police employees are expensive to have on the payroll. They are characterized by excessive tardiness and absences. You are apt to find that they are difficult to supervise. They have a tendency to upset the morale of the work group. Consequently, you should worry about (1) hiring a problem employee in the first place, (2) handling him or her on the job so that he or she reaches maximum productivity with the least disruption of the team's overall performance, and (3) determining whether a problem employee has become so seriously maladjusted that he or she needs professional attention.

This section focuses on the police employee who is causing internal problems. The following section centers on the police employee who is generating external problems for the department. Obviously, both categories overlap and there is not any clear demarcation—except when an officer commits a crime. That is really a worst-case problem employee.

## Recognizing Problem Employees

Many problem employees fall into these categories: They are perpetually dissatisfied, are given to baseless worries, tire easily, are suspicious, are sure that superiors withhold promotions or that their associates gossip maliciously about them. Some are characterized by drinking sprees, are insubordinate, or have ungovernable tempers.

Among themselves, problem employees differ widely, just as more normal people do. But within the framework of their symptoms, they are surprisingly alike in their reactions.

The behavior of a psychotic or neurotic employee can become your concern. Both terms sound pretty ominous. But only the police officer with a psychosis is seriously ill. The most common type of psychosis is schizophrenia, or "split personality." A schizophrenic lives partly in a world of his imagination. Especially when the world seems threatening to him, he withdraws. He may be able to adjust to life, even have a successful career. But when he loses his grip, his problem is beyond the scope of a supervisor.

Conversely, most of us are neurotic to a degree. People who have exaggerated fears, who feel the need to prove themselves, or who are irritable, hostile, opinionated, timid, or aggressive (which somewhere along the line describes most of us) have the seeds of neurosis in them. It's when this condition becomes exaggerated that a neurotic employee becomes a problem to associates and to the supervisor.

A couple of samples of neurotic employees: The officer who boasts about his drinking and sexual prowess. The supervisor who gets pleasure from reprimanding a police employee in front of others. The detective who visits a medical doctor every other day with some minor ailment. The dispatcher who meticulously arranges his or her workplace in the same manner every day, who can't begin his or her job unless everything is exactly as he or she wants it.

## Recognizing Problem Supervisors and Managers

A few years ago a police supervisor began to counsel one of his officers on some minor rule infractions. The officer listened for a few moments, jumped to his feet, ran to an open window, crawled out onto a roof and up a twenty foot communications tower. It took eight hours to convince him to climb down. (He was armed.) He said, "My supervisor stressed me."

Yes, there are supervisors and police managers who preach too much, who are rigid in their interpretation of policy, who enjoy assigning employees to jobs they particularly dislike, or who continually hold some sort of threat, veiled or otherwise, over their employees' heads.

Then, too, you and your boss especially are beset with more than ordinary obstacles at work. And not only do they have their own phobias to contend with, they must listen to and try to assuage those of their employees. Is it any wonder that a supervisor or police manager becomes a problem employee?

## Helping the Problem Employee

The psychotic or highly neurotic employee requires professional assistance. Many police departments have either full-time or on-call psychiatrists and clinical psychologists. With your superior's approval, you should refer these unfortunate people to such specialists.

You can help the problem police employee toward better adjustment only after you have reassured the officer that you are trying to help him or her keep his or her job—not looking for an excuse to get rid of him or her. No approach does more harm with a person of this nature than the "better get yourself straightened out or you will lose your job" attitude on a supervisor's part. You have to believe, and make the employee believe, that your intentions are good, that you want to help him or her. Then you must give the officer every opportunity to help himself or herself. This approach is called counseling, and there are fifteen rules for you to follow.

1. Listen patiently to what the employee has to say before making any comment of your own. This act on your part may be sufficient to resolve the difficulties.
2. Refrain from criticizing or offering hasty advice on the employee's problem.
3. Never argue with a police employee while you are in the process of counseling.
4. Give your undivided attention to the employee.
5. Look beyond the mere words of what the employee says; listen to see if the officer's trying to tell you something deeper than what appears on the surface.
6. Recognize what you are counseling an employee for. And don't look for immediate results. Never mix up the counseling interview with some other action you may want to take, such as discipline.
7. Find a reasonably quiet place where you're sure you won't be interrupted and won't be overheard. Try to put the employee at ease. Don't jump into a cross-examination.
8. Depending on the nature of the situation, multiple sessions may be necessary. They should last from fifteen to thirty minutes per session.
9. If after two counseling sessions you are not making progress, you should consult with your manager concerning referral to a professional therapist.
10. Get conditioned to the fact that it is your job and you can't run away from it.
11. Look at your task as a fact-finding one, just as in handling grievances.
12. Control your own emotions and opinions while dealing with the employee.
13. Be absolutely sold on the value of listening rather than preaching.
14. Recognize your own limits in handling these situations. You're not a clinical psychologist. You're a person responsible for getting results out of your assigned officers.
15. If all else fails, then you still have your prerogative to use discipline.

Make no mistake: Handling a police employee who has become a problem isn't easy. Sometimes it can become downright unpleasant. But the sooner you face up to this key supervisory responsibility, the sooner the problems get solved.

The belief that employees are basically good and can be constructively corrected is one of the most widely held beliefs in formal organizations. Yet it is both untrue and destructive. Those who believe in innate human goodness view the battle for a better employee as primarily a struggle between the individual and society. In our opinion, the battle is between the individual and his or her character.

We have stressed that the problem employee represents a very small percentage of the department. We believe that many of them can and will correct their wrongful behavior. We also believe that, unfortunately, a few are losers. And there is nothing that you can do about it—no matter how hard you try. What you can and must do is assist them in exiting the department. W. C. Fields, the late comedian, quipped, "When at first you don't succeed, try and try again. Then if you don't succeed, give up. Don't be a damned fool about it."

## PROBLEM EMPLOYEES: CITIZEN RELATIONS

*In order to strengthen administrative review and control, responsibility should formally be delegated to the police for developing comprehensive administrative policies and rules governing the duties and responsibilities of police officers together with procedures and sanctions for ensuring that these duties and responsibilities are met.*

—American Bar Association, *The Urban Police Function* (Washington, D.C.: American Bar Association, 1973), p. 163

One of the main reasons for your job is to strengthen agency review and control of police conduct. Plainly, it is impossible to construct an effective system of accountability (see Figure 10-1) without a strong and functional mechanism for maintaining behavioral control over police personnel. While the exclusionary rule, criminal and civil actions against police officers, and other external remedies serve as important constraints, you must accept primary responsibility for controlling the vast discretionary power of police officers.

Unfortunately, some police supervisors have not yet accepted this challenge, and this is the basic reason why there has been constant pressure for civilian review boards, ombudsmen, and other such external review agencies.

Your agency may be efficient and large enough to afford an "internal investigations" or "professional responsibilities" unit. Nevertheless, the creation of an internal investigation unit *does not* relieve you of the need to maintain discipline. On the contrary, it strengthens it by providing assistance to supervisors *on request*, in the investigation of alleged misconduct of their team members.

### Drawing the Lines

While the community may disagree with or be vague about what constitutes police misconduct, the police cannot. Granted, without community consensus on this subject the problem is a highly perplexing one for our police.

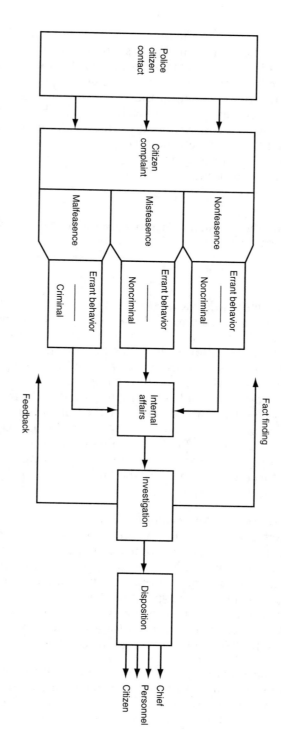

**Figure 10-1** Internal Discipline: A System of Accountability (Paul Whisenand and Fred Ferguson, *The Managing of Police Organizations*, 2nd ed., © 1978, p. 349. Reprinted by permission of Prentice Hall, Inc., Englewood Cliffs, N.J.)

Nonetheless, wrongdoing must be *defined* and *policies* must be set by the agency. Lines must be clearly drawn. Essentially these lines should encompass three forms of misconduct: (1) legalistic, (2) professional, and (3) moralistic. The first involves criminal considerations; the second may or may not be criminal in nature but does entail professional considerations; and the third may or may not include professional canons, but does embody personal ethics. Each form of errant behavior is examined further in the following paragraphs. It will be noted that there is a descending degree of clarity or precision with each type of wrongdoing. Conversely, there is an ascending degree of managerial ambiguity on police and procedural violations.

———◆•※•◆———

While the community may disagree with or be vague about what constitutes police misconduct, the police cannot.

———◆•※•◆———

**LEGALISTIC MISCONDUCT.**     This type of misconduct is also commonly referred to as "corruption." Police corruption is an extremely complex and demoralizing crime problem, and it is not new to our generation of police personnel. Police corruption includes (1) the misuse of police authority for the police employee's personal gain; (2) activity of the police employee that compromises, or has the potential to compromise, his or her ability to enforce the law or provide other police service impartially; (3) the protection of illicit activities from police enforcement, whether or not the police employee receives something of value in return; and (4) the police employee's involvement in promoting the business of one person while discouraging that of another person. Police corruption means, therefore, acts involving the misuse of authority by a police officer in a manner designed to produce *personal gain for the officer or for others*. And this is illegal!

**PROFESSIONAL MISCONDUCT.**     This form of misconduct can range from physical to verbal abuse of a citizen. On the one hand, a criminal or civil violation may have occurred, while, on the other, agency standards of professional conduct may be at issue. The possibilities for wrongdoing in this instance can fall within two rubrics: the law and professional conduct "unbecoming an officer." The distinction, again, between this type of wrongdoing and corruption is that no personal gain for the officer or others is involved. The key question is: What conduct is permissible? Hence, there is a need for established policies, procedures, rules, and sanctions that explicitly encompass the conduct of police employees.

**MORALISTIC MISCONDUCT.**     If an officer thinks certain citizens are deserving of aggressive police practices, the likelihood of his behaving aggressively is enhanced, perhaps to the point of overreaction or even physical abuse. Or if the officer thinks certain citizens are deserving of no police attention, the likelihood of his or her behaving passively is increased, perhaps to the extent of no reaction, and thus the possibility of corruption occurs. Space does not allow adequate coverage of this subject. Nonetheless, it is at the very crux of other forms of misconduct.

## *Structured Exercise 10-2*

Please evaluate the following three cases, each of which includes conflict. First of all, decide which one or more of the three types of misconduct is involved. Then decide what should be done to resolve each situation. This exercise is best conducted in a group setting.

**PROBLEM 1.**   You are currently enrolled as a public administration major at the local university. After having acquired your bachelor of science degree in Criminal Justice last year, you desired to continue your education. As a result, you entered the School of Public Administration as a part-time student at the graduate level. Your graduation plans call for the awarding of a master of science degree in Public Administration within three years. Upon walking into your first class on campus, you were pleased to see four co-workers from your agency in the class. The remainder of the graduate seminar is comprised of seventeen full- and part-time students representing a broad spectrum of public-service interests.

Professor Esoteric, a new member of the faculty, spent the first class session reviewing his philosophy on the administrative ethic. Near the end of the class he asked each student to discuss his or her personal and professional background. When one of your co-workers mentioned that he worked for a police department, Esoteric interrupted and commented, "Dammit, isn't it possible to do anything in today's world without surveillance by the Gestapo?"

During the next four weeks at each three-hour class session, Dr. Esoteric made brief, but caustic, remarks about the American police. Casual conversation has revealed that there are currently eight hundred majors in the graduate program. Of the eight hundred, fifty-six represent local law-enforcement agencies.

At the last class meeting, Dr. Esoteric returned to you a graded written examination. He gave you a letter grade of D without any further written comment. After class you learned from your co-workers that they had also received D's. The four of you approached Professor Esoteric and inquired as to the reason for the failing grades. His reply was, "Don't threaten me! I am prepared to immediately go to your City Council and inform them that I am being harassed."

Your chief of police has a master of science degree in Business Administration and encourages members of your department to attend college courses. The university that you are attending is the only one within seventy-five miles of your agency. Furthermore, there is an academic pay incentive program of 5 percent for a master of science degree. When comparing your grade-point average to your co-workers', it was found that the mean average was 3.54. Also, you have discovered that the sister of the dean of public administration is a member of your city council. You have submitted a written report to the chief who, in turn, asked the Task Force to make a recommendation(s).

**PROBLEM 2.** Officer Errant had been repeatedly warned about his misconduct over the four years he was on the department. While most of the criticisms were verbal and proffered by his immediate supervisor, some did appear in writing and were now a part of his personnel folder. In the main, Officer Errant had garnered five citizen complaints for abusive language, two court actions (not guilty) for use of excessive force during an arrest, ten instances of tardiness to roll call, four instances of grossly erroneous crime reports, and two minor situations involving insubordination to command officers.

Yesterday his sergeant was called to the scene of a civil disturbance. Errant had requested assistance at the location and Sergeant Rectitude responded. Upon his arrival he observed that Errant had two subjects in custody, handcuffed, and standing by the patrol car. Rectitude asked what was happening, and Errant replied, "These two —holes kept arguing so I decided to book their hips." It was discovered that they were husband and wife, and the dispute was minor. Rectitude took immediate action and essentially apologized for the mistake. Errant, in turn, called Rectitude a "spineless kiss—."

The situation was reported, in writing, to the chief. The chief summoned both Rectitude and Errant to his office. After having heard from both of the involved parties, Chief Unequivocal stated that, in his judgment, Errant should be penalized for insubordination. With that Errant blurted out, "You out-of-touch jerk! You can go to hell." The chief loudly retorted, "I'm not going to hell; on the contrary I'm staying around long enough to see you fired!" The meeting then ended.

The following day Chief Unequivocal received a registered special delivery letter from Errant's attorney. Basically it stated that Errant (1) had been unjustly threatened, (2) his fundamental rights had been violated, and (3) he would seek legal redress if the chief decided to sanction Errant. What should the chief do?

**PROBLEM 3.** It has come to the attention of the chief that an increasing number of police officers are holding a second full- or part-time job over and above their department employment. Second jobs are particularly common among field officers who are working a four-day forty-hour week. While there is a great debate among the police managers and supervisors about the actual effect on job performance of the second job, all are agreed that they do not like the general idea because they feel officers do not have the proper enthusiasm for their police jobs. Additionally, there have been at least two instances in which the outside employment represented a potential conflict-of-interest situation. The department has just announced a policy under which police employees must secure prior approval of any outside employment. The police union that represents the department's officers immediately issued a statement that challenged the legality of the policy, charging that it infringes on the civil rights and constitutional guarantees of its members. The only law regarding outside job employment prohibits a person from having two government jobs at the same time. How should this matter be handled?

# CITIZEN COMPLAINTS

Frequently you will be the first to hear a citizen's complaint. "I want to see your supervisor" is a pervasive request on the part of a citizen who feels he or she has been mistreated. A complaint starts with its *receipt*, then proceeds to an investigation, and concludes with *adjudication*. More specifically, the three phases are as follows:[2]

## Phase 1: Complaint Receipt

1. A viable complaint reception provides you with a useful tool for officer performance evaluation.
2. It is imperative that all complaints (letters, telephone, in person) be investigated.
3. A form should be designed and used for complaint processing (see Figure 10-2).
4. The complaining citizen should be given a completed copy of the form as a receipt.
5. Results of the investigation should be submitted to the complaining party.
6. If the citizen complaint is found to be intentionally malicious, then the officer has legal redress available.

## Phase 2: Investigation

1. All supervisors assigned should be given specific training in investigating internal discipline complaints and should be provided with written investigative procedures.
2. Every police agency should establish formal procedures for investigating internal misconduct allegations.
3. Every supervisor should conduct internal investigations in a manner that best reveals the facts while preserving the dignity of all persons and maintaining the confidential nature of the investigation.
4. Every police agency should provide at the time of employment and, again, prior to the specific investigation all its employees with a written statement of their duties and rights when they are the subject of an internal discipline investigation.
5. Every police chief should have legal authority during an internal discipline investigation to relieve police employees from their duties when it is in the interests of the public and the police agency.
6. All internal discipline investigations should be concluded 30 days from the date the complaint is made unless an extension is granted by the chief executive of the agency.

---

[2]This section is excerpted from the National Advisory Commission on Criminal Justice Standards and Goals, *Police* (Washington, D.C.: U.S. Government Printing Office, 1973), p. 483.

CITY OF ANAHEIM, CALIFORNIA
Police Department

## MESSAGE FROM THE CHIEF OF POLICE

The Police Officer of today works in an extremely complex society. A goal of the Anaheim Police Department is to ensure that the public is served in a most efficient and effective manner by highly trained Police Officers.

To assist us in achieving this goal, you, as an individual, can help by letting us know if you have a complaint. Rest assured that your complaint will be quickly, professionally, and objectively investigated in order to arrive at all the facts which will clear the Officer's name or substantiate the individual's complaint, whichever is appropriate.

Randall W. Gaston
Chief of Police

## POLICE COMPLAINT PROCEDURE

HOW DO I FILE A COMPLAINT? If you wish to file a formal complaint, it will be necessary for you to complete a Personnel Complaint form. You may obtain this form at the front counter of the Police Department, the City Clerk's Office, any Anaheim Public Library, the Community Services Office, or by calling or writing the Anaheim Police Department and requesting that a form be sent to you. When the Personnel Complaint form is filled out, it should be delivered to the Anaheim Police Department, 425 South Harbor Boulevard, or mailed to P.O. Box 3369, Anaheim, CA 92803-3369.

WHAT WILL HAPPEN TO THE OFFICER? It will depend on what the Officer did. If the Officer's actions were criminal, he/she could be dealt with in the same way as any other citizen. If the Officer's actions were improper but not criminal, he/she may be disciplined by the Chief of Police. If the Officer is falsely accused, the complainant may face civil and/or criminal action.

WILL I BE TOLD OF THE RESULTS OF THE INVESTIGATION? Yes. You will receive a letter from the Chief of Police advising you of the disposition of your complaint.

MESCHIEF.RWG                                                                                              JR:RWG:ml

P. O. Box 3369, Anaheim, California 92803-3369

**Figure 10-2**   (Courtesy of the Anaheim Police Department)

CITY OF ANAHEIM, CALIFORNIA
Police Department

## UN MENSAJE DEL JEFE DE POLICIA

El policia de hoy en dia trabaja en una sociedad compleja. Una de las metas del Departamento de Policia de Anaheim, es la de asegurar que al publico se le sirva de manera eficiente y efectiva por un Cuerpo de Policia lo mas altamente entrenado posible.

Usted, como una persona particular, puede ayudarnos a lograr esta meta, haciendonos saber si tiene alguna queja, la cual se investigara rapidamente, profesionalmente y objectivamente, para asi poder descubrir los hechos que absolveran de toda culpa el nombre del agente de la Policia, o justificaran la queja de la persona particular, cualquiera de las dos que sea la apropiada.

Randall W. Gaston
Jefe de Policia

## PROCEDIMIENTO PARA PRESENTAR UNA QUEJA

¿COMO REGISTRO UNA QUEJA? Si usted desea registrar una queja formal, sera necesario que complete una forma que usted puede obtener en la oficina de la policia de la ciudad de Anaheim, la oficina del escribano de la ciudad (office of the City Clerk), cualquier sucursal de la biblioteca, la oficina de servicios de la comunidad, o puede llamar o escribir al departamento de policia de Anaheim para solicitar una forma por correo. Cuando complete la forma, devuelva al departamento de policia de Anaheim, 425 South Harbor Boulevard, o mandela por correo al P.O. Box 3369, Anaheim, CA  92803-3369.

¿QUE LE PASARA AL AGENTE DE LA POLICIA? Esto depende en lo que haya hecho. Si cometio una accion criminal, se le tratara igualmente como cualquier otra persona que haya cometido una accion similar. Si fue una accion impropia, el Jefe de la Policia se encargara de disciplinarlo. Si por el contrario, se determina que usted hizo una queja falsa a sabiendas, se le puede someter a un proceso civil o criminal.

¿ME DIRAN EL RESULTADO DE LA INVESTIGACION? Si. Usted recibira una carta del Jefe de la Policia, donde la comunicaran la accion que tomo tocante su queja.

MESCHIEF.RWG

JR.RWG:ml

P. O. Box 3369, Anaheim, California 92803-3369

**Figure 10-2** *(Continued)*

ANAHEIM POLICE DEPARTMENT

PERSONNEL COMPLAINT/QUEJA DEL PERSONAL     File Number:

Print your NAME, ADDRESS and PHONE NUMBERS, BUSINESS & HOME / En Letra de Molde Escriba su Nombre, Domicilio, y Numeros de Telefono, Trabajo Y Casa

Print the DATE, TIME and LOCATION OF THE INCIDENT / Fecha, hora y Sitio del incidente

Print the NAMES, ADDRESSES and PHONE NUMBER OF any Witnesses / Nombres, Domicilios y Numeros de Telefonos de Testigos

DESCRIBE the incident in detail. Begin in the space below and if more space / Describa en detalle el incidente. Empiece en el espacio de abajo, y si necesita mas espacio, is needed, continue on a second sheet. Sign all pages.     continue en una segunda hoja. Firme todas las paginas.

YOU HAVE THE RIGHT TO MAKE A COMPLAINT AGAINST A POLICE OFFICER FOR ANY IMPROPER POLICE CONDUCT. CALIFORNIA LAW REQUIRES THIS AGENCY TO HAVE A PROCEDURE TO INVESTIGATE CITIZENS' COMPLAINTS. YOU HAVE THE RIGHT TO A WRITTEN DESCRIPTION OF THIS PROCEDURE. THIS AGENCY MAY FIND, AFTER INVESTIGATION, THAT THERE IS NOT ENOUGH EVIDENCE TO WARRANT ACTION ON YOUR COMPLAINT. EVEN IF THAT IS THE CASE, YOU HAVE THE RIGHT TO MAKE THE COMPLAINT AND HAVE IT INVESTIGATED IF YOU BELIEVE AN OFFICER BEHAVED IMPROPERLY. CITIZEN COMPLAINTS AND ANY REPORTS OR FINDINGS RELATING TO COMPLAINTS MUST BE RETAINED BY THIS AGENCY FOR AT LEAST FIVE YEARS. IT IS AGAINST THE LAW TO MAKE A COMPLAINT THAT YOU KNOW TO BE FALSE. IF YOU MAKE A COMPLAINT AGAINST AN OFFICER KNOWING THAT IT IS FALSE, YOU CAN BE PROSECUTED ON A MISDEMEANOR CHARGE.

I have read and understood the above statements, and have presented true and accurate facts. I understand that if I knowingly make a false accusation. I may be subject to criminal or civil action.

USTED TIENE EL DERECHO DE HACER UNA DEMANDA EN CONTRA DE UN OFICIAL DE POLICIA POR CUALQUIER CONDUCTO INAPROPIADO. LA LEY DE EL ESTADO DE CALIFORNIA REQUIERE QUE ESTA AGENCIA TENGA UN PROCESO PARA INVESTIGAR DEMANDAS DE CIUDADANOS. USTED TIENE EL DERECHO A UNA DESCRIPCION ESCRITA DE ESTE PROCESO. ESTA AGENCIA PUEDE ENCONTRAR, DESPUES DE INVESTIGAR, QUE NO HAY DEMASIADA EVIDENCIA PARA TOMAR ACCION EN SU DEMANDA. AUNQUE ESO SEA EL CASO, USTED TIENE EL DERECHO PARA HACER LA DEMANDA Y TENERLA INVESTIGADA, SI USTED CREE QUE UN OFICIAL DE POLICIA SE COMPORTO INAPROPIADO. DEMANDAS DE CIUDADANOS Y CUALQUIER REPORTES O ENCUENTROS RELACIONADOS A DEMANDAS TIENEN QUE SER MANTENIDAS POR ESTA AGENCIA POR LO MENOS DE CINCO AÑOS. ES ENCONTRA DE LA LEY HACER UNA DEMANDA QUE USTED SEPA QUE ES FALSA. SI USTED HACE UNA DEMANDA EN CONTRA DE UN OFICIAL DE POLICIA, SABIENDO QUE ES FALSA, USTED PUEDE SER PROCESADO(A) POR UN CARGO DE LEY.

Yo e leido y entiendo los datos de harriba, y e presentado datos eficientes y verdaderos. Yo entiendo que si ago una acusacion falsa sabida, yo estoy subjeto a accion criminal o civil.

Signature/Firma _____     Date / Fecha _____

FORM ISSUED BY: _____     DATE: _____

FORM RECEIVED BY: _____     DATE: _____

ASSIGNED TO: _____     TIME: _____

APD-296  Rev. 1/96

DISTRIBUTION:  WHITE - Special Investigations, GREEN - Chief, CANARY - Division Commander, PINK - Watch/Bureau Commander, GOLDENROD - Complainant

**Figure 10-2**   (Continued)

The role of the supervisor during phase 3 is normally in an advisory role to the police manager. More than anyone else, the immediate supervisor should be able to evaluate the overall conduct and performance level of his or her staff and, if a penalty is indicated, to determine how severe it should be. Or, conversely, the supervisor may argue that (1) the officer should be exonerated, (2) unfounded (the act did not occur), or (3) not sustained (insufficient facts to make a determination). If the charge against the officer is sustained, then the supervisor can recommend one of the following penalties:[3]

- Oral reprimand
- Written reprimand
- Remedial training
- Loss of time or of annual leave in lieu of suspension
- Suspension up to thirty days (but no longer)
- Removal from service

## Phase 3: Adjudication

1. A complaint disposition should be classified as sustained, not sustained, exonerated, unfounded, or misconduct not based on the original complaint.
2. Adjudication and, if warranted, disciplinary action should be based partially on recommendations of the involved employee's immediate supervisor.
3. An administrative fact-finding trial board should be available to all police agencies to assist in the adjudication phase. It should be activated when necessary in the interests of the police agency, the public, or the accused employee, and should be available at the direction of the police chief or upon the request of any employee who is being penalized in any manner that exceeds verbal or written reprimand. It should be advisory to the chief.
4. The accused employee should be entitled to representation and logistical support equal to that afforded the person representing the agency in a trial board proceeding.
5. Police employees should be allowed to appeal a chief's decision. The police agency should not provide the resources or funds for appeal.
6. The chief should establish written policy on the retention of internal discipline complaint investigation reports. Only the reports of sustained and, if appealed, upheld investigations should become a part of the accused employee's personnel folder. All disciplinary investigations should be kept confidential.
7. Administrative adjudication of internal discipline complaints involving a violation of law should neither depend on nor curtail criminal prosecution. Regardless of the administrative adjudication, every police agency should refer all complaints that involve violations of law to the prosecuting agency for the decision to prosecute criminally. Police employees should not be treated differently from other members of the community in cases involving violations of the law.

[3]Ibid., p. 492.

## Structured Exercise 10-3

Your Name _____

Organizational Unit Assessed _____

**INSTRUCTIONS.** The purpose of this index is to permit you to assess your organization with regard to its conflict-management climate. On each of the following rating scales, indicate how you see your organization as it actually is right now, not how you think it should be or how you believe others would see it. Circle the number that indicates your sense of where the organization is on each dimension of the Conflict-Management Climate Index.

### 1. Balance of Power

| 1 | 2 | 3 | 4 | 5 | 6 |
|---|---|---|---|---|---|

Power is massed either at the top or at the bottom of the organization.

Power is distributed evenly and appropriately throughout the organization.

### 2. Expression of Feelings

| 1 | 2 | 3 | 4 | 5 | 6 |
|---|---|---|---|---|---|

Expressing strong feelings is costly and not accepted.

Expressing strong feelings is valued and easy to do.

### 3. Conflict-Management Procedures

| 1 | 2 | 3 | 4 | 5 | 6 |
|---|---|---|---|---|---|

There are no clear conflict-resolution procedures that many people use.

Everyone knows about, and many people use, a conflict-resolution procedure.

### 4. Attitudes toward Open Disagreement

| 1 | 2 | 3 | 4 | 5 | 6 |
|---|---|---|---|---|---|

People here do not openly disagree very much. "Going along to get along" is the motto.

People feel free to disagree openly on important issues without fear of consequences.

### 5. Use of Third Parties

| 1 | 2 | 3 | 4 | 5 | 6 |
|---|---|---|---|---|---|

No one here uses third parties to help resolve conflicts.

Third parties are used frequently to help resolve conflicts.

## 6. Power of Third Parties

| 1 | 2 | 3 | 4 | 5 | 6 |
|---|---|---|---|---|---|

Third parties are usually superiors in the organization.

Third parties are always people of equal or lower rank.

## 7. Neutrality of Third Parties

| 1 | 2 | 3 | 4 | 5 | 6 |
|---|---|---|---|---|---|

Third parties are never neutral, but serve as advocates for a certain outcome.

Third parties are always neutral as to substantive issues and conflict-resolution methods used.

## 8. Your Leader's Conflict-Resolution Style

| 1 | 2 | 3 | 4 | 5 | 6 |
|---|---|---|---|---|---|

The leader does not deal openly with conflict but works behind the scenes to resolve it.

The leader confronts conflicts directly and works openly with those involved to resolve them.

## 9. How Your Leader Receives Negative Feedback

| 1 | 2 | 3 | 4 | 5 | 6 |
|---|---|---|---|---|---|

The leader is defensive and/or closed and seeks vengeance on those who criticize him or her.

The leader receives criticism easily and even seeks it as an opportunity to grow and learn.

## 10. Follow-Up

| 1 | 2 | 3 | 4 | 5 | 6 |
|---|---|---|---|---|---|

Agreements always fall through the cracks; the same problems must be solved again and again.

Accountability is built into every conflict-resolution agreement.

## 11. Feedback Procedures

| 1 | 2 | 3 | 4 | 5 | 6 |
|---|---|---|---|---|---|

No effort is made to solicit and understand reactions to decisions.

Feedback channels for soliciting reactions to all major decisions are known and used.

## 12. Communication Skills

| 1 | 2 | 3 | 4 | 5 | 6 |
|---|---|---|---|---|---|

Few, if any, people possess basic communication skills or at least do not practice them.

Everyone in the organization possesses and uses good communication skills.

## 13. Track Record

| 1 | 2 | 3 | 4 | 5 | 6 |
|---|---|---|---|---|---|

Very few, if any, successful
conflict-resolution experiences
have occurred in the recent past.

Many stories are available of
successful conflict-resolution
experiences in the recent past.

### Conflict-Management Climate Index Scoring and Interpretation Sheet

**INSTRUCTIONS:** To arrive at your overall Conflict-Management Climate Index, total the ratings that you assigned to the thirteen separate scales. The highest possible score is 78 and the lowest is 13. Then compare your score with the following conflict-resolution-readiness index range.

| Index range | Indication |
|---|---|
| 60–78 | Ready to work on conflict with little or no work on climate. |
| 31–59 | Possible with some commitment to work on climate. |
| 13–30 | Very risky without unanimous commitment to work on climate issues. |

Assess your overall score. If in a group setting, compare your bottom-line results to others in your group. Attempt to explain your lowest and highest scores per item. Use case examples when possible.

---

## PREVENTING THE PROBLEM EMPLOYEE

*Leadership is the lifting of a man's vision to higher sights, the raising of a man's performance to a higher standard, the building of a man's personality beyond its normal limitations. Nothing better prepares the ground for such leadership than a spirit of management that confirms in the day-to-day practices of the organization strict principles of conduct and responsibility, high standards of performance, and respect for the individual and his work.*

—Peter F. Drucker
*Management* (New York: Harper and Row, 1974), p. 5

As a supervisor, you hold a responsibility for producing the type of leadership that Drucker writes about. Quickly reread his admonition to you. Now recognize and keep this in focus as you supervise others: Some problem employees simply do not want to change their negative attitudes and malcontent behavior. And, in spite of your efforts, they won't. That's the bad news. However, with time many will cast off their negative shell. That's the good news!

---

Your difficult workers are likely to be few in number.

---

All the preceding chapters are focused on helping you in "problem employee prevention." Furthermore, if it should occur, how to correct a person's counterproductive attitude and behavior was discussed. Your difficult workers are likely to be few in number. Nonetheless, you'll find yourself expending considerable energy and thought in bringing them back on board the team.

## MOST OFTEN . . .

Most often you are likely to experience reasonably cooperative individuals forming into perfectly difficult groups. These groups come in all sizes and possess a wide range of values and purposes. Sometimes the values and purposes are confusing, even covert in nature: for example, the leader of a neighborhood watch program that patiently seeks burglary prevention, but in reality is attempting to build a political base to eventually run for a city council seat. At times the values and purposes conflict with existing departmental policies and professional ethics. A case in point here are police associations and unions; for example, they may tell their members "reduce your productivity," while you are telling them not to. (Paradoxically, you may be a union member.)

## SEXUAL HARASSMENT

Since 1977, police managers have had to deal with increased employee rights, civil litigation and recruiting problems. But no issue is more complex than sexual harassment in the police environment. Currently, it is estimated that 15% of the sworn personnel are female, and this percentage will continue to increase. We predict that by the year 2000, one in five officers will be female. (The Equal Employment Opportunity Commission [EEOC] has targeted police agencies to have staff of which 50 percent will be women by the year 2000.)

### Legal Definition

Let us review how the legal definition of the term has evolved.

**1964**     *Civil Rights Act of 1964* is enacted. It contains a provocatively novel amendment banning job discrimination on the basis of sex, which foes of the law had hoped would derail it.

**1975**     *In the first reported sexual-harassment decision* under the new law, involving two women who claimed they suffered repeated verbal and physical abuse advances from a supervisor; Arizona federal district court rules the act does not cover such a claim.

**1977**     *Washington, federal appeals court rules that sexual harassment is discrimination* under the act, in a case in which a woman alleged that her job was abolished in retaliation for refusing a supervisor's sexual advances.

| 1980 | The EEOC issues *landmark sexual-harassment guidelines* prohibiting unwelcome sexual advances or requests that are made a condition of employment, and conduct that creates a hostile work environment. |
|---|---|
| 1986 | *U.S. Supreme Court upholds validity the EEOC guidelines* and rules that sexual harassment that creates a hostile or abusive work environment is a violation of the act. |
| 1991 | A Florida federal district court rules that nude pinups in the workplace can create *an atmosphere that constitutes sexual harassment;* a California federal appeals court rules that a hostile environment should be evaluated from the standpoint not of a "reasonable person" but of a *"reasonable woman."* |
| 1993 | U.S. Supreme Court rules that a hostile work environment need not be psychologically injurious but only *reasonably perceived as abusive.* |

## Compliance

The U.S. Supreme Court (*Meritor Savings Bank* v. *Vinson*–447 U.S. 57, 1986) decided that the policy of "no unwanted sexual advances between employees and that employees must report this type of unwanted conduct to management," will not comply with all the mandates cited by the Vinson Ruling.

What can police agencies do to comply? Establishing preventive policies and training will lessen the likelihood of liability if a complaint is filed.

Sexual harassment is more than supervisory employees making demands for sex on the threat of adverse employment decisions. Employers may also be liable for physical and verbal conduct of a sexual nature that has the purpose or effect of creating a hostile work environment. It is behavior that is indicative of a "hostile atmosphere" such as sexually stereotyped insults and jokes, demeaning propositions and remarks, indecent or vulgar comments, staring or ogling that causes discomfort or humiliation, demands for dates that are viewed as offensive, and physical harassment.

Sexual harassment is behavior that has been admitted where the question was hostile environment. This is proved when there is evidence that other employees were treated in the same manner and when employees of the same sex as the offender found the conduct offensive.

> Sexual harassment is more than supervisory employees making demands for sex on the threat of adverse employment decisions.

## Protection

How can a department protect itself from this liability?

- Have an explicit anti-harassment policy.
- Publicize and enforce the policy.
- Make clear that the hostile environment-type of harassment is covered.
- Regularly and repeatedly publish the policy.
- Establish a grievance system that allows employees to report all incidents of sexual harassment.
- Administratively and promptly investigate all allegations. If the allegations are sustained and warrant the discipline of the offending employee, you should consider entering into a compromise with the offended employee to reduce the chance that he or she would seek further remedy outside the department.
- Communicate the facts and the resulting discipline to the relevant employees (don't use names). Re-enforce that this type of behavior will not be tolerated and that discipline can result.

## NEGOTIATIONS: GETTING TO YES

If you will commit yourself to the supervisor's role and hope to approach its fulfillment, then the following is equally logical and practical in respect to coping with difficult groups of people. First, think of yourself as a change agent, better still—a negotiator. Second, act like one.

Whether a work group or a group of citizens, they will on occasion pose for you, as a supervisor, problems, issues, conflicts, obstacles, and confrontations. It is up to you, and perhaps some others, to perform the following:

| Dysfunctional | Supervisor Negotiates | Functional |
|---|---|---|
| Problems | into | Potentialities |
| Issues | into | Initiatives |
| Conflicts | into | Challenges |
| Obstacles | into | Opportunities |
| Confrontations | into | Cooperation |

Being an adept negotiator is important to your success as a supervisor because (1) you are destined to experience conflicting situations and groups, and (2) you are in a front-line position to convert potentially negative conflict into positive problem solving.

## GENERAL APPROACH FOR NEGOTIATING DIFFERENCES

Negotiation is a basic means of getting what you want from others. It is back-and-forth communication designed to reach an agreement when you and the other side have some interests that are shared and others that are opposed. More and more occasions require negotiation; conflict is a growth industry. Everyone wants to participate in decisions that affect them; fewer and fewer people will accept decisions dictated by someone else. People differ, and they use negotiation to handle their differences.

Conflict resolution techniques may be applied at any of several pressure points. Their effectiveness and appropriateness depend on the nature of the conflict and on the supervisor's style of supervision. The major challenge, however, is not the elimination of conflict and ambiguity from organizational life; it is the containment of these conditions at levels and in forms that are at least humane, tolerable, and low in cost and which at best might be positive in contribution to individual and organization.

Because of the wide range of problems to be solved by the supervisor, the *process* of resolving conflicts rather than particular issues will be emphasized. Once the process has been mastered, actual problem solving should become all the easier. From this point on we will refer to the supervisor when seeking to resolve conflict as a third-party *intervener*. The strategy, in turn, can be called *process intervention*. More often than not, when intervening the supervisor will find that to solve the problem, she or he must develop the following: direct structural changes into the organization, new criteria of selection and placement, tolerance and coping abilities of individuals, and a stronger interpersonal bond among organizational members.

### Intervention: Where, When, and How?

Where, when, and how to intervene in a dispute, if at all, are the most fundamental choices to be made by the supervisor. Even before these decisions must come the realization that she or he cannot wait for others to request that intervention in a dispute. Moreover, the supervisor must not become a silent observer of "people" problems. The police supervisor—that is, the effective supervisor—has to be alert for organizational arguments and, once they are detected, must rapidly attempt to resolve them. The supervisor must, in a single work, *intervene*! Once the police supervisor has decided to intervene, follow-up decisions must be made:

- Should the place of conflict resolution be entirely neutral to all parties (the disputants and the supervisor), or should it be geared to assist one or the other? For example, if the supervisor decides to hold the meeting in his or her office, the location would tend to reflect that aura. But if the supervisor chooses to resolve the participants' problems at a social meeting, personal power would be manifested.
- Should the place of conflict resolution be formal or informal? To illustrate, if the supervisor insists on job titles being used during group interaction, then considerable formality occurs. But if the situation permits the use of first names, informality will result. (It is just as easy, and much more effective, to state, "Joe, you're wrong!" as compared to "Officer Cline, the department is hereby and herein reprimanding you for inappropriate activities.")

- Should the time period allowed for conflict resolution be short or long? By this we mean, "You two have a problem—please think it through and, when decided, report back to me" or "You two are constantly arguing—resolve your difficulties before the day is over!"
- Should the supervisor include himself or herself and/or others in the argumentative dialogue, or is it best limited to the disputants? This is to say, "It's just the two of you—closet yourselves and please come forth with a reasonable solution to your problems."

Based on the preceding decisions, certain additional activities on the part of the police supervisor become necessary:

- Refereeing the discussion (often heated) between employees
- Recommending a format that should be followed during the dialogue
- Providing clarification of information important to one another
- Assisting in the discussion by offering feedback
- Seeking to identify the issues that caused the conflict
- Suggesting a means of communication that would promote discussion
- Indicating the problems in interpersonal communications
- Constant counseling relative to the primary goals and standards of the department as they impact on the conflict

The aim of "creative" conflict resolution is integration that allows both parties to achieve their objectives. The basic goal is a win-win approach rather than a win-lose approach. However, the latter is much more common in our competitive society, and it does indeed take creative conflict management to find integrative solutions. A confrontation mode might or might not facilitate achieving integrative results. It can mean getting all the cards on the table, expressing goodwill in empathizing with alternative viewpoints, and actively seeking solutions that satisfy both (or all) protagonists. Obviously not easily done, but certainly possible.

## Intervention: Supervisory Attributes

Certain attributes of the supervisor and of his or her relations with the disputants influence the supervisor's ability to perform the functions and implement the interventions described previously. The following attributes are required of the third party (supervisor): establishing professional expertise, exerting power, and manifesting neutrality and candor.

PROFESSIONAL EXPERTISE.    The supervisory attributes that give the principals confidence in entering an open confrontation and facilitate confrontation processes include (1) diagnostic skill, (2) behavioral skills in breaking impasses and interrupting repetitive interchange, (3) attitudes of acceptance, and (4) a personal capacity to provide emotional support and reassurance to all involved.

**PERSONAL POWER.** The real or perceived power of the supervisor and her or his general knowledge of the principals, issues, and background factors are important attributes. At least moderate knowledge of the principals, issues, and historical factors usually is an advantage. It not only enhances the supervisor's credibility with the principals but also increases the likelihood that her or his intervention will be on target. Also, the prior knowledge reduces the amount of time that the principals spend talking to the supervisor rather than each other (this admittedly is not always an advantage). One factor arguing against a supervisor's being highly knowledgeable about the issues and persons involved is that it is harder for the principals to believe she or he does not have her or his own opinions, about either the issues or the persons' views, which disqualify her or him as a disinterested party.

**NEUTRALITY.** Naturally, differences in the supervisor's relationships to the two principals can influence effectiveness. Three different types of supervisory justice and balance are critical: Is the supervisor neutral with respect to outcome? Is the supervisor attitudinally equally distant from the parties in a personal sense? Does the supervisor eliminate rules for handling differences that would inadvertently create an advantage for one and a disadvantage for the other?

**SELF-REALITY.** "To thine own self be true" is the crux of the message contained herein. It is *not* important that the supervisor's personal style or the way she or he comes across to others be taken into account to more fully understand her or his power. Moreover, it *is* critical for the general theory and practice of conflict resolution to know that such personal attributes and styles do condition the role and the behavior of the person. Those involved in the process have to believe that the supervisor is attempting to impartially and accurately "redress the balance" between the differing parties.

### Interventions: Conflict "Prevention"

Since conflict is inherent in organizations, what can the police supervisor do in the face of the inevitable? If the supervisor is wise, he or she will be alert to the demands imposed on his or her subordinates and offer them the support of his or her authority and position and his or her knowledge and experience in resolving conflict. The supervisor must also review conflicting demands frequently, for they will not remain static over time. As the organization and its members adjust to changes in technology, personnel practices, and the types of people joining the organization, the expectations of those who impose demands will change as well. Therefore, detection of group and interpersonal conflict requires periodic analysis and definition of position content.

Frequent consultation with subordinates, open communication between organizational levels, joint problem-solving meetings, and management by objectives are all means to detect the existence of role conflict. Once the nature of recurring conflicts is understood, it is possible to collect information useful in resolving them.

## SEVEN STEPS YOU CAN TAKE FOR GETTING TO YES

*Candor, when properly used, is one of the most powerful, effective—and underused—negotiating techniques I know of.*

—Mark H. McCormack
*What They Don't Teach at Harvard Business School*
(New York: Bantam Books, 1984), p. 16

Whether in police work, personal business transaction, or our own family, we reach most decisions through negotiation. Even if we go to court, we almost always negotiate a settlement before trial. Although negotiation takes place every day, it is not easy to do successfully. Our natural approaches for negotiation often leave us and others dissatisfied, fatigued, or withdrawn—and frequently all three.

---◆◆◆◆◆---

Whether in police work, personal business transactions, or our own family, we reach most decisions through negotiation.

---◆◆◆◆◆---

We find ourselves in a "Catch 22." We envision two ways to negotiate, easy or tough. The easy negotiator wants to avoid personal conflict and so makes concessions readily in order to reach agreement. This person wants an amicable resolution; yet he or she often ends up exploited and feeling bitter. The tough negotiator perceives any situation as a highly competitive contest of wills in which the side that takes the more extreme positions and perseveres *wins*. Such people need to win; yet they often end up creating an equally tough response, which exhausts them and their resources and harms their relationship with the other side. Other typical negotiating strategies fall between tough and easy, but *each includes an attempted trade-off between getting what you want and getting along with people.*

### A Better Way

There is a third and better way for you as a supervisor to negotiate. It is neither tough nor easy, but oddly *both*! It can be referred to as *principled negotiations*.[4] This approach strives to decide the issues on their merit rather than who wins. It urges that you look for mutual gains wherever possible and that, where your

[4]Much of the methodology described in this section is excerpted from Roger Fisher and William Ury, *Getting to Yes: Negotiating Agreement Without Giving In* (Boston: Houghton Mifflin, 1976).

interests conflict, you should agree that the result be based on fair standards, independent of your will and that of your adversary. The method of principled negotiations is tough on the merits, easy on the people. It employs no tricks and no posturing.

Principled negotiation shows you and your opponent how to obtain what you are entitled to and still be civil. It enables you to be equitable while protecting both of you against being taken advantage of. What follows is an all-purpose strategy. Unlike almost all other conflict-resolution strategies, if your adversaries learn this one, it does not become more difficult to use; it becomes easier. If they read this chapter, all the better for the two of you.

### First: Don't Bargain Over Positions

When we bargain over our positions, we tend to lock ourselves into those positions. The more we clarify our position and defend it against attack, the more committed we become to it. As more attention is paid to positions, less attention is devoted to meeting our underlying concerns. Agreement becomes less likely. Any agreement reached may reflect a mechanical balance of the difference between final positions, rather than a solution carefully forged to meet our legitimate interests.

1. Arguing over positions creates, at best, unsatisfactory agreements.
2. Arguing over positions is inefficient because the conflicting parties usually start at an extreme position and stubbornly hold to it, while at times making small concessions. This is highly time-consuming and thus inefficient.
3. Arguing over positions endangers an ongoing relationship because each side tries to *force* the other to change its position.
4. When there are many parties involved, all of the above is compounded because coalitions are formed.

### Second: Being Nice Is Not the Answer

Many people understand the high costs of hard positional bargaining, particularly on the parties and their relationship. They hope to avoid them by following a more pleasant style of negotiation. Instead of seeing the other side as adversaries, they prefer to see them as "friends." Rather than emphasizing a goal of victory, they emphasize the necessity of reaching agreement. In a soft negotiation game the standard moves are to make offers and concessions, to trust the other side, to be totally affable, and to yield as necessary to avoid confrontation. However, any negotiation focused on the relationship runs the risk of producing a weak agreement. More seriously, pursuing a soft and friendly form of positional bargaining makes you vulnerable to someone who plays a hard game of positional bargaining. In positional bargaining, a hard game dominates a soft one. The remedy for playing hardball is *not* pitching marshmallows.

The answer to the question of whether to use soft positional bargaining or hard is "neither." Change the game! The new game proposed to you is referred to as principled negotiation or negotiation on the merits. It consists of four basic points. Each point deals with a basic element of negotiation and suggests what you should do about it.

**1.** People: Separate the people from the conflict.
**2.** Interests: Concentrate on interests, not positions.
**3.** Options: Generate a variety of options before deciding what to do.
**4.** Criteria: Insist that the solution be based on some objective standard.

Each point is examined further in the sections that follow.

### Third: Separate the People from the Conflict

This point acknowledges that you and I are creatures of strong emotions who often have radically different perceptions and have difficulty communicating clearly. Emotions typically become entangled with the objective merits of the problem. Taking positions just makes this worse because people's egos become identified with their positions. Hence, before working on the substantive problem, the "people problem" should be disentangled from it and dealt with separately. We should see ourselves as working side by side, attacking the problem, not each other. Hence the first proposition: Separate the people from the conflict.

### Fourth: Concentrate on Interests, Not Positions

The second point is designed to overcome the drawback of concentrating on people's stated positions when the object of a negotiation is to satisfy their underlying interests. A negotiating position often obscures what you really want in a conflicting set of situations. Compromising between positions is not likely to produce an agreement that will effectively take care of the human needs that led people to adopt these positions. The second basic element of the method is to *concentrate on interests, not positions.*

### Fifth: Generate a Number of Options

The third point responds to the difficulty of designing optimal solutions while under pressure. Trying to decide in the presence of an adversary narrows your vision. Having a lot at stake inhibits creativity. So does searching for the right answers. Keep in mind that, usually, there is more than a single right solution or answer to the conflict.

Set aside a designated time within which to think up a wide range of possible solutions that advance shared interests and creatively reconcile differing interest. Hence, the third basic point: Before trying to reach agreement, invent numerous options for mutual gain.

### Sixth: Adopt Objective Criteria

Where interests are directly opposed, an officer may be able to obtain a favorable result simply by being stubborn. That method tends to reward intransigence and produce arbitrary results. However, as a sergeant you can counter such an officer by insisting that his or her single say-so is not enough and that the agreement must reflect some fair standard independent of the naked will of either side. This does not mean insisting that the terms be based on the standard you select, but only that some fair standard such as custom, expert opinion, prior decisions, or law determine the outcome.

By discussing a fair criteria rather than what the parties are willing or unwilling to do, neither party need give in to the other; both can defer to a fair solution. Hence the fourth basic point: Adopt objective criteria.

## Seventh: Take Three More Steps

The four basic propositions of principled negotiations are relevant from the time you begin to think about negotiating a solution to a conflict until the time either an agreement is reached or you decide to stop the effort. That period can be divided into three steps: analysis, planning, and discussion.

1. *Analysis.* During the analysis step you are simply trying to diagnose the situation—to gather information, organize it, and think about it. You will want to consider the people problems of biased perceptions, hostile emotions, and unclear communication, as well as to identify your interests and those of the other side. You will want to note options already on the table and identify any criteria already suggested as a basis for agreement. (Because police personnel are trained investigators, this step could be a natural one.)

2. *Planning.* During the planning step you deal with the same four elements a second time, both generating ideas and deciding what to do. How do you propose to handle the people problems? Of your interests, which are most important? And what are some realistic departmental objectives? You will want to generate additional options and additional criteria for deciding among them.

3. *Discussion.* Again during the discussion step, when the parties communicate back and forth looking toward agreement, the same four elements are the best subjects to discuss. Differences in perception, feelings of frustration and anger, and confusion in communication can be acknowledged and addressed. Each side should come to comprehend the interests of the other. Both can then jointly generate options that are mutually beneficial and seek agreement on objective standards for resolving opposed interests.

Remember that "anger" is only one letter away from "danger."

## Structured Exercise 10-4

Tackle the following cases using the "seven steps for getting to yes." Have one member of your group serve as an observer and recorder of the deliberations. When finished with each case, critique your problem-solving process in respect to the seven steps.

**PROBLEM 1.** Ten workers, all over fifty years of age, from the department's Communications and Data Processing Unit have submitted a letter of complaint to the chief about the status of the older workers in their unit. As they explain it, the nature of the communications and data processing systems operation is such that college-trained younger people are constantly being brought into the unit to work on a part-time basis. These youngsters, in their view, are more interested in short-term benefits and working procedures than are the older workers. When initially receiving the complaint, the chief told them that considerable savings are achieved by the employment of the younger workers. The older employees have hinted they may seek redress through the Fair Employment Practices Commission. What should the chief say and do at this point?

**PROBLEM 2.** The captain in command of Uniform Field Operations Bureau (patrol and traffic) has complained bitterly to the chief on two occasions that the department's Special Operations Bureau (SOB) has significantly reduced the quality of police–citizen relationships. He has asserted that the personnel in his unit are making every effort to provide just and effective law enforcement. The captain finds that the SOB, however, disrupts the development of a mutually supportive police–community relation by its heavy-handed tactics. When questioned, the lieutenant in charge of the SOB indicated that his special enforcement staff was clearly successful in reducing major felonies. Furthermore, he implied that perhaps the captain was getting "soft" and could best be assigned elsewhere. The chief is convinced that both individuals are dedicated and professional individuals. Also, both have highly commendable performance records with the department. How should the chief resolve this situation?

**PROBLEM 3.** Sixty percent of the detectives in the investigations unit filed a grievance regarding their performance evaluations. The percentage of grievances has been going steadily upward. The chief is beginning to think that the reason for this occurrence is that a grieving employee almost always gets some portion of his rating raised. Increasingly it appears that the feeling among the detectives seems to be "why not" or "if the other guy does it, I had better also." How should the immediate situation be handled? What should be done in the long run?

---

## SUMMARY

In contrast to positional bargaining, the principled negotiation method of emphasizing basic interests, mutually satisfying options, and fair standards normally produces a wise agreement. The method permits you to reach a solid consensus on a joint decision efficiently without all the emotional costs of digging into positions only to have to dig yourself out of them. And removing people from the problem allows you to deal directly with the other negotiator as a human being, thus making possible a fair agreement.

## KEY POINTS

- Human conflict is a natural, and therefore a normal, phenomenon.
- It is up to the supervisor to convert dysfunctional conflict into productive energy.
- The first person to motivate is—yourself!
- Conflicts emanate from (1) existing conditions; (2) our attitudes; (3) our thoughts; and (4) our behavior.
- The creation of an internal investigations unit does *not* relieve the supervisor of his disciplinary duties.
- Citizen complaints start with the receipt of the complaint. Next comes an investigation, and finally an adjudication.
- As a conflict resolver, the supervisor usually negotiates between opposing factions.
- When intervening in a conflict, a supervisor should rely on his or her professional expertise, personal power, neutrality, and self-reality.
- In negotiating ("getting to yes"), do not bargain over positions or believe that being nice will resolve the conflict.
- Furthermore, in negotiating separate the people from the conflict; concentrate on interests, not positions; generate a number of options; adopt objective criteria; and analyze, plan, and discuss the proposed solution to the conflict.

## DISCUSSION

1. Have you witnessed conflict being a plus for an organization? If so, describe how it occurred and what the results were.
2. How have you dealt with a problem employee (co-worker, boss, subordinate) of late? Were you successful or not? Why?
3. Conflict can be a positive force. Why? Give examples.
4. Of the four supervisory attributes needed for successful intervention (professional expertise, etc.), which is the most and least important for success?
5. Why not bargain over positions? Any examples?
6. Develop an actual or hypothetical conflict. Now apply the key steps in principled negotiations to it. Critique the results.

# RESPONSIBILITY ELEVEN

———◆»x«◆———

# *Stress*

The police supervisor is responsible for combating distress and maintaining wellness within the work group.

*The height of human wisdom is to bring our tempers down to our circumstances, and to make a calm within, under the weight of the greatest storm without.*

—Daniel Defoe

Being motivated (R-6), setting goals (R-7), sharing power (R-8), and handling conflicts (R-10), together are an interactive and dynamic force which entails a lot of change—and with change comes stress (R-11).

Victor Frankl was a psychiatrist and a Jew. He was imprisoned in the death camps of Nazi Germany, where he directly experienced the living hell of the Holocaust. Except for his sister, his entire family died. He suffered torture and the daily uncertainty of being sent to the gas ovens. (At this point, we're disclosing the ultimate in *distress*.)

One day, naked and alone in a small room, he became aware that his Nazi captors *could not take away his freedom or power to choose, within himself, how all of the threats, punishment, and injustices were going to affect him.*

Through his disciplined mind, and applying mainly his memory and imagination, he exercised his freedom of choice until he actually had more freedom than his captors. He survived the death camps, and wrote and lectured about his experiences for many years thereafter.

Why this story? Every day we have many choices facing us. One choice is for using stress or incoming demands for change as a positive force for wellness.

## STRESS: THE DEMAND FOR CHANGE

All of us have been, are now, and will continue to be stressed. Some of us can control stress, which is the nonspecific response to a demand for change, better than others. Some people can anticipate it in some situations, while it surprises others. How one copes with stress—and there are certainly a number of things to cause stress that are associated with police supervision—determines how one behaves, thinks, and feels. Too much stress is clearly not good and, ironically, too little stress is not healthy. Unless stress is harnessed and converted into a "steady state," over time, stress will make one ill—perhaps very ill.

―――――◆◆◆◆◆◆◆◆―――――

Stress is the nonspecific response to a demand for change.

―――――◆◆◆◆◆◆◆◆―――――

Stress, the demand for change, can either arrive from an external source or may be generated from within. The main thing to do is to recognize that every-one is destined to be stressed. First, it is critical that one be aware of being stressed. There are scientifically documented signs and events that can disclose when one is being stressed and to what extent or degree. Second, there are proven techniques not only for coping with *distress* (the injurious type), but, more importantly, converting it into *eustress* (the favorable type). Relaxation exercises are one example of a method for controlling stress. We have a choice, to either cope with and thus master stress or to allow it to wear and tear us.

## RESPONSIBILITY OF THE POLICE SUPERVISOR

The responsibility of the police supervisor is to understand and effectively deal with the individual and organizational implications of stress in police work.

### Individual Implications

There seems to be a "stress fad" or syndrome in police organizations today. Granted, police work is a stressful occupation. But so are many others. We can assure you that the business supervisor, fire captain, supervising nurse, con-struction supervisor, and so on, experience stress in their daily activities. What counts is that the supervisor (1) know when stress has become too much or too little, and (2) maintain a stress reduction or wellness program. This applies to both the supervisor and his or her assigned personnel.

―――――◆◆◆◆◆◆◆◆―――――

Stress in daily life is natural.

―――――◆◆◆◆◆◆◆◆―――――

Police supervision is largely a constant process of adaptation to the "spice of life" that is change. The prescription for health and happiness is (1) to successfully adapt to everchanging circumstances, and (2) to remember that the penalties for failure to adjust to change are illness (physical and mental) and unhappiness. Interestingly, the very same stressful event or level of stress that may make a person ill can be a motivating experience for someone else. It is through the *general adaptation syndrome* (GAS) that the various internal organs, especially the endocrine glands and the nervous system, help one (1) to adapt to the constant changes that occur in and around one and (2) to navigate a reasonably steady course toward whatever one considers a meaningful purpose.

As a police supervisor, then, you should understand that:

- Stress in daily life is natural, pervasive, unavoidable, and thus to be expected.
- Depending on how one copes with stressful events, the experience of stress can be positive (healthy and happy) or negative (sick and unhappy).
- Since people differ in a variety of ways, each person's means and success in coping with stressful incidents will vary.
- There is a mental–physiological mechanism, known as the general adaptation syndrome, that assists one to adjust to demands for change.
- By definition, stress is the nonspecific response of the body to any demand for change. The demand can be from within, or from one's surrounding environment.
- Police supervisors are subjected to megachanges. As a result, they typically experience high levels of stress.
- The supervisor is in a key position to help others cope with stressful events.

## Organizational Implications

A major concern for the police manager and supervisor is the effects of stress on job performance. The stress–performance relationship resembles an inverted bell-shaped curve, as shown in Figure 11-1. At low stress levels, individuals maintain their current level of performance. Under these conditions, individuals are not activated, do not experience any stress-related physical strain, and probably see no reason to change their performance level. If not supervised well, a person could become bored, lazy, and a poor performer.

On the other hand, under conditions of moderate stress, studies indicate that people are activated sufficiently to motivate them to increase performance. Stress, in modest amounts, acts as a stimulus for the individual, as when a police supervisor has a tough problem to solve. The toughness of the problem often pushes supervisors to their performance limits. Similarly, mild stress can also be responsible for creative activities in police personnel as they try to solve challenging (stressful) problems.

Finally, under conditions of excessive stress, individual performance drops markedly. Here the severity of the stress consumes attention and energies, and individuals focus considerable effort on attempting to reduce the  stress. Little

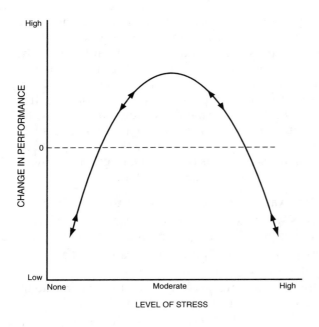

**Figure 11-1** Relationship between Stress and Job Performance

energy is left to devote to job performance, with obvious results. Some refer to this as *burnout*.

Here it is important for the supervisor to recognize that

- Stress has a significant relationship to job performance.
- Very low or very high stress levels can be counterproductive.
- Moderate amounts of stress can be a positive influence in a work setting.

## STRESS AS A DEMAND FOR CHANGE

Stress is essentially reflected in the rate of all the wear and tear caused by life. Although stress cannot be avoided, a great deal has been learned about how to keep its damaging side effect, which is distress, to a minimum. For instance, it has been demonstrated that many common diseases are largely due to errors in the adaptive response to stress of humans, rather than being due to direct damage by germs, poisons, or life experience. In this sense, many nervous and emotional disturbances, high blood pressure, gastric and duodenal ulcers, and certain types of sexual, allergic, and cardiovascular disorders appear to be essentially *diseases of adaptation*.

### Medical Findings

Research on stress was limited because there were no objective, measurable indexes to assess it, until it was found that stress causes certain changes in the structure and chemical composition of the body, which can be accurately studied. Some of these changes are merely signs of *damage;* others are indications of the body's *adaptive reactions* (its mechanism of defense against stress). The totality of these changes, the GAS, develops in three stages: (1) the alarm reaction, (2) the stage of resistance, and (3) the stage of exhaustion.

The *nervous system* and the *endocrine* (or hormonal) *system* play particularly important parts in maintaining resistance to stress. They assist in keeping the structure and function of the body steady, despite exposure to stressor agents (e.g., tension, wounds, infections, and poisons). This steady state is defined as *homeostasis*.

In summary, the response to stress involves a threefold mechanism, consisting of (1) the direct effect of the stressor on the body, (2) internal responses that stimulate tissue defense or help to destroy damaging substances, and (3) internal responses that cause tissue surrender by inhibiting unnecessary or excessive defense. Resistance and adaptation depend on a proper balance of these three factors. Specific steps to protect yourself and your personnel are covered later in the section on "wellness." But, for now, realize the most standard medical textbooks attribute anywhere from 50 to 80 percent of all disease to psychosomatic or stress-related origins. And stress-related psychological and physiological disorders have become the major social and health problem in the last decade. Stress-induced disorders have long since replaced epidemics of infectious disease as the major medical problem of the postindustrial nations.

## Turbulent Changes, Supervising, and Stress

*Stress that is handled properly can be an invigorating force in relationships, at work, and in self-development, providing one knows how to control its negative effects.*

—Sidney Lecker, M.D.
*The Natural Ways to Stress Control* (New York: Grosset and Dunlap, 1978), p. 6

————◆◆◆◆◆————

Planning for change, not just for the sake of change, but for survival, is more than a new discipline—it's a whole new theory.

————◆◆◆◆◆————

The promise of the future for any person in a police supervisor role is a life of increased change and thus increased stress. The accelerating rate of change is a reality. Toffler's *Future Shock* and Naisbett's *Megatrends* are present and operating in our lives. Planning for change, not just for the sake of change but for survival, is more than a new discipline—it's a whole new theory. If we are to better control situations of stress, we must place more emphasis on the better control of self and the police work we must do to enhance our professional growth and development.

Selye writes:

> *Many scientific studies were performed to establish the stressor effects of executive responsibilities in middle and top management, relative to that of subordinate employees in various occupations. Undoubtedly, executive responsibilities, if taken very seriously, produce severe distress with somatic and psychic manifestations often*

*conducive to actual disease. However, here, as in all considerations of stress mani-festations, conditioning factors must be taken into account, for whatever a person's position in the hierarchy of command, the stressor effect of his decision-making depends mainly upon the way he reacts to it.*[1]

## Structured Exercise 11-1

The way to reduce physical stress is relatively simple. The principle underlying physical stress control is that it is impossible for anyone to exist in two contra-dictory states simultaneously. You cannot be short and tall at the same time. You cannot be pregnant and not pregnant concurrently. Vigor and fatigue cannot coexist. Similarly, it is impossible to be stressed and physically relaxed at the same time. If you know how to find a state of physical relaxation and how to sustain it, you will be better able to prevent the occurrence of physical stress overload, and you will be able to control excessive tension once it has occurred.

A stress-control formula is useful here. You need to learn how to focus on phys-ically relaxed states, how to rehearse physical relaxation responses until they can be achieved quickly and with ease, and then learn when and how to implement the physical relaxation response at a time preceding or during a stressful event.

Focusing on a physically relaxed state is achieved by three means:

First, use diaphragmatic breathing in slow, four-second "in" and four-second "out" excursions to assist the relaxation process. Lie down on a flat surface, facing up, and place your hand on your stomach. When you breathe in, your stomach should slowly rise, because the diaphragm, acting like a piston, moves out of the chest cavity to suck air into your lungs. At the same time, the diaphragm descends into the abdominal cavity, pushing your intestines down and forward—the cause of your rising stomach. Exhale slowly, and your stomach falls. Your rib cage should be quite still. It is only needed during extreme exertion. Breathing to a count of four on each inhalation and exhalation is a restful breathing pattern.

Second, you must learn to relax your muscles and blood vessels. When your blood vessels are relaxed, your hands feel warm. When the blood vessels in your body are tense, your hands feel cold and clammy. You can increase the warmth of your hands by focusing on the sensations in your hand as it rests on the arm of the chair beside you. You can feel the texture of the arm of the chair upon which your hand rests. Whatever the room temperature may be, your hands can feel the sensations of airy coolness as well as of warmth. If you wish to intensify the warmth, simply keep "warmth" in a relaxed focus in your mind. Imagine lying on a sunny beach with the sun beating down on your hand. Imagine your body filling up with warmth from the toes on up.

[1] Hans Selye, *The Stress of Life,* 2nd ed. (New York: McGraw-Hill, 1976), p. 15. Chapter 5 is primarily based on Selye's research and writings on stress—and appropriately so. Selye "discov-ered" stress in 1936. Often referred to as "Dr. Stress," Selye has been a member of the University of Montreal faculty for over thirty years and in 1978 founded the International Institute of Stress in Montreal. He continued to add to the growing body of knowledge on stress until nearly eighty years of age.

To relax your muscles, you can take the hand that is gently resting on the arm of the chair beside you and tense all your fingers without pressing them into the chair. Your hand will feel like it is hovering just above the arm of the chair. Tense muscles make your limbs feel light. Now relax your arm, wrist, and fingers. The limb will feel heavy as it slouches on the arm on the chair.

Third, starting from the top of your head and proceeding through every muscle and joint in your body down to your toes, contract each muscle to feel the sensation of tension—the lightness—and then feel the weight and heaviness associated with muscular relaxation.

You must now learn to rehearse warming your hands, relaxing your muscles and joints, and breathing slowly with your diaphragm. Take about twenty minutes to do so. Do not watch the clock—just guess at a time span of roughly twenty minutes, and rehearse the relaxation of your breathing, blood vessels, and muscles.

While relaxing your body, you may wish to simultaneously relax your mind by using a mind-focusing exercise. When I practice relaxation, I breathe in cycles of three breaths repeating in my mind.

*Breath 1.* Give up caring
*Breath 2.* Heavy and warm
*Breath 3.* Breathe and relax

As distractions enter my consciousness, I do not let them trouble me, even if they temporarily throw me off my pattern. I simply resume my slow, three-breath cycle of

*Breath 1.* Give up caring
*Breath 2.* Heavy and warm
*Breath 3.* Breathe and relax

When you have rehearsed these relaxation exercises for a period of several days, you can then begin to implement them in your daily life.

---

## SOURCES AND FORMS OF STRESS: THE STRESSORS

The police supervisor will experience stress from one of three sources: personal, environmental, and organizational/social. The first source is within the individual; the latter two are external. Most often they present their demands for change in combination with one another. Let us explore the sources in more detail and then focus our attention on the four types of stress they produce for all employees in a police organization.

### Three Sources of Stress

**PERSONAL.** A review of all the possible personal or inner stressors would be impossible here. They can range from sexual disorders, through grief due to the loss of a loved one, to a fear of flying. We will center on those that are directly or potentially job related. Roughly, they can be assigned to one of two categories: our emotions and our power base.

**EMOTIONS.** The majority of us have received absolutely no training in how to deal with our own emotions. At best, we have probably been given some advice on what to do during emotional periods; for example, being told that "there is nothing to fear but fear itself" when we are feeling frightened. Such advice is rarely ever truly helpful in overcoming the effects of the emotion. There are five very potent emotions that you should be able to recognize and deal with: depression, anxiety, guilt, failure, and disapproval. More will be said about these five emotions later when we discuss stress-reduction methods.

Responsibility One covered this subject. You may recall that a value is an enduring belief that a particular course of action (means or goal) is to be preferred over an alternate one and that values cause us to *behave* in certain ways, to *want* to behave in certain ways, to *think* in certain ways, and to *feel* in certain ways. Obviously, they are extremely important to us. Hence, "we are what we value." Values can induce stress when there is a conflict between one's own needs and the need for one's own values, and the alarm called anxiety may go off. Many people do not know how to use this alarm and either fear or idealize it, instead of understanding that it is simply a signal that is calling attention to some process. When one sets one's values too high or exacting, one then becomes vulnerable to feelings of failure and guilt, and if one fails to identify or consider one's values, one opens oneself to depression.

**POWER.** The position of supervisor involves both the *right* to supervise and the *opportunity* to lead others. The right to supervise is centered in the position of police-supervisor, while the opportunity to provide leadership is centered in one's personal ability to do so. Since supervision and power are closely allied, they both involve stress and responsibility. Police supervisors who feel the pangs of stress are usually responding to the use of supervisor power (by them or others) to cause change. For some, the term "Power" suggests a negative action. We look at it as a potential force for good.

**ENVIRONMENTAL.** The environmental stressors can be labeled as either technological, economic, or political. Frequently, an environmental stressor can be assigned to all three. For example, the computer is causing numerous and profound technological changes for the police manager (interactive terminals in the office). Economically, they require capital outlay and maintenance. And politically, they imply power. Pollution in the work setting can be stressful (noise, air, filth, etc.). Insufficient work space often elevates tension. We could continue, but we believe you know what they are because you're probably experiencing some of them right now.

**ORGANIZATIONAL/SOCIAL.** In this instance we will catalog the stressors as too much, too little, uncertain conditions, and problem personalities. Although posed in a job sense, many demands for change will occur via the family and other nondepartmental relationships.

**Too Much.** There are two types of input overload or hyperstress: quantitative and qualitative. *Quantitative input overload* is a result of simple demands, but too many of them for the time allotted—for example, too many phone calls to make, memos to read, or meetings to run in the time allowed. Increases in blood pressure, pulse rate, and cholesterol are associated with quantitative input overload. *Qualitative input overload* is a result of complexity and of limited time. There are not as many jobs, but the time allotted to do these jobs is less than is needed to do them up to standard.

**Too Little.** Low levels of mental and physical activity can cause hypostress; that is, hypostress is caused by quantitative and qualitative input underloads. Naturally, certain forms of hypostress (such as recreation and self-reflection) are eustressful (desirable); but if a protracted period of nothingness is experienced, one may be confronted with hypostress, which is distressful (undesirable). Similar to hyperstress, hypostress can be either good or bad, depending on how one adjusts to its demands.

**Uncertain Conditions.** A police supervisor is responsible for making decisions (often high-risk ones) under above-average conditions of uncertainty. Herbert A. Simon alluded to this situation when he described programmable decisions in comparison with nonprogrammable decisions. (The supervisor frequently experiences an arena of nonroutine, nonprogrammable, high-risk decision making.)

Clearly, the bureaucratic, decision-making, operational turf of a police supervisor is filled with ambiguity and confusion, which may be stress inducing.

**Problem Personalities.** Certain types of personalities commonly act as stressors. We realize that a police supervisor often simply cannot stay clear of these types of personalities; indeed, his or her agency may be plagued with more than its fair share of them, and the supervisor may find them in his or her primary social groups. However, whenever feasible, you should minimize your exposure to them. Who are these problem personalities? (Some introspection may be helpful here, in that you ought to ask yourself if you are one of those defined.)

- *Type A behavior.* Aggressive, competition for the joy of competing, in a hurry, impatient, tense, concentration on self-interest.
- *The worrier.* Rehearsing disaster scenarios, dependent, fatalist, frequent pain.
- *The guilt-tripper.* Overdose of conscience, rear-view-mirror thinking, cynical, contrite at all costs, humble to a fault.
- *The perfectionist.* Can be done better, faster, cheaper; drugged in optimism; ignores success and focuses on failure.
- *The winner.* Addicted to winning, number one at all costs; nothing for fun, all for victory; creates competitive situations; belittles the loser.
- *WSM.* The Whining, Sniveling, Malcontent; every organization has a few. WSMs actively seeks opportunities to carp, complain, and voice displeasure. Conversely, the WSMs are never available to correct any of the reasons for their constant woes.

## Four Types of Stress

Figure 11-2 depicts the four major dimensions that comprise stress or change:

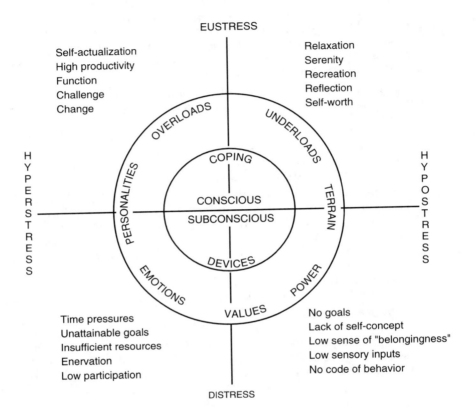

**Figure 11-2**  Coping with Stress

**1.** *Hyperstress.* Overloaded with change

**2.** *Hypostress.* Underloaded with change

**3.** *Eustress.* Favorable or positive changes

**4.** *Distress.* Unfavorable or negative changes

The main sources of stress (see again Figure 11-1) are implicit in each section of Figure 11-2.

Our coping mechanisms are divided into two basic categories: the subconscious and the conscious. Space does not permit adequate treatment of the subconscious mechanisms, but, essentially, the subconscious coping techniques are developed through our formative years and we have learned to rely on one or more much like a reflexive action. The conscious coping techniques are those that one can test and use to reduce stress and perhaps even to convert distress into eustress.

## DETECTING ONE'S STRESS LEVEL

### General Signs of Stress

Our mind and body report stress in many ways. For example, when stressed we may experience the following discomforting feelings:

- Dry throat
- Nervous tic
- Stomach disorders
- Pounding of the heart
- Elevated blood pressure
- Inability to concentrate
- Muscle spasm
- Insomnia
- Sweating
- Migraine headaches

Unfortunately, many of these symptoms are either ignored or fail to alert our senses. We may be experiencing excessive stress, not coping well if at all, and thus exposing ourselves to any number of diseases.

*Clearly, it is important for the police supervisor to develop a perceptual capability for accurately detecting signs and symptoms of distress within himself or herself and others.*

### Specific Signs of Stress

We now offer you an opportunity to assess your own and others' existing stress level. The four questionnaires should be self-administered (1) once a year, (2) at the time of frequent and/or major changes in your life, or (3) when you notice certain telltale signs of mounting tension or uneasiness in you or members of your department. The scales probe for hyperstress (eustress and distress). Hypostress cannot be effectively dealt with in the pages allotted for this subject. (The majority of police supervisors rarely experience this form of stress.) The data presented following these instruments include scores with which to compare your scores.

Listed in Structured Exercise 11-2 are many organizational events that have been found to stimulate stress reactions in employees. The numerical value of each event reflects the degree of disruption it causes in the average person's life. Generally, the higher the score, the greater the probability of a significant health change in the near future. (*Note:* Because individuals vary in their tolerance for stress, the total score should be taken as a rough guide only.)

For each of the events listed in Structured Exercise 11-2 that you have experienced during the *past twelve months,* place its Value in the My Score column. If you have experienced an event more than once within the past twelve months, you may record its value *twice.* Then add all the numbers in the My Score column to obtain your total episodic, work-related stress score.

### *Structured Exercise 11-2*

**Episodic, Work-Related Stress Evaluation**

| Event | Value | My Score |
|---|---|---|
| 1. Being transferred against my will to a new assignment | 81 | _____ |
| 2. Being assigned a less important job | 79 | _____ |
| 3. Experiencing a decrease in status | 68 | _____ |
| 4. Being disciplined/reprimanded by my boss | 67 | _____ |
| 5. Having my request to transfer to a better job rejected | 65 | _____ |
| 6. Sustaining an abrupt and major change in the nature of my work | 60 | _____ |
| 7. Learning of the cancellation of an important project I was involved in | 60 | _____ |
| 8. Encountering major and/or frequent changes in policies or procedures | 59 | _____ |
| 9. Being promoted/advanced at a slower rate than planned | 58 | _____ |
| 10. Voluntarily transferred to a new position or assignment (not a promotion) | 52 | _____ |
| 11. My forthcoming retirement | 47 | _____ |
| 12. Experiencing a major reorganization in my unit | 46 | _____ |
| 13. Experiencing a sudden reduction in the number of positive strokes for my work accomplishments | 46 | _____ |
| 14. Encountering a major change (increase or decrease) in the technology affecting my job (computers, techniques) | 46 | _____ |

15. Giving a major briefing (not roll call) or formal presentation     46     _____

16. Encountering a significant deterioration in environmental conditions such as lighting, noise, temperature, space, and filth     45     _____

17. Acquiring a new boss     45     _____

18. Sustaining an immediate, significant *decrease* in the pace of my work     43     _____

19. Sustaining an immediate, significant *increase* in the pace of my work     43     _____

20. Undergoing a major physical relocation of my workplace     31     _____

21. Acquiring an increase in status     30     _____

22. Being compelled to work more hours per week than usual     29     _____

23. Experiencing the transfer, resignation, termination, or retirement of a close co-worker     24     _____

24. Being promoted or advanced at a faster rate than I expected     24     _____

25. Acquiring new subordinates     23     _____

26. Receiving a major change in my work schedule     23     _____

27. Acquiring new co-workers (peers)     21     _____

28. Experiencing an increase in the number of positive strokes for my accomplishments     20     _____

29. Encountering a significant improvement in environmental conditions such as lighting, noise, temperature, and space     17     _____

30. Undergoing a minor physical relocation of my workplace     5     _____

Total episodic, work-related stress score     _____

Listed in Structured Exercise 11-3 are many nonwork events in life that have been found to produce stress for us. The scale value of each event reflects the degree of disruption it causes in the average person's life. Generally, the higher the score, the greater is the probability of a significant health change in the near future. The severity of health change also tends to increase with higher scores. (Again, since individuals vary in their tolerance for stress, the total episodic, nonwork-related stress score should be taken as a rough guide only.)

Stressful day-to-day conditions, such as those listed in Structured Exercise 11-4, exist at work. Indicate the relative frequency with which you experience each of the following sources of stress by assigning the correct number.

**Frequency Scale**

1. Never
2. Infrequently
3. Occasionally
4. Frequently
5. Always

Listed in Structured Exercise 11-5 are several potentially stressful conditions of life at home and in our society generally. Indicate how stressful each is for you personally by selecting a number from the severity scale.

**Severity Scale**

1. Not stressful
2. Somewhat stressful
3. Moderately stressful
4. Very stressful
5. Extremely stressful

To summarize, stress both on and off the job causes disruptions, triggers a chain reaction, and requires a certain amount of personal adjustment. The more often we trigger the stress response with either kind of change event, the more likely it is that we will become ill. Although specific kinds of stress usually cannot be linked to specific diseases, with excessive stress our latent tendencies to become ill or psychologically distressed are more likely to become manifest.

Long-term stress, even after we become accustomed to it, causes pressures that induce illness, lowers our feelings of satisfaction, and inhibits growth and work effectiveness. When many *episodes* involving work-related change occur in an organization in which people are already working in long-term, highly stressful conditions, the occurrence of sick leave and the seriousness of illness, accidents, and inattention to work can increase rapidly.

## Structured Exercise 11-3

### Episodic, Nonwork-Related Stress Evaluation

| Event | Value | My Score |
|---|---|---|
| Death of spouse | 100 | |
| Divorce | 73 | |
| Marital separation | 65 | |
| Jail term | 63 | |
| Death of close family member | 63 | |
| Personal injury or illness | 53 | |
| Marriage | 50 | |
| Fired from work | 47 | |
| Marital reconciliation | 45 | |
| Retirement | 45 | |
| Change in family member's health | 44 | |
| Pregnancy | 40 | |
| Sex difficulties | 39 | |
| Addition to family | 39 | |
| Business readjustment | 39 | |
| Change in financial status | 38 | |
| Death of close friend | 37 | |
| Change to different line of work | 36 | |
| Change in number of marital arguments | 35 | |
| Mortgage or loan over $10,000 | 31 | |
| Foreclosure of mortgage or loan | 30 | |
| Change in work responsibilities | 29 | |
| Son or daughter leaving home | 29 | |
| Trouble with in-laws | 29 | |
| Outstanding personal achievement | 28 | |
| Spouse begins or stops work | 26 | |
| Starting or finishing school | 26 | |
| Change in living conditions | 25 | |
| Revision of personal habits | 24 | |
| Trouble with boss | 23 | |
| Change in work hours or conditions | 20 | |
| Change in residence | 20 | |
| Change in schools | 20 | |

| | | |
|---|---|---|
| Change in recreational habits | 19 | _____ |
| Change in church activities | 19 | _____ |
| Change in social activities | 18 | _____ |
| Mortgage or loan under $10,000 | 17 | _____ |
| Change in sleeping habits | 16 | _____ |
| Change in number of family gatherings | 15 | _____ |
| Change in eating habits | 15 | _____ |
| Vacation | 13 | _____ |
| Christmas season | 12 | _____ |
| Minor violation of the law | 11 | _____ |
| Total episodic, nonwork-related stress score | | _____ |

From *Mind as Healer, Mind as Slayer* by Kenneth R. Pelletier, Ph.D. Copyright © 1977 by Kenneth R. Pelletier. Used by permission of Delacorte Press/Seymour Lawrence, a division of Bantam Doubleday Dell Publishing Group, Inc.

———◆━◆━◆———

## Structured Exercise 11-4

———◆━◆━◆———

## Long-Term Work Related Stress Evaluation

| Frequency | Condition |
|---|---|
| _____ | 1. I am uncertain about what is expected of me. |
| _____ | 2. My peers appear unclear about what my role is. |
| _____ | 3. I have differences of opinion with my superiors. |
| _____ | 4. The demands of others for my time are in conflict. |
| _____ | 5. I lack confidence in top management. |
| _____ | 6. My boss expects me to interrupt my assigned work for new priorities. |
| _____ | 7. Conflict exists between my unit and others it must work with. |
| _____ | 8. I get feedback only when my work is unsatisfactory. |
| _____ | 9. Decisions or changes that affect me are made without my knowledge or involvement. |

_____ 10. I am expected to endorse the decisions of management without being informed of their rationale.

_____ 11. I must attend meetings to get my work done.

_____ 12. I am cautious about what I say in meetings.

_____ 13. I have too much to do and too little time in which to do it.

_____ 14. I do not have enough work to do.

_____ 15. I feel overqualified for the job I have.

_____ 16. I feel underqualified for the job I have.

_____ 17. The personnel I supervise are trained in a field that is different from mine.

_____ 18. I must go to other units (bureaus) to get my job done.

_____ 19. I have unsettled conflicts with my peers.

_____ 20. I get no personal support from my peers.

_____ 21. I spend my time "fighting fires" rather than working according to a plan.

_____ 22. I do not have the right amount of interaction (too much or too little) with others (bosses, peers, staff).

_____ 23. I do not receive the right amount of supervision (too much or too little).

_____ 24. I do not have the opportunity to use my knowledge and skills.

_____ 25. 1 do not receive meaningful work assignments.

_____ Total

List below any ongoing sources of stress you experience at work that are not included in the evaluation form.

_____

_____

_____

_____

_____

_____

## Structured Exercise 11-5

### Long-Term Nonwork-Related Stress Evaluation

| Severity | Condition |
|---|---|
| _____ | **1.** Noise (traffic, airplanes, neighbors, etc.) |
| _____ | **2.** Pollution (air, water, toxic waste, etc.) |
| _____ | **3.** Personal standard of living and ability to make ends meet financially |
| _____ | **4.** Crime and vandalism in immediate neighborhood |
| _____ | **5.** Law and order in society |
| _____ | **6.** Personal, long-term ill health |
| _____ | **7.** Long-term ill health of family member or close friend |
| _____ | **8.** Racial tensions |
| _____ | **9.** Regular drug or alcohol abuse of family member or close friend |
| _____ | **10.** Concern over future of my own career |
| _____ | **11.** Concern over values or behaviors of family members |
| _____ | **12.** Political situation in this country |
| _____ | **13.** Possibility of war |
| _____ | **14.** Concern over financing my own retirement, my children's education, and so on |
| _____ | **15.** Economic situation in this country |
| _____ | **16.** Changing morals in our society (regarding family life, sexuality, and so on) |
| _____ | Total |

List here any ongoing nonwork-related sources of stress you experience that are not included in the evaluation form.

_____

_____

_____

_____

- The four evaluation sheets have been included to help determine sources of stress.
- Is there any pattern to the four set of results?
- Is one type or source of stress more prevalent than the others?
- Discussing scores with a friend or police colleague should provide additional insights.

### Reliable Data

The four scales that you've completed vary in their reliability. But we are not implying that they are unreliable. On the contrary, many have discovered that they accurately forecast degrees of our human wellness (or lack of same). How they vary is in accordance with the individual longevity of their scientific validation. The first scale, in particular, is exceptionally well known and accepted; it has over thirty years of hard data to demonstrate its potency to detect distress.

The first step in any stress management or wellness program is to secure reliable data. The bottom-line scores are *indicants* (not guarantees) of health or, conversely, ill health. From our professional perspective and human experience, the following scores or higher should cause you reflective concern:

- Episodic, work-related      300 points
- Episodic, nonwork-related      150 points
- Long-term, work-related      64 points
- Long-term, nonwork-related      33 points

Our observations plus scientific validation of the four scales give us cause to alert you to their predictiveness. If we self-administered the scales (and we do annually), and discovered our scores on one (and especially more) of the scales to be above those cited above (ours have been so on a few occasions), then we would immediately check for signs of distress and simultaneously implement a program of wellness (we've done this too).

If practical, compare the scores you've posted with other people who have completed the scales. Focus on common and dissimilar results and particular stressors. Also, share your thoughts and feelings about the levels and types of stress you are now experiencing. Afterward, proceed to the next section, which describes some of the methods for coping with distress.

## CONVERTING STRESS INTO WELLNESS

Now that we have learned about the sources, effects, and our own stress levels, we can consider stress management and our desire for wellness. Keep in mind that *a healthy police supervisor is in much better shape to be an effective one.* Obviously, this holds true for all employees of the police agency.

Although many people associate wellness only with fitness, nutrition or stress reduction, wellness is really much more. *Wellness brings people into a domain of self-responsibility and self-empowerment.*

---

Wellness brings people into a domain of self-responsibility and self-empowerment.

---

*Set goals for wellness;* they keep you on course. And more than that, goals are like magnets—they tend to attract people and resources that help get them accomplished. It's almost magical how this happens. Often people set their sights too high and then quit completely when they don't make the grade. Approach these "impossible" goals by breaking them down into manageable parts. One part should be (we think) a keen sense of humor.

## *Structured Exercise 11-6*

---

Ed Wynn sang, "I love to laugh. It gets worse every year," in the venerable motion picture *Mary Poppins*. We can recall his laughter, sparking it ourselves. The more fun he had, the happier he became and so did we. Fun and laughter are de-stressors. There is a law—an axiom—*if you learn to laugh at yourself, you'll never run out of material.*

Norman Cousins, the former editor of *Saturday Review of Literature,* was informed by a battery of medical doctors in the 1970s that he would die within six months of a rare and untreatable disease. He tells the story of being informed and then immediately checking out of the hospital. He registered at a deluxe hotel, rented a VCR and a very humorous movie. Mr. Cousins proceeded to laugh himself well. (He also consumed 3,000 units of vitamin C a day.) After three months, the doctors reexamined him, and the terminal disease had evaporated.

There are psychobiological explanations for this miracle. The bottom line is—fun and humor are healthy for us. (By the way, Mr. Cousins laughed his way to nearly eighty years of age.)

Let us see if we can start you on a humor kick. The animals and insects in the jungle divided their ranks into two football teams. The large jungle animals were on one team, and the smaller jungle animals and insects were on the second. At half time, the large animals were ahead 28–0. The large animals received the kickoff to start the second half. On the first play, the large animals were sacked for a six-yard loss. When the players unpiled, at the bottom was a tiny centipede. The large animals sent the elephant off-tackle on the next play. Again, a loss of four yards. At the bottom of the heap was the centipede. In desperation, on third down, they ran the cheetah around end. Bang! Down he went for a seven-yard loss. Who's at the bottom of the pile—the centipede. The coach of the small animals and insects called time-out and had his team come to the sidelines. He looked at the centipede and asked, "Where in the hell were you during the first half when we needed you?" The centipede frowned and said, "Coach, I was taping my ankles."

We laughed at this cute story—it made us feel better—relaxed and non-stressed.

⬥⬦⬥

## Step 1: Affixing Responsibility

Twenty-four centuries ago in Greece, Hippocrates, the Father of Medicine, told his disciples that disease is not only suffering (*pathos*), but also work (*ponos*); that is, disease is the fight of the body to restore itself to normal. This is an important point, and one that, although being constantly reinforced during the intervening centuries, is not yet generally acknowledged even today. Disease is not a mere surrender to attack; it is also a fight for health. *Unless there is fight, there is no disease.* Or, to state this another way, our health is our *responsibility.* And we must work at it!

## Step 2: Reliable Data

While medical science continues to develop new means to keep us alive, we nullify such efforts by refusing to slow down, relax, and consume less. Our American way of life is killing people at an early age. The United States is sixteenth among countries in the world for male longevity and eighth for female longevity. (The greatest life expectancy in the industrialized world is in Sweden.) It appears that it is our life style, as well as fear of old age, that is killing us off before we reach our longevity potential. An undisciplined, random, fast-paced existence is dangerous to our wellness. It is essential that we know our varying levels of change. The two sections on general and specific stress signs afford us the opportunity to reliably measure our life change units. In knowing ourself we can, if we choose, know our stress. And, in knowing our stress factors, we are in a position to take accurate and positive action. In other words, by assuming the responsibility for your health, you automatically create the need for *reliable data* about it.

## Step 3: An Action Plan for Wellness

It seems that everyone has a particular stress-reduction program that he or she wants others to use. What works for one person, may not work for the other. Jogging, for example, may be helpful stress therapy for one public employee, while another may find it harmful to one's knees. Hence, a stress management and wellness program must be *custom designed* to meet the specific requirements of the individual.

⬥⬦⬥

A stress management and wellness program must be custom designed . . .

⬥⬦⬥

Our review of the literature on wellness and the successful adaptation to the accelerating thrust of change leads us to propose five fundamental coping strategies. The astute police supervisor will select components from one or more of these strategies and *act on them*. Briefly, here are the coping strategies to maintain our wellness and defeat the harm consequences of distress and burnout.

### SUPPORTIVE RELATIONSHIPS

- Build supportive structures in one's home, which will include sacred times, family rituals, and protected settings for recuperation. Build supportive structures within oneself, which are associated with one's own attitude toward discomfort, work, personnel needs, and the like.
- "No person is an island": This statement has proved to be an axiom in terms of mental health and coping with stressors. Each person *needs* people, especially helpful people, who will give support when one is depressed, anxious, unhappy, angry, or simply distressed. Whom do you turn to at midnight when you are experiencing a strong sense of impending failure?
- Such thinking as "Oh, I can handle that myself" or "Dealing with this problem alone will make me stronger" is not only erroneous, it can be dangerous to the point of possible injury to oneself.
- In establishing a supportive relationship, one should remember two things: (1) A supportive relationship requires cultivation; if it is unattended, it may dissolve; and (2) be certain that the relationship is reciprocal, that is, that there is both giving and taking,
- Finally, it takes *positive strokes* to develop emotionally healthy persons with a sense of OKness. Without supportive relationships the latter would be impossible.

### MENTAL DISCIPLINE

- *Step 1.* Learning to reduce the complexity and the number of tasks that confront you will help to reduce stress. You will cope more effectively when problems are handled one by one, on a priority system and in manageable installments. As we have seen displayed on car bumpers and office walls, "One day at a time."
- *Step 2.* Learning to reduce the time pressures on yourself will help to reduce stress. Nature has been good enough to give us a natural reflex for reducing time pressures when faced by overwhelming stress, but many of us fight nature's automatic mental stress-control mechanism. The old adage, "Who's going to know the difference in 100 years?" seems proper here.
- *Step 3.* Mind-focusing exercises are very helpful ways of reducing mental stress. Various meditative methods have been developed and promoted to help people unload tensions by focusing their minds on neutral thoughts, such as a mantra, a number, or deep breathing (a deep-breathing exercise concludes this chapter). In effect, meditation allows you to put down your mental burdens several times a day, to rest your mind for twenty minutes, and then to pick up your burdens once again with more mental energy. It has

been found that people who practice mind-focusing or meditation respond better to stress, and they seem to recover much more rapidly from the effects of stress than do nonmeditators.

**A Safe and Happy Place.** All of us need a comfort zone, which causes one to feel good, to feel secure, and indeed, allows one to feel one's feelings. A "safe and happy place" (SHP) should be one of your own choosing, but you must find one if you have not already done so. Your SHP may be a particular room, a camper van, a fishing stream, an athletic club, a mountain trail, a book—anything, anyplace. Moments to undergo self-renewal, relaxation, introspection, and serenity can and frequently do occur there.

### OTHERNESS

- *Step 1.* Develop the skills to read the signs of distress, anger, and depression in yourself and others.
- *Step 2.* Develop skills to listen. Most police supervisors who are concerned about doing or solving something forget how powerful and helpful it is just to be a concerned and active listener.
- *Step 3.* Tend to the people issues that are associated with changes. Remember that change is the cause of stress, so there needs to be more than just preparation for the change. There must also be aftercare, which concerns such things as listening and understanding the processes that unfold in individuals and groups after significant changes. This is not working harder, but smarter.
- *Step 4.* Put issues into words. Words are structures in themselves. Sometimes they need to be written down, particularly when one is working to build supportive structures for oneself or one's family. Problems that are terribly difficult to manage and that hang over one's head for weeks or even for years may surprisingly dissolve once they have been cast into words.

### THE THREE R'S

- *Step 1. Reading* for fun and enjoyment
- *Step 2. Relaxation* as a voluntary control of stress
- *Step 3. Recreation* as a release and as a revitalization

### ALTRUISTIC EGOISM

- Hans Selye coined the expression and advanced the practice of "altruistic egoism," which basically is *looking out for oneself,* but in an altogether different frame of reference than one might initially suspect.[3] Selye went on to reveal that this self-ism is to be developed in and around being necessary to others. Eliciting the support and goodwill of others is a key ingredient in the practice of altruistic egoism.

[3]Selye, *The Stress of Life,* pp. 452, 453.

- "Earn thy neighbor's love." This motto, unlike love on command, is compatible with our natural structure and, although it is based on altruistic egoism, it could hardly be attacked as unethical. Who would blame anyone who wants to assure his or her own homeostasis and happiness by accumulating the treasure of other people's benevolence? Yet this makes the person virtually unassailable, for nobody wants to attack and destroy those upon whom he or she depends. People are social beings. Avoid remaining alone in the midst of the overcrowded society that surrounds you. Trust people, despite their apparent untrustworthiness, or you will have no friends, no support. If you have earned your neighbor's love, you will never be alone.

### *Structured Exercise 11-7*

There are some tabloids that report on events such as "Mother Gives Birth to Eighty-Year-Old Twins." You'll find them at newsstands and markets. Recently, one of us spotted a front-page headline, "The Ultimate Secret to Stress Reduction." For $0.50 how could I go wrong? Here is what I learned.

A fellow in Canton, Ohio, buys an enormous amount of jello. When distressed, he puts it into his bathtub, gets in, and lays there until it congeals. He assured me, the reader, that it works. His worries were removed, no more troubles, aches and pains gone.

Well, I didn't try it. It made for amusing reading, though. Do you know, it probably helped him. The reason for this scenario is simply: What works for one person may not work for another.

Now, here is what I learned. Wellness programs must be custom designed. What works for me may not help you. Nonetheless, you must identify and apply those highways that avoid the barriers of distress and provide the carriers of success. At this point, construct your own unique wellness program. Good luck!

## THE GOOD NEWS

The query, "As a police supervisor, do I need to live with unusually high levels of stress?" or the assertion that "My work environment generates unavoidable distress" can be responded to with an unequivocal answer—no! Fortunately, each person has a considerable freedom of choice. Included within this infinite set of choices is one that deals with stress. Plainly put, do you, as a police supervisor, want behavioral patterns that possibly lessen your ability to cope with stress? Similarly, do you, as a police supervisor, want others to mismanage their life unit changes? Again, the obvious answer is no! Supervising police employees requires the effective managing of one's stress. This chapter has been designed to assist you to deal better with the pervasive phenomenon of stress—more specifically, *the stress of management.*

## KEY POINTS

- Stress is a demand for change.
- Stress is a natural phenomenon.
- When stress is mismanaged, it can be harmful.
- There are three sources of stress: (1) personal, (2) environmental, and (3) organizational/social.
- There are four types of stress: (1) hyperstress, (2) hypostress, (3) eustress, and (4) distress.
- Due to the very nature of the job, a police supervisor is assured of experiencing all four types of stress—especially hyperstress.
- Distress can seriously reduce the effectiveness of a police supervisor.
- The police supervisor should be alert for the general and specific symptoms of distress.
- The supervisor should maintain a program of wellness by (1) recognizing that he or she is responsible for his or her health, (2) collecting reliable data on one's stress level, and (3) designing and using a custom-designed plan for wellness.

## DISCUSSION

1. An earlier section dealt with the reality of "turbulent changes." As a group, identify the five major changes affecting you or your work group.
2. Of the four stressors listed as organizational/social, which one seems to dominate in your organization?
3. In terms of Episodic, Work-Related Stress events, to cite three events you personally feel to be the most stressful. Discuss them as a group. Be alert for similarities and uniqueness. Discuss them as a group. Be alert for similarities and uniqueness.
4. Drawing from the six strategies for wellness, custom design a stress management action plan for yourself.

# PART THREE

# *External Partnerships*

## RESPONSIBILITIES

- Twelve—Organizing

- Thirteen—Teamwork

- Fourteen—Community-oriented Policing, and Problem-oriented Policing

- Fifteen—Anticipation

# RESPONSIBILITY TWELVE

# *Organizing*

The police supervisor is responsible for designing a work structure that facilitates all employees, making a maximum contribution to accomplishing the mission of the department.

*And Moses chose able men out of Israel, and made them heads over the people, rulers of thousands, rulers of hundreds, rulers of fifties, and rulers of tens.*

*And they judged the people at all seasons: the hard causes they brought unto Moses, but every small matter they judged themselves.*

—Exodus 25-26

With all prior responsibilities attended to, the supervisor is now faced with organizing the staff into a cohesive, focused, and dynamic work unit that is capable of implementing a community-oriented policing program.

As with everything else in our lives, organizations are changing. When speaking about change today, we often hear the word "revolutionary"; for example, the revolution in communications technology. Additionally, the type or frequency of change is usually referred to as "chaotic" (or some other synonym).

Organizational change is certainly not revolutionary. At best, it has been evolutionary for some organizations. Many organizations have resisted even evolutionary or minor changes. Regardless of an organization welcoming or stonewalling change, chaos plagues organizations in their endeavors to adapt to new ways or hold fast to the old.

A lot of police organizations are making a full commitment to the implementation of community-oriented policing (COP). Some of them realize that in doing so they must change their "culture" or attitudes and skills. We agree that beliefs, attitudes, and skills need to be modified in order to support a COP effort. But unless there is also a shift in governance (how we distribute power, purpose, and rewards), the efforts will be more cosmetic than foundational.

Many of us live two lives. One life is personal with choices, freedom, interdependency, caring, loyalty, and trust. The other life is organizational with directions, control, dependency, indifference, and self-serving.

This chapter is on aspects of the police organization that have been most resistant to change, namely the distribution of power, purpose, and rewards. It seeks to reintegrate parts of ourselves with the mission of our police agencies. We start by more fully examining the concept of governance.

## GOVERNANCE

In previous chapters we have referred to management (supervision) and leadership. The concept of governance recognizes the political nature of our lives and workplace, and serves as an umbrella for both. A leader must cope with decisions on how to govern an organization. Again, governance encompasses questions about service, community, power, commitment, purpose, and achievement.

---

The concept of governance recognizes the political nature of our lives and workplace, and serves as an umbrella for both.

---

If those who govern (manager and/or leader) answer these questions based on a top-down, bureaucratic, hierarchical point of view, you'll get one set of answers. Those who answer with a bottom-up, agile, share form of governance give us a totally opposite approach. Top-down or bottom-up, which is best? Let us explore both types of governance, all the while recognizing that they exist in various combinations in all organizational settings.

### Top-Down Governance

The top-down organization on paper looks like a rigid pyramid. It consists of many layers of managers and prestigious job titles; it thrives on written policies and rules; it emphasizes complexity. The manager is the boss, and authority is top-down. We refer to this as the bureaucratic organization.

- *Service.* The managers decide on what types and quality of services are best for the community.
- *Community.* The people served are seen and served as being one, a sameness.
- *Power.* Power is viewed as having clearly defined boundaries. It is centralized at the top of the department.

- *Commitment.* There is top managerial commitment to their bosses and elite work groups.
- *Purpose.* The purpose of the department and its divisions is defined by top management.
- *Achievements/Advancements.* Opportunity to achieve and be rewarded for it (e.g., promotion, a better job) are limited to those that daily demonstrate a commitment to the top managers.

(Top-down governance relies on a bureaucratic organization to get the mission accomplished. Also, management is primary and leadership secondary when using this type of governance.

---

Top-down governance relies on a bureaucratic organization to get the mission accomplished.

---

## Bottom-Up Governance

The bottom-up organization on paper looks like a fluid frisbee. It consists of a few layers of leaders-managers with little attention to official emblems of rank; it thrives on flexibility and action; it emphasizes simplicity. The leader is the senior partner and authority is bottom-up. We refer to this as the agile organization.

- *Service.* The leader, in concert with his or her work team, communicates with the community to decide what is best for the customers.
- *Community.* The people served are viewed and served as individuals, as singularly unique.
- *Power.* Power is understood as being infinite. It is dispersed throughout the agency. Every employee is empowered.
- *Commitment.* Similar to power, there is an equal commitment by the department to the welfare of all employees.
- *Purpose.* The purpose of the department and its divisions is determined by people representing all levels and job assignments within the agency.
- *Achievements/Advancements.* The changes of career growth and job accomplishments are unlimited and not tied to a particular manager or preferred supervisory style.

Bottom-up governance depends on an agile organization for mission fulfillment. Further, leadership is primary and management secondary in this governance system.

---

Bottom-up governance depends on an agile organization for mission fulfillment.

---

Visualize an organization—one that you currently work for, or one that you worked for in the past. Next, respond to the following questions about the various dimensions by encircling the most appropriate number.

**1.** Service mix decided                                     Service mix decided
   at the top.                                                 by everyone.

     1      2      3      4      5      6      7

**2.** Community seen                                          Community seen
   as a whole.                                                comprised of
                                                              individuals.

     1      2      3      4      5      6      7

**3.** Power is centralized.                                   Power is dispersed.

     1      2      3      4      5      6      7

**4.** Commitment is to                                        Commitment is to
   top management                                             all employees.

     1      2      3      4      5      6      7

**5.** Purpose defined by                                      Purpose defined by
   top management.                                            all levels in the department.

     1      2      3      4      5      6      7

**6.** Achievement is judged                                   Achievement is judged
   by management standards.                                   by individual contributions.

     1      2      3      4      5      6      7

Add up the numbers. The higher the sum (36+), the more likely you are working for a governance system that is agile and in need of leader-managers. The lower the score (24−), the governance system is highly structured and in need of manager-leaders.

————●◦●◦●————

**Which One Is Best?**

All things considered, and all things being equal, the bottom-up or agile organization is the most beneficial of the two for the delivery of high-quality police services. However, in the real world of police work, not all things are considered, and all things are not equal. Thus, before a decision on what form of a governance system is best for an agency, the following questions or issues must be explored.

- How much tolerance is there for mistakes—taking risks?
- What is the nature of the community and what do they expect from their police?
- What is the skill level of the personnel?
- Do the employees support the mission of the department?
- How motivated is the staff?
- How ethical is the staff?
- How much trust is there among the personnel and among the work units?

Once the above questions have been answered and evaluated, those in power can decide on either a manager-leader or a leader-manager governance system.

---

The type of governance system selected determines which organizational design should be used.

---

The type of governance system selected determines which organizational design should be used. If manager-leader, then the bureaucratic or top-down organization is required. If leader-manager, then the agile or bottom-up organization is called for. A revolt will occur if the wrong organizational system is applied. Manager-leaders will struggle, if not fail, within an agile organizational setting. And, leader-managers will flop in a bureaucratic environment.

Structured exercise 12-2 is a *keystone for the final part of this section. Review it carefully.*

## Structured Exercise 12-2

---

Several years ago, one of your authors was a police officer and, as such, he remembers a particular patrol roll call. A newly appointed sergeant appeared and introduced himself to the twelve of us. He went on to say, "This isn't a democracy. I believe in participative supervision. I'm going to supervise, and you're going to participate. I run a benign dictatorship."

Later on that evening while on patrol, my partner remarked, "It appears that this sergeant is the same as the last. Clearly, he is not interested in our ideas or opinions. He's big into control. And, if we want to get along okay with him, then we best comply with his orders."

Several years afterward, I recalled this episode. I saw a gross paradox in our daily lives as compared to our organizational lives. First of all we live with political institutions that celebrate the rights of individuals to express themselves, to assemble, to pursue happiness and individual purposes, to pick their own political leaders. We pay enormous attention to the rights and procedures of due process. At times, we seem to be on the edge of anarchy and yet we tenaciously cling to our political beliefs. Conversely, when we shift into our occupational life, those beliefs are best ignored. Consistency, control, and compliance become the dominant values.

For many years, I faced the frustrating dilemma of how to most effectively govern an organization. I was convinced that democracy would not work. Can you imagine voting on whether we should wear uniforms; who works what assignments; ethical standards; whether to evaluate employee performance or not? I was equally convinced that while a bottom-down autocracy could work, it was filled with such pitfalls as transparent loyalty, weak commitment, low trust, poor communications, and zero risk taking.

If neither one of the above governance systems are relevant, then come the questions: What might prove successful? What is the most reliable alternative? Before reading further, think about these questions. What is your answer? Discuss it with your co-workers. The alternative follows.

———•◦✦◦•———

## The Alternative

When you empower employees, you are automatically creating a series of partnerships within an agency. Responsibility Eight, Empowerment, covered this in detail. You should recall that community-oriented policing (COP) hinged on a police department empowering its personnel. When this occurs, you have an organization comprised of interlocking partnerships.

Partnerships pave the road to an agile organization, which we mentioned earlier and will describe in detail later.

**SENIOR PARTNERS.** The agile organization with its leader-manager form of governance is not a democracy. However, we can observe several democratic principles at work in an agile organization. For example, via teamwork, the employees are encouraged to express their concerns on decisions that are going to affect them. Police associations/unions typically elect their leaders. Value statements and ethical standards usually include tenets such as justice, respect, loyalty, honor, and the like, for everyone and not a chosen few.

———•◦✦◦•———

The agile organization with its leader-manager form of governance is not a democracy.

———•◦✦◦•———

There are business firms and, on an informal basis, a few public agencies that operate as partnerships. Within each partnership, there are people identified as *senior partners*. The buck stops with the senior partner. *It is the senior partner who has overall accountability for the direction and welfare of the police department.* The senior partner is the quarterback of the team. The rest of the players share in the responsibility for winning. And they're constantly informing the quarterback on what they think is the best strategy for doing so.

---

It is the senior partner who has overall accountability for the direction and welfare of the police department.

---

- The supervisor is one of several senior partners.
- Senior partners have the ranks of sergeant, lieutenant, and so on.
- They function best in an agile organization.
- Senior partners emphasize the traits of a leader while using those of a manager on occasion.
- Senior partners are expected to empower their staff, thereby establishing a partnership.

**PARTNERS.** Community-oriented policing (Responsibility Fourteen) is in essence a partnership between the police and its community for achieving value-added, quality services. Within the agency, partnerships are also formed to undergird the overarching goal of COP.

Few occupations produce stronger working relationships than those comprising the police service. The very nature of police work generates enormous group and interpersonal cohesiveness in lateral, but seldom vertical, directions. As with everything, cohesiveness has its plus's and minus's.

*Lateral partnerships.* Line-level police officers and civilian employees are very supportive of one another. At times, their physical safety, to the point of their very life, depends on the immediate assistance of their partners in patrol, detective, traffic, and the like. The status differences between sworn and civilian employees are being erased as both realize they need each other to get the job done safely and effectively. With each rung upward, there exist partnerships among supervisors, lieutenants, and so on. However, with each advancing rank, there is more internal politics. Consequently, in many departments you will find less cooperation and more competition over resources, rewards, and recognition.

*Vertical partnerships.* Teamwork is the game plan for developing winning partnerships. Within the ranks of similar job classes, this is relatively easy to accomplish. Between ranks and job classes, it is a significant challenge, frequently frustrating the best of supervisors and managers.

At the supervisory level, teamwork is hampered and partnerships are curtailed because of the following. One of the first things a new supervisor hears is that "You're no longer one of the troops. You're a supervisor now—you're different than they are!" Second, they are trained and evaluated on their ability to get compliance within their staff by constant vigilance and control. Obviously, such supervisory behavior eliminates any hope of empowerment, which is the fuel and substance of teamwork. And, with no teamwork, forget vertical partnerships.

The good news is that many leader-managers are encouraging their police and civilian supervisors to avoid the we-they vigilance-control-compliance syndrome. *Empowerment, teamwork, and vertical partnerships are making headway. This is indeed good news for COP.*

**Groupthink.** The main threat to a governance system built on interlocking partnerships is *groupthink*. Groupthink is a terminal disease of agreement. It is teamwork in a fortress sense—up with the drawbridge when evening approaches. It is the one best way that everyone must endorse. It is a code of silence. Any disagreement means expulsion as a nonconformist—a malcontent is not to be trusted. Many of the earlier responsibilities resist and expose groupthink. Responsibility Eight, Empowerment, is especially potent in combating groupthink.

## ORGANIZATIONS

*Organizations* are social units (human groupings) deliberately constructed and reconstructed to seek specific goals. Business corporations, military units, schools, churches, and police departments are included; ethnic groups, friendship groups, and family groups are excluded. An organization is characterized by (1) goals; (2) a division of labor, authority, power, and communication responsibilities in a rationally planned, rather than a random or traditionally patterned manner; (3) a set of rules and norms; (4) the presence of one or more authority centers which control the efforts of the organization and direct them toward its goals.

### The Bureaucratic Organization

*It is only through enforced standardization of methods, enforced cooperation that this faster work can be assured. And the duty enforcing the adaptation of standards and of enforcing this cooperation rests with the management alone...*

—Frederick W. Taylor

Most police organizations are bureaucratic in nature and foster top-down governance, manager-leader systems. Nonetheless, one normally will find a few pockets of agility thinking and leader-managers in charge.

Bureaucracies are organizations that have numerous *formalized rules* and regulations. They are among the most important institutions in the world because they not only provide employment for a very significant fraction of the world's 5.6 billion population but also make critical decisions that shape the economic, educational, political, social, moral, and even religious lives of nearly everyone on Earth.

**THE FOUR CORNERSTONES OF BUREAUCRACY.** The bureaucratic organization developed over a number of centuries and finally matured in the 1930s. It is exemplified in Luther Gulick's essay "Notes on the Theory of Organization,"[1] in Mooney and Reiley's *Principles of Organization*,[2] and in Max Weber's writing on bureaucracy.[3] All these theorists were strongly oriented toward economy, efficiency, and executive control. These values, when combined, create a bureaucratic organization that has four cornerstones—division of labor, hierarchy of authority, structure, and span of control.

---

Of the four, division of labor is the most important.

---

Of the four, division of labor is the most important; in fact, the other three are dependent on it for their very existence. The hierarchy of authority is the legitimate vertical network for gaining compliance. Essentially, it includes the chain of command, the sharing of authority and responsibility, the unity of command, and the obligation to report. Structure is the logical relationship of positions and functions in an organization, arranged to accomplish the objectives of organization. Classical organization theory usually works with two basic structures, the line and the staff. Both structures can be arranged four ways: purpose, process, people (clientele), and place where services are rendered. The span of control concept deals with the number of subordinates a superior can effectively supervise. It has significance, in part, for the shape of the organization. Wide span yields a flat structure; short span results in a tall structure.

The modern bureaucratic organization evolved from the thinking and practice of

- Max Weber, who emphasized the need for rationality
- Frederick W. Taylor who concentrated on its scientific aspects
- Luther Gulick and Lyndall Urwick, who formulated principles

**WEBER: RATIONALITY.** Max Weber was a founder of modern sociology as well as a pioneer in administrative thought. Weber probed bureaucracy, here essentially synonymous with "large organization," to uncover the rational relationship of bureaucratic structure to its goals. His analysis led him to conclude

[1]Luther Gulick, "Notes on the Theory of Organization," in *Papers on the Science of Administration*, ed. Luther Gulick and Lyndall Urwick (New York: Institute of Public Administration, 1937), pp. 1–45.

[2]James D. Mooney and Alan C. Reiley, *Principles of Organization* (New York: Harper & Row, Publishers, 1939).

[3]The best-known translation of Max Weber's writing on bureaucracy is H. H. Gerth and C. Wright Mills, trans. *From Max Weber: Essays in Sociology* (New York: Oxford University Press, 1946).

that there were three types of organizational power centers: (1) traditional—subjects accept the orders of a supervisor as justified on the grounds that it is the way things have always been done; (2) charismatic—subjects accept a superior's order as justified because of the influence of his or her personality; and (3) rational-legal—subjects accept a superior's order as justified because it agrees with more abstract rules which are considered legitimate.

***Power and authority.*** The type of power employed determines the degree of alienation on the part of the subject. If the subject perceives the power as legitimate, he or she is more willing to comply. And, if power is considered legitimate, then according to Weber, it becomes authority. Hence, Weber's three power centers can be translated into authority centers. Of the three types of authority, Weber recommended that rational structural relationships be obtained through the rational-legal form. He felt that the other two forms lacked systematic division of labor, specialization, and stability and had non-relevant political and administrative relationships.

***Six safeguards.*** In each principle of bureaucracy described below, Weber's constant concern about the frailness of a rational-legal bureaucracy is apparent. His primary motive, therefore, was to build into the bureaucratic structure safeguards against external and internal pressures so that the bureaucracy could at all times sustain its autonomy. Paraphrasing Weber, a bureaucratic structure, to be rational, must contain these elements.

1. *Rulification and routinization.* A continuous organization of official functions bound by *rules.* Rational organization is the opposite of temporary, unstable relations, thus the stress on continuity. Rules save effort by eliminating the need for deriving a new solution for every situation. They also facilitate standard and equal treatment of similar situations.

2. *Division of labor.* A specific sphere of competence. This involves a sphere of obligation to perform functions which have been marked off as part of a systematic division of labor. It provides the incumbent with the necessary means of compulsion clearly defined, and their use is subject to definite conditions.

3. *Hierarchy of authority.* The organization of offices follows the principle of hierarchy; that is, each lower office is under the control and supervision of a higher one.

4. *Expertise.* The rules which regulate the conduct of an office many be *technical* rules or norms. In both cases, if their application is to be fully rational, special training is necessary. It is thus normally true that only a person who has demonstrated an adequate technical training is qualified to be a member of the administrative staff.

5. *Written rules.* Administrative acts, decisions, and rules are formulated and recorded in writing.

6. *Separation of ownership.* It is a matter of principle that the members of the administrative staff should be completely separated from ownership of the means of production or administration. There exists, furthermore, in principle, complete separation of the property belonging to the organization, which is controlled within the spheres of the office, and the personal property of the official.

Weber did not expect any bureaucracy to have all the safeguards he listed. The greater the number and the intensity of them an organization possessed, however, the more rational and, therefore, the more efficient the organization would be.

TAYLOR: SCIENTIFIC MANAGEMENT.    Frederick W. Taylor, production specialist, business executive, and consultant, applied the scientific method to the solution of factory problems and from these analyses established principles which could be substituted for the trial-and-error methods then in use. The advent of Taylor's thinking in the early 1900s, opened a new era, that of *scientific management*.

*Contributions.*    Taylor's enormous contributions lay, first, in his large-scale application of the analytical, scientific approach to improving production methods. Second, while he did not feel that management could ever become an exact science in the same sense as physics and chemistry, he believed strongly that management could be an organized body of knowledge and that it could be taught and learned. Third, he originated the term and concept of *functional supervision*. Taylor felt that the job of supervision was too complicated to be handled effectively by one supervisor and should therefore be delegated to as many as eight specialized foremen. Finally, Taylor believed that his major contribution lay in a new  philosophy of motivating workers and management.

*Enforced cooperation.*    Taylor consistently maintained—and successfully demonstrated—that through the use of his techniques it would be possible to obtain appreciable increases in a worker's efficiency. Furthermore, he firmly believed that management, and management alone, should be responsible for putting these techniques into effect. Although it is important to obtain the cooperation of the workers, it must be "enforced cooperation."

*Five methods.*    Taylor prescribed five methods for "scientifically" managing an organization. First, management must carefully study the worker's body movements to discover the one best method for accomplishing work in the shortest possible time. Second, management must standardize its tools based on the requirements of specific jobs. Third, management must select and train each worker for the job for which he or she is best suited. Fourth, management must abandon the traditional unity-of-command principle and substitute functional supervision. As already mentioned, Taylor advocated that a worker receive his or her orders from as many as eight supervisors. Four of these supervisors were to serve on the shop floor (inspector, repair foreman, speed boss, and gang boss) and the other four in the planning room (routing, instruction, time and costs, and discipline). Fifth, management must pay the worker in accordance with his or her individual output.

*Impact.*    Taylor's general approach to management is widely accepted today in production-oriented business organizations. Scientific management became a movement, which still has a tremendous influence on industrial practice. More specifically, it had a major effect on the reform and economy movements in public administration and thus also influenced police administration. Its impact on public organizations is readily apparent at the present time: One can find numerous managers and supervisors (private and public alike) who firmly believe that if material rewards are directly related to work efforts, the worker consistently responds with maximum performance.

**GULICK AND URWICK: PRINCIPLES.** While the followers of Taylor developed more scientific techniques of management and work, others were conceptualizing broad principles for the most effective design of organizational structure. Luther Gulick and Lyndall Urwick were leaders in formulating principles of formal organization.

***The first and main principle.*** Gulick and Urwick proposed eight principles, the first of which underlies and influences the seven others—*division of labor.* Their approach rests firmly on the assumption that the more specific function can be divided into its simplest parts, the more specialized (e.g., homicide investigation) and, therefore, the more skilled a worker can become in carrying out his or her part of the job. They emphasized that any division of labor must be in strict accordance with one of the following four rationales.

- The major *purpose* the worker is serving, such as designing microprocessors, controlling crime, or teaching
- The *process* the worker is using, such as engineering, medicine, carpentry, programming, or accounting
- The *person* or *things* dealt with or served, such as immigrants, victims, minorities, mines, parks, farmers, automobiles, or the poor
- The *place* where the worker renders his service, such as Hawaii, Washington, Rocky Mountains, beach resorts, college campuses, or sports arenas

### *Structured Exercise 12-3*

Small police agencies (ten or fewer employees) have little specialization. The majority of the employees are generalists, with one or two being assigned the job of chief supervisor, and clerk/dispatcher. In the medium- to large-scale departments, we find a lot of specializations (e.g., motorcycles, K-9 units, SWAT teams, field evidence technicians, field training officers and more). Now the question—*Which one of the four above rationales is most appropriate for determining how to divide the work (division of labor) in a police agency?* Think about it; discuss it. Once you have reached a conclusion, proceed with your reading. The answer follows.

No single rationale is better than the others! In practice, the rationales often overlap, are sometimes incompatible with one another, and are quite vague. For example, when looking at a police organization, it would be difficult not to conclude that the four rationales fail to provide a satisfactory guide to division of labor in that organization. Furthermore, it can be seen that the four rationales are prescriptive rather than descriptive, that they state how work should be divided rather than how work is actually divided. The planning of the division of labor in a given organization is affected by many considerations not covered by the four principles. The division may be determined by the culture in which the organization is situated, by the environment of the organization, by the availability and type of personnel, and by political factors. Organizations are made up of a combination of various layers which differ in their type of division. The lower layers tend to be organized according to area or clientele, and the higher ones by purpose or process. Even this statement however, should be viewed only as a probability. In a police organization, all four rationales operate at the same time.

**Seven additional principles.** Gulick and Urwick went on to underscore seven more principles for organizing.

1. *Unity of command.* A man cannot serve two masters. This principle is offered as a balance to the division of labor and reflects Taylor's "functional supervision."

2. *Fitting people to the structure.* People should be assigned to their organizational positions "in a cold-blooded, detached spirit," like the preparation of an engineering design, regardless of the needs of that particular individual or of those individuals who may now be in the organization.

3. *One top executive (manager).* Gulick and Urwick both strongly supported the principle of one-person administrative responsibility in an organization. Hence they warned against the use of committees and would have choked on the word "teamwork" or "partners."

4. *Staff: General and special.* The classical writers' concern about staff assistance to top management deserves special attention. When management expressed a need for help from larger and larger numbers of experts and specialists, this need immediately raised the question of the relation of these specialists to the regular line supervisors and employees. In this instance, Gulick recommended that the staff specialist obtain results from the line through influence and persuasion and that the staff not be given authority over the line. The next question to be answered was that of coordination. Top management would have more people to supervise, since they would be responsible for not only the line but also the special staff. The Gulick-Urwick answer to this problem was to provide help through "general staff" as distinguished from "special staff" assistance. Significantly, general staff are not limited to the proffering of advice. They may draw up and transmit orders, check on operations, and iron out difficulties. In doing so, they act not on their own but as representatives of their superior and within the confines of decisions made by him or her. Thus, they allow their superior to exercise a broader span of control.

5. *Delegation.* They emphasized that "lack of the courage to delegate properly and of knowledge how to do it is one of the most general causes of failure in organization." In larger organizations, we must even delegate the right to delegate.

6. *Matching authority and responsibility.* They dealt with both sides of the authority–responsibility relationship. It is wrong to hold people accountable for

certain activities if the necessary authority to discharge that responsibility is not granted. On the other side, the responsibilities of all persons exercising authority should be absolute within the defined terms of that authority. Managers should be personally accountable for all actions taken by subordinates. They set forth the widely quoted axiom that "at all levels authority and responsibility should be continuous and coequal."

7. *Span of control.* Gulick and Urwick asserted that no supervisor can supervise directly the work of more than five or, at the most, six subordinates whose work interlocks. When the number of subordinates increases arithmetically, there is a geometrical increase in all the possible combinations of relationship which may demand the attention of the supervisor.

**POSDCORB.** Gulick took the concept of "management" and defined it as consisting of seven activities—which spelled out *POSDCORB.*

- *Planning:* working out in broad outline what needs to be done and the methods for doing it to accomplish the purpose set for the enterprise;
- *Organizing:* the establishment of a formal structure of authority through which work subdivisions are arranged, defined, and coordinated for the defined objective;
- *Staffing:* the whole personnel function of bringing in and training the staff and maintaining favorable conditions of work;
- *Directing:* the continuous task of making decisions, embodying them in specific and general orders and instructions, and serving as the leader of the enterprise;
- *Coordinating:* the all-important duty of interrelating the various parts of the organization;
- *Reporting:* keeping those to whom the executive is responsible informed as to what is going on, which includes keeping him or herself and subordinates informed through records, research, and inspection;
- *Budgeting:* all that goes with budgeting in the form of fiscal planning, accounting, and control.

**BUREAUCRACY IN REVIEW.** The words "bureaucracy" and "bureaucrat" have negative connotations. If we do not like an organization, we can label it a "bureaucracy." If we do not like a government worker, we can call him or her "bureaucratic." This is an injustice to both the organization and the person. To use these terms belies the fact that all organizations of a few or more people, and all workers are to some degree bureaucracies and bureaucrats—even the agile ones and leader-managers/partnerships. While at times inefficient and frustrating, we need them to convert disorder into order.

<hr />

It is the "one right way" of thinking that gets bureaucracies into trouble.

<hr />

The theoretical underpinnings of bureaucracy were built on three inter-locking cornerstones: rationality of structure, scientific management, and principles of organization. One way of classifying these three concepts is as follows: First, *Weber's writing was primarily descriptive;* however, it did indicate that a particular form of organizational structure was preferable. Second, the theories of both *Taylor and the Gulick-Urwick team were prescriptive;* that is, they expressed the *one right way* to manage and organize a body of people. It is the "one right way" thinking that gets bureaucracies into trouble. The agile organization rejects such thinking with its motto "there are many right ways."

## The Agile Organization

*AN ORGANIZATIONAL STRUCTURE, once created, should be flexible and responsive to the developing needs of the organization and changes.*

—David Packard

Success today and in the future depends on police organizations that can create new knowledge that results in value-added services. Success now and in the future will depend on police employees who have a passion for the profession, who generate new ideas—ways of doing things that result in new knowledge, which in turn result in innovative and unique services. With these current and future demands, do we want to place our bet on consistency, control, and compliance?

The agile organization and its partnership form of governance are not an idle, idealistic dream. They exist. Admittedly, most of them are in the private sector. They are beginning to emerge in government—we see police agencies evolving as agile organizations.

CONTINUITY AND CHANGE. The governance system of an agile organization is constantly reconfiguring in order to balance continuity (its core values) and change (internal and external cultural and technological demands). The agile organization and its primary components are shown in Figure 12-1. The subsections that follow briefly describe each of the seven components.

————◆▸◉◂◆————

The governance system of an agile organization is constantly reconfiguring in order to balance continuity and change.

————◆▸◉◂◆————

### Speed
- Today's environment, with its virtually real-time information exchanges, demands that an institution embrace speed.
- Faster, in almost every case, is better! From decision making to performance making to communications to services, speed, more often than not, ends up being the success differentiator.
- If it's worth doing, it's worth doing poorly.

# THE AGILE ORGANIZATION

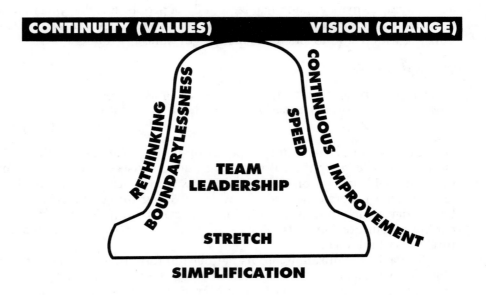

**Figure 12-1**  The Agile Organization

### *Boundarylessness*

- An obsession for finding a better way—a better idea—be it a source, a colleague, another organizational unit, or a neighboring organization, or one on the other side of the globe that will share its ideas and practices.
- Aligned with boundarylessness behavior is a rewards system that recognizes the adaptor or implementer of an idea as much as the originator.
- Creating this open, sharing element magnifies the enormous and unique strength of an organization—an endless stream of new ideas and best practices.
- Deploy "seam teams." These are work teams that link-up, integrate two or more operations. For example, traffic units that work as a common unit to combat a drug infested area.
- Bureaucracy bashing is insuring that written rules, memorandums and the like do not hamper operational efficiency. The larger the operations manual, the more it will burden an agency.
- Tier trashing is keeping the number of horizontal levels to a minimum. The more tiers the more inefficiency. Remember keep it simple, keep it lean.

### *Stretch*

- In an organization where *boundarylessness,* openness, informality, and the use of ideas from anywhere—and *speed*—with its bias for action—are increasingly a way of life, an overarching operating principle—*stretch*—is a natural outgrowth.
- Stretch, in its simplest form, says, "Nothing is impossible," and the setting of stretch targets inspires people and captures their imaginations.
- Stretch *does not* mean "commitments are out." Stretch can occur only in an environment where everyone is totally committed to a rigid set of core values—integrity, trust, quality, boundaryless behavior—and to outperforming every one of it global competitors in every market environment.
- Stretch *does* mean we are not fixated on a meaningless, internally derived, annual budget number that does nothing but make bureaucrats comfortable.
- A stretch atmosphere replaces a grim, heads-down determination to be as good as you *have* to be, and asks, instead, how good *can* you be?

### *Simplification*

- The overlay for speed, boundarylessness, stretch, and everything else you do is simplification!
- De-complicate everything you do.
- Straightforward communications to one another and even simpler to your customers.
- The efficacy of statistics, budget data, and the like will be measured by their simplicity; and that simplicity will improve their quality, their cost, and their speed in reaching the intended consumer.

### *Rethinking*

- At least annually, compare the performance of an operation or an agency with the performance of all others (benchmarking) with the best becoming the standard to be met by all the following year.
- Conventional policy making ranks programs and activities according to their good intentions; rethinking ranks them according to results.
- On a routine basis reinventions should be expected and not celebrated as unique.
- Downsizing *per se* is not rethinking—it may cause "amputation before diagnosis." It can be a casualty rather than a cure.
- Rethinking is identifying the activities that are productive, those that should be strengthened, promoted, and expanded.
- Rethinking does not give us answers but forces us to ask the right questions.
- Particular focus on
  —performance objectives
  —quality objectives
  —cost objectives
- See "continuous improvement."

### Continuous improvement
- Ongoing evaluation of everything that you do.
- Particular focus on:
  —performance objectives
  —quality objectives
  —cost objectives
- Link the improvements to some form of an incentive or recognition.
- Incremental improvements *before* the service reaches a peak or goal.

### Team leadership
- Team leadership = a swarm of people acting as one; folks that have left behind their self-interest; they manage things and lead people; and with people, fast is slow and slow is fast—it takes time.

---

With people, fast is slow and slow is fast.

---

- There is no place for halfhearted interest or halfhearted effort.
- Even the most capable managers have trouble in transiting from an emphasis of command-and-control type managing (micromanaging) to team leadership. Cause: Simple human nature—reclaiming the sandbox for themselves—reverting to old habits. "Corecracking of a team is like having a baby tiger given to you; it does a wonderful job of keeping the mice away for about twelve months, and then it starts to eat the kids."
- Transitional tips: (1) Don't be afraid to admit ignorance; (2) think about what you take on, not what you give up; (3) learn when and where to intervene; (4) get used to learning on the job; and (5) learn to really share (let go) power.

AGILITY IN REVIEW.    Some of the elements of agile organizations are often in place. We frequently see innovative personnel rating systems, self-managing teams, total quality efforts, partnerships, customer attentiveness, and flattened pyramids. They are rarely, however, put together in a pervasive governance strategy. As a result, we end up too often working against ourselves. We share control with the left hand and take it back with the right. One moment we are on the fast track toward agility and the next moment we are instituting more bureaucratic controls.

Figure 12-1 depicts the pivotal role that the team leader-manager has in striking a balance between continuity (core values) and vision (change). The demand for change is constant. Those managers and supervisors who are overly comfortable in their jobs prefer a rigid and stable organization as compared to a flexible and agile one.

One organization confronted such a situation as follows.

## *Structured Exercise 12-4*

————◆·❈·◆————

It was at our team-building sessions that it became clear that some of the rhetoric heard at the top level—about involvement and excitement and turning people loose—did not match the reality of life at the line level. The problem was that some of our managers and supervisors were unwilling, or unable, to abandon big department, big-shot autocracy and embrace the values we were trying to grow. So we defined our leader-manager styles, or "types," and how they furthered or blocked our values. And then we acted.

Type I not only delivers on performance commitments but also believes in and furthers our values. The trajectory of this group is "onward and upward," and men and women who comprise it will represent the core of our senior leadership into the next century.

Type II does not meet commitments, nor share our values—nor will it last long here.

Type III believes in the values but sometimes misses commitments. We encourage taking swings, and type III is typically given another chance.

Type IV. The "calls" on the first two types are easy. Type III takes some judgment; but Type IV is the most difficult. One is always tempted to avoid taking action, because Type IV's deliver short-term results. But Type IV's do so without regard to values and, in fact, often diminish them by grinding people down, squeezing them, stifling them. Some of these learned to change; most couldn't. The decision to begin removing Type IV's was a watershed—the ultimate test of our ability to "walk the talk" but it had to be done if we wanted our employees to be open, to speak up, to share and to act boldly outside traditional "lines of authority" and "functional boxes" in this new learning, sharing environment.

————◆·❈·◆————

## A CASE FOR AGILE ORGANIZATIONS

The way a police department is structured affects individual motivation and performance. There are bureaucratic organizations in which the person at the top issues an order and it is passed on down the line until the person at the bottom does as he or she is told without question or reason. This is precisely the type of police organization we are arguing against. We are convinced that the objectives of COP can best be achieved by people who understand and support them and who are allowed flexibility in working toward common goals in ways that they help determine are best for their operation and their department.

## KEY POINTS

- Governance includes leadership and management plus the political nature of our organizational lives.
- Top-down governance is found in bureaucratic organizations.
- Bottom-up governance is found in agile organizations.
- A bottom-up or leader-manager style of governance is not a democracy.
- It is imperative that there is a fit between the type of governance and the type of organizational structure.
- Senior partners are accountable for the overall mission of the department.
- Of all the cornerstones and principles of bureaucracy—division of labor is the most important.
- The agile organization maintains a balance between consistency and change.

## DISCUSSION

1. How can authority be bottom-up?
2. How do partnerships differ from democratic organizations? And what is the responsibility of the senior partners?
3. Thinking about your organization, how bureaucratic is it? How agile is it?
4. We intentionally did not pose any questions about Structured Exercise 12.4. Reread the exercise and discuss the merits and downside of this department's approach for achieving value compliance.

# RESPONSIBILITY THIRTEEN

---◆━✕━◆---

# *Teamwork*

The police supervisor is responsible for leading a group of independently minded employees, with all of their vast diversity, and blend them into an interdependent team.

*We must all hang together, else we shall hang separately.*

—Benjamin Franklin, on signing the Declaration of Independence

All of the prior responsibilities (R-1 to R-12) are now fused with mutual trust and team training in order to effectively deliver community-oriented police (R-14) services.

---

One of a baby's earliest words is "mine." We enter the world totally dependent on others for our very survival. Most of us are encouraged as we grow up to be independent—to be self-sufficient, to be competitive. We place a high value on being independent. But, Steve Covey argues that being *interdependent* is a higher value than being dependent.

As we grow and mature, we become increasingly aware that all of nature is interdependent, that there is an ecological system that governs nature including society and the organizations within it. We further discover that human life also is interdependent.

Let us look at maturity as a continuum.

- Dependence is seeing the world in terms of *you*—you take care of me; you help me; you're responsible for me.
- Independence is seeing the world in respect to *I*—I can do it; I am responsible; I can choose.

- Interdependence is the model of *we*—we can do it; we can cooperate; we are responsible.

Dependent people need others to get what they want. Independent people can get what they want by their own effort. Interdependent people combine their efforts—form a team—to achieve their goals.

It is the successful supervisor who realizes the need for the best thinking, a coordinated effort, mutual support to be truly effective. Independent supervisors who do not have the maturity to think and act interdependently may be good individual producers, but *they won't be good leaders or team players.*

Teamwork depends on people who are willing to function as interdependent contributors. For this to occur, they must first trust one another and then be trained to operate as a team. This section centers on the need for *interdependency* as compared to independence or dependency. In the two sections that follow, we'll cover the important advantages of team performance. We then deal with the *trust* and *training*, which are the two essential underpinnings for team building. Finally, we will direct our attention to the major hurdle confronted by any endeavor to foster teamwork—*cultural diversity.* Work groups that are trained in interdependency evolve into teams. This team approach will be the hallmark of the great police departments of the twenty-first century. We are convinced of it.

## WHY TEAMS?

————◆·✕·◆————

> Police services are too complex and the respective technologies too specialized for any one individual to accomplish alone.

————◆·✕·◆————

Although establishing teams frequently involves much hard work, the effort provides three important factors to group effectiveness: (1) synergy, (2) interdependence, (3) and a support base. What energy is to the individual, synergy is to groups. The synergy of a group is always potentially greater than the sum of the combined energies of its members. Thus, it is not infrequent in laboratory exercises that a group effort results in a better performance than that achieved by the group's most competent member. If you doubt it, have three people independently make a bed. Then have them make three beds jointly.

Effective teams are made up of highly independent individuals who must combine their separate efforts in order to produce an organizational result. The focus of the team effort is on combining, rather than on coordinating resources. *Interdependence* in today's organizations is a simple reality. Police services are too complex and the respective technologies too specialized for any one individual to accomplish alone. The team concept provides the necessary link to approach departmental objectives from a position of strength and creativity.

It is no overstatement that we spend most of our waking hours in a work setting. It is also a reality that the individual carries all his or her needs with him or her at all times, regardless of the location or situation. From this perspective, the quality of life must be attended to in the work setting as much as in the home setting. And the supervisor shares a responsibility for doing so.

The police team constructed for alignment has the potential to provide social and emotional support for its members, producing a more satisfying and work-productive environment. It is important to note that, for a group truly to function as a support base, the group norms that emerge for any specific team *must* originate from within the team itself and not represent a set of "shoulds" from the behavioral sciences or other social institutions. Sometimes, also, it is simply more fun to work with someone else than to work alone!

## TEAM BUILDING

*I've always found that the speed of the boss is the speed of the team.*

—Lee Iacocca

As an internationally acknowledged successful manager, Iacocca is quick to underscore the importance of training for *teamwork*. Furthermore, he stresses that as the boss goes (in this case a supervisor), so goes the team.

You are likely to find that training for teamwork is one of your most difficult and intriguing chores. But the results will far offset your efforts. As you mold a group of individual officers into a cohesive team, you will find out why.

———◆·•·◆———

Training for teamwork is one of your most difficult and intriguing chores.

———◆·•·◆———

Briefly, you'll discover that the term "team" means:

T ogether
E veryone
A chieves
M uch

A team is a group of individuals who must work interdependently in order to attain their individual and organizational objectives.

The most obvious example of a team is an athletic team. The members have a purpose, which gives them an identity. Each player has a unique function (position) that must be integrated with that of the other members. The players are aware and supportive of the need for interdependent interaction, and the team usually operates within the framework of a larger organization (a league). A few years ago the Boston Celtics won the championship of the National Basketball Association. During an interview, the coach was asked, "What was the major difference between your team and the one you defeated?" He responded, "We had alignment!"

Not all working groups, however, are teams, nor should they necessarily be. The faculty of a department in a university is a good contrast to an athletic team. Other examples of work groups that are not teams are committees, in which the purpose is representation, rather than interdependence, and training groups, for which no charter exists.

There are several necessary assumptions concerning the nature of teams. The first assumption is that all the talent necessary to allow the team to be anything it wishes is already present within the group. The second is that everyone already knows what he or she wants to do; the prime focus is on how the members are stopping themselves from doing what they want. Third, the team's maximum potential for strength and effectiveness is limited only by the limitations each individual member sets on his or her potential. And, fourth, the work itself is potentially exciting. Clearly, police work fully meets or comes close to meeting these four assumptions.

## Team Effectiveness

Team building and effectiveness occur through your leadership and the facilitation of group dynamics.

**LEADERSHIP.** Much has been written and spoken advocating the participative leadership approach as the one best way to manage team development; currently, the participative approach is highly favored in public and private business settings. Nevertheless, autocracy or any other particular leadership style is not precluded from being effective: One has only to look at the sports team to see that this is true. It is highly unlikely that the Miami Dolphins football team would vote as a team, prior to each game, on what plays will be run.

More important than the particular leadership style is your ability to combine individual efforts into group output, provide the necessary liaison between your team and the total police organization, and accomplish this in a manner consistent with professional values.

**GROUP DYNAMICS.** The very nature of teamwork depends on the effectiveness of the interaction among team members. The concepts of contact, role, and values are elements of effective team interaction. Good *contact* is based on authenticity among team members. It implies that each individual is aware of his or her individuality and is willing to state views and ideas clearly and to support the principles of openness and conscious choice. An environment that encourages the open expression of disagreement, as well as agreement, accepts the reality that an individual may like some co-workers more than others. This is legitimate as long as openly stated preferences do not result in discriminatory, unfair, or task-destructive behavior.

Two elements, function and relationship, are combined in the concept of *role*. Function is the specific task each member is there to perform; relationship relates to the interaction necessary to get the task completed—with whom each member must interact and how the interaction occurs. In the well-functioning team, role clarity is evident. The team's objectives are clear and agreed on, and each team member knows each member's unique contribution to those objectives, thus eliminating any duplication of effort. Usually, the effective team is comprised of individuals who have complementary, rather than similar, talents and approaches.

All decisions, whether made by individuals or by groups, are based on *values*. Three specific values seem to identify good working police teams: (1) task effectiveness, (2) dealing in the present, and (3) conflict viewed as an asset.

1. *Task effectiveness.* The well-functioning group of police officers places a high value on task effectiveness, with greater emphasis on *doing the right things*, rather than on doing things right. The value implies that the team also focuses on the objective, or end result, rather than only on the team's ongoing activity.

2. *Dealing in the present.* The effective team focuses on "right here, right now," an emphasis that allows a flexible response to changing conditions within the team itself and within the larger organization. The team can make more appropriate decisions when it is concentrating on *what* is happening rather than *why* it is happening.

3. *Conflict viewed as an asset.* Conflict provides two very necessary elements to the effective work group. First, it is the prime source of energy in systems, and, second, it is the major source of creativity. Since conflict is absolutely unavoidable, in any case, an effective team's approach to dealing with it is to use it rather than to try to resolve, avoid, or suppress it. More potential for ineffectiveness and marginal performance exists in avoiding conflict than in conflict itself. When conflict is seen as an asset, the preferred approach is to deal with it through collaboration, although competition or even compromise is not precluded, when called for by the situation.

Self-administer the questionnaire in Structured Exercise 13-1 and share the results.

## ADVANTAGES

Despite the potential advantages to creating a shared-responsibility team, many supervisors express strongly negative sentiments about teams, groups, committees, and meetings. They associate teams with delays, endless talk (or false, constrained politeness), avoidance of responsibility, and other unpleasant outcomes. Indeed, too few management teams now function in ways that could produce enthusiasm and encourage emulation.

———◆•✦•◆———

Many supervisors express strongly negative sentiments about teams.

———◆•✦•◆———

## Structured Exercise 13-1

# WORK-GROUP-EFFECTIVENESS INVENTORY

Work Group:_____
Date:_____

Circle one number for each statement:

| | Strongly Disagree | Disagree | Undecided | Agree | Strongly Agree |
|---|---|---|---|---|---|

1. I have been speaking frankly here about the things that have been uppermost in my mind.

    1    2    3    4    5

2. The other members of this team have been speaking frankly about the things that have been uppermost in their minds.

    1    2    3    4    5

3. I have been careful to speak directly and to the point.

    1    2    3    4    5

4. The other members of this team have been speaking directly and to the point.

    1    2    3    4    5

5. I have been listening carefully to the other member's of this team, and I have been paying special attention to those who have expressed strong agreement or disagreement.

    1    2    3    4    5

6. The other members of this team have been listening carefully to me and to each other, and they have been paying special attention to strongly expressed views.

    1    2    3    4    5

7. I have been asking for and receiving constructive feedback regarding my influence on the team.

    1    2    3    4    5

**8.** I have been providing constructive feedback to those who have requested it—to help them keep track of their influence on me and the other team members.

   1     2     3     4     5

**9.** Decisions regarding our team's operating procedures and organization have been changed rapidly whenever more useful structures or procedures have been discovered.

   1     2     3     4     5

**10.** Everyone on the team has been helping the team keep track of its effectiveness.

   1     2     3     4     5

**11.** Members of this team have been listening carefully to each other, and we have been paying special attention to strongly expressed values.

   1     2     3     4     5

**12.** We have been speaking frankly to each other about the things that have been uppermost in our minds.

   1     2     3     4     5

**13.** We have been speaking directly and to the point.

   1     2     3     4     5

**14.** We have been helping our team keep track of its own effectiveness.

   1     2     3     4     5

**15.** Our team's internal organization and procedures have been adjusted when necessary to keep pace with changing conditions or new requirements.

   1     2     3     4     5

**16.** All members of this team understand the team's goals.

   1     2     3     4     5

**17.** Each member of our team understands how he or she can contribute to the team's effectiveness in reaching its goals.

   1     2     3     4     5

| | Strongly Disagree | Disagree | Undecided | Agree | Strongly Agree |
|---|---|---|---|---|---|
| 18. Each of us is aware of the potential contribution of the other team members. | 1 | 2 | 3 | 4 | 5 |
| 19. We recognize each other's problems and help each other to make a maximum contribution. | 1 | 2 | 3 | 4 | 5 |
| 20. As a team, we pay attention to our own decision-making and problem-solving processes. | 1 | 2 | 3 | 4 | 5 |

Suppose, however, that your direct subordinates could function as a team with the following characteristics:

- Everyone knows his or her own and others' tasks well enough so that nothing falls through the cracks; everyone knows who is, and who should be, doing what.
- Trust is so high that the group does not need to meet on every issue. Each member is confident that no one, including the boss, would act without consultation unless there was a good reason—such as prior general agreement, special expertise, legitimate time pressures, or unavailability of affected parties. And the person who does act would know that others would back any action.
- Such a group would not be very "groupy" or clingy, and would not waste time meeting on trivial issues or limiting those who had taken individual initiative.
- Members who were clearly more expert than the others, in certain areas, would be given great latitude to make the decisions on those matters.
- Nevertheless, if issues cross several areas or affect the department as a whole, members would seriously address the issues together, fight hard and openly for their beliefs, insist that their concerns be addressed, yet also pay attention to the needs of the department as a whole. Everyone would be comfortable wearing at least two hats, one for his or her area and one for the department.

- Although skilled at persuasion and willing to fight hard over important differences, members would feel no obligation to oppose automatically initiatives from other members or the manager. There would be no competition for competition's sake. Members would enthusiastically support the positions or ideas of others when they happened to agree.

- Despite members' willingness to fight when necessary, the climate is pervasively supportive, encouraging members to ask one another for help, acknowledge their mistakes, share resources (people, information, or equipment), and generally further everybody's performance and learning.

- The group pays attention to successful task achievement and to individual members' learning; members are not restricted to areas where they have total competence and hence can't acquire new expertise, nor are they so overloaded with learning experiences that group performance seriously suffers.

- Perhaps most important, the group has self-correcting mechanisms; when things aren't going well, all members are ready to examine the group's processes, discuss what is wrong, and take corrective action. Whatever the problems—overly lengthy meetings, inappropriate agenda items, unclear responsibilities, lack of team effort, overly parochial participation, or even poor leadership practices—the group takes time out to assess its way of operating and to make midcourse corrections. Individual members as well as the manager feel free to raise questions of team performance.

Does this team profile sound too ideal? Is the well-developed team a fantasy projection that will remain frustratingly out of reach in the real world of petty politics, indirection, waffling, and hushed-corridor cabals? It could be but not necessarily. We've seen police teams achieve this level of alignment. If you want a team effort, develop one. *Trust and training are a two-seated vehicle for pursuing teamwork.*

## TRUST

In Responsibility Four, we underscored trust by discussing the concept of trust banking accounts (TBAs). Please return to that section now and refresh your memory. What was stated there has clear applications here.

There is no foolproof formula for establishing and maintaining trust in a work group. Nonetheless, here are some steps that have proven valid in funding TBAs.

### Believing

Police leaders (managers and supervisors) must have an enduring belief that *most* people want to do a good job and that it is important for them to enjoy their work. Closely coupled with this is a strong belief that *all* individuals be treated with consideration and respect and that their achievements be recognized. This belief should encourage a work culture where each person in the department counts, and every job counts.

---

*Most people want to do a good job.*

---

## Personality

One should not base one's work relationship on another person's personality, chemistry, or enjoyment. He or she may be a fun person, clever, bright, and more. But this doesn't mean you can trust that person. People who rely only on similar tastes, on personalities that mesh, or on the right chemistry, and who ignore character and values, are setting themselves up for great disappointment.

## Values—Theirs

Find out what the other person's values are. Have a dialogue with the person and probe his or her values. How important are goodness, honesty, and unselfishness to the person? What, if anything, is more important to the person than personal happiness? Not only are the person's answers to these questions important, but it is also revealing if the person gets annoyed when such issues are raised.

Finally, ask yourself: If you had to prove to someone who never met your co-worker how decent a person he or she is, what concrete evidence could you submit?

## Behavior

Pay at least as much attention to how the person treats others, especially people from whom he or she needs nothing, as to how the person treats you. Watch, for example, how your co-worker treats a customer. Does the person treat the server as an inferior human being, to be ordered around?

---

*Pay at least as much attention to how the person treats others.*

---

People generally treat decently those from whom they want something—a better assignment, help, approval, or a special favor. That someone treats you well may therefore reveal nothing about character (and therefore may not indicate how that individual will treat you later).

## Values—Yours

Know your own values (Responsibility One). If you don't have strong values yourself, or you do but cannot clearly articulate them, the two previous suggestions may not be very helpful. How can you inquire or talk about values that you yourself either don't hold or can't identify? Thus, the stronger and more focused your values become, the less likely you are to trust people with poor values.

Having the right values serves a selfish purpose. Those who live by values that are higher than themselves tend to bring such people into teams. And such employees are a great deal less likely to disappoint us as teammates.

In summary, you can best determine who to trust or not by following these rules.

**1.** Do not trust co-workers based on personality, chemistry, or enjoyment alone.

**2.** Find out what the other person's values are. While values are not enough to ensure a good working relationship, they can guide you in terms of whom to trust.

**3.** Pay careful attention to how the co-worker treats others, especially others from whom he or she needs nothing, and how the person treats you.

**4.** Know your own values. If you do not have firmly held values, and cannot clearly articulate them, the above rules are useless.

## TRAINING

It is a paradox that while everyone seems to be in favor of teamwork, there isn't a lot of it around. Trust building and team building are synergistic. You push for one and the other responds as well. Hence, if you start training employees as a team, they are likely to trust each other more and function as a team.

Regretfully, the majority of police training is individual-based. One person heads for a problem-oriented policing seminar and another for an ethics course. The majority of police training today at all levels in a department constrains team building. The best model for enhancing team performance in a police agency is the athletic one. Basically, diverse people are brought together and trained to be mutually supportive of one another. The more team training, the better the morale and the better the quality of services.

———◆◆◆———

Much of your success or failure as a supervisor hinges on your ability to *train*—especially teamwork.

———◆◆◆———

As a trainer (or developer of human resources), you influence an officer's values, attitudes, perceptions, learning, motivation, job satisfaction, stress, and wellness. Furthermore, as a trainer, you sway group dynamics, communications, and followership (your leadership). Likewise, as a trainer, you affect goal setting, planning, MBO, performance appraisal, discipline, conflict resolution, community relations, labor relations, and one's professional success. Pointedly, then, much of your success or failure as a supervisor hinges on your ability to *train*—especially teamwork.

## Responsibility of the Police Supervisor

The police supervisor is in a most advantageous position to influence personal and organizational development in a local law-enforcement agency. Hence our basic premise—the police supervisor has a responsibility for the improvement of the human resources within his or her purview and in line with attaining the goals of the agency.

Many police agencies have established a field training officer's (FTO) position. This officer is usually provided with some form of incentive to "coach" a newer officer in the performance of his or her duties while on the job (on-the-job training, OJT). We are, in turn, proposing that the supervisor be assigned the responsibility for training his or her subordinates. Similarly, the supervisor should become involved in decisions affecting his or her team members' education, career progress, and organizational development. It is recognized that all of these concepts are, if not vague, certainly overlapping in their very nature.

Some clarification of these concepts will be attempted in subsequent sections of this chapter. To reemphasize, the supervisor should have *the* primary charge for personal and organizational team development of his or her work unit.

## Training Goals

Training, as we see it, has two fundamental goals: To make lasting *improvements in the performance* of one's organizational role and to *develop one's capacity* for handling higher levels of responsibility. In other words, training to help a person do her or his job better, while at the same time prepare her or him for more challenging duties. Consequently, training means a change; that is, a change on the part of the individual and the organization. Both are interdependent partners in any process of change. Furthermore, training means integration; that is, unifying people and the organization in a concerted attempt to more effectively achieve assigned goals.

Underlying its goals and characteristics is a certain philosophy or perhaps better, attitude, of what training is. Six key attitudes underscore police training goals today.

1. Motivations attached to skills lead to action. Skills are acquired through practice.
2. Learning is a complex function of the motivation and capacity of the individual, the norms of the training group, the training methods and the behavior of the trainers, and the general climate of the police organization.
3. Improvement on the job is a complex function of individual learning, the norms of the working group, and the general climate of the organization. Individual learning, unused, leads to frustration.
4. Training is the responsibility of three partners: the organization, the trainee, and the trainer. It has preparatory, pretraining, and posttraining phases.
5. Training is a continuous process and a vehicle for consistently updating the skills of the individual human resources.
6. Training is also a continuous process and a vehicle for consistently improving the capacity of the individual officers to behave as a team.

These goals and attitudes, in turn, have produced the following set of training objectives:

1. Required entry-level information of a technical and a social nature
2. New information on a sustained and planned basis
3. Developmental learning and training experiences for all members in the department that promote and reinforce teamwork
4. Required work experience and training for upper levels before the person is promoted
5. The police supervisor has the major responsibility for training and developing his or her subordinates
6. The police training officer has the responsibility for planning a total program including all members—officers, supervisors, and managers—of the police agency in a set of learning experiences both within and without the organization

Note again the fifth objective. Essentially we are saying that if you, as a police supervisor, separate training from the rest of the work experience and are concerned only with its contribution to the output of the police organization, the chances of effective training are sharply reduced. This latter point is extremely important. Nothing contributes so much to job satisfaction and morale as a sincere interest on the part of the first-line supervisor.

The preceding is not intended to ignore or challenge the viability of the field training officer (FTO) program. Agency after agency has found the FTO program most helpful in assisting a new police officer to quickly build proper job attitudes and behavior. Briefly, an FTO program provides close coaching and monitoring of a new officer's demeanor by a senior officer who has received *special instruction* on doing so. Untrained FTOs can create as much damage as benefit to a department. An FTO program should be used by a police supervisor as one of many training methods for ensuring the agency that his or her assigned staff are peak performers.

## Training: The Process

*For thousands of years people have been talking about improving teaching—to no avail. It was not until the early years of this century, however, that an educator asked, "What is the end product?" Then the answer was obvious. It is not teaching. It is, of course, learning.*

—Peter F. Drucker
*The Effective Executive* (New York: Harper and Row 1957), p. 30

At the focal point of training is the trainee. The changes in her or his behavior are the measure of the effectiveness of training. To produce needed behavioral changes, training subjects the participant to a process of change that includes three overlapping and circular stages: preparation, implementation, and evaluation (follow-up and repreparation). Naturally, participants other than the trainee are involved; that is, the organization and the trainer. The presence of all three is required to identify their relevant training needs.

Many of us have experienced a lag in our attention to a training session. In most cases, this lag in attention is caused by a lack of trainee need fulfillment.

This lag can be avoided by involving the trainee in deciding which needs should be met through both formal programs and developmental experiences.

The trainee and the organization are subjected to the same stages in the process but with different purposes in mind. The function of the trainer relates to her or his style. In regard to the trainee, we find (1) Preparation: The trainee identifies needs and develops certain expectations and levels of motivation concerning the program; (2) Implementation: The trainee selects the items she or he feels she or he must learn; and (3) Evaluation: The trainee transfers the learning to application. Concerning the organization, we find (1) Preparation: The organization identifies its needs and selects and motivates the trainees; (2) Implementation: The organization provides an environment conducive to learning; and (3) Evaluation: The organization provides support for the transfer of learning into application.

## Effective Training

In practice, the aims of training are external to the process itself, that is, the goals to be achieved are modifications in organizational performance or capabilities. Furthermore, the results obtained from training are ultimately assessed in terms of organizational criteria and not by standards that are an inherent part of training itself. In short, *the common quality of training is its intended aim of moving something from an initial state in which problems or needs exist to an end state in which the problems have been solved or the needs met.*

---

The goals to be achieved are modifications in organizational performance or capabilities.

---

One finds in this section various strategies now practiced in the field of training. However, the consideration of strategies for training involves the broader issue of effectiveness. In other words, the desire for effective training structures the entire program, including the employee strategies. Hence, we turn briefly to an examination of what is meant by effective training.

First, effective police training requires proper selection of both courses and trainees. This means that all concerned, trainees and their supervisors, should know the objectives of the course. It also means that the selection decision should consider the employee's training needs in his or her present job and in his or her career development.

Second, to be effective, police training must support operations. In other words, both trainees and supervisors should be able to specify in advance how the employee is expected to use the training in his or her work. Furthermore, if the training has been effective, they should be able at some later date to point to ways in which the trainee has used it.

Third, effectiveness of police training depends on positive action, not only by the trainee but also by the police supervisor. The aim of training is to change a person's behavior. However, the effects of training evaporate unless supervision and management are prepared to accept the changed person and have changed the work situation to accommodate him or her. As has been pointed out more than once, the organizational climate must reinforce the training experience, thereby increasing the probability that the employee will apply the training in his or her work.

**HOW DO WE KNOW?** Effective training calls, therefore, for clarity of objectives and means. Both the ends and the means must be appropriate to the purpose. Relating them demands clear specifications for each part of the training task, including the time, skill, and facilities required to complete it. Ensuring this clarity is a primary responsibility of the police supervisor. Unless this task has been accomplished, a new police training program is launched into a void, doomed to problems and failure.

One final question remains, however, "How do you know when we have succeeded in providing an effective training program?" The answer is obvious— by evaluating the training effort! In summary, then, effective training calls for (1) establishing relevant training objectives, (2) defining training specifications, (3) selecting the appropriate strategy, (4) creating suitable structural arrangements, and (5) evaluating and improving the program.

### *Structured Exercise 13-2*

Learning Needs Questionnaire

*Directions.* Circle the number that you feel best represents your experience.

| | | |
|---|---|---|
| I am not well prepared for my job. | 1　2　3　4　5 | I am fully prepared for my job. |
| I lack essential skills for my job. | 1　2　3　4　5 | I have all the necessary skills for my job. |
| I was not carefully introduced to my job. | 1　2　3　4　5 | I was carefully introduced to my job. |
| I found it difficult to learn my job. | 1　2　3　4　5 | I learned my job with minimal difficulty. |
| I have no opportunities for development. | 1　2　3　4　5 | I have good opportunities for development. |
| I have far too little proper training. | 1　2　3　4　5 | I have sufficient training. |
| My boss is not concerned about training needs. | 1　2　3　4　5 | My boss is concerned about training needs. |

**ESTABLISHING TRAINING OBJECTIVES.** Since any training objective is based on the objectives of the police department, the main question is whether the department's objectives are realistic. Furthermore, is the training input of the program envisaged also realistic? Or is training in danger of being misused? For example, is it too little and too late? All this is to say that (1) the training objectives must support organizational activities, and (2) the training objectives must be realistic. These two basic needs suggest that four steps are necessary to ensure that departmental and training objectives are met.

1. Be certain that a needed change calls for training. What many police organizations need is not training, at least not immediately, but lots of detailed operational planning and implementation of plans. Training at this stage would be a disservice if it deprived the organization of skilled people currently needed for action.
2. Define the part that police training can play in the change. What new competences does the department require and which of these can be acquired through systematic training? Training strategy determines which goals can reasonably be achieved through a training program and which cannot. And, vice versa, the goals determine which training strategy is most appropriate.
3. The third step is more taxing and worthy of the most careful consideration; it concerns questions of quantities and levels of police personnel to be trained, and of timing and training as well.
4. The fourth step involves training for teamwork. *People who work together should be trained together.* The truly effective work groups are trained like any successful sports team. All members know what their job consists of, and what they should provide and can expect of others.

**TRAINING STRATEGIES.** Any attempt to train, that is, to change, an individual automatically means a *freezing-up of relations* between people. The freezing-up of relations involves three stages: *unfreezing, moving,* and *refreezing.*

Unfreezing is necessary because the police officer (and his or her organization, family, and locality) comes up with habits, values, and practices, the very opposite of a clean slate. To affect him or her through training, normal habits have first to be questioned and disturbed, or unfrozen.

Training can do this by focusing on needs that police trainees cannot satisfy by habitual behavior. The supervisor then introduces other events that allow participants to try new ways of behaving, that is, changing. If the police trainees find the new behavior more useful in meeting the "new" needs, they can then be helped to make it habitual. Each officer thus gains a new set of behavioral patterns, which he or she then freezes.

The guiding principles for training strategies lie in these dynamics of the development process and in the minimum critical concentration of effort required at each stage of it. Training differences occur along two axes. The first axis delineates the subject matter that police officers are to learn. At one extreme it points toward learning about a specific task or piece of knowledge, such as the pros and cons of using certain investigative techniques. This kind of knowledge is *content*. At the other extreme are general understanding and insight into how people and things function. This kind of knowledge is *process*. For example, participants could learn how investigative techniques are developed and the principles that underlie them. This first axis then has content for one extreme and process for the other.

The second axis shows the basic function of police training. Is it to be used for constructing new concepts and theory? That would be one extreme, which we call *concept*. Or is it to improve action on the job? That extreme we call *job*. Along these two axes are six major training strategies.

The selection of a strategy depends on a number of factors. One is the training goals. Once the police department is clear about its goals, it can choose a strategy that leads to them. The second consideration when choosing a strategy is the resources (human, physical, and financial) available for training.

---

The selection of a training strategy depends on training goals.

---

**YOUR DELIVERY OF TRAINING.** As a police supervisor, you are responsible for the delivery of needed training to your personnel. While the style may vary from a stand-up, roll-call lecture to ride-along coaching, train you must.

It is not sufficient to make police training supplemental to work; police work must be organized to facilitate training and development. Several factors support this conclusion. First, any help in training provided by the police agency must be welcome because the training demands are ever expanding in local law enforcement. Second, we live in an age of revolution in processes, systems, and products in public and private organizations. The training burdens are great. Increasingly, training must be part and parcel of the work itself, and it should be increasingly supplied and directly monitored by the immediate supervisor.

If your department is astute, they are rating your performance as a police supervisor, to a major extent, on your ability to *deliver* timely and useful training to others. Trainers and supervisors are one and the same. Effective trainers and effective supervisors build teams.

**EVALUATING YOUR ACCOMPLISHMENTS.** The evaluation of training frequently falls prey to its becoming a popularity contest and/or merely an entertaining event. The key questions are, or should be,

- What, precisely, did you learn?
- Why is it important to you and your agency?
- How do you plan to use it?
- When and where will the new learning be applied?

Asking these pointed questions demands follow-up and feedback on your part. A final critical and, at times, risky question is, How can I, as your supervisor, improve as a trainer?

## DIVERSITY IN THE WORKPLACE

Until the 1950s, American law enforcement primarily consisted of white, male employees representing two to three generations. The few females were relegated to clerical and technical jobs. Hence, police departments were homogeneous in appearance. Obviously, the employees did differ due to their own unique individuality. As a result, supervising diversity was relatively simple. The opposite is real today.

### Defining Diversity

Managing or supervising diversity is creating and maintaining a work environment in which each person is *respected because of his or her differences*, and where *all can contribute and be rewarded based on their results*.

—————◆•※•◆—————

Supervising diversity includes self respect and respect of others and all can contribute.

—————◆•※•◆—————

"Respected because of their differences" means that we need to understand, first, that different does not mean less than and, second, that different approaches and different opinions can be beneficial to making decisions and providing service delivery to a diverse customer base.

"Rewarded on the basis of their results" means that people should be rewarded on the basis of what they do and how they produce, not on the basis of who they know or what they look like.

Our definition of work-force diversity suggests four harmful misconceptions.

**MISCONCEPTION 1. MANAGING DIVERSITY IS A DISGUISE FOR AFFIRMATIVE ACTION PROGRAMS.** Often, in an organization where perceptions and behaviors are not managed carefully, some people express and act out the opinion that the organization's goals for managing diversity simply are an attempt to sneak in affirmative action goals and quotas.

**MISCONCEPTION 2. MANAGING DIVERSITY IS CULTURAL DIVERSITY TRAINING.** Some may think that managing diversity is simply teaching appropriate behaviors to use when interacting with people of specific races, national origins, mental or physical abilities, sexual orientations, or lifestyles.

Managing diversity goes beyond learning to act out a prescribed behavior. For some organizations or work teams, it will mean a basic change in the way people communicate, interact, process information, make decisions, and serve customers. It is not a quick-fix recipe!

**MISCONCEPTION 3. MANAGING DIVERSITY IS SENSITIVITY TRAINING.** Managing diversity is not some touchy-feely training session. Managing diversity is a way for us to understand and appreciate ourselves better so we can understand the factors and situations that motivate our personal beliefs, values, and behaviors. This allows us to accept, then respect, others who may have different beliefs, values, lifestyles, and ways of doing things at work.

**MISCONCEPTION 4. MANAGING DIVERSITY IS AN EFFORT TO MIRROR OUR CUSTOMERS OR CITIZEN BASE.** At times, managers and organization leaders feel it is important that we mirror, or look like, the customers or citizens we serve. While it may give us some initial comfort, merely having work teams that look like those we serve cannot represent the ultimate goal for achieving success.

When we manage diversity effectively, we discover that added personal differences or personal similarities cannot be attributed necessarily to race, gender, or lifestyle. We get better at recognizing the differences, respecting the differences, and expecting the differences to enrich our relationship and contribute to better quality performance and behavior results.

## Everyone Belongs to a Minority Group

The all-male work force is history. Sameness of sex and ethnicity is out, and differences are in.

In sheer numbers women dominate the information society. Eighty-four percent of working women are part of the information-service sector. Of the people whose job title falls under the category of "professional"—versus clerical, technical, laborer—the majority are women. Forty-four percent of adult working women (ages twenty-five to sixty-four) are college educated, compared with 20 percent in 1965. Further, six out of ten joining the work force right now are female.

As the twentieth century closes, white men are already less than half of the labor force. By 2010, married couples will no longer be a majority of households. Asians will outnumber Jews by a margin of two to one, and Hispanics will lead blacks as the nation's largest minority.

By 2020, immigration will become more important to U.S. population growth than natural increase (the growth that occurs because births outnumber deaths). The population will diversify even more rapidly.

## Dangerous Delusions

No other nation is as challenged as the United States in bringing large numbers of highly diverse people together in organizational settings and then expecting our managers and supervisors to build cooperative and happy work teams. Unfortunately, some of us have been deluded by the false hopes or assumptions that follow.

**LAWS AND POLICIES.** Legislating and policy making are not the answers to worker diversity! Granted, we need laws and policies concerning hate crimes, discrimination in age, sexual harassment, and other such illegal behavior. But, they do not work when it comes to *thinking* anti-racist, -sexist, -religious thoughts. The ideal we seek is best approached by encouraging individuals to share and resolve their differences.

**POLITICAL CORRECTNESS.** Political correctness (PC) is the suppression of "hate speech," which is loosely defined as anything that any recognized minority or victim group chooses to find offensive. Hence, there is considerable latitude in determining what is or is not PC. For example, we might use the term "female athlete" which is not "in" today ("woman" should be used) and thus we're not PC. In our opinion, PC is insincere, deceitful, and dysfunctional.

A more honest alternative for genuinely building solid working relationships is being *professionally correct* (PRO-C). If PRO-C, then you are automatically behaving in accordance with ethical standards and common decency. You, in turn, are being truthful to yourself and others, while simultaneously being sensitive to human feelings.

**GIVE ME THE LIST.** Some of us are deluded by assuming that you can get a laundry list of do's and don'ts and that following that list will help you be PC and avoid blunders. In matters of humor or just ordinary topics of discussion, "you have to shed knee-jerk assumptions." Not every African-American plays basketball. Everyone with a Latino surname doesn't speak Spanish. All Asians are not Chinese. For that matter, not all whites come from the ruling class. As a consequence, assume nothing about the person except that he or she has values and you must understand them to be successful in your job as supervisor and leader.

**DIVERSITY FOR PROFIT.** There are consultants, lecturers, tests, films—an entire industry has been born to fuel and feed off of the privilege of a lifetime—being who you are.

American civil society, long founded on the notion of "from many, one," *e pluribus unum*, is being deluded into a poisonous flood tide of negation, sectarianism, self-pity, confrontation, vulgarity, and flat-out, old-fashioned hatred.

One of the most obvious is also the most disheartening: Almost a hundred years after the last great immigration wave changed the face of American society, vast numbers of Americans—including, sadly, the best educated—are again being taught to identify themselves with the qualifying adjectives of race, religion, generation, and gender. Our self-identity is not shaped by will, choice, reason, intelligence, and desire, but by membership in groups. We are not individuals, but components of categories. Those in the so-called diversity business love it as we divide and collide.

### What Can the Police Leader Do?

- First, the police leader has to remember and appreciate that each one of us, including him or herself, is diverse—we're individuals with unique value systems.
- Second, when one's values are being assaulted, conflict will ensue.
- Third, in many cases what may be referred to as a diversity problem (e.g., male versus female) is in reality a supervisory problem such as status differences (e.g., sworn officers demeaning the work of civilian dispatchers). What

may be a work issue may be cleverly masked as a diversity issue and thus made worse by using the wrong approach to it.

- Four, the three core values for both avoiding and solving employee diversity are caring, trusting, and communications/understanding.
- Five, police supervisors will have to be especially adroit in leading a more diverse work force. We would urge that all supervisors recognize the enormous power that is unleashed by a diverse work force. In our opinion, it is one of this nation's paramount strengths, and this should hold true for its police agencies.

In conclusion: *We are what we value and we will manage our diversity and the diversity of others accordingly!*

## KEY POINTS

- Teamwork requires interdependency of thinking and effort.
- The main purpose for teamwork is that through alignment, synergy is produced within the work group.
- Team effectiveness occurs through leadership and the facilitation of group dynamics.
- Teamwork can occur only if there is mutual trust and training as a team.
- Trust should be based on knowing the other person's values as well as your own.
- Training is a key responsibility of a police supervisor.
- An FTO program does not diminish or detract from a supervisor's training function.
- The training process incorporates three essential partners: department, trainer, and trainee.
- Effective training is defined by the clarity of objectives *and* means of delivery.
- Training objectives should be set according to (1) is training really required, (2) what part is it to play, and (3) how many and who should participate?
- Your training style will emphasize one of four behaviors: (1) excellence, (2) power, (3) efficiency, and (4) affability.
- Your training strategy depends on goals and available resources.
- Your delivery of training should be subjected to constant evaluation by your boss and yourself.
- The most difficult of all training goals for the supervisor is that of building and maintaining a work *team*.
- The number one challenge in promoting trust and team training is the enormous amount of diversity among today's police employees.

## DISCUSSION

1. Why is an interdependent work group so important? How can interdependency avoid the pitfall of "groupthink"?

2. Review the steps mentioned for building trust. Are there steps that should have been included? If so, what are they? Can I like you and not trust you? What about the reverse—trust but not like you?

3. In your opinion, what are (in rank order) the major training needs of a police officer today?

4. "Feedback is the breakfast of champions." Why?

5. What is being done in your department or work unit to respect diversity (our individuality) while forging a team effort? What else should be done?

# Community-oriented and Problem-oriented Policing

Community-oriented policing is a strategy for forging a partnership between the police and its customers. Problem-oriented policing is a set of tactics for making it work.

*Community partnerships and problem solving—the two core components of community policing—can be accomplished in a variety of ways.*

—"Community Policing Strategies"
National Institute of Justice
U.S. Department of Justice

Community- and problem-oriented policing (R-14) are both a culmination and a starting point. All of the previous responsibilities (R-1 to R-13) serve as a platform for COP and POP to be possible. At this point, it is up to the supervisor to step forward and make it a reality.

*Community-oriented policing (COP) depends on police supervisors who lead their lives and manage their relationships around values and ethics.* They see and believe in a mission that is devoted to serving and helping their customers. They exercise self-discipline and are not afraid of hard work. They know how and where to allocate their time. They also know that individual effectiveness precedes organizational effectiveness.

COP gives us a destination while POP provides answers on how to get there.

Problem-oriented policing (POP) depends on police supervisors who can translate COP into operational reality. They take the goals of a mission statement and cast them into very specific and attainable objectives and projects. POP is a logical and practical extension of COP.

In summary, COP gives us a destination while POP provides answers on how to get there.

## COMMUNITY-ORIENTED POLICING

Although the acronyms COP (community-oriented policing) and POP (problem-oriented policing) are relatively new to many, some basic elements, such as citizen participation, officers knowledgeable in the values and traditions of the area they serve, police officer–citizen communication, and the like, are not. They were present to one extent or another in earlier policing in the United States, whether by design or individual style, especially in the late nineteenth and early twentieth centuries, and especially in large cities with dense populations.

During the late 1960s and 1970s, following recommendations from the President's Commission on Law Enforcement and Administration of justice, a proliferation of federally funded police–community relations models sprang up throughout the country. The purpose was to bring police officers closer to the community, to promote mutual support, to encourage communication, and so on.

Some programs experienced relative success; others did not. Most were relegated to test areas and specific officer assignments, as opposed to total departmental understanding, involvement, and support. Even those programs held up as positive examples were, in almost every case, gradually phased out or modified in such a way as to become isolated from the mainstream of their respective agencies. The programs did little to strengthen relationships between the community and response-oriented police officers, or even between police officers assigned to "community relations" and other officers.

The 1970s also gave birth and often death to some form of *team policing*. Early team policing programs were burdened by lack of documented successes and failures. Those who experimented with team policing were not aware that elements of team policing would prove to be incompatible with preventive patrol and rapid response to calls for service. It would be implemented, voluntarily assigned officers and citizens would like it, it would have an initial impact on crime, and then traditional habits would overwhelm it and the program would disappear.

In the early 1970s, the Holyoke, Massachusetts, Police Department instituted a program considered by many to be the showcase of federally funded team policing programs. It was almost unbelievably successful. The team consisted of fifteen highly motivated, people-conscious officers: one captain, two sergeants, twelve patrolmen—all volunteers. Working in identifiable blazers out of a storefront located in the high-crime-rate 235-acre Ward One, the team was responsible for providing 24-hour police service for the 7,000 occupants of mixed racial backgrounds who had a common distrust of police.

In addition to routine police functions, the focus was on human relations, language, and traditional cultures of those residing in the ward. These officers were in for the duration (no transfers) and they got to know the people and to be known by the people. And they became effective. However, after a time with a substantial infusion of more federal dollars, the program was expanded, ward by ward, and ward by ward it began to fail—and did fail.

Officers assigned to the new teams were not all volunteers. Transfers were routine. Reportedly many were "old-timers" who simply would not or could not change, and they were not motivated or motivatable. Some were said to be simply insensitive. A "we–they" attitude prevailed.

There were other problems, of course. Some were blamed on what were perceived to be unqualified or improperly tuned-in political nonpolice background appointments in key positions. At any rate, for whatever reasons, a very well-designed and -staffed, successful pilot program went the way of most of the early programs.

Moreover, the lessons about innovation and excellence that Peters and Waterman brought together in *In Search of Excellence* were not then available to police administrators. Current innovators have an advantage in that they have seized the opportunity to learn from the proven successes and failures of the past. And they're looking for facts and are not content merely with studying innovation and management in policing.

If conditions in the past indicated the need for such programs, social conditions of the 1990s dictate an imperative: the burgeoning immigration of different races and cultures, clustering together in crowded, often substandard housing areas, where the police and citizens do not share common beliefs, do not know or trust one another, or even speak a common language; and where it is not understood that success of each in his or her personal role is predicated, at least in part, upon mutual respect and assistance from the other.

## Why COP?

There are four driving forces pushing COP: (1) citizen frustration with police services, (2) research conducted during the 1970s, (3) increased social conflicts of the 1990s, and (4) dissatisfaction with the traditional role of the police officer.

**FRUSTRATION WITH POLICE SERVICES.** Citizens respect most police officers. Most people enjoy contact with police. However, some people continue to be frustrated by police who whisk in and out of their neighborhoods, with little sensitivity to community norms and values. Regardless of where one asks, people want both the familiarity and accountability that characterize foot patrol. More and more people are demanding increased participation with police in the determination of police priorities in their neighborhood security and a means of opting for different police services.

**RESEARCH.** Research in the 1970s showed that preventive patrol in patrol cars had little effect on crime, citizen levels of fear, or citizen satisfaction with police. Rapid response to calls for service also had little impact on arrests, citizen satisfaction with police, or levels of citizen fear.

**INCREASED SOCIAL CONFLICTS.** Social conflicts between patrol officers and citizens have increased in the 1990s for a variety of reasons, not the least of which is that officers often find themselves hurrying from call to call, with no real opportunity for closure. People want police *help* and it doesn't always happen. The growing proliferation of foreign-born immigrants of many races, values, and languages is compounded by different life experiences with police.

**ROLE OF THE PATROL OFFICER.** Finally, patrol officers are frustrated with their traditional role. Despite the lip service that patrol is the "backbone of policing," every police officer knows that, at best, patrol is what officers do until they become detectives or are promoted. Patrol officers have the most important mission in police departments—they handle the public's most pressing problems and must make complex decisions almost instantaneously. Patrol officers are general practitioners who make house calls. Even so, police administrators continue to treat patrol officers as if they were the "buttbone" of the agency, not the "backbone."

## *Structured Exercise 14-1*

This is a group exercise for six to eight people. Draft a memorandum for your chief or sheriff to sign that explains his or her reasons for installing a COP program.

### Central Mission

The central mission of the police is to control crime. Crime fighting enjoys public support as the basic strategy of policing precisely because it embodies a deep commitment to this objective. In contrast, other proposed strategies such as problem solving or community policing appear to ignore this focus.

The central mission of the police is to control crime.

Professional crime fighting now relies predominantly on three tactics: (1) motorized patrol, (2) rapid response to calls for service, and (3) follow-up investigation of crimes. The police focus on serious crime has also been sharpened by screening calls for service, targeting patrol, and developing forensic technology (e.g. automated fingerprint systems, computerized criminal record files, etc.).

Although these tactics have scored their successes, they have been criticized within and outside policing for being reactive rather than proactive.

Reactive tactics have some merits, of course. The police go where crimes have occurred and when citizens have summoned them. They keep their distance from the community and thereby retain their impartiality. They do not develop the sorts of relationships with citizens that could bias their responses to crime incidents. The reactive tactics do have preventive effects—at least in theory. The prospect of the police arriving at a crime in progress is thought to deter crimes.

Finally, many police forces have developed *proactive* tactics to deal with crime problems that could not be handled through traditional reactive methods. In drug dealing, organized crime, and vice enforcement, for example, where no immediate victims exist to alert the police, the police have developed special units that rely on informants, covert surveillance, and undercover investigations rather than responses to calls for service. In the area of juvenile offenses, the police have created athletic leagues, and formed partnerships with schools to deal with drug abuse, gang activity, truancy, and so on. *It is not accurate, then, to define policing as entirely reactive.*

The greatest potential for improved crime control does not lie in the continued enhancement of response times, patrol tactics, and investigative techniques. Rather, improved crime control can be achieved by (1) diagnosing and managing problems in the community that produce crimes; (2) fostering closer relations with the community to facilitate crime solving; and (3) building self-defense capabilities within the community itself. Among the results may be increased apprehension of criminals. To the extent that problem-solving or community strategies of policing prepare the police to use local knowledge and capacity to control crime, they will be supportive of the future of policing.

**Case for Quality**

In the 1980s, police agencies began to explore the crime-fighting effectiveness of tactics that build on previous approaches. At the same time, they sought to extend them by looking behind offenses to the precipitating causes of crimes. They endeavored to build closer relations with the community and enhance the self-defense capacities of the communities themselves.

Their guiding theory was that the effectiveness of existing tactics can be enhanced if the police increase the quantity and *quality* of their contacts with citizens (both individuals and neighborhood groups) and conditionally include in their responses to crime problems thoughtful analyses of the root causes of the offenses. The expectation is that this will both enhance the direct effectiveness of the police and enable them to leverage the resources of citizen groups and other public agencies to control crime.

The 1980s saw, therefore, many police agencies attempting to "work smarter and not harder" and to "do more with less." What still remains unanswered is the consequence of shifting a whole department to a different style of policing. For example, if officers are taken from patrol and detective units to do problem-oriented or, community policing, it is fairly certain that response times would lengthen—at least until the problem-solving efforts decreased the demands for service by removing the problem that was producing the calls for service. And even though longer response times do not necessarily indicate a loss in crime-fighting effectiveness, it would be *perceived* as such because the public and the police consider rapid response to crime calls as crime-control effectiveness.

What is inviting, of course, is to avoid deciding between these strategies, and to adopt the strengths of these various approaches while avoiding their weaknesses. This could be seen in decisions to create special units to do COP within existing organizations whose traditions and main forces remained committed to traditional patrol and investigation tactics. But this means more resources, which means more money, and more money is darned difficult to acquire.

Community-oriented policing is not merely a matter of budget dollars. It is also a matter of philosophy, administrative style, and structure. COP requires a greater degree of decentralization than does the current policing strategy. It depends more on the initiative of the officers. And they reach out for a close rather than a distant relationship with community. It is very different from the kind of current administrative posture that stresses centralization, control, and professional separation from the community, and has a very different mission statement. Mission statements are revised to reflect the transition to community policing. The protection of life and of property are still important, but the emphasis is changed from the police enforcing laws and making arrests to co-active partnerships with the community to solve problems (Figure 14-1).

———◦•◊•◦———

The emphasis is changed from the police enforcing laws and making arrests to co-active partnerships.

———◦•◊•◦———

| Old Mission Statement | | New Mission Statement |
|---|---|---|
| "The Bureau of Police is responsible for the preservation of the public peace, protection of the rights of persons and property, the prevention of crime, and the enforcement of all Federal laws, Oregon state statutes and city ordinances within the boundaries of the City of Portland." | *TRANSITION* | "The mission of the Portland Police Bureau is to work with all citizens to preserve life, maintain human rights, protect property, and promote individual responsibility and community commitment." |

**Figure 14-1** Comparison of Portland's old and new mission statements.

Most basically, then, COP includes a likelihood of a need for more money and certitude of a need for administrative change, with organizational and community support, with the understanding and belief that crime is everyone's business—that the cops really *cannot* do it alone.

## Who's Really Responsible?

If we believe that the police are the first line of defense against disorder and crime, and the source of strength for maintaining the quality of life, what should its strategy be? The traditional view is that the police are a community's professional defense against crime and disorder: Citizens should leave control of crime and maintenance of order to police. The COP strategy is that police are to promote and buttress a community's ability to create livable neighborhoods and protect them from criminals.

What about neighborhoods in which criminality prevails—where, for example, drug dealers take over and openly deal drugs and threaten citizens? Clearly, our police must play a leading role defending such communities. Should they do so on their own, however?

Oddly enough, when the police move in to attack dangerous street crime aggressively, the very neighborhoods plagued by disorder reject their approach. The citizens are not ready to surrender control of their neighborhoods to remote police who show them little respect. Are police the first line of defense in a neighborhood? No—citizens are! And if they are, law enforcement must first provide communities with sufficient information—in a manner that will be accepted—to understand and develop interest in the "new" relationship with community protection and the police. And then law enforcement must provide proper training and continuing education to ensure that communities are prepared to assume the new responsible role and to work within specified parameters. We have been advised that new entries into a COP program should be cognizant of the likelihood that like some new police recruits, some neighborhood participants in their enthusiasm may become overzealous and step beyond the boundaries, at times dangerously so.

## Will COP Succeed?

There are four reasons for believing that COP will continue to grow among police agencies.

- Citizen response thus far to the new strategy
- Ongoing research on police effectiveness
- Recent experiences the police have had with COP
- Values of the new generation of police managers and supervision

CITIZEN RESPONSE.   Overwhelming public response to community and problem-solving policing has been positive, regardless of where it has been instituted. Police and citizens alike are now able to say yes or no to COP based on documented experiences in such places as Boston, Massachusetts; Flint,

Michigan; Kansas City, Missouri; Houston, Texas; Arapaho County, Colorado; and Santa Ana, California.

**NEW RESEARCH ON EFFECTIVENESS.** Research conducted during the early and mid-1970s frustrated police executives. It generally showed what did not work. Research performed during the 1970s and early 1980s was different. By showing what new tactics did work, it fueled the move to renovate policing. This research provided police with the following guidance:

- Foot patrol can reduce citizen fear of crime, improve the relationship between police and citizens, and increase citizen satisfaction with police.
- The productivity of detectives can be enhanced if patrol officers carefully interview neighborhood residents about criminal events, get the information to detectives, and detectives use it wisely.
- Citizen fear can be substantially reduced by police tactics that emphasize increasing the quantity and improving the quality of citizen–police interaction.
- Street-level enforcement of heroin and cocaine laws can reduce serious crime in the area of enforcement, without being displaced to adjacent areas.
- Problem-oriented policing can be used to reduce thefts from cars, problems associated with drug trafficking, and household burglaries.

**EXPERIENCE WITH INNOVATION.** The desire to improve policing is not new with this generation of innovators. Before COP there were two major efforts to form a police–community partnership. In the 1960s, it was labeled "police community relations" (PCR). It went down the drain when the citizens saw it mainly as a public relations scheme. The 1970s gave birth and death to "team policing." The early team-policing programs were burdened by a lack of documented successes and failures. Those who experimented with team policing were not aware that elements of team policing were simply incompatible with preventive patrol and rapid response to calls for service. It would be implemented, officers and citizens would like it, it would have an initial impact on crime, and then traditional habits would overwhelm it—the program would disappear.

But lest we forget, many innovators and innovations of the past were very successful and are still with us or cycling upward as technologies change. But these successes were for the most part in the nature of things (tools), not people; and even failures provide valuable data.

**NEW POLICE LEADERSHIP.** The new police leadership is unique in the history of American policing. Unlike the tendency in the past for chiefs and sheriffs to be local and inbred, chiefs and sheriffs of this generation are knowledgeable and sophisticated. In our opinion, they are every bit as skilled and creative as their private-sector counterparts. With growing criminality and a worldwide drug problem, they've been compelled into *thinking smarter*. And, with an ever-greater competition for budget dollars, they've been forced into *doing more with less*. Our police leadership, in every way, is looking better each and every day.

---

*Our police leadership, in every way, is looking better each and every day.*

---

## IMPLEMENTATION

Changing from one style of policing to another takes time and it is not easy. In terms of time, COP requires three to five years before significant results can be seen. And, it is no simple matter to change a department's (1) mission, (2) culture, (3) supervisory style, (4) structure, and (5) programs.

**A NEW MISSION.** This first step is the most crucial. It sets the tone and substance for everything that follows. The forging of a new mission must not be the exclusive responsibility of a few managers and supervisors. Everyone in the organization should be held accountable for its development. This takes patience and persistence, and it is worth it. If it is the intention of the agency to truly form a partnership with its customers, then they too should be involved. If it sounds like a lot of work, it is. *Again, the results are worth it.*

When creating a COP mission statement, remember that you are wrestling with decisions about the core values of your department. The values should at minimum address:

- Value-added quality services via a
- Community–police partnership which is
- Problem centered and thus ensured by
- Empowered police personnel

**A NEW CULTURE.** The second step focuses on culture which consists of groundwork, results versus process, values, accountability, and training.

***Groundwork.*** One of the main reasons that COP flops is inadequate groundwork or preparation. The seeds to plant include some of the following:

- Involve everyone in the change process
- Openly address any and all concerns about COP
- Break down barriers to change
- Educate its leaders and line employees on the merits of COP
- Reassure the line employees that the COP concepts being adopted had not been imported from outside the department but, instead, were an outgrowth of existing programs
- Address problems on a small scale before making the full transition to COP
- Demonstrate to the public and elected officials the benefits of COP
- Provide a training ground for COP concepts and strategies
- Free up a willingness to experiment with new ideas

***Results versus process.*** The first component of the COP attitude is an orientation toward *problem solving*. Embracing the pioneering work of Herman Goldstein (see the section on problem-oriented policing), COP focuses on *results* as well as process. Incorporated into routine operations are the techniques of problem identification, problem analysis, and problem resolution.

***Values.*** COP also relies heavily on values that incorporate citizen involvement in matters that directly affect the safety and quality of neighborhood life. The culture of the police department becomes one that not only recognizes the merits of community involvement, but moreover organizes and manages departmental affairs in ways that are consistent with such beliefs.

***Accountability.*** Because different neighborhoods have different needs and priorities, it is necessary to have an adequate understanding of what is important to a specific neighborhood. To acquire such an understanding, officers must interact with residents on a routine basis and keep them informed of police efforts to fight and prevent neighborhood crime. This ensures accountability to the community, as well as to the department.

***Training.*** Under COP the attitude toward officer training is changed. At the recruit level, cadets are provided information about the complexities and dynamics of the community and how the police fit into the larger picture. Cadet training also enables the future officer to develop community-organizing skills. Supervisory training is designed to provide the skills needed to facilitate the problem-solving process. This is accomplished by training supervisors to solve problems, coordinating officers' activities, planning community-organizing activities, and mapping out criminal investigation. Management training focuses on leadership, vision, and values.

**A NEW SUPERVISORY STYLE.** The COP supervisor will be held accountable for evolving a new philosophy of supervision; empowering line personnel; changing the role of a supervisor; and emphasizing the delivery of quality police services.

***Philosophy of supervision.*** COP is a way of thinking about how to supervise one's self and others to:

- Ensure mutual support among various departmental functions
- Ensure alignment between officers and citizens so that a consensus can be reached on what needs to be done to improve the quality of neighborhood life
- Integrate the expectations of citizens with the actions taken by the police to identify and address conditions that have a negative effect on the quality of neighborhood life
- Ensure that all actions are designed to produce intended results

***Empowerment of beat officers.*** Rather than simply patrolling the streets, beat officers are encouraged to initiate creative responses to neighborhood problems. Beat officers must become actively involved in the affairs of the community. They must be given the authority to make decisions, based on the circumstances of the situation. This empowerment reflects the trust that police leaders have in their officers' ability to make appropriate decisions.

***Supervision and management.*** *Under COP, the role of persons at all levels within the organization changes.* For example, the patrol officer becomes the "manager" of his beat, whereas the supervisor assumes responsibility for facilitating the problem-solving process by training, coaching, coordinating, and evaluating the officers. Management's role is to support the process by mobilizing the resources needed to address citizen concerns and problems.

***Quality police services.*** In COP, the supervisor serves as the quality control checkpoint. Our nation is in a *total quality management* (TQM) movement. We are striving to make our products and services not merely work, but work very well, and more importantly, better than anyone else's. Customers are searching for quality in what they pay for, whether at the retail center or in taxes. Today they have options—even when it comes to policing (e.g., contracting for police services with another agency).

In latter years of life, the father of TQM, Dr. W. Edwards Deming, urged us to look more deeply into quality, to understand what it was truly about. He stated that quality was about the human spirit. "Spirit" comes from the Latin word for breath — breath as a symbol of life.

**A NEW STRUCTURE.** The organization will be reconfigured as a decentralized and power sharing delivery system.

***Decentralization.*** The decentralization of authority and structure is another component of COP. Roles are changed as the authority to participate in the decision-making process expands significantly. The expansion of such empowerment makes it necessary to adjust organizational functions throughout the department.

***Power sharing.*** Responsibility for making decisions is shared by the police and the community after a valid *partnership*—one that encourages *active* citizen involvement in policing efforts—between the two groups has been established. *Passive* citizen involvement will not suffice. Power sharing means that the community is allowed to participate in the decision-making process unless the law specifically gives that authority to the police alone.

**NEW PROGRAMS.** Some of the new programs to be considered are as follows:

***Problem-oriented policing.*** This is the subject of the second half of this responsibility.

***Investigations.*** Neighborhood crime is best solved with information provided by residents. COP makes it necessary to decentralize the investigative function and focus on neighborhood, or area-specific, investigations. Centralized investigations, however, cannot be eliminated entirely as these are needed to conduct pattern- or suspect-specific *citywide* investigations.

***Beat redesign.*** Beat boundaries are drawn to coincide with natural neighborhood boundaries rather than in an arbitrary fashion that meets the needs of the police department. Individual neighborhoods are not placed in multiple beats.

***Permanent assignments.*** Under COP, shift and beat assignments are issued on a permanent, rather than a rotating, basis. This allows the beat officer to become an integral part of the community that he or she has been assigned to protect. When a beat officer is reassigned to another area, his or her replacement is required to participate in an orientation period with the outgoing officer.

***Performance evaluation.*** With the modified roles for all personnel comes the need for a revised system for evaluating officer performance. Rather than simply counting numbers (e.g., number of citations issued, number of arrests made, number of calls handled), performance quality is based on the officer's ability to solve problems and involve the community in the department's crime-fighting efforts.

***Managing calls for service.*** Inherent in COP is the understanding that all police resources will be managed, organized, and directed in a manner that facilitates problem solving. For example, taking of incident reports over the telephone, by mail, or in person at police facilities; holding lower-priority calls; and having officers make appointments with an individual or a group. This provides the officers or deputies more time to interact with "their citizens."

### Structured Exercise 14-2

———◆◆◆◆———

The implementation road is full of barriers and potholes. What should the agency do to reduce and overcome any resistance to COP?

———◆◆◆◆———

## Who Benefits?

———◆◆◆◆———

COP will benefit both the public and the police.

———◆◆◆◆———

If done correctly, COP will benefit both the public and the police. Some of the benefits to the public are

- *A commitment to crime prevention.* Unlike traditional policing, which focuses on the efficient means of *reacting* to incidents, COP strives to confirm that the basic mission of the police is to *prevent* crime and disorder.
- *Public scrutiny of police operations.* Because citizens will be involved with the police, they will be exposed to the "what," " why," and "how" of police work. This is almost certain to prompt critical discussions about the responsiveness of police operations.
- *Accountability to the public.* Until the advent of COP, officers were accountable for their actions only to police management. Now officers also will be accountable to the public with whom they have formed a partnership.
- *Customized police service.* Because police services will be localized, officers will be required to increase their responsiveness to neighborhood problems. As

police–citizen partnerships are formed and nurtured, the two groups will be better equipped to work together to identify and address *specific* problems that affect the quality of neighborhood life.

- *Community organization.* The degree to which the community is involved in police efforts to evaluate neighborhood problems has a significant bearing on the effectiveness of those efforts. The success of any crime-prevention effort depends on the police and citizens working in concert—not on one or the other carrying the entire load alone.

The benefits of COP to the police are

- *Greater citizen support.* As people spend more time working with the police, they learn more about the police function. Experience has shown that as people's knowledge of the police function increases, their respect for the police increases as well. This increased respect, in turn, leads to greater support for the police.
- *Shared responsibility.* Historically, the police have accepted the responsibility for resolving the problem of crime in the community. Under community policing, however, citizens develop a sense of *shared* responsibility.
- *Greater job satisfaction.* Because officers are able to resolve issues and problems within a reasonable amount of time, they see the results of their efforts more quickly.
- *Better internal relationships.* Communication problems among units and shifts have been a chronic problem in police agencies. Because COP focuses on problem solving and accountability, it also increases cooperation among the various segments of the department.
- *Support for organizational change.* COP requires a vast restructuring of the department's organizational structure to ensure the integration of various functions, such as patrol and investigations. The needed changes are new management systems, new training curriculums and delivery mechanisms, a new performance evaluation system, a new disciplinary process, a new reward system, and new ways of managing calls for service.

### *Structured Exercise 14-3*

Are there any additional benefits that should be added to those cited above? Conversely, what are the disadvantages of COP?

## PROBLEM-ORIENTED POLICING

One should view COP as an overall departmental strategy for improving police work. Similarly, POP should be treated as a tactical method for making COP work.

Problem-oriented policing (POP) emphasizes the value of being able to diagnose the continuing problems that lie behind the repeated incidents that are reported to police employees and to design and implement solutions to those problems. Herman Goldstein, one of the foremost thinkers in the police field, defines a police department as practicing POP when it

- Identifies substantive community problems
- Inquires systematically into their nature
- Analyzes community interest and special interest in each problem
- Assesses current responses
- Conducts an uninhibited search for tailor-made solutions
- Takes initiative in implementing solutions
- Evaluates the effectiveness of solutions

---

POP should be treated as a tactical method for making COP work.

---

Many police departments concentrate on one incident at a time as they respond to calls for service. They neglect to assemble into a single picture the separate symptoms they treat. A neighborhood may be experiencing a flood of troubles—street fights, insults to passersby, solicitation by prostitutes, pick-pocketing, and drunken driving—but the department does not recognize their sources in a sports bar. When the sole police response to a community problem is to arrest the current troublemakers, that department is not engaging in POP.

## A Departmental Strategy

Assuming that your department has a mission statement, a strategy or strategies for pursuing its attainment becomes paramount. A strategy includes unique operational programs and a particular management/supervisory style for fulfilling your mission. We earlier described the strategy that guided and helped the police from an arena of amateurism—and all the baggage that entails—to an arena of professionalism. It earned the name *professional crime fighting*. More recently, it has acquired an additional label, *incident driven*.

INCIDENT DRIVEN. Current police practice is primarily incident driven. That is, most police activities are aimed at resolving individual incidents rather than groups of incidents or problems. The incident-driven police department has four characteristics.

First, *it is reactive*. Most of the workload of patrol officers and detectives consists of handling crimes that have been committed: disturbances in progress, traffic violations, and the like. The exceptions—crime prevention and narcotics investigations, for example—make up but a small portion of police work.

Incident-driven police work *relies on limited information*, gathered mostly from victims, witnesses, and suspects. Only limited information is needed because the police objectives are limited: Patrol officers and detectives are trying only to resolve the incident at hand. The primary means of resolving incidents is to *invoke the criminal justice process.* Even when an officer manages to resolve an incident without arresting or citing anyone, it is often the threat of enforcing the law that is the key to resolution. Alternative means of resolution are seldom invoked.

Finally, incident-driven police departments *use aggregate statistics to measure performance.* The department is doing a good job when the citywide crime rate is low, or the citywide arrest rate is high. The best officers are those who make many arrests or service many calls.

Remember, a police agency is not constrained to one strategy for accomplishing its mission. It is important, however, that if two or more strategies are adopted, they be compatible and not confrontational, and one cannot successfully subordinate another. See Figures 14-2 and 14-3 for a comparison of incident-driven and problem-oriented policing.

**PROBLEM DRIVEN.** The practice of POP seeks to improve on other professional crime-fighting models by adding *pro-activeness* and *thoughtfulness.* It differs from COP by the emphasis of an analytic effort. It differs from professional crime fighting/incident driven, which focuses on discovering offenders and apprehending them. It assumes that this alone prevents crime. Also, it assumes that the police can position themselves to see offenses and respond to them quickly.

Problem-oriented policing takes a different posture about crime. In POP it is not automatically accepted that crimes are caused by predatory offenders. (True, in all crimes there will be an offender.) But POP makes the assumption that crimes could be caused by particular continuing problems in a community such as drug dealing. Hence crimes might be controlled, or even prevented, by actions other than the arrest of particular individuals. For example, the police might be able to resolve a chronic dispute or restore order to a disorderly street. Arrest and prosecution remain crucially important tools of policing. But ideas about the causes of crime and methods for controlling it are expanded substantially.

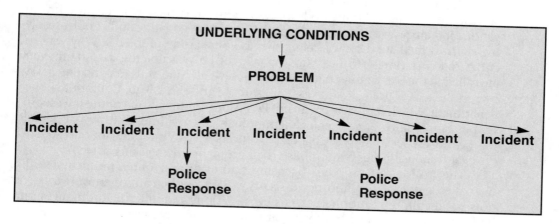

**Figure 14-2**   Incident-driven policing

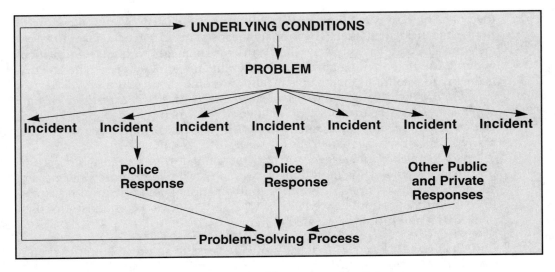

**Figure 14-3**   Problem-oriented policing

---

In POP, the applied imagination of police employees, sworn and civilian alike, is galvanized as a crime-fighting tool.

---

In POP, the applied imagination of police employees, sworn and civilian alike, is galvanized as a crime-fighting tool. Problem identification and problem definition are essential steps in POP. The superficial symptoms of crime are avoided while the root causes are fervently sought. The common linkage of POP, COP, and the professional crime-fighting incident-driven model, however, remains the same—crime control!

The subtle but fundamental switch in perspective requires police and sheriff agencies to broaden their methods for responding to crime beyond patrol, investigation, and arrests. For example, the police can use negotiating and conflict-resolving skills to mediate disputes before they become crime problems. Why wait for crime to occur? Moreover, the police can take corrective action the second time they are called to the scene rather than the sixth or seventh time, thus making timely savings in the use of police resources. For example, the San Diego, California, police department, which has been practicing POP since 1988, has one of the lowest officer per capita ratios of any major metropolitan city, resulting in heavy workloads for the officers. Despite these challenges, officers have found time not only to handle beat responsibilities but to polish their problem-solving skills as well.

The police can use civil licensing authority and other municipal ordinances to enhance neighborhood security. Bars can be cautioned on excessive noise, and children cautioned on curfew violations and loitering ordinances can be expanded to reduce situations that require police involvement.

Further, other local agencies can help to deal with existing or potential criminal offenses. The fire department can be asked to inspect "crack houses" for fire safety regulations. The public works department can be asked to inspect buildings and property for code violations. To the extent that problem solving depends on the initiative and skills of officers and civilians in defining problems and devising solutions, the administrative style of the organization must change. Since POP depends on individual initiative, the agency must decentralize.

Once again, attempts should be made to give full recognition and enhanced rewards to the job of patrol officer. Patrol work has to be seen as a springboard and not a millstone. Recognition and rewards will promote this goal.

## Why POP?

At first blush POP may appear to be another label for crime prevention. Or, it may look like several clever tactics for "cracking down" on a specific police problem. POP is much, much more than this. In fact, it involves an organization-wide and in-depth shift in policies, practices, and thinking. In a few words— *POP places effectiveness first and efficiency second*

There are eight reasons for POP.

1. *Lack of success.* There is an old adage that, "Nothing succeeds so much as a successful failure." The professional crime-fighting strategy, although not a disaster, has not proven itself effective in crime control. Herman Goldstein and a few others pointed this out and in 1979 started their quest to refine an alternative policing approach.

2. *Efficiency has been inefficient.* Police management has been preoccupied with the internal operations and "doing things right." "Right" statistics, "right" training, "right" procedures, and looking "right." POP addresses the highly value-laden question of "why?" Or, rather than simply doing things right, "Are we doing the right things?"

3. *Scarce resources.* Whatever the budget, there is never enough to do the *entire* job. Hence, some demands for service may go begging. POP seeks to establish police priorities. If drug trafficking is the most significant problem, then the first allocation of resources goes to that, and so on. POP means priorities!

4. *Reaction.* It seems that everyone today is talking about, and doing little about, *proactivity.* POP requires self-initiative on the part of the police to prevent or reduce community problems.

5. *Community partnership.* POP encompasses COP or vice versa. The past has seen this partnership attempted in a random or haphazard way. POP is based on a systematic and continuing working relationship between the police and its public.

6. *Brainpower.* POP depends on the thinking of everyone in the department (sworn, civilian, part-time employees, whatever). Once more, we return to the need for *empowerment.* Unfortunately, many police agencies function as if the only "good ideas" come from the top. POP operates on the premise that good ideas can come from anyone, and must be encouraged and rewarded.

7. *Culture.* POP requires that the old ways of doing things be carefully replaced with a different organizational structure and management ethic. This is difficult because most new ideas or systems are suspect of being grossly inefficient or plainly stupid. Usually, the first reaction to POP is—"Big deal, we've been doing this for years." The POP culture is keyed to effectiveness and not efficiency.

8. *Expanded mission.* POP envisions an altered and much better articulated police mission. Earlier, we discussed the police mission and mission statements. It is vital to POP and POP to the department that everyone is "reading off the same music sheet." In other words, the police employee, the department, the policy makers, and the community must understand and, it is hoped, appreciate what the police are accountable for doing.

---

POP places effectiveness first and efficiency second.

---

For many agencies, the mission is no longer limited to the efficient control of street crime. It also includes (1) a strengthened attack on dangerous offenders, organized criminal groups, and white-collar offenders; (2) a more determined effort to resolve the problems that underlie incidents reported to the police; and (3) a heightened concern for fear, disorder, and other problems that communities designate as high-priority issues. The mission at times includes police action on community problems such as drugs in schools, drunk driving, public drunkenness, unsupervised children, and other medical and social crises. Although it is by no means easy for a chief or sheriff to create an organization that can accommodate these diverse purposes, there does not seem to be any fundamental contradiction among these missions. Indeed, many departments are already pursuing these diverse missions with encouraging degrees of success.

## Origins of POP

It is said that police scholar Herman Goldstein, who first described the concept of problem-oriented policing in 1979, is the father of POP. If this is so, the Police Executive Research Forum (PERF) is surely the incubator. PERF has diligently encouraged, nurtured, and guided law-enforcement studies and applications of Goldstein's problem-solving concepts. Many police agencies throughout the justice system—San Diego being the largest metropolitan area—have been the recipients. PERF has provided staff and direction and continues to study in-place applications of strong problem-solving elements in a number of organizations.

## Five Ways to Solve a Problem

There are five ways that problems can be solved, and the measure of effectiveness depends in large part on the characteristics of the problem. These are summarized on the next page:

1. A problem can be solved by eliminating it totally.
2. A problem can be solved by reducing the number of incidents it creates.
3. A problem can be solved by reducing the seriousness of the incidents it creates.
4. A problem can be solved by designing methods for better handling the incidents.
5. A problem can be solved by removing it from police consideration.

## Application Principles

The five principles that serve as a guideline for the application of a successful POP program are:

1. The final process must involve all department members—all ranks and units, all sworn officers and non-sworn department members—in the identification, study, and resolution of problems.
2. The final process must foster the use of a wide variety of data sources—from internal records and officers' knowledge to other government agencies and private individuals and organizations—to understand the causes and consequences of problems.
3. The final process must encourage police department members to work with members of other public and private agencies to devise effective, longlasting solutions to problems.
4. The final process must be capable of becoming an integral part of police decision making, without creating special units or requiring additional resources.
5. The final process must be capable of being applied to other law-enforcement agencies.

## Problem Analysis Guide: SARA

In the late 1980s, the Police Executive Research Foundation and Newport News Police Department designed and tested a problem solving process called SARA. SARA stands for:

1. *Scanning*: identifying the problem
2. *Analysis*: learning the problem's causes, scope, and effects
3. *Response*: acting to alleviate the problem
4. *Assessment*: determining whether the response worked

In addition, a *Problem Analysis Guide* was formulated which suggested potential information sources (see Figure 14-4). The guide plus a *Problem Analysis Report* (Figure 14-5) should be helpful when completing Structured Exercise 14-4. The Problem Analysis Report is based on a hypothetical situation. Insert your facts as presented in the Structured Exercise.

## Structured Exercise 14-4

To: PAAC Committee
From: Lieutenant S. Barrett
Subject: Gay Time Disco

***Details:*** In the last four years, the Gay Time Disco, 1132 Hollywood Boulevard, has had a greater increase in calls for service and reported offense violations than any other liquor-serving establishment in the area.

On September 30, 1998, Officer N. Traub submitted a problem analysis report to the PAAC committee, The majority of the complaints occurred on Wednesday nights between the hours of 2100 and 0230. On Wednesdays the Gay Time featured "ladies night" with $1 draft beer special. The complaints ranged from overcrowding, disorderly persons, fights, drinking in public, drunk persons, loitering, and firearms violations.

A statistical analysis of the Gay Time and eight other liquor establishments in the area was conducted by Officers Traub and J. Baker. During the period of January 1 through June 30, 1998, in comparison to the eight liquor establishments located in the north end of the city, the Gay Time had 42% of the calls for service. From March 1997 to March 1998, the Gay Time had 102 calls for service, with 51 calls occurring on a Wednesday night. Of the 51 calls, the majority were for fights, disorderly and intoxicated persons, and firearms violations.

The problem analysis form was approved by Sergeant T. Smith on August 17, 1998, after supervising the investigative work and analysis done by Officer Traub. (Officer Traub had enlisted the help of Officers Baker and R. Ramos.)

On September 21, 1998, Officer N. Traub with Officers B. Christofferson and D. Phipps arrived at the establishment in plainclothes to review the inside problems. On the exterior, videotaping was conducted of violations in the area.

## Using SARA

At this point, scanning and analysis have occurred. Your job is to consider the R (response) of SARA, and later the A (assessment). Each participant should list a number of possible responses, including violations, other perspectives that should be considered, who should be involved (other agencies, etc.), and strategies.

With a chalkboard (more preferably, a newsprint tablet) appoint someone to list each participant's responses, one participant at a time. For each repeat, add one mark.

Your group is now the Problem Analysis Advisory Committee (PAAC). Review all inputs and delete those that the committee does not support. Remember, the number must be manageable and the response must be logical—doable.

For our purpose, assessment will be PAAC's perception of the desirable and probable outcomes. At the conclusion, each participant is to score his or her responses against the final PAAC selection. Give yourself 10 points for each agreement.

## The Problem Analysis Guide
### (List of topic headings)

- **Actors**
  - Victims
    - Life-style
    - Security measures taken
    - Victimization history
  - Offenders
    - Identity and physical description
    - Life style, education, employment history
    - Criminal history
  - Third parties
    - Personal data
    - Connection to victimization
- **Incidents**
  - Sequence of events
    - Events preceding act
    - Event itself
    - Events following criminal act
  - Physical context
    - Time
    - Location
    - Access control and surveillance
  - Social context
    - Likelihood and probable actions of witnesses
    - Apparent attitude of residents toward neighborhood
  - Immediate results of incidents
    - Harm done to victim
    - Gain to offender
    - Legal issues
- **Responses**
  - Community
    - Neighborhood affected by problem
    - City as a whole
    - People outside the city
  - Institutional
    - Criminal justice system
    - Other public agencies
    - Mass media
    - Business sector
  - Seriousness
    - Public perceptions
    - Perception of others

**Figure 14-4**   Problem Analysis Guide

OXNARD POLICE DEPARTMENT
PROBLEM ANALYSIS REPORT

1. SUBMITTED BY:___B. Kelley_____     ID#___3399_____
2. Date Submitted:___07-03-94_____

## A.  PROBLEM IDENTIFICATION (SCANNING):

3. Describe the Problem: (Who, what, when, where, how, and why)
   Drug usage and dealing from a location historically known as "The Fence".
   Actual address is 232 Avenida Gaviota.

4. Problem Reported by _____Officers on patrol_____
5. Location of Problem (circle) BEAT  1  ②  3  4  5  6  7
6. Date(s) and Time(s) Problem(s) Occurring _Problem has existed in_____

   ___various degrees for 30 years._____

## B.  PROBLEM EXAMINATION (ANALYSIS):

7. Shifts affected: (Circle)     I     II     III     IV
8. Division affected: ___Patrol_____Investigations_____

9. Information Sources: (This list does not include all possible information sources.
   There may be other places where you can get information.) Please indicate <u>all</u>
   sources.

   [xx] Crime Ananlysis Unit        [xx] Parole Office
   [xx] Vice                        [xx] Investigations
   [xx] Crime Watch                 [xx] Neighborhood Canvass
   [  ] Literature Search           [xx] Citizen Complaints
   [xx] Personal Observations       [  ] Surveys
   [xx] Police Informants           [  ] Churches
   [  ] Schools                     [  ] Media
   [  ] Central Records             [xx] Community Leaders
   [xx] Local Businesses            [  ] DMV
   [  ] Other Law Enforcement Agencies
   [  ] Government Agencies, list _____

   _____

10. Findings: (Based on the information you have collected, describe the problem.)
    Historically a location that is a gathering point for those persons
    involved in narcotic usage, dealing and other illegal activities.
    Suspects gather on private property behind a wooden picket-type fence
    for purposes primarily to illegally use and deal controlled substances.
    These persons gather with the consent of the resident. Assaults, muggings,
    etc. have occurred to passerbys at the location. Numerous arrests and
    selective enforcement has not eliminated the problem.

**Figure 14-5**    Problem Analysis Report

## C. STRATEGIES (Responses):

11. Goals and Objectives: (What do you expect to accomplish?)

Eliminate the gathering of persons for illegal activities at the location.

12. Recommended strategies: (how do you expect to obtain the above result?)

The non-resident owner of the rental property has been located and has agreed to abate the problem. Officer Kelley, the property owner, and the resident have met and the resident has agreed not to allow loiters, placed a lock on the gate and to

13. Date and time for implementation: __08-15-94__                                    (con't)
14. Expected date and time for termination: ____continual____
15. Expected number of officers needed: _routine patrol to monitor_
16. Expected number of vehicles needed: __same__ Types: _____

## D. SUPERVISORY REVIEW OF STRATEGIES:

[ ] Approved          [ ] Disapproved

Recommendations:

Date: __08-17-94__     Supervisor: _RKelley LT_

## E. EVALUATION (Assessment):

17. Did you get the results you expected?

[ ] Yes      [ ] No      [ ] Partially      [ ] Temporarily

18. Actual number of Officers Used: _Routine patrol_
19. Actual number of Vehicles Used: _____
20. Actual Number of Hours Used: _____
21. Describe the results of what happened.

22. Is any further action required? If yes, explain.

Continued monotoring of activities at the location.

23. Additional comments:

(12) con't.

sign complaints against trespassers.

**Figure 14-5**   *(Continued)*

## IMPLEMENTATION

To implement POP, you must operationalize eleven interrelated program components. The components fall into one of three phases:

**1.** Identification of problems
**2.** Analysis of problems
**3.** Options

### Identification of Problems

The identification and definition of police problems encompasses components 1 to 3. It has been often stated that problem identification is two thirds of the effort in getting a solution. We concur. We also agree that if an option exists, problems ought to be explored as close to the operating level as possible.

**WHO IDENTIFIES PROBLEMS.** In general, problems will be surfaced by (1) the community, (2) police management, and (3) line employees.

***Community.*** Community involvement in problem identification has benefits and downsides. On the one hand, community members will express their needs and frustrations. On the other, their problems may not involve situations that the police are equipped or obligated to handle. Bluntly, it may be someone else's problem. For example, a needed traffic signal near a senior citizen home is not likely to be something the police can resolve. They may help— but some other agency is actually responsible for installing it. This is where candor and openness count.

***Police management.*** Police managers and supervisors are in a position to see the so-called big picture. We covered the importance of vision earlier. The perceptive, aware manager and supervisor can supply vital input to POP.

***Line employees.*** Of the three, the line employees are in the best position to identify problems. We spoke of empowerment earlier. Employees should be not only encouraged but also *rewarded* for their observations and ideas. When we use the term "employees" we include everyone working—paid workers and volunteers, sworn servants and civilians—for the agency.

**PROBLEMS ARE LIMITLESS.** Typically, more problems will outcrop than time or resources can address. Once a list has been created, then the problems must be rank ordered. Some of the criteria for achieving this are as follows:

**1.** Is it really a police problem or not?
**2.** What is its impact (size and cost) to the community?
**3.** How much support can be anticipated from the community in tackling it?
**4.** Does it in any way threaten our civil rights?
**5.** How much enthusiasm do the police employees possess in combating it?
**6.** Is it indeed something that can be solved with existing resources?

**COMPONENT 1: GROUPING INCIDENTS AS PROBLEMS.**   Police incidents are usually dealt with as stand-alone, unique events. Hence, the first component of POP is to move beyond just incident handling. It requires that incidents be looked on as *symptoms of a problem*. The police have to probe for relationships (how do incidents connect with one another) and conditions (what is the real cause of the problem).

**COMPONENT 2: FOCUS ON SUBSTANTIVE PROBLEMS.**   Reoccurring problems are substantive problems—or what we think of as *police work*. Police are prone to identify substantive problems in terms of internal management (e.g., not enough staff, poor training, malingering officers, low pay). Simply, but importantly, substantive problems are those very problems that justify establishing a police agency in the first place. Making this happen is not easy. The "internal management" habit is tough to break. It takes time and practice. As a supervisor, you're responsible for making the transition.

**COMPONENT 3: EFFECTIVENESS FIRST.**   Some would attempt to define effectiveness in terms of solving a problem—making something stop or go away. To do this in police work is ridiculous and even counterproductive. After all, zero crime is impossible. Some agencies point with pride to statistics that reveal a reduced increase in crime rates over last year. Effectiveness is defining for a specific agency, in a particular community, what ought to be tackled and in what order of priority.

## Analysis of Problems

This phase involves components 4 to 7. The analysis of problems includes (1) types of information, (2) sources of information, and (3) scientific rules.

**TYPES OF INFORMATION.**   Those who identified the problem in the first place are likely to be the best resource for deciding what kinds of information are needed to solve it. Brainstorming is an excellent technique for arriving at what's required.

**SOURCES OF INFORMATION.**   Some of the sources are

1. Existing literature (research reports, current journals, and the like)
2. Police files
3. Knowledge of line employees
4. Victims
5. Community
6. Perpetrators
7. Other agencies (general government and criminal justice)

**SCIENTIFIC RULES.**   By their very nature, our police are "applied social scientists." They are constantly being challenged to think, act logically, and be objective. Long and detailed reports are turn-offs to many people. POP doesn't demand time-consuming and profound reports. A page or two is sufficient—if it adheres to the facts, and is objective and logical. The police employee must be alert to such deficiencies as inadequate police files. The current responses to a problem may be confusing and very hard to describe.

**Component 4: Setting Up a System.**   Once the seemingly random incidents have been categorized into groups, a system for the collection of pertinent facts and their analysis must be designed. Crime and service statistics are helpful but much too limited. Systematic analysis includes (1) telephone questionnaire and individual surveys of those who might know something about the problem (e.g., citizens, victims, officers, offenders, other governmental personnel); and (2) literature searches of government and private-sector repositories. Essentially, social scientific tools are applied at this juncture.

**Component 5: Redefining Problems.**   What at first blush may be a traffic problem on further analysis should be categorized as a drug problem. *Problem definition can make or break a POP program.* Is there any doubt that attempting to solve a traffic problem versus a drug problem involves different methods and training? Additionally, there is an enormous difference between thinking tactically about dealing with burglars from a legal viewpoint and coping with burglary as it exists in the community. How we perceive and label a problem ultimately determines how we go after it.

**Component 6: Who's Interested (or Should Be)?**   Simply viewing conduct as illegal is not efficient in constructing a response to a problem. Because we mentioned gangs earlier (Oxnard), let's consider it as one example. To determine who is or ought to be interested in gang activity, we'd ask: Why is the community concerned? What are the social costs? Who is being harmed and to what degree? There are obviously many more questions of a similar bent. For the police to invent a successful plan to deal with gangs (or any other problem), they must find out who is interested in it. From this set of multiple interests will emerge a plan of attack.

**Component 7: What's Working Now.**   We have witnessed police agencies discard successful operational practices. They tend to leap from one fad or technique to another. Frequently, the officers have the answer, but management fails to ask them. It is here that POP surfaces one of its major strengths—"If it's not broke, don't fix it." If the agency's approach to "espousal abuse" is successful then, unless some other tactic can nearly guarantee an improvement, don't fuss with it.

### Options

The development of optional choices encompasses components 8 to 11. All right, we've found and analyzed the problem—what now are the options for hammering it? Obviously, the choices are infinite. To gain some focus here, we'll lump them into nine groups while emphasizing that there is a lot of leakage and overlap.

1. *Frequent offenders.* Those few who create many incidents.

2. *Interagency cooperation.* The problem can be handed to another agency or jointly handled.

3. *Conflict management.* "Getting to yes" via mediation and negotiation.

4. *Process of making "public" public information.* This is an underused but potentially highly potent problem-solving tool. Here are some of the uses: (1) reduces fear; (2) helps people solve their own problems; (3) educates people about their rights and responsibilities as citizens; (4) warns possible victims; (5) develops cooperation and support; and (6) indicates what the police can and cannot do.

5. *Galvanizing of citizens.* POP depends on it! It goes beyond informing them to include organizing their support.

6. *Existing controls.* Means authority figures deploying their influence. Examples are teacher–student; apartment manager–renter; parent–child; employer–employee.

7. *Defensible space.* Denotes attempts to fortify our physical environment in some fashion, thus making crime and undesirable behavior more difficult, if not impossible. Alarm systems, antitampering packaging, lighting, and locking systems are a few examples.

8. *Increased or expanded regulations.* Requires a lot of imagination and risk taking. Some police agencies have used city building codes and land-use regulations to combat drug and prostitution problems. One city (Monrovia, California) enacted an ordinance that specifically prohibits loitering in drug-trafficking areas.

9. *Legal intervention.* Also requires experimentation and a willingness to take a chance. For example, some police agencies are placing public inebriates and the mentally ill under "temporary detention." Some are using decoys and sting operations. Some may target or saturate a crime problem such as gang violence. Some may intervene without making an arrest (traffic violations) or making an arrest without intending to prosecute (civil disturbance violations, e.g., "right to life"). More and more police agencies are aggressively confiscating property that aids in, or is the result of, a crime ("asset forfeiture").

**COMPONENT 8. CUSTOMIZED OR CANNED?** In the 1970s, the criminal justice system was filled with talk of "technology transfer." If a piece of equipment or a program functioned well in one organization, then it could be easily lifted and inserted into another. Many departments borrowed or purchased "turn-key" computers, helicopters, modified work weeks (4-40, 3-12, 5-9, and so on) and a variety of operational programs (e.g., team policing, neighborhood watch, Drug Abuse Resistance and Education). Most found that canned approaches when incorporated in an agency had to be retrofitted, redesigned, and restudied. POP relies on a tailor-made response. Problems are specific to an agency and any method of resolving them must be specific. POP is not saying, however, that agencies should shun the innovations of others. On the contrary, they should be avidly sought out and rigorously examined for potential use. At the same time,

POP would caution the interested user—if it appears helpful, then test it and modify it in strict accordance with your department's particular problem.

**COMPONENT 9: TAKE THE OFFENSIVE.** Taking the offensive is accomplished in three ways. First, the initial identification of problems must be constant and systematic. Second, the police must be active in educating the public and placing choices before it. Third, the police should be advocates for the community (reporting if garbage is uncollected, potholes are unfilled, or vehicles are abandoned).

**COMPONENT 10: DECISION VISIBILITY.** More and more we're seeing the officer educating the public on why certain things are or are not done. Decisions are explained. It assists the public in understanding that the police do not have as much authority as they think, and they'll take risks and sometimes fail—they're not infallible.

**COMPONENT 11: EVALUATION AND FEEDBACK.** Evaluation and feedback are not a concluding POP step. They are designed to support all of the other components in making incremental adjustments and improvements. For example, a reliable evaluation should be able to inform the department if its original grouping of problems was valid. Without this component, POP is likely to fail.

### Structured Exercise 14-5

The exercises that follow are best handled in groups of six to eight persons.

1. *Problem analysis report.* Return to the Problem Analysis Report (Figure 14-5). Identify a problem that your agency is confronted with and complete it. If you do not work for a police agency, then seek to secure the cooperation of a department in completing it. (You may be doing them a big favor.)

2. *Rank ordering problems.* We listed six criteria for rank ordering problems. Apply the criteria to the following problems: (1) armed robbery, (2) drug trafficking, (3) homelessness, (4) child abuse, and (5) police corruption. What does your ranking look like?

3. *Options—A.* Earlier we conceptualized at least nine avenues or options for coping with a problem. Can you add one or two more options to our list?

4. *Options—B.* Imagine that you work for a very honest, bright, and outspoken sheriff. His demeanor has irritated your major newspaper to the extent that it blasts him at every opportunity. When he gets the chance, he hits the paper back verbally. He is in charge of the highly successful regional drug-enforcement team.

   The captain that manages the unit has just informed him that three supervisory employees of the paper are trafficking in cocaine (estimated sales $7,000 per day). The users identified so far number thirty-four, most of whom work for the paper.

What options does he have? Which one is the best?

5. *Options—C.* Now imagine that you work for one of the leading police chiefs in your state. He reveals to you and a few others that the city manager and city council informed him that the graffiti problem had grown to the point that the city is losing revenues. In the last three years, he has used POP to decrease all part 1 crimes. Nonetheless, they've indicated that his job hinges on him stopping the graffiti. What are his options? Which one is best?

—•••◦•—

## CONCLUDING THOUGHT

If POP is approached as a method for improving the police, it will fail. If, however, it is looked on as a way to *solve community problems*, it has a chance of working. The agencies now using POP have demonstrated a willingness to cooperate with others in solving community problems. Further, they've resisted dwelling on the internal shortcomings of their organization. Quality and effectiveness are being redefined, thanks to POP, from "response times" and "crime rates" to *getting solutions*.

## KEY POINTS

- Although not identical, POP and COP are highly complementary of one another.
- A strategy encompasses the operational programs and management style for achieving the department's mission.
- A police agency can adopt more than one crime-control strategy—but they must be compatible.
- POP improves on the professional crime strategy by adding *protectiveness* and *thoughtfulness*.
- The common linkage between POP, COP, and the professional crime fighting model is crime control.
- Patrol work has to be given enhanced status and rewards for POP to be successful.
- POP places effectiveness over efficiency in importance.
- POP is comprised of eleven component parts that commence with the *grouping of incidents together* and ends with *evaluation and feedback*.
- Problems should be identified and defined as close to the line level as possible.
- Those who identified the problem are probably in the best position to decide what kinds of information are needed to solve it.
- There are at least nine options for handling a problem.

## DISCUSSION

1. What are the similarities and differences between POP and COP?

2. The professional crime-fighting strategy contained two significant flaws. What are they? How does POP avoid them?

3. How does POP differ from the professional crime-fighting strategy?

4. What type of structural changes must be made in an organization as it moves toward POP?

5. What can be done to make patrol work more appealing and prestigious?

6. Which one of the several ingredients of POP is the most important?

7. Eight reasons for POP were listed earlier. Rank order them in terms of their influence on causing POP to happen in police work today.

8. What are "substantive problems"? Can you cite some examples of such a problem?

9. What are the benefits and disadvantages to having the community involved in problem identification?

# RESPONSIBILITY FIFTEEN

# *Anticipation*

The police supervisor is responsible for sensing, clarifying, and adapting to evolving trends in his or her work environment and career field.

*There is nothing more difficult to take in hand, more perilous to conduct or more uncertain in its success than to take the lead in the introduction of a new order of things.*

—Machiavelli

Responsibilities 1 to 14 are relatively enduring. They have a proven staying power. On occasion, the winds of change will add in or modify the steps a supervisor should consider taking when fulfilling a responsibility. Anticipating trends that signal the need for change is by far superior to reacting to them.

A television sports commentator remarked about a highly rated team that suffered a dismal loss, "Once is an accident. Twice is a trend."

The celebrated futurist, John Naisbett, cautions us that we must endeavor to distinguish fads from trends. He related that fads are explosive and accompanied by a lot of hype and gimmicks. Fads are short-lived and frequently emanate from Washington, D.C. Conversely, trends emerge quietly without much fanfare. You have to concentrate on the horizon to spot them. Trends are conceptualized and take root where we live and work. The advice of the sports commentator can be relied on here. Once may be a quirk, but if you see it twice or more, then you may be looking at a trend.

## WHY ANTICIPATION

Being highly alert to developing trends and incoming demands for change and adaption is the prerequisite for anticipation. Once I see or feel a trend on the move, I am able to anticipate its consequences for me as a supervisor and those in my work unit. In essence, I am able to get ahead of it, perhaps harness it, and respond to it after thoughtful consideration. Trend spotting guarantees me the time and opportunity to initiate action that is likely to succeed. Hence, one reason for enhancing your anticipatory capacity is to make early and better decisions on what to do in light of an identified trend.

Another reason for a police supervisor to be mentally anticipative is to predict trends. Predicting trends is different than spotting them after they have surfaced. It is also much more esoteric and the error factor is higher. There is less risk in discovering a trend and then anticipating the consequences of your choices about how to cope with it. When you anticipate that which is unseen, you are entering the arena of future-gazing. Anticipating future trends is a blend of some luck and a lot of labor.

Community-oriented policing (COP) is not a fad, it is a trend. Thus, you can anticipate its consequences for you and your department. A more demanding anticipation of you is—what next? What type of a police services model can you anticipate eventually supplanting COP? Similarly, what might we anticipate as the next major thorn in the side of our police system?

## WAYS TO ANTICIPATE

Many of the preceding responsibilities contain ideas or ways to enhance your ability to anticipate incoming events and trends. See in particular the section on problem-oriented policing and the SARA method.

Anticipation begins with a heightened perception of the way our lives move forward. We suspend our doubts and distractions in order to glimpse events starting to unfold. Typically, it is accompanied by a profound sense of restlessness.

Anticipation occurs when we become conscious of the *coincidences* in our lives. When we organize them and correctly interpret them, trends can be detected. Being acutely aware of who you are, where you are, and what you are doing is critical. Where we are today is not just the evaluation of technology; it is the evaluation of thought.

Watch for coincidences, ask why, and your capacity to anticipate will be measurably enhanced.

## TREND ONE—CAREER PATH CIVILIANS

The question is not, "Will we employ civilians?" but "Where and how many civilians will be employed?"

In the 1950s, some police agencies discovered that civilian employees were beneficial. Basically, civilian employees freed the sworn officer to do "real" police work. Their numbers gradually grew to the point that police departments are now one civilian to every three police officers.

This trend does not pertain to their number but their power. Civilians in police agencies are paving career paths. They are promoting upward and will continue to do so. This trend will result in major divisions of a police agency being commanded by a civilian employee. Civilians will supervise sworn personnel.

Civilian staff are a reality. How much power they will assert is at issue. Analyzing this trend indicates that the civilian employee, civilian supervisor, and civilian manager are becoming a significant force in the operations of our police agencies.

## TREND TWO—TECHNOLOGY AND TOUCH

The use and influence of technology in police work will accelerate. Electronic files, laptop (palmtop) data processing, miniaturization of hardware, increased microprocessing speeds, portable digital communication devices, and more will proliferate. The information super highway will take shape. The majority of our mail will be e-mail or fax. We'll be defined by our World Wide Web site. We'll be a cold fact, a set of impersonal numbers. Incidently, those that believe data processing technology will create a "paperless" society are going to be surprised. There will be more, not less, paper.

The police supervisor will be asked to counter our loss of "self." Overriding all of the virtual reality, touchless technology will be a human being. The police supervisor will be expected to forge a human linkage between the officer and his department. The supervisor will be more than ever before asked to instill a feeling of warmth and care into a cold and technology-driven working environment.

## TREND THREE—WORK-FORCE DIVERSITY

Work-force diversity is a well-recognized trend. The vast majority of police organizations are comprised of both genders, more than one race, two to three generations and much more. In some parts of our country, there is no majority, everyone represents one or more minorities. One should expect that this trend will expand and accelerate. For one example, a few years ago, there were a few civilians or a few female officers in our departments. Now there are many. Many police agencies report that one in three employees are civilians and females in supervisory and management jobs.

What can and should be done to understand diversity? To begin with, do not limit your thinking or approach to the notion of "cultural diversity." Workplace diversity is much more encompassing.

Being a successful supervisor in a work environment that consists of diverse employees demands that you first know yourself, and then those who work for you, very well. The majority of this text is intended to help you do just that.

## Trend Four—Ethical Dilemmas

A person we know often comments, "I can resist everything except temptation." By our very nature, all of us experience temptation. Temptations can range from ordering a second piece of pie to stealing evidence from the property room. With all of the temptations bombarding us daily, our judgments are constantly being tested.

Our ability to rationalize or shift accountability exacerbates our problem in dealing with ethical dilemmas.

A police agency can and should anticipate that more employees will succumb to temptations that are unethical and/or unlawful. Fortunately, this trend can be countered, and even erased. Better recruitment and selection is one approach. Of equal importance is training! We are quick to acknowledge that integrity and ethics can't be taught. On the other hand, we know that integrity and ethics can be learned! We learn our integrity and ethics by example and constant training and retraining on doing what is right when confronted by an ethical dilemma.

## Trend Five—Fewer Qualified Job Seekers

Demographics tell us that, in our nation, there will be fewer people available to work. Behind the "baby boomers" is a generation that does not contain as many folks. When you consider this in light of the large number of police employees who will retire within the next five years, there is going to be a scramble for available talent. Police agencies can and should anticipate a serious challenge in recruiting and selecting police officers and civilian employees.

Not only will there be shortfall in the sheer number of employable people, those qualified to do police work are likely to diminish. Drug abuse and an absence of "life experiences" are two culprits that reduce the talent pool.

Police agencies can expect to commit an enormous amount of time and energy to attracting and then insuring they are hiring honest and responsible employees who can be trained to do good police work.

## Trend Six—Modified Workweek

The modified workweek is an established and rapidly growing trend. We see: 4:10, 3:12, 9:80, and more. Telecommuting is a reality in some jobs. There are obvious advantages to the agency (e.g, peak period deployment) and the employee (e.g., less commuting time to work).

A supervisor can and should anticipate obstacles in the endeavor to rate his or her staff's performance. Some work schedules severely inhibit a supervisor's ability to accurately evaluate assigned personnel. Many supervisors are frustrated by not having enough contact with a person under review. Rating systems are breaking down due to the supervisor not being in a position to make judgments about someone's behavior. Modified workweeks, vacation time, rotation among shifts, and the like, seriously decrease the exposure that a supervisor has to the work efforts of subordinates.

Many techniques are being applied to overcome this situation. Multiple raters (two or more supervisors) are being used to rate a single police employee. Much better are the deployment schedules that keep the supervisor attached to his or her work unit. If concrete steps are not taken to offset the negative aspects of this trend, performance evaluations will be at least meaningless or, worse yet, harmful.

## TREND SEVEN—COMMUNITY-ORIENTED POLICING

Community-oriented policing (COP) and problem-oriented policing (POP) are not fads, but trends. Granted, some COP and/or POP programs are paper tigers. Nonetheless, many agencies are exerting enormous energy to make them operable and, thus, a reality. (Responsibility Fourteen covered this subject.)

The police supervisor can and should anticipate COP and POP to change. In other words, how might they be made better? Are there any new programs or tactics that would make them more effective? Such thinking confutes the adage, "If it isn't broke, don't fix it.... As soon as anything proves workable, start anticipating how you can improve it.

## TREND EIGHT—SERVICE EVALUATION

It's small, but we believe we see a trend toward service evaluation. Some police agencies, like their business counterparts, are systematically asking their customers, "How are we doing?"

A police supervisor can and should anticipate designing and implementing a method for reaching out to those that they serve and asking such questions as:

Rate the following questions from 1 through 7, 7 is high.

- My sense of security in our community?
    1    2    3    4    5    6    7

- The quality of our police services?
    1    2    3    4    5    6    7

- My chance of being the victim of a major crime?
    1    2    3    4    5    6    7

- Overall I would rate my police agency?
    1    2    3    4    5    6    7

There are three major ways to elicit feedback on a service evaluation questionnaire—telephone, mail, and a direct handout to those contacted. Those agencies that have employed such a feedback instrument have found the results reinforcing, rewarding, and helpful in anticipating evolving community needs.

## TREND NINE—BUSINESSLIKE

Since its inception, the American police have looked at their assigned turf as a monopoly. "When it comes to police service, we're the only choice in town." Additionally, they emphasized a bottom line of crime statistics. "When it comes to judging us, focus on these hard data and percentages." Finally, our police have used the fear of crime to leverage their requests for more and better resources.

All of the above is changing. Police departments are being operated as businesses. Being the only game in town is no longer true. There are options. Cities can contract for police services with other cities, sheriff's departments, state police; they can combine city departments into regional police agencies, and more. Police departments have shifted their bottom-line emphasis to one of a process of quality and service. Police departments are learning to do more with less, simplify, stretch, and use the synergy of teamwork to produce results.

The police supervisor can and should anticipate new ways for police service to be more businesslike.

## TREND TEN—YOUR TURN

We've identified nine trends and then briefly anticipated their impacts on the police supervisor and the police agency. Now it's your turn to envision a trend and then anticipate its consequences for the supervisor and the department.

The tenth trend is up to you. So is the daily privilege and effort to fulfill all FIFTEEN RESPONSIBILITIES up to you. We have no doubt that you and other police supervisors will do so and thus succeed in making police work all the more professional.

# Index

## A

Accountability, 1, 3
  community-oriented policing (COP) and, 332, 334
  integrity and, 43
  leadership and, 76
Adams, J. Stacy, 140
Adjudication of complaints, 237
Affirmative action programs, 318
Agile organization, 295–99
Alderfer's ERG theory, 135–36
All-channel network, 96–97
Alternatives, setting objectives and, 164
Altruistic egoism, 275
Analysis:
  negotiations and, 250
  of problems, problem-oriented policing (POP) and, 347–48
  Anticipation, 13, 353–58
  reasons for, 354
Attention through vision, 70–71
Attitudes, 19
Authority, 57
  as bottom up, 66
  matching responsibility and, 293–94
Autocracy, 5
Avoidance of conflict, 224

## B

Bargaining over positions, 248
Beat assignments, community-oriented policing (COP) and, 333
Beat boundaries, community-oriented policing (COP) and, 333
Behaviorally anchored rating scales (BARS), 210, 211
Behavioral theory of leadership, 60, 61
Believing, trust and, 309
Bennis, Warren, 57, 60, 68, 75
Blanchard, Ken, 109
Body language, 87
Boundarylessness, 110–11, 296
Budgets, 156
Bureaucracies, 92, 288–95
  cornerstones of, 289
  Weber on, 289–91, 295
Burnout, 148
Businesslike police service, 358

## C

Caring, delegation and, 179
Category II activities, 116, 117
  becoming a Category II police supervisor, 118–23
  action and being flexible, 123
  goals, 120–21
  mission statement, 119–20
  roles, 120
  schedule, 121–22
Central-tendency errors, 197
Chain network, 95–96
Change (changing), 7–9
  managing, 7–8
  resistance to, 8–9
  stress as demand for, 254, 256
  values, 22–23
Channel blockage, coping with, 104
Circle network, 96
Citizen complaints, 233–37
Citizen relations, problem employees and, 228–31
Civilian employees, 354–55

for change, stress as, 254, 256
  of communications, 82
Deming, W. Edwards, 10, 333
Dependency, partnership and, 6
Direction of behavior, as element of motivation, 131
Discussion, negotiations and, 250
Dissatisfaction, change in values and, 22–23
Distress, 262, 263
Diversity in the workplace, 318–21, 355
Division of labor, 289, 292, 293
Downward flow of communications, 90–91
Drucker, Peter F., 12, 158, 240
Ducking, empowerment and, 169–70

**E**

Education. *See also* Training
  ethical, 46–48
Effort, as element of motivation, 131
Einstein, Albert, 109–10
Emotional indicators, values as, 25
Emotions:
  as barrier to communication, 102
  as stressors, 260
Empathic listening, 87–89
Empowerment, 12, 168–83
  "all or none" approach to, 170
  community-oriented policing (COP) and, 332
  decision making and, 169, 170
  delegation and, 171, 173–79
  benefits of delegation, 174–75
  context of delegation, 175
  letting go, 173–74, 178
  lonership versus ownership delegation, 176–78
  objections to delegating, 173
  trust and, 178
  obstacles to, 169–71
  participation and, 171, 180–83
  partnership and, 4, 6
  problem-oriented policing (POP) and, 339
  through stewardship, 77
Environmental stressors, 260
Equity theory of motivation, 140
Ethical code, 41, 42
Ethics (ethical issues), 11, 34, 37–55, 356. *See also*
    Integrity; Values
  anticipating problems, 48
  belief in innate human goodness and, 49
  collaboration and, 45–46
  decision making and, 41
  defined, 38
  exercises, 38, 40, 41, 47–48
  inspiration and, 44–45
  integration and, 49–50

laws and, 39–40
  as own reward, 48
  paradigms and, 50
  recognition and early detection of, 46–47
  temptations and, 49
  training and education in, 43–50
Ethos, 37–38
Eustress, 262, 263
Evaluation:
  in objective-setting process, 165
  of problem-oriented policing (POP), 350
  service, 357
Example, leadership by, 58
Expectancy theory of motivation, 138–39
Expectations, communication and, 82
Expertise:
  bureaucracy and, 290
  power to lead and, 58
External partnerships, 12

**F**

Face-to-face communication, 94, 100
Fair play, 71
Feedback:
  communicating, 90, 91
    on individual needs, 93
    on objectives and methods, 92
    on policies and practices, 92
  in objective-setting process, 165
  performance evaluation and, 213
  in problem-oriented policing (POP), 350
  values and, 31
Field training officer (FTO), 312, 313
Filtering, as barrier to communication, 102
Filters, values as, 24
Flexibility, 9
Forcing, conflict resolution by, 225
Formal communication channels, 83–84
Formal leaders, 58–59
Frankl, Victor, 253
Freezing-up of relations between people, 316
Functional supervision, 291

**G**

Gates, Bill, 101
General adaptation syndrome (GAS), 255, 257
Generation gap, values and, 24
Global rating scales (GRS), 193–97
Goals, 12, 150–67. *See also* Objectives
  clarification of, 92
  communicating, 91
  management by objectives (MBO) and, 157
  motivation and, 147

Lonership delegation, 176–77
Loop in downward communications, 91

# M

Management:
  activities of, 294
  community-oriented policing (COP) and, 333
  scientific, 291
  total quality (TQM), 333
Management by objectives (MBO), 92, 156–62
  dynamics of, 159–60
  goals and objectives and, 157–58
  obstacles to, 166–67
  performance evaluation and, 213
  philosophy of management and supervision
    and, 162
  self-discipline and, 161–62
  setting objectives, 160–61
  specific objectives, 160
Managing by wandering around (MBWA), 94–95,
    101, 102, 117
Maslow's hierarchy of needs, 135, 137
MBO. See Management by objectives
MBWA (managing by wandering around), 94–95,
    101, 102, 117
McClelland's achievement, power, and affiliation
    theory, 137
Meaning:
  communication as movement and understand-
    ing of, 81
  through communication, 71–72
Meetings, 100
Memoranda, 99
Message blockage, reducing, 103
Messages. See also Communication(s)
  types of, 98–102
  volume of, 97–98
Minority groups, 319
Misconduct, police, 228. See also Citizen com-
    plaints
  legalistic, 230
  moralistic, 230–31
  professional, 230
Mission. See also Goals
  departmental and personal, 66–67
  of the police, 326
  of problem-oriented policing (POP), 340
Mission statements, 67–69, 150
  for community-oriented policing (COP), 331
  performance evaluation and, 214
Mistakes, positive self- and other-regard and, 75
Modeling, 21
Mooney, James D., 289
Moralistic misconduct, 230–31

Motivation, 12, 129–49
  defined, 130–31
  goal setting and, 147
  individual differences and, 146
  job satisfaction and, 143
  matching people to jobs and, 146
  performance differentiated from, 131–32
  questions and answers about, 141–42
  reasons for paying attention to, 130
  rewards and, 147
  intrinsic and extrinsic, 132–33, 146
  theories of, 135–41
  Alderfer's ERG theory, 135–36
  equity theory of motivation, 140
  expectancy theory, 138–39
  Herzberg's motivation-hygiene theory, 137
  Maslow's hierarchy of needs, 135, 137
  McClelland's achievement, power, and affilia-
    tion theory, 137
  need theories, 135–38
  procedural justice theory, 141
  value system and, 25
  winning environment and, 146
Motivation-hygiene theory, Herzberg's, 137
Motives, ethics and, 49

# N

Naisbett, John, 353
Needs, Maslow's hierarchy of, 135–37
Need theories of motivation, 135–38
Negotiations, 243–50
  adopting objective criteria, 249–50
  analysis and, 250
  bargaining over positions, 248
  being nice, 248–49
  concentrating on interests, not positions, 249
  discussion and, 250
  general approach to, 243
  generating a number of options, 249
  planning and, 250
  principled, 247–48
  separating the people from the conflict, 249
Networks, communication, 95–97
Neurotic employees, 226
Neutrality, conflict resolution and, 246
Nonverbal communications, 87
Nonverbal signs, as barrier to communication,
    102

# O

Objective criteria, negotiations and, 249
Objectives. See also Goals
  communicating, 92

Responsibilities (*Continued*):
  groups of, 11–13
  overview of, 1–2
Rethinking, 297
Rewards, 147
  authority to administer, 57
  intrinsic and extrinsic, 132–33, 146
Roles, group dynamics and, 304–5
Routine reports, 98–99
Routinization, bureaucracy and, 290
Rules:
  bureaucracy and, 290
  limitations of, 45

## S

Safe and happy place (SHP), 275
Sanctions, authority to issue, 57
SARA problem solving process, 341, 342
Schizophrenic employees, 226
Scientific management, 291
Self-discipline, management by objectives (MBO) and, 161–62
Self-interest, 2, 4, 6
  ethics and, 47
Self-reality, conflict resolution and, 246
Self-regard, positive, 74–76
Self-supervision, 1
Selye, Hans, 257–58, 275
Sender blockage, overcoming, 103
Sensitivity training, 318–19
Sermonizing, 46
Service:
  partnership and, 6–7
  partnership and commitment to, 4
Sexual harassment, 241–43
Sharing, 182
Significant, 213
Significant emotional events (SEEs), change in values and, 22
Simon, Herbert A., 261
Simplification, 297
Situational theory of leadership, 60, 62–64
Smoothing, 224–25
Socialization, 21–22
Span of control, 294
Speed, 9, 295
Standards, value system as a set of, 25
Steiner, George A., 155
Stewardship, 77
Strategic planning, 155
Strategy, departmental, 336
Stress, 12, 253–77
  converting into wellness, 271–76
  as demand for change, 254, 256
  detecting one's level of, 263–71
  medical findings on, 256–57
  responsibility of the police supervisor, 254–59
  sources of, 259–61
  types of, 262–63
Stress management, 271–76
Stretch, 297
Strictness errors, 196
Subformal channels of communication, 84–85
Subjective time, 110, 111
Superordinate goals, conflict resolution and, 224
Supervision:
  functional, 291
  leadership and, 56, 59–60
Supervision by objectives (SBO), 12, 162
Supportive relationships, 274
Symbol blockage, decreasing, 103

## T

Task effectiveness, 305
Taylor, 295
Taylor, Frederick W., 289, 291
Team leadership, 298
Team policing, 324, 330
Teams, 302–5
  advantages of, 305, 308–9
  building, 303–5
  effectiveness of, 304–5
  training, 311–17
    delivery of training, 317
    effective training, 314–15
    establishing objectives, 316
    evaluation of training, 317
    goals of training, 312–13
    lag in attention, 313–14
    process of training, 313–14
    responsibility of the police supervisor, 312
    strategies, 316
Teamwork, 13, 71, 116, 160, 185, 301–22. *See also* Teams
  group dynamics and, 304–5
Technological communications, 101–2
Technology, 355
Telephone conversations, 100
Time, 107–25
  boundaryless, 110–11
  performance appraisal and, 190
  productivity and, 111–12
  self-mastery of, 109–11
  subjective, 110, 111
  wasters of, 117–18
Time dimension, 109
Time management, 11
  Category II activities, 116–23

becoming a Category II police supervisor, 118–123
fast versus slow decisions, 115
four generations of, 115–16
involvement of the total you in, 108
Job-Time Analysis Form, 122
matrix of, 116–17
overloads and, 112
Time pressures, 110
as barrier to communication, 102
Total quality management (TQM), 333
Training:
community-oriented policing (COP) and, 332
ethics, 43–50
teamwork and. *See* Teams, training
Trait theory of leadership, 60, 61
Trends, anticipating, 354–58
Trust:
communication and, 81
delegation and, 178
teamwork and, 308, 309–11
through positioning, 72–74
values and, 310
Trust bank account (TBA), 72–73, 81
Trust banking accounts (TBAs), 309

# U

Uncertainty:
accepting, 8
as stressor, 261
Understanding:
empathic listening and, 87–89
values, 18–19
Unifying the group, collaboration and, 45
Unity of command, principle of, 293
Upward communications, 92–93
Urwick, Lyndall, 292–94

# V

Value Indicator List, 28–29
Values (value systems), 11, 17–36. *See also* Ethics
changing, 22–23
choosing, 27
clarification of your, 26–29
exercises, 28–29, 32–33
community-oriented policing (COP) and, 332
as conflict resolvers, 25
defined, 18, 20
as emotional indicators, 25

ethics and, 34
failing to act on, 30
feedback and, 31
as filters, 24
functions of, 23–26
generation gap and, 24
individual differences in, 24–25
as motivators, 25–26
organizational and environmental, 31
overview of, 18
as pattern of life, 28
performance of, 27–28, 31
position of police supervisor as value driven, 30–32
prizing, 27
public affirmation of, 27
responsibilities as, 31
sources of, 20–22
as standards, 25
of teams, 305
as thought provokers, 25
trust and, 310–11
uses of the word, 19–20
Values statements, 33–35
Vision, 66–67
attention through, 70–71
Vision statements, 67–68
Volume of messages, 97–98
Voluntary organizations, police departments as, 66

# W

Wallenda factor, 75
Weber, Max, 289–91, 295
Wellness, converting stress into, 271–76
Wheel network, 96
Whining, Sniveling, Malcontents (WSMs), 220–21, 261
Winning environment, motivation and, 146
Win-win attitude, empathic listening and, 88
Worker motivation. *See* Motivation
Workmanship, 153
Workweek, modified, 356–57
Written communications, 86–87
Written reports, 98–100
Written rules, bureaucracy and, 290

# XYZ

Y network, 96